Percy Melville Thornton

The Stuart dynasty

short studies of its rise, course, and early exile.

Percy Melville Thornton

The Stuart dynasty
short studies of its rise, course, and early exile.

ISBN/EAN: 9783744737128

Printed in Europe, USA, Canada, Australia, Japan

Cover: Foto ©ninafisch / pixelio.de

More available books at **www.hansebooks.com**

THE STUART DYNASTY:

SHORT STUDIES OF

ITS RISE, COURSE, AND EARLY EXILE.

THE LATTER DRAWN

FROM PAPERS IN HER MAJESTY'S POSSESSION AT WINDSOR CASTLE.

BY

PERCY M. THORNTON,

AUTHOR OF
'FOREIGN SECRETARIES OF THE NINETEENTH CENTURY'; 'HARROW SCHOOL
AND ITS SURROUNDINGS'; 'THE BRUNSWICK ACCESSION';
ETC., ETC.

LONDON:
WILLIAM RIDGWAY, 169, PICCADILLY, W.
1891.

To

HER MOST GRACIOUS MAJESTY VICTORIA,

QUEEN OF GREAT BRITAIN AND IRELAND,

EMPRESS OF INDIA,

THESE RESEARCHES

AMONG ANCESTRAL RECORDS OF

THE ROYAL HOUSE OF STUART

ARE, BY PERMISSION, INSCRIBED BY

HER MAJESTY'S

DUTIFUL AND DEVOTED SUBJECT AND SERVANT,

PERCY MELVILLE THORNTON.

PREFACE TO THE SECOND EDITION.

A FAVOURABLE reception, quite beyond expectation, has induced me to publish an edition of this work at a popular price. In so doing I shall not attempt to cope in detail with the opinions of some sixty too lenient critics, but content myself with a justification of that *via media* which I claim to have taken in regard to the controversy which continues between the two schools who respectively laud and execrate the Stuart name. That I am not so far from the truth in my estimate as some critics suppose, is, I think, manifest from the strong objection taken to my conclusions by the White Rose organs on one hand, and the *Daily News* and several journals in sympathy with it on the other; while the fact that a majority of my critics have expressed themselves in favour of a *juste milieu* being observed in estimating the merits and demerits of the unfortunate Stuart race, leads one to believe that some protest against the *ipse dixit* school of historians was needed.

Study of European history has led me to the conclusion that if the microscope of modern inquiry had been directed against any other dynasty, regnant or extinct, in the same minute and unsparing fashion in which it has been held over the Stuarts, there would have been opportunity for brilliant penmanship to present a picture quite as dark and repulsive as that which writers of the last few decades have painted of Mary Queen of Scots and her descendants.

On the other hand, the excellent writers in the *Royalist* seem to me to favour an ideal conception of monarchy, anti-popular in its nature, which would, rightly or wrongly, destroy that estimable institution in all quarters of the globe. At the same time they utterly ignore the fact that Henry, Cardinal of

York, the last royal Stuart, practically transferred his family rights to his cousins, the present holders of England's Crown.

The *Spectator* having done me the honour to suggest that certain views expressed in this volume might reflect those of Her Most Gracious Majesty, it is my plain duty to declare most distinctly that all opinions herein set forth have been adopted or formed on my own responsibility, and as a result of my own deliberate judgment. That a contrary idea should have gained credence is perhaps owing to that good-fortune which has brought me my Sovereign's approval, signified by a graceful gift ever to be dearly prized.

Of the general popularity of this subject, aroused doubtless by the Exhibition of 1888-9, I was apprised by no less a person than the Right Honourable W. E. Gladstone, who, on March 8, 1890, wrote to me regarding the Stuarts and the publication of this book, using the following words:—

"That family, on account of its primacy in calamity, which Voltaire has so strikingly pointed out, will always form a historical subject of profound interest."

It is fair, however, to state that Mr. Gladstone further expressed the opinion that the relations of the Stuarts "with this island" had been "prevailingly unhappy"—a phrase which, whether we agree with it or not, does not imply sympathy with the spirit of bitter severity lately prevalent.

It seems to have escaped comment that the Stuart Papers in Appendix I. prove that the Chevalier de St. George and his advisers were as ignorant as other onlookers of Lords Oxford's and Bolingbroke's intentions before Queen Anne's death. Anyhow, Mr. John Morley's averment that evidence of their resolution to restore the Stuarts forthwith "was then hidden in the despatch-boxes at St. Germain,"* falls to the ground in the light of sentences such as these of the Duke of Berwick:—

"I hardly believe Harley will open himself entirely."
"They are unwilling of trusting anybody with their secret."
"If Harley is a knave at the bottom," &c., &c.

* Morley's 'Walpole,' p. 43.

Preface to the Second Edition.

The uncertainty herein, as elsewhere in the Stuart Papers, expressed, is quite in unison with what we learn from Walpole's Secret Committee of Inquiry, where nothing definite was ever proved, although every available document had been ransacked, and the report took five hours in reading. Hence it is that Swift's version of the story in his 'Four Last Years of Queen Anne' has gained credence, and most men now believe that the Tory Government desired to sustain their party, and not to effect a dynastic *coup d'état*.

Time alone can decide satisfactorily as to the opinion set forth in the *Athenæum* and the *Spectator*, that I have gauged the historical value of papers drawn from the Stuart collection too highly. I am, however, certainly at one with the writer in the latter journal in not attaching paramount importance to the great Duke of Marlborough either sending money to St. Germain, or soliciting a pardon in that quarter. Taken by themselves, these actions weigh but little when we know that a like duplicity had from time to time characterised the Captain-General's conduct ever since he helped to bring about the Revolution of 1688.

The pages of Macpherson reveal this; while the uncontradicted statements therein made, stand in strange contrast to those contemporaneous effusions breathing devotion to the Elector of Hanover, before he became George I., which are to be found amongst the famous Hanover papers.

Moreover, Marlborough was but employing tactics which, alas, were in those days familiar to nearly all the public men, Whig or Tory. The view I have taken—that the danger to the Government and rule of George I. was greater than had been believed before these Stuart documents were carefully sifted—is, I still believe, perfectly sound. For it is after a study of the subsidiary portion of the correspondence that the truth appears, rather in the taking for granted the determining nature of Marlborough's complicity in Jacobite schemes, than from explicit statements. For instance, the Lord North and Grey, a Blenheim veteran who announced his adherence to the Chevalier through Lord Bolingbroke, was either at that moment military governor of Portsmouth, or had just vacated the post, while the Duke of Shrewsbury, to whom Queen Anne on her death-bed entrusted the Treasurer's staff, is also found promising to serve the son of James II.

Again, in a letter from a Colonel Parker (previously famous as a Jacobite organiser in 1691) to the Chevalier when at Urbino, in 1718, I found an account of how, both at Leeds and Halifax, horse, arms, and money, were in the possession of men preparing to act in concert with those in Scotland, at Preston, Bristol, and the West. Under such circumstances I contend there was supreme cause for disquiet at St. James's in 1715, hitherto unsuspected, even if the Duke of Marlborough did not cherish the design of becoming a second Monk.

I can assure a writer in the *Scots Observer*, that a careful search through the 'Calendars of State Documents' and the Exchequer Rolls* does not disturb the estimate I have arrived at regarding the Stuart Princes reigning in Scotland, the new matter disclosed in those pages bearing reference to events of general history rather than to the conduct of the national dynasty.

A review in the *Times* of September 20th, 1890, has relieved me from again calling more than passing attention to the remarkable letters of Lord Bolingbroke which appear in the Appendix; while this occasion seems opportune for mentioning the fact that the House of Lords' unpublished papers, dealing with the reigns of William III. and Anne, contain some curious revelations regarding the secret service money paid to noble waverers who were in sympathy with St. Germain. Amongst these we find the Duke of Ormond during 1691 (as might then be expected, when exempted from pardon by James II.) receiving 5630*l.* a year; while John Earl of Mar, the future Jacobite general of 1715, was also a large pensioner. Probably when Mr. F. Skene and Mr. E. F. Taylor have finished this portion of their already fruitful labours, the instability of leading politicians, who flourished between 1691 and 1714, will receive further elucidation.

* One fact, derived from the last-named source, has alone escaped notice: namely, that after the murder of James the First of Scotland, which took place at Perth, in 1437, his heart was—like that of his great ancestor, Robert Bruce—removed from his body before burial, and conveyed on a pilgrimage to the East, whence it was brought back, in 1443, to the Carthusian monastery at Perth. See the Exchequer Rolls of Scotland, pp. 156 and 179.

Preface to the Second Edition.

I have to thank the writer of the review in the *Athenæum* for pointing out some clerical slips and minor errors; from which I trust this edition will be free. A word of defence must be uttered as to the genealogical sheet. The republished *skeleton* Pedigree does not pretend to be an exhaustive record of the whole race of Stuarts, but an aid to the genealogy of the sovereigns of that line, showing, also, the family connection with the House of Brunswick.

A word in conclusion concerning the future publication of documents at Windsor which deal with the Rebellion of 1745. So many have been the public suggestions that my work should be extended in this direction, that I have made a preliminary search, and am convinced that although both the late Lord Stanhope's 'History' and Browne's 'History of the Highlands,' contain documents culled from the unique collection in Her Majesty's possession, the romantic story of Charles Edward Stuart's venture might be further elucidated by the production of his unpublished letters, together with a few more of his father's, as well as those of their adherents.

PERCY M. THORNTON.

BATTERSEA RISE, S.W.,
December 1890.

CONTENTS.

	PAGE
PREFACE	v

CHAPTER I.

THE STEWARDS OF SCOTLAND, 1124—1370 1

CHAPTER II.

UNDER TWO KINGS:—
    Robert II., 1370-1390 11
    Robert III., 1390-1406 15

CHAPTER III.

TWO SUCCESSIVE REGENTS, AND ONE GREAT MONARCH:—
    Robert, Duke of Albany, 1406-1419 23
    Murdoch, Duke of Albany, 1419-1424 26
    James I. of Scotland, 1424-1437 27

CHAPTER IV.

STUART, OR DOUGLAS?—
    James II., 1437-1460 37
KING, OR NOBILITY?—
    James III., 1460-1488 46

CHAPTER V.

THE ANCIENT LEAGUE WITH FRANCE:—
    James IV., 1488-1513 55
    Childhood of James V., 1513-1528 67

CHAPTER VI.

THE CHURCH AT BAY:—
    James V., King in Fact, 1528-1542 . 76
    Minority of Mary Stuart, 1542-1560 .. 85

CHAPTER VII.
Mary Queen of Scots. Her Reign. 1560–1567 95

CHAPTER VIII.
Mary Stuart's Captivity and Death, 1567–1587 115

CHAPTER IX.
Feudalism on the Wane:—
James I. and Charles I., 1587–1649 135

CHAPTER X.
Broken Purposes:—
Charles II., 1649–1685 156

CHAPTER XI.
King and Exile:—
James II. of England and VII. of Scotland, 1685–1701 172

APPENDIX I.
Introduction, followed by Selection from the Stuart Papers in Possession of Her Majesty at Windsor Castle 203

APPENDIX II.
The Birth and Childhood of James VI. of Scotland and I. of Great Britain and Ireland 283

APPENDIX III.
The Casket Letters 286

APPENDIX IV.
Dying Declaration of Margaret Dawson, Bedchamber Woman of Mary of Modena, regarding the Birth of the Chevalier de St. George 290

Index 291

THE STUART DYNASTY.

CHAPTER I.

THE STEWARDS OF SCOTLAND.

1124-1370.

THE founder of the Stuart family, first known as the Stewards of Scotland, is said to have been Fleance, son of the Banquo who is believed to have been murdered by Macbeth A.D. 1043; but the tradition has no sure foundation.*

Lord Hailes, perhaps better known as Sir David Dalrymple, the distinguished student of antiquities, exploded this theory early in the eighteenth century, and at the same time showed several fabulous narratives concerning this family to be incompatible with ascertained facts.

Walter, son of Fleance, and Alan his successor, assumed to have been the earliest of these shadowy Stewards of Scotland, were—the former a courtier at Edward the Confessor's court, the latter a Crusader under Godfrey de Bouillon.†

In fact, the origin of the royal Stuarts cannot be traced on firm ground further back than the reign of David I., who governed Scotland between the years 1124 and 1153, but from that epoch onward the path is safe and the tracks are clear, the truth of the record being beyond all question. In short, Walter Fitzalan, Steward of Scotland in this reign, is a genuine historical personage.

Alan, the son of Flaald or Flathald, a Norman, obtained from the Conqueror the castle of Oswestry in Shropshire. He was a person of great consequence when Henry I. came to the throne in 1100. It is believed that he came over from Normandy with William the Conqueror, and was one of his leading men. Alan married the daughter of Warine, sheriff of Shropshire, and had three sons:—(1) William, progenitor

---

* A. Stuart's 'Genealogical History of the Stewarts,' pp. 1, 2. † Ibid., p. 4.

of the Fitzalans, Earls of Arundel and Lords of Oswestry (from whom the Dukes of Norfolk inherit—through an heiress—the title of Earls of Arundel); (2) Walter, High Steward of Scotland, who married Eschina de Londiniis, heiress of Molla and Huntlaw in Roxburghshire; and (3) Simon, alleged ancestor of the family of the Boyds, Earls of Kilmarnock, now represented by the Earls of Erroll.*

The descent of the House of Stuart from Alan is established as follows:—

Richard Fitzalan, Earl of Arundel, the eighth in descent from Alan, Lord of Oswestry, being in Scotland with King Edward III. in 1335, and claiming to be Steward of that realm *by hereditary right*, made over his whole title thereto, for a grant of 1000 merks, to be received out of the King's Exchequer at Caernarvon. Dugdale's 'Baronage' was the authority relied on, but the late Mr. Chalmers, not trusting Dugdale for such a transaction, found in the Tower of London a verification of the record in question, and in addition discovered that King Edward had obtained the confirmation of his purchase, so anxious was he to secure this title of Steward of Scotland.†

How such a title could be substantiated when no direct descent from Walter, who is called the first Steward, was possible, and the dignity seemed to be the sole property of a younger branch, it is difficult to comprehend. Possibly Richard Fitzalan may have invented or believed the tradition connecting Banquo and his son Fleance with the origin of Stewards of Scotland. Be that as it may, Edward III. thought the position of Steward worth acquiring when seeking to assert a suzerainty over the Scottish king; while in the transaction whereby he became possessed of this questionable title, he acknowledged Richard Fitzalan's strange claim.

The title of Seniscalcus (steward) is said to have been derived from the German *seniscalc*, "oldest of the servants," and signified not only the office of chief of the household, but also entailed much power, provided that the sovereign retained confidence in the holder. For in feudal times the collection and management of the revenue, together with administration of justice, and even chief direction of war, co-operated with constant contiguity to the throne in elevating the individual enjoying such advantages to a very exalted position in the realm. And, indeed, in France this office was considered to be too vast a one to be filled by one man.‡

* Douglas's 'Peerage,' vol. i. p. 42. † Ibid., p. 43. ‡ Ibid.

King Malcolm IV. of Scotland, who reigned between 1153 and 1163, confirmed a charter in favour of Walter, son of Alan, conferring on him lands in Renfrewshire, together with the Stewardship, both originally granted by David I.

It is also known that the first Steward of Scotland founded the Abbey of Paisley in 1164.*

The traveller proceeding from Glasgow down the lovely Clyde would pass within sight of the ancient patrimony of the Stuart Kings; and when the shores of Renfrewshire sink out of sight, the fair prospects in and around Bute may recall other memories of the same royal line, inasmuch as that attractive island became in 1255 a portion of the Stuart property. Indeed, it is probable that the geographical position of Renfrewshire, intermediate between the Highlands, the Isles of the West, and the Lowlands, gave the Stuarts an original advantage in their rivalry with the House of Douglas, whose reputation for conducting forays into England, and as supreme lords of the Border, was scarcely realised amongst the wild warriors who, living north of Inverary, had yet from time to time come into personal contact with several of the Stewards of Scotland.

Alan, the second Steward, succeeded his above-mentioned father Walter, holding his position for twenty-seven years; being twice married, first to Eva, daughter of Swan, son of Thor, Lord of Tippermuir and Tranent, progenitor of the Ruthvens; but by this marriage the Steward had no children, and a second time entered the marriage state with Alesta, daughter of Morgand, Earl of Mar, the origin of whose house is lost in the mists of antiquity. The son and heir, Walter, by this marriage, was third holder of the Stewardship, and flourished in that capacity between 1204 and 1246, being himself allied to Beatrix, daughter of Gilchrist, who then held the title of Angus.†

Walter's son, Alexander, the fourth Steward, appears to have developed military talent, for he commanded the Scottish army at the battle of Largs on Oct. 2, 1263.‡ This Alexander, serving Alexander III. as General on this occasion, was, in all probability, defending his own interests

---

* A. Stuart's 'Genealogical History of the Stewarts,' p. 3; also Sir David Dalrymple's (Lord Hailes) 'Annals of Scotland,' third edition, 1819, vol. i. p. 363.

† A. Stuart's 'Genealogical History of the Stewarts,' p. 8; also Douglas's 'Peerage,' vol. i. p. 44.

‡ Douglas's 'Peerage,' vol. i. p. 44.

when Haco, King of Norway, made himself master of Bute and Arran, and then appeared with a great navy off the village of Largs in Cunningham, where, the weather proving unpropitious, many of the vessels either got stranded or entangled one with the other. Haco, however, landed what troops he could collect, and the Norwegians, being in a disorganised state and much outnumbered by their foes, suffered a great disaster, and their King escaped to the Orkneys with the remnant of his fleet, only to die there under the shadow of St. Magnus's shrine.*

Alexander, the fourth Steward, married, in the year 1255, Jean, daughter and heiress of James, son of Angus Macroryr, or Roderick, Lord of Bute.†

A brother of Alexander, the fourth Steward, was Walter of Menteith, who adopted his wife's name, by which his family has been known ever since; a representative existing in the person of Sir James Stuart Menteith, Bart.

In the year 1283, at the age of sixty-nine, the successful general, Alexander, the fourth Steward, died a natural death and was buried at Paisley. He was succeeded by his eldest son James, the fifth Steward, who held the office from 1283 to 1309, when he died, aged sixty-six. James was one of the Regents after the death of Alexander III. in 1287, when his infant grandchild—known in history as the Maid of Norway—was sole heiress to the Scottish throne.‡

Never in the history of nations has any more anxious dynastic crisis threatened to disintegrate a nation by reason of disputed succession than that which menaced Scotland when the Maid of Norway, landing in Orkney on her way to take possession of her crown, died there during September 1290. Her grandfather, Alexander III., by an alliance with a daughter of Henry III. of England, had paved the way as it were for the union of the two crowns, which the prescient Edward I. thought might afford a short cut to the practical possession of Scotland, in endeavouring to gain which object so much of that great English sovereign's life was spent. When, therefore, amidst circumstances of much national hope and rejoicing, the sad tidings reached Scotland's shores, a feeling akin to despair took possession of her rulers, who saw in the ensuing contest between Robert Bruce and John Baliol—the Cumyns having resigned their claim in favour

* Burton's 'History of Scotland,' vol. ii. pp. 34, 35.
† Douglas's 'Peerage,' vol. i. p. 44.
‡ Burton's 'History of Scotland,' vol. ii. p. 43.

of the latter—the seeds of future civil war, the fomenting of which Edward I. made thenceforth a leading part of his policy.

James, the fifth Steward, like his father before him, served the monarchy with courage, skill, and fidelity, for we find him associated with Sir William Wallace in 1297, and subsequently standing surety for Robert Bruce's good behaviour, when that monarch had undertaken to deliver up Marjory, his only daughter, to the English. His recognition of Bruce's right to the throne, doubtless strengthened his family position in the State. His wife was Cecilia, daughter of Patrick, Earl of Dunbar and March.

A brother of James, the fifth Steward, Sir John by name, married Margaret, daughter of Sir Alexander Bonkyl, and became progenitor of several noble houses, including that of Darnley, Earls of Lennox, to which house belonged Henry, Lord Darnley, Queen Mary's husband. Sir John Stuart was also ancestor of the Earls of Galloway.

Walter, the second son of James, the fifth Steward, became the sixth of his race who served the royal line of William the Lion, and was destined himself to be the means of founding a dynasty, although the purple never descended on to his shoulders. Andrew, his elder brother, being sent as a hostage to Edward I., in England, and dying there, Walter Stuart became the head of the family. He had a great reputation for bravery, and held a prominent command at Bannockburn in 1314, when, under the shadow of Stirling's fortressed height, the nationality of Scotland was saved. His prowess on this great occasion is thus celebrated by the poet Barbour, once chaplain to David II. :—

> " Valtir, steward of scotland, syne,
> That than wes bot ane berdlas hyne,
> Com vith a rout of nobill men,
> That all be coutynans mycht ken." *

The Steward's contingent was evidently composed of aristocratic elements; while Barbour further tell us:—

> " And syne the thrid battale he gaf
> To valtir stewart for to leid,
> And till dowglas douchty of deid." †

After Bannockburn, Walter, the sixth Steward of Scotland, was appointed to receive Elizabeth, Queen of Robert Bruce,

* Barbour's ' Robert Bruce,' p. 266 (Skeat).
† Ibid., p. 269; A. Stuart's 'Genealogical History of the Stewarts,' pp. 17-18.

Marjory his daughter, and other illustrious prisoners then released from captivity in England. He then, having lost his first wife, Alice, formed the attachment to Marjory Bruce which led in 1315 to their marriage, the issue whereof became entitled to the throne in his mother's right.*

Traditions of Walter and Marjory Stuart's residence at Paisley live to this day, and in the centre of the semi-ruined Abbey church may be seen the tomb of the "lass," as James V. had it, with whom the crown came to the Stuarts. This Princess was riding between Paisley and Renfrew on Shrove Tuesday, 1316, and falling from horseback fractured her neck, the child, afterwards Robert II., coming into the world by means of what is known as the Cæsarean operation.† In the bitterness of this terrible sorrow, Walter Stuart went to the Border wars, seeking to drown his grief by serving the national cause. He survived his wife, formerly Marjory Bruce, ten years, and died in 1326, aged thirty-three.

Sir Walter Scott has rendered apt testimony to the bravery of Walter the sixth Steward ‡—a quality which may be considered hereditary, as the course of this narrative must show.

One of the results of Bannockburn seems to have been the capture of Berwick by the Scots in 1318, a place of arms which the English resolutely endeavoured to recapture, encountering Walter Stuart as governor of the fortress, in which capacity he displayed great courage, rushing through the flames of a burning gate, and by his example rallying the Scots, and saving the place.§

The child of Walter Stuart and Marjory Bruce was named Robert, and could not be considered as born to higher destiny than that of his predecessors in the Stewardship, because, although his contingent right to the succession had been proclaimed at Bruce's suggestion shortly before the national hero expired, yet his son David II., Marjory Bruce's brother, having a prior claim, had all the world before him.

It could scarcely be expected that neither of this King's wives—Joanna, Princess of England, and the mysterious Margaret Logie—should bear children, but such was the case; and in consequence of this failure of issue, when David

---

* Douglas's 'Peerage,' vol. i. pp. 45–46.
† Crawford and Semple's 'History of Renfrewshire,' part i. p. 25.
‡ 'Tales of a Grandfather,' edition 1880, p. 55.
§ Sir David Dalrymple's (Lord Hailes) 'Annals of Scotland,' third edition, 1819, vol. ii. p. 112.

died, at the age of forty-seven, in the Castle of Edinburgh, Feb. 22, 1370,* the male line of the Bruces became extinct, and that of Stuart inherited the throne in the person of Robert the seventh Steward. His early career was brilliant and full of interest.

When only seventeen years of age, in 1333, the youthful Robert Stuart led a division of Scots against the English at Halidon Hill, and was subsequently one of the first leading men who made a stand against Baliol, after he had, in the following year, again invaded Scotland. The Stuart property in Renfrew had been confiscated, and the Steward forced to take refuge under concealment in Bute.† Thence he escaped to Dumbarton Castle in a boat brought to Rothesay by two old family vassals, Gibson and Heriot. On learning this intelligence the retainers of the Stuarts, in and around the district, flew to arms forthwith. Robert put himself at their head, and, acting in conjunction with Colin Campbell of Lochow, stormed and took the Castle of Dunoon. Nor did the reaction against Baliol stop there, for, continuing his advance and gathering adherents daily, the Steward of Scotland regained for David II. Annandale and the lower parts of Clydesdale, while Renfrew, Carrick, and Cunningham were freed from the enemy's occupation.‡

For these services, rendered in the years 1336 and 1337, Robert Stuart, although only twenty years of age, reaped the high reward of becoming joint Regent over loyal Scotland with Sir Andrew Moray. The Steward's success, however, proved to be but temporary; for in 1337 Baliol and Edward III. swept away all opposition, and overran most of the kingdom.

In 1338, on Sir Andrew Moray's death, the Steward became sole Regent,§ whereupon he immediately applied to Philip of France, the first King of the House of Valois, for assistance, which promptly came in 1339, when five French men-of-war, having on board a body of men-at-arms under the command of Arnold Audineham, Marshal of France, appeared in the Forth. A sanguinary and devastating struggle followed, wherein the country around Perth being absolutely desolated, the Steward took possession of the city for David II., then an exile in France.

---

* Scott's 'Tales of a Grandfather,' edition 1880, p. 54.
† Tytler's 'History of Scotland,' edition 1841, vol. ii. p. 35.
‡ Ibid., p. 37.
§ Ibid., p. 55. Burton speaks as if the Steward had not previously been co-regent.—'History of Scotland,' vol. ii. p. 323. He gives no reference.

A siege of Stirling followed, which resulted favourably for the Steward's arms in 1339, although, despite a strategic success which every one acquainted with the country will appreciate, no well-wisher of Scotland could do otherwise than commiserate her dreadful condition at this period. Law and order obtained only where armed forces existed to preserve the country from rapine and consequent confusion,* while the very deer of the forest browsed where man had formerly fixed his dwelling. However, the situation, for all its gloom, contained the elements of a settlement favourable to the national party. In the first place, Edward Baliol had taken his departure into England, conscious that, with Perth, Fife, and the north in Scots hands, and Stirling in dire peril of capture, the future of Scotland was to be decided by its own inhabitants. It was late in 1339, a few months after Baliol left Scotland, that the Steward won Stirling. Edinburgh was recovered in 1341, and Roxburgh in 1342.† This consummation became inevitable when Edward III. determined to invade France, and concentrated his resources there. The Steward had now arrived at a critical period of his eventful career. Fordun, the Scotch historian of the fourteenth century, thus describes the young Regent who became King Robert II.: "He was a comely youth, tall and robust, modest, liberal, gay, and courteous." Fordun adds that he was much beloved amongst his countrymen.‡

This irresistible young hero, in the full flush of hope, met Elizabeth, the beautiful daughter of Sir Adam Mure of Rowallan, representative of an old Ayrshire family. The two young people fell violently in love with one another, overlooking the fact that they were distant cousins in the third and fourth degrees of affinity, and in the fourth degree of consanguinity,§ and therefore, by the existing canon law of the Church, prohibited from marriage unless a dispensation were given from Rome. There is no reason to think that the Pope would have hesitated, had the lovers consented to await his decision, but, heedless of the future, and conscious only of the affection which bound them together, they ventured upon a step which threatened in after years to disturb the Succession.

It is said that one Roger Macadam, a priest, probably

* Tytler's 'History of Scotland,' edition 1841, vol. ii. p. 59.
† Burton's 'History of Scotland,' new edition, vol. ii. p. 325.
‡ A. Stuart's 'Genealogical History of the Stewarts,' p. 33.
§ Riddell's 'Stewartia,' p. 1.

about 1337, married Robert Stuart and Elizabeth Mure at Dundonald Castle, near Ayr,* where the bridegroom lived in early youth; and, indeed, the distance of the relationship being so great, the fact itself was probably, if not forgotten altogether, at least passed over in silence, when there must have been a disposition evinced to ignore such extravagant Papal pretensions. At any rate not a word appears in any of the chronicles threatening the young Steward's title to the throne, although Clement VI., elected Pope in 1342, gave the marriage dispensation about 1347. Indeed the Regency must have been conferred within a very few months of the marriage.

The chroniclers are silent as to the precise age of John, known as Robert III., eldest child of this marriage; but his brother, the famous Duke of Albany, was born in 1339,† and it seems probable that Robert Stuart and Elizabeth Mure joined their fortunes in 1337, just after the campaign against Baliol, which gained for the Steward of Scotland the position of joint Regent with Sir A. Moray. It is curious that the Papal dispensation was lost, and not put in evidence until 1789, after the Stuarts had ceased to strive for the recovery of the British throne; and the fact gave rise to some strange quibbles from time to time.

In 1341 King David returned from France with his Queen Joanna, and received obeisance from the Regents, who straightway rendered up the government—despite the fact that a youth of seventeen was manifestly unequal to the cares of an unsettled State, such as Scotland was at this period. It is well known how David II., fired with the unpractical spirit of chivalry with which he had become imbued in France, and incited by the king of that country, his ally, was fatuous enough to advance across the Border with an army in the year 1346, and attempt to emulate on English soil the deeds of his great father Robert Bruce— a project which ended disastrously at Nevil's Cross, near Durham.

The defeat of the Scots was such that their King fell into the enemy's hands, and only one division remained intact under the Steward's command, so that enemies to the dynasty soon to be founded averred that Robert Stuart failed to do his duty towards his royal uncle on that occasion.

* Crawford and Semple's 'History of Renfrewshire,' p. 14.
† Burton ('History of Scotland,' vol. ii. p. 395) says he died in 1419, aged 80.

10   *The Stuart Dynasty.*

How Scotland could have benefited by the almost certain loss of its remaining armed force, together with the death or captivity of its chosen alternative ruler, it would be difficult to show. But it is not to be wondered at that the Steward should have been judged harshly by David II., who had suffered the disgrace of being paraded through London as a set-off against the English humiliation at Bannockburn.

It is said that David II. never forgave this assumed desertion, and his subsequent desire to place the English Duke of Clarence next in the Scotch Succession has been thus accounted for; but we know on the other hand, as the result of later research, that Robert Stuart honourably preserved the kingdom for his uncle until he returned from captivity in 1357, although the general unsettlement which then prevailed might have furnished excuse for a more ambitious course.* This fidelity was maintained even when David's marriage with Margaret Logie rendered the Stuart prospects more uncertain; although, as David II. manifested distrust and dislike of his heir-presumptive, due security was taken to provide that the Succession, as determined by Robert Bruce, should not be disturbed. However, in 1363, the King cherished the design of setting the Stuarts aside, with the result that the country came into imminent danger of civil war.

A bond was entered into between the Steward, the Earls of March and Douglas, the Steward's sons, and others, who warned David II. that he must stand by the legitimate Succession or himself abandon the throne. The controversy, however, ended amicably, as the Steward renewed his vow to the King, who in turn recognised that the royal title was to descend from Bruce through the female line to the Stuarts, and conferred the Earldom of Carrick on the prince who afterwards became Robert III.†

Divorced mysteriously from Margaret Logie, and still childless, David II. reigned until February 1370, but, during the last seven years of his life, nothing happened which is worthy of note.

* Burton's 'History of Scotland,' new edition, vol. ii. p. 330.
† Tytler's 'History of Scotland,' edition 1841, vol. ii. p. 120.

CHAPTER II.

UNDER TWO KINGS.

1370–1406.

Robert II., 1370-90; Robert III., 1390-1406.

It certainly speaks volumes for the fidelity to Robert Bruce's memory which his countrymen displayed, that they acquiesced quietly in the elevation of Robert II., first sovereign of the house of Stuart. Not only was the country generally in apparently inextricable confusion, but a war with England had been now raging, now smouldering, for nearly eighty years; while it was whispered that William, Earl of Douglas —the head of that romantic family, himself a prominent warrior, and acknowledged as military leader of the nation— was ready to take also upon his shoulders the royal cares of State. The late Mr. Hill Burton* speaks to this effect of the candidature of the Earl of Douglas, while other authorities regard it as an established fact, though it does not appear in the chronicles.

King Robert had reached fifty-five years of age when he was crowned at Scone, and the narrative of that eventful and warlike life given in the last chapter will itself give the reason why he desired thus comparatively early, as regards age, to take refuge from camps and seek such ease as his position might confer. But this shrinking from active responsibility was totally out of place at the time in Scotland, and it is wonderful that things went on so well as they did during the reign of Robert II. There were, it is true, perpetual combats on and around those wild Border lands so justly renowned in Scotch story: while the Lowlands suffered severely from invasion in 1385. Moreover, in some quarters, as future events were to show, there was a doubt as to the Succession.

It will be remembered that Robert II. had married Elizabeth Mure, his distant cousin, and so needed a Papal dispensation to confirm their union, the issue of which numbered

* 'History of Scotland,' vol. ii. p. 343.

no less than four sons and six daughters, the latter married to men of influence in the realm. There was, however, another family by his second wife, Euphemia Ross, two sons and four daughters, the assumed claims of which branch of the Stuarts were destined more than once in future times to threaten commotion and incite to civil war. They seem to have known nothing of the Pope's dispensation, which is first mentioned in literature by A. Stuart, in his 'Genealogical History of the Stewarts.'

The reign opened by the traditional connection between France and Scotland being confirmed by Charles V. of France and his newly elevated brother Robert II. of Scotland. The old league between the kingdoms was renewed with solemnity, an embassy going to Paris, under Sir Archibald Douglas, for the purpose.*

Edward III. of England had on hand so severe a task in coping with the French on their own territory, that the combats and Border forays which occurred at the commencement of the Stuart régime were unimportant and practically without result, ending as they did in a welcome truce between 1381 and 1384. At the conclusion of the truce in 1384, John of Gaunt marched to the Border with a powerful army professedly to preserve peace.† The year following, however, John de Vienne, Admiral of France and her most famous soldier, appeared in the Firth of Forth with 2000 men, half of them mounted, together with a thousand stand of armour and arms. As a set-off against the gathering of the Lowlands, which took place around this nucleus of a formidable Franco-Scotch army, the young King of England, Richard II., put himself at the head of seventy thousand men, and marched to the Border.

Fortunately for those interested in the period, Froissart, the French chronicler, was a witness of the events that ensued, and it is to his attractive pages that the facts here related owe their preservation. After a dispute between Vienne and Douglas as to the mode of campaign, it was resolved to ignore the approaching English. King Robert II. appears on this occasion as a respectable figurehead, surrounded by—according to Froissart—"nine sons who loved arms;" ‡ but his state of health precluded the

---

* Burton's 'History of Scotland,' new edition, vol. ii. p. 348.
† Ibid., p. 350.
‡ Froissart, translated edition, 1808, vol. vii. p. 53. Three natural sons according to Tytler.

monarch from taking the field in person, as he was suffering from an affection of the eyes—" red bleared eyes " as the chronicler has it*—so that when by summons he had collected thirty thousand men, he bade them god-speed, and awaited results in Edinburgh.

Vienne and his Scotch allies proceeded to the south through Melrose and Roxburgh, the fortress of which they disregarded, and ultimately halting half-way between Berwick and Newcastle, burned several villages of the Percys on the route. Thence, however, hearing that the English were advancing, they made an uneventful retreat over the same ground.†

It is not generally realised, because historians have minimised the facts, that King Richard II. entered Scotland in this year 1385, at the head of seventy thousand men, burnt Melrose, wasted the country around, and quartered himself in Edinburgh, whence after five days he took his departure, having destroyed the city by fire, the castle alone remaining intact for Robert II. The English then marched on Dunfermline, and afterwards besieged Stirling, which resisted them successfully; so that if the King o'Scots was a fugitive his handiwork was apparent in the salvation of the State, for as Steward of Scotland he had wrested the fortress from the party of Baliol during the year 1339.

After burning Perth, Richard sent an advanced guard to Aberdeen, which, however, feeling insecure so far from its base of operations, did no damage to the city, and retired on the main body. But as in each invasion of Scotland it was always found difficult to pass northwards without taking Stirling, so on this occasion did the English, unsuccessful in their endeavours before that fortress, learn the necessity of making a retrograde movement, or running the risk of having their communications cut off, for they had put the river Forth between themselves and England.‡

Nor were the French and Scots idle, for they made raids into Cumberland and Westmoreland, burning villages and laying the country waste until, the district having been drained of its resources by the English army, they sat down before Carlisle. Finding themselves unable to subdue this place, they retired across the Border. Truly, an inconsequent conclusion for both nations. But the poor French fared worst of all, inasmuch as the Scots declared they

---

* Froissart, translated edition, 1808, vol. vii. p. 53.
† Ibid., p. 57. ‡ Ibid., pp. 69, 70.

had injured their allies much more than the English enemy they were present to repel, because in crossing the fields crops had been destroyed. In requital for these losses they detained John de Vienne and the other French barons, who had narrowly escaped annihilation by the returning English. But the opportunity was missed owing to inaction caused by the internal dissensions of King Richard's followers.* Little wonder that the French were glad to return to their own country.

These details, belonging more to the national records of the sister kingdom than to a history of the Stuart dynasty, have been given here in order that the state of Scotland at the close of the fourteenth century may be apparent, and those interested may form an idea of the turbulent state of the kingdom which Robert II. nominally governed.

The following extract gives a vivid picture of the condition of the peasantry. "The French and Scots marched back the way they had come. When arrived in the lowlands, they found the whole country ruined; but the people of the country made light of it, saying that with six or eight stakes they would soon have new houses, and find cattle enow for provision."†

Froissart tells us that advantage was taken of a quarrel between the Percys and Nevilles to invade Northumberland in 1388, without consulting the King at all, on the ground that "he knew nothing about war."‡ But the charge of negligence as regards the interests of his kingdom, to which this amounts, cannot be substantiated, because, in all probability, this combination of the barons for an invasion of England in 1388 was that designed and led by Robert, Earl of Fife, second son of Robert II., afterwards famous as the Regent Albany, who, a year after the battle of Otterburn had been fought, received as a reward at his father's hands, when fifty years of age, the formal governorship of the kingdom.§

This is not the place to give any detailed account of the romantic moonlight defence of the Scotch camp of Otterburn, near Newcastle, in 1388, where brave Earl Douglas, after capturing the Percy pennon, died a hero's death in the very hour of victory—a victory gained by the display of his famous banner. The story of this interesting battle has been

* Froissart, translated edition, 1808, vol. vii. p. 74.
† Ibid., p. 75. ‡ Ibid., vol. ix. p. 238.
§ Tytler's 'History of Scotland,' edition 1841, vol. iii. p. 54.

inimitably narrated by Froissart. During the latter portion of this reign the executive government was guided by that mysterious but able member of the Stuart family, Robert, Earl of Fife, who never really lost grasp of power until his death in 1419. He seems to have conducted a raid into England in 1389, but the incidents were unimportant; and a truce which followed in the same year cheered the last days of the old King, who, dying in 1390, aged 74 years, in the words of Scotland's latest historian, " left the character of a peaceful ruler over a quarrelsome people." * He is known in history more especially as the first sovereign of the Stuart line, although the previous chapter contains evidence that before his elevation to the throne, and when Steward of Scotland, this high-minded peace-loving King underwent a career of hardship and warlike adventure, which made him a prominent figure in the times wherein he lived. The remains of Robert II. were buried in the Abbey of Scone on August 13, 1390, and the following day saw the coronation of Robert III. celebrated with great pomp and solemnity. Next day his wife Annabella, a daughter of the noble house of Drummond, was anointed Queen; and then the assembled prelates and nobles took the oath of allegiance to the new sovereign, who rejected the name of John because it had been that of the anti-national claimant for the sovereignty, Baliol, and was consequently adjudged " ominous and unpopular." †

When quite a youth the King received a kick from a horse at a tournament, and was rendered little better than a cripple for life, and so was doomed to inactivity when war's alarms were sounded. Moreover, his character was in some degree similar to that of Robert II. Amiable and full of good sense, the second Stuart sovereign did not lack discretion, although a love of pacific, not to say domestic, life tended to make him hesitate sometimes when decision was most needed. ‡

Trusting, then, the affairs of State generally to the Earl of Fife, his brother, and appointing a half-brother the Earl of Buchan, with his son (the King's nephew), to control the Highlands and the north, Robert III. sank into a state of dignified repose which enabled him to display to his subjects the gentleness and chivalric nature which made mankind love him, but did not realise the ideal which those

* Burton's 'History of Scotland,' new edition, vol. ii. p. 369.
† Tytler's 'History of Scotland,' edition 1841, vol. iii. p. 60.
‡ Ibid., pp. 60, 61.

best able to judge longed to behold in a King o' Scots at this period.

The weakness of the situation thus created became apparent when in the first place the northern Viceroy, the Earl of Buchan, displayed a savagery which seriously damaged the popularity of the throne which he misrepresented:* and had it not been for the address with which the Earl of Fife renewed the league with France, whereby truce between the three countries was prolonged and ratified by the King, Scotland might have been confronted with the direst peril. †

The public safety seems to have been preserved at this time by the forethought of the Earl of Fife—a statesman whose record can by no means be purged of all self-seeking, or cleared decisively of stains which suspicion casts upon his character, but whose hand is visible in securing many benefits for his country. But the state of barbarism to be dealt with was simply inconceivable in a land where Christianity had held sway for more than eight hundred years, and where the dictates of chivalry were recognised, and its civilising influence admired and welcomed.

Indeed we find the high-minded King persuaded to preside over an exhibition of barbarism early in his reign. A quarrel between the Highland clans Kay and Quete (or Chattan) threatened to convulse the mountain country above Perth, so thirty champions from each bellicose faction were marshalled on the North Inch at Perth. It is a beautiful piece of level ground, by which the river Tay passes rippling on with music sweet. The spectacle of the Scottish King enthroned on a platform as umpire in these strange Highland games were doubtless impressive. But the bloodshed which ensued must have been revolting to the gentle King Robert III., who doubtless commiserated in his heart the recalcitrant deserter from the clan Chattan who cast himself into the Tay, and swimming across fled to the woods. Nor, with all knightly respect for bravery such as that of the Perth armourer, Henry of the Wynd, who filled up the gap,

---

* Tytler's 'History of Scotland,' edition 1841, vol. iii. p. 64. Evidence of the Buchan's vandalism is, alas! apparent in Elgin Cathedral, which this so-called Wolf of Badenoch partially gave to the flames. He burnt the beautiful choir, and much of Elgin itself, in June 1390, to revenge a private grudge against the Bishop, Barr by name.—'Survey of Province of Moray,' edition 1808, p. 81.

† 'Records of the Parliament of Scotland,' A.D. 1390, p. 136.

could the merciful sovereign of Scotland rejoice over a carnage which left the clan Quete (or Chattan) supreme— the Perth tradesman and ten other stout men-at-arms surviving, while one solitary individual remained to carry tidings of defeat to the men and women who fought under the Kay tartan.* This strange event occurred on October 23, 1396. About this time the chronicles are full of complaints on the part of the poorer people who needed protection from the marauding parties of disbanded soldiery which infested the country. Such protection could alone be received from a strong Government, and not therefore from that of King Robert; for, in addition to his ordinary causes of embarrassment, a rivalry was fast rising up between the heir to the throne, the young Earl of Carrick, who became the Steward of Scotland, and the Earl of Fife, on whom the King relied for the direction of the royal policy. Great as were the difficulties of the Stuart dynasty at that period, an early mitigation might have been expected from the increase of intercourse between England and Scotland, which was sure to result from peace between these countries.

Not only was there coming and going of the nobility, merchants, and students, and Churchmen, which for a century had been impossible, by reason of the perpetual state of warlike confusion on the Border, but the spread of chivalry rendered Scotland the chosen arena for magnificent tournaments and mock trials of arms, such as were calculated to bring money into the country, and temporarily provided a healthy substitute for the perpetual feudal conflicts which had plagued the land.

Prominent amongst these chivalric displays appeared the person of the youthful heir to the throne, whose manly bearing, gentle manners, and knightly accomplishments combined with great personal beauty to enlist the sympathies of his father's subjects.

A fondness for poetry and a certain acquaintance with literature, on the other hand, alienated this youth of high birth, but woful destiny, from the fierce barons who made up the court of Robert III.; and hence it was that Fife, the Governor, always had a party amongst the nobility favourable to the continuance of his sway. Nor did the spoilt and petted son of the recluse king, Robert III., fail to give ample

* Burton's 'History of Scotland,' new edition, vol. ii. p. 369; also Tytler's 'History of Scotland,' edition 1841, vol. ii. p. 67. This incident is employed to great advantage by Sir Walter Scott in 'The Fair Maid of Perth.'

cause of offence which might warrant a prescient statesman in withholding from the lawful heir to the throne the rights and privileges which were his birthright.

The young Earl of Carrick was terribly profligate, and by his disregard of ordinary restraints to which even monarchs' sons were subjected in the fourteenth century, gave occasion for his enemies to plot and conspire against him.

The King attempted to satisfy the ambition both of brother and son by importing the title of Duke from France and England into Scotland, creating Fife Duke of Albany, and the prince Duke of Rothesay; but the latter, having been initiated into the practice of government in the Highlands, was not in a mood to brook his uncle's continued preeminence. This Albany recognised by calling a Parliament at Perth on January 27, 1398, whereat the Duke of Rothesay was made the King's lieutenant, and Albany relegated to a principal place in the royal council.*

Duke Robert of Albany has been charged by most historians who have undertaken the narration of succeeding events, with the crime of supplanting, ruining, and at last cruelly doing to death this attractive but erring nephew, his rival. Wynton, prior of Lochleven—a contemporary—alone of the chroniclers gives denial to this averment, although later writers, Hill Burton especially, have in the absence of direct evidence spoken with uncertainty. The facts are as follows.

The Queen very naturally thought that a well-chosen wife might be the means of steadying her son the Duke of Rothesay, and bringing to an end the period of his profligacy, and a daughter of the powerful Earl of March was chosen for the bride; but a stronger claimant for the royal alliance appeared in the person of Archibald, Earl of Douglas, whose daughter Elizabeth became Rothesay's wife. This disappointment so weighed on the Earl of March that he sought an interview with the King, whereat he is said to have expressed himself more intemperately than became a subject, demanding redress and the restoration of a sum of money he had paid as a dower.† King Robert's answer being of an evasive character, March repaired to England and offered his services to the new King, Henry IV., who had usurped the throne and imprisoned Richard II. Henry, at the moment bent on invading Scotland, proceeded to do so with

---

* Tytler's 'History of Scotland,' vol. iii. p. 76.
† Preface to Drummond's 'History of Scotland.'

a large army, summoning Robert of Scotland to appear before him as a liegeman and vassal. How far the exceptional information regarding the country which March could give helped the English on this occasion is not recorded.

Henry IV. conducted a processional invasion up to the gates of Edinburgh in this year 1400, refraining, however, from burning or pillage, but was unable to capture the castle, in which the Duke of Rothesay was ensconced as commander. After some hesitation the English sovereign retired, while Albany, who was posted with an army within a day's march at Calder Moor, adopted a Fabian policy and fought no decisive battle for the relief of Rothesay, a cause of abiding offence to the partisans of that unfortunate prince. But the military position by no means warranted their charges against his uncle, whose tactics were undoubtedly justified by the result. However, the bad blood between these two princes was destined to bring about a terrible tragedy, the circumstances connected with which are known but in outline. The conduct of Rothesay did not, unfortunately, improve with marriage, and his neglect of his wife alienated the favour of his powerful father-in-law, Archibald Douglas, whose influence was henceforth thrown into the scale against him when the re-establishment of Albany's authority was in question. Hearing, therefore, from influential men of his court, Douglas amongst the number, that it was necessary to subject the Duke of Rothesay to some restraint, the King gave way in the matter so far as to tolerate his son's temporary captivity, and to leave the future practically to Albany's guidance.

By the assistance of a certain Sir John Ramorny, the prince was captured on the road to St. Andrews, and committed to prison in the castle of Falkland in Fifeshire.

The Queen had died early in this ill-omened year 1401, and the poor prince was bereft of his noble mother's powerful advocacy, and left to the mercy of his aggrieved father-in-law the Douglas, and his uncle Albany, the two acting in concert for the occasion.

It is said that the prince was left without food for fifteen days, and that for a short interval he survived after that period, because a poor woman surreptitiously brought food to the dungeon; but at lost nature gave way, and the inanimate body was found in an emaciated state too horrible for mention.*

* Goodall's edition of Fordun, vol. ii. p. 431.

Public indignation against Albany rising fast, a Parliament was called at Holyrood in May 1402, before which assembly Albany and Douglas were examined and acquitted, but in language which did not clear their characters from the foulest suspicions. It is declared by the Parliament "that the young prince died by the visitation of Providence," Albany and Douglas being indemnified, and persons forbidden to repeat calumnious rumours regarding them.*

Unfortunately the dictum of a Scotch Parliament at this period is open to two objections. In the first place, each gathering was determined by the needs of Government to enable them to proceed in their executive task, or remove some present difficulty, rather than by reason of any legal obligation to discuss the affairs of the nation, and it was a recurrence to such a state of things which injured the Stuart prospects so sorely when they ruled England in the seventeenth century. Secondly, the assemblage of barons, Churchmen, and commoners holding of the King, which made up Parliament in Scotland, sat in a single chamber, and no second House could check its proceedings in any way. Hence its rulings were always liable to the suspicion of having been prompted by some great noble whose royal favour enabled him to gain a majority, and for this reason men will continue to look askance on the conduct of Robert Duke of Albany and the famous fighting Douglas (who was afterwards taken prisoner at Shrewsbury) regarding the Duke of Rothesay, although the amount of provocation, and the measure of danger which the country encountered through the wild levities of the heir-apparent, should be weighed in the balance. As to the King himself, historians are at one in absolving him from any complicity in his son's death; although the pliability which led him to listen to Douglas and Albany was unfortunate in the same proportion as were the monarch's disabilities, natural and acquired, which prevented him from fulfilling the rough duties of his position.†

* Burton's 'History of Scotland,' new edition, vol. ii. p. 381. The late historiographer for Scotland thought this matter very obscure.

† Tradition, in Edinburgh at least, is adverse to the Duke of Albany in this matter, for a graceful chapel in St. Giles's, which takes the name of Albany's Aisle, is said by Dr. Cameron Lees, historian of that cathedral, to have been erected by the Regent in expiation of Rothesay's murder.—'St. Giles's Church and Cathedral, Edinburgh,' by J. Cameron Lees, D.D. (W. & R. Chambers, 1889.)

The concluding years of Robert III. were indeed gloomy. His army was defeated at Homildon Hill, by the skill of the English archers, on September 14, 1402, both the Earl of Douglas and Murdoch Stuart, the Duke of Albany's son, becoming the prisoners of Henry IV. Direst stroke of all —a similar fate awaited the Scotch monarch's surviving son. James—who had just been despatched to France for education there, as well as to place him beyond the reach of hostile intrigue at home—was captured on his outward voyage by an armed merchantman off Flamborough Head, and taken to London.

This event occurred on Palm Sunday, 1405, which fell on the 12th of April, Wynton the chronicler showing that the truce had not expired.*

Prince James had been placed by his guardian, Sir David Fleming, upon the Bass Rock opposite to North Berwick, pending his removal by ship to France. Sir David, returning through Haddingtonshire, was attacked and murdered by James Douglas of Balveny. The prince embarked on a ship from Leith, and off Flamborough, as has been said, fell into English hands.†

Although the narrative of the young prince's life will be told in due course, it is necessary to mention this fact here, as bearing on the closing days of his father's life; and to pay a passing tribute to the loyal service which Wardlaw, Bishop of St. Andrews, performed, both as faithful friend to the dying Stuart King, and as counsellor of his child.

It cannot be doubted that James I. had the foundations of his great learning laid when under the influence of this remarkable man.‡ The news of his son's captivity was brought to Robert III. when about to sup in his ancestral home at Rothesay in Bute. The unhappy widower lived but a few months afterwards, so dire was the shock inflicted by the intelligence of the greatest family calamity which, short of the heir's death, could have overtaken the second Stuart King at this crisis. For, whatever else might be hidden in the darkness of the future, Robert III. could not hope to look on his boy's face again.

Thus died the second sovereign of the Stuart line, and was buried amongst his forefathers in the Abbey Church at Paisley.

* Chalmers's 'Poetical Remains of the Scottish Kings,' edition 1824, p. 3.
† Ibid.
‡ Henry's 'History of Great Britain,' second edition, vol. x. p. 141.

"In person," says Tytler, "Robert was tall, and of a princely presence; his countenance was somewhat florid, but pleasing and animated, whilst a beard of great length, and silvery whiteness, flowed down his breast, and gave a look of singular sanctity to his appearance." *

Excessive humility, a virtue estimable at all times, seems to have been carried to such an extent that it destroyed his usefulness as a feudal ruler, although as a Christian man (apart from the youthful amours to which we have alluded, p. 12 *note*) his record stands clear.

It is said that Queen Annabella once desired that, like his father and grandfather, he should provide a monument for himself, but that the King declined "a proud tomb for his miserable remains." " Cheerfully (said he) would I be buried in the meanest shed on earth, could I thus secure rest to my soul in the day of the Lord." †

* 'History of Scotland,' edition 1841, vol. iii. p. 136.
† Ibid.

CHAPTER III.

TWO SUCCESSIVE REGENTS, AND ONE GREAT MONARCH.

Robert, Duke of Albany, 1406-1419;
Murdoch, Duke of Albany, 1419-1424;
James I., 1424-1437.

IT remains uncertain whether the elder branch of the Stuart dynasty was or was not at this period in danger of succumbing to a kindred usurpation to that which had taken place in England when Henry IV., by popular favour and as the result of an insurrection which ushered in the fifteenth century, became King of England. Robert, Duke of Albany, in complete possession of power, might find specious excuses for holding the same when he scanned the horizon of Scottish politics; to say nothing of the example afforded him by the success of Henry IV. in elevating a third branch of the Plantagenets over the second, when the nation had rejected the first of that name.

In Scotland the executive Government needed a strong arm to guide its course, and the heir was a prisoner in England; the Duke of Albany being helpless to deliver him, in spite of all that has been written to the contrary. For in the year 1413, a negotiation was set on foot for the deliverance of the King, and a safe-conduct granted by the new English sovereign Henry V. (for Henry IV. had passed away on March 20, 1413), to five commissioners from Scotland so that they might remain in England to treat. But these efforts proved ineffectual.*

That the Regent must have been cognisant of such action is shown by the commanding position he held in the Government: and the fact that the English did in 1415, in exchange for Hotspur, release Albany's son, Murdoch—a prisoner of less importance than the King of Scotland—by no means warrants the common assumption that the Regent was privy to his sovereign's continued detention in a foreign country.

* Henry's 'History of Great Britain,' second edition, vol. ix. p. 297; Dr. Henry quotes Rymer, vol. ix. p. 5.

It is scarcely possible to improve on Dr. Hill Burton's summing up of this matter. The heir to the throne was taken prisoner, as if exactly to suit his (Albany's) projects; yet he could well say to any accuser, "Thou canst not say I did it." * Nor is it surprising that the dark rumour of the manner in which the late Duke of Rothesay had been starved to death at his uncle's instance, or at least with his silent concurrence, should blind men to the loyal services which Robert Duke of Albany, Regent of Scotland, subsequently performed. Chief amongst these stands the energy whereby the Earl of Mar was sent to cope with the wild hosts of Donald of the Isles, who was brought to bay at the ever-to-be-remembered village of Harlaw, on the water of Urie, close to its junction with the Don not far from Aberdeen. The battle there contested on July 24, 1411, was one of the most important fought within the limits of Caledonian soil.

Donald of the Isles, checked in his southward progress, retired baffled and cowed to his mountain fortresses; while Albany, displaying great vigour, conducted an army to Dingwall in the following year, and secured the earldom of Ross, which Donald claimed, to his own son the Earl of Buchan.†

The question at issue was whether Euphemia, Countess of Ross, could resign the earldom in favour of the Earl of Buchan when she had retired into a convent. Donald of the Isles contended that by taking the veil she became civilly dead, and, as brother-in-law of the late earl, claimed the title and estates himself.‡

The Regent Albany supported the Earl of Buchan's claim with all the resources of Scotland, apparently not being anxious for Donald's particular form of Home Rule in the Isles, but the conflict which ensued at Harlaw checked the encroachments of a barbarous domination.

On the whole, Robert Duke of Albany's régime must be characterised as successful so far as the condition of Scotland allowed, although the cruel burning of John Resby, the Wycliffite preacher, in 1408, conspired with an ineffectual raid on Roxburgh and Berwick in 1416 to give hostile writers ground for criticism.

On the other hand, contemporary testimony of Wynton, prior of Lochleven, affords ground for taking a more lenient view of the Duke's conduct than history has hitherto allowed;

---

* Burton's 'History of Scotland,' new edition, vol. ii. p. 395.
† Tytler's 'History of Scotland,' edition 1841, vol. iii. p. 153.
‡ Ibid., p. 146.

but it is necessary to follow the example of Dr. Hill Burton, and, while fully admitting the force of such considerations, to relegate this controversy to those who make a special study of the matter in question, and who are not merely giving an account in outline of a long period.

It is certainly strange that through the whole of his actual regency, Albany should have held an assumed counterpoise to the captivity of James I. in England, inasmuch as within the dominions of Donald of the Isles appeared, in 1404, an individual styling himself Richard II. of England, who was said to have escaped from Pontefract Castle instead of having died therein mysteriously four years before.

To Donald himself, the ally of England, the pretended English King asserted no such identity; but as neither Tytler nor Hill Burton were satisfied that this mysterious captive was not Richard II., it is impossible to settle the question here.*

On the other hand, the fact of a pretender to their throne being in Albany's hands probably rendered both Henry IV. and Henry V. of England obdurate when the question of rendering up James I. was mooted.

In the same year, 1419, which saw the Regent Robert of Albany's long life of eighty years closed at Stirling, this pretended (or *bonâ fide*) son of the Black Prince was buried in the Dominican Friars' church in the same royal burgh. The inscription on his tomb was as follows:—"Angliæ Ricardus iacet hic Rex ipso sepultus." †

It will be seen that the view indicated as possibly tenable but yet deprecated by Dr. Hill Burton has been avoided here. No attractive picture has been painted of Robert, Duke of Albany, in a stainless garb of innocence—depicted, in short, as his clerical admirer, Prior Wynton of Lochleven, would have desired. It is enough to say that considerble obscurity still surrounds the events of this lengthened career. It is indeed impossible to deny that the Government made itself respected at home, while maintenance of the French League formed the keystone of Albany's foreign policy. Learning the while advanced in some degree, and was nurtured by the foundation of St. Andrews University in the year 1411. This fact is attested in Fordun's chronicle 'Scotichron.,' bk. xv. ch. xxii.

Duke Robert of Albany married first, the Countess of

* See Burton's 'History of Scotland,' new edition, vol. ii. p. 383.
† Ibid.

Menteith, a distant cousin, the union requiring a Papal dispensation similar to that given in 1361 at Avignon by Pope Innocent VI. The Earls of Castle-Stewart claim to be representatives of this branch. Secondly, the Regent Robert of Albany married in 1407 Muriella, daughter of Sir William de Keith. Although a son by this marriage was the famous Earl of Buchan, who won the battle of Beauge in 1421 and fell at Verneuil in 1424, the line is extinct.*

Duke Murdoch of Albany called no Parliament together when his father died, and therefore committed an act of treason when he calmly assumed a regency which his abilities precluded him from exercising as his father had done. The Government was therefore only held together by allowing certain supporters amongst the nobles to seize estates and hold them without legal title, so that illegality was rampant throughout the land.

But for the fact that James I. in his prison at Windsor was from time to time in correspondence with leading men amongst his own subjects, this state of things might have lasted much longer, but the King o' Scots, armed with his conspicuous abilities, was a match for the feeble Regent, who whiled away his time in hawking and other amusements, while the honour and fame of Scotland were lowered, at least at home.

For at Beauge, in France, in March, 1421, it is right to record, did the Earl of Buchan, Duke Murdoch's half-brother, score the first success achieved in this generation against the English invaders of France. At the head of six thousand Scots he overcame the Duke of Clarence; a triumph obliterated, however, in August 1424 by the Duke of Bedford, when Buchan and most of his army died on the field of Verneuil.†

But this latter event occurred several months after the accession of James I., which had been hastened because the Regent Murdoch could neither guide the State nor control his own sons; and indeed, according to Sir Walter Scott and Drummond (in the preface to his 'History of Scotland),' it was the wanton destruction of a favourite falcon by Murdoch's son Walter, who had asked for the bird and had been refused, which led to the final and successful negotiations with

* See 'Pedigree of the House of Stuart,' compiled by W. A. Lindsay, Esq., for the Stuart Exhibition in London. Also Burke's 'Peerage.'
† For a succinct account see Sir W. Scott's 'Tales of a Grandfather,' edition 1880, p. 61.

England for the release of James I. in consideration of a large ransom. "Since thou wilt give me neither reverence nor obedience, I will fetch home one whom we must all obey," is said to have been the sentence announcing this decision. The retiring Regent had gauged the character of his sovereign aright.

JAMES I., 1424–1437.

It is no exaggeration to say that James I. of Scotland was the most illustrious Stuart sovereign who ruled over the northern country before the two crowns were united. The King of England, conscious of the value of the prize that had fallen into his hands, guarded the future sovereign of Scotland during his captivity with the greatest care.

He was taken in the first instance, on April 12, 1405, to the Tower of London, and kept a close prisoner there until June 10, 1407, when Nottingham was chosen as the place of confinement, wherein nearly seven years were destined to be spent.*

The first day of March 1414 saw James Stuart relegated back to the Tower, where he was kept for five months. In the following August he found a refuge at Windsor, and there first saw his future Queen, Jane Beaufort. It happened that the royal captive inhabited the tower which is known as that of Edward III., and casting his eyes towards the garden, he beheld walking therein with her ladies the fair one whose destiny was to be so closely linked to his own. The mutual attachment which ensued gave the romantic flavour to this transaction which the Scots looked for when their sovereign married; while as an affair of State the alliance promised to bring strength and influence to the northern throne.

Jane Beaufort was daughter of the Earl of Somerset, brother of Henry IV. of England, so that the two reigning families of England and Scotland became very closely allied in blood by means of this love-match. For love-match it certainly was, celebrated by the royal bridegroom in graceful verse couched in the ancient language of his own nation, and therefore ill-adapted for popular criticism, although adjudged worthy of a more advanced school of poetry than that in vogue during the fifteenth century in Britain. Speaking of the first glimpse of Jane Beaufort, the royal poet says, in the

* Henry's 'History of Great Britain,' edition 1788, vol. x. p. 140.

'King's Quhair' (as quoted in Chalmers's 'Poetical Remains of the Scottish Kings,' p. 40) :—

> "And therewith cast I down mine eye again,
> Where as I saw walking under the tower full secretly
> * * * *
> The fairest or the freshest young flower
> That ever I saw methout before that hour."

It was in February of the year 1424 that James I. married Jane Beaufort in the Church of St. Mary Overy, Southwark, the alliance being celebrated by a feast given in the palace of the bride's uncle, Cardinal Beaufort, a man of vast wealth and ambition.*

In the year 1420 the captive King James accompanied Henry V. into France as a counterpoise to the presence in that kingdom of 7000 Scots under John Stuart, Earl of Buchan, who afterwards, by his victory at Beauge on March 22, 1421, demonstrated the possibility of stemming the tide of English invasion.

Henry's aim was to interpose the King of Scotland's authority to oblige the Scots to return home, and although the Earl of Buchan repudiated an authority urged by his sovereign when acting under compulsion, an excuse was afforded for Henry V. treating all Scotchmen opposed to him in France as rebels.†

This period of James's life spent across the Channel is little commented on by the chroniclers, French or English, and presents one of the by-paths of history open to the efforts of modern explorers. He is known to have been at the coronation of Catherine Queen of France, in 1420, while two years later Rymer the chronicler speaks of the captive King o' Scots as being in that country.‡ Nor was the return of James I. to his own dominions effected without long negotiations, resulting in a treaty which called for considerable sacrifice on the part of the smaller kingdom.

It is difficult to realise how highly the Scotch people in the fifteenth century valued their monarchical institutions. Strong evidence of their loyal devotion remains, however, recorded. For we know that the following individuals of title and station were prepared to enter England as hostages

---

* Tytler's 'History of Scotland,' edition 1841, vol. iii. p. 169.
† Rapin's 'History of England,' fourth edition, vol. iv. p. 281.
‡ Chalmers's 'Poetical Remains of the Scottish Kings,' edition 1824, p. 9.

for payment of the 40,000*l.* which James I. had engaged to render to the sovereign of that country. James himself gave a bond for the full amount, whilst the nobility amongst them guaranteed the debt more than twice over. The actual hostages were:—

	Marks.		£
David, heir to Earl of Athole, guaranteed	1,200	about	8,000
Earl of Moray	1,000	,,	6,666
Earl of Crawford	1,000	,,	6,666
Duncan, Lord of Argyll	1,500	,,	10,000
William, heir of Lord Dalkeith	1,500	,,	10,000
Eldest son of William, Constable of Scotland	800	,,	5,338
Robert, Marischal of Scotland	800	,,	5,338
Robert, Lord Erskine	1,000	,,	6,666
Walter, Lord Dirleton	800	,,	5,338
Thomas Boyd, Lord Kilmarnock	500	,,	3,333
Patrick, Lord Cumnock	500	,,	3,333
Alexander, Lord Gordon	400	,,	2,666
William, Lord Abernethy	500	,,	3,333
James Dunbar, Lord Frendrath	500	,,	3,333
Andrew Gray of Foulls	600	,,	4,000
Robert, Lord Livingstone	400	,,	2,666
John Lindesay	500	,,	3,333
Robert, Lord Lisle	300	,,	2,000
James, Lord of Caldor	400	,,	2,666
James, Lord of Cadzo	500	,,	3,333
William, Lord Ruthven (or Ruthvane)	400	,,	2,666
George, heir of Hugh Campel (or Campbell)	300	,,	2,000
Robert, heir of Lord Maitland	400	,,	2,666
David Menzies	200	,,	1,333
David Ogilby (or Ogilvy)	200	,,	1,333
David, heir of John Lyon	300	,,	2,000
Total			£110,006

All these men swore that they would remain in the power of Henry VI. until the various parts of the treaty were fulfilled, so that some were committed to the Tower of London, Dover Castle, and other fortresses in the south of England.

The towns of Perth, Dundee, and Aberdeen also gave bonds equal to 50,000*l.*, so the English held pretty good security for payment of the 40,000*l.* demanded to indemnify them for the expenses of James I. during his captivity.

The above table gives an idea of the means which the Scotch aristocracy possessed; and, when we consider the

30   *The Stuart Dynasty.*

enormous difference in the value of a pound in the fifteenth century and the same amount in our own day, it will be seen that broad acres conferred wealth as well as responsibility in Scotland. Moreover, loyalty north of the Tweed is clearly hereditary. The details are to be found in Henry's 'History of Great Britain,' vol. ix. pp. 306-8, quoting Rymer's 'Fœdera,' vol. x. pp. 294-300; he (Rymer) was historiographer to Charles II., and made deep researches into Scotch history.

James I. found Scotland a veritable nest of robbers, and cannot be blamed for the resolve to subjugate independent chieftains, Lowland and Highland, who carried on their lawless depredations openly before the world. Moreover, to effect this it was natural that he should seek to guard himself against the intrigues of Murdoch, Duke of Albany, his cousin, who had for five years tolerated the complete subservience of Scotland to England, while Henry V. agreed in return to retain James in captivity.

The retribution which fell on Murdoch and his supporters was not limited to loss of political power, but extended to loss of life.

The King appears to have made his position sure by means of the Lords of Articles, whereby measures were presented to the Scotch Parliament in a practicable form after previous preparation by the Royal Council, the Constitution enabling the King to utilise such means before striking at these enemies of his own household; and if compelled to doubt the justice of the severe reprisals which ensued, we cannot deny the worldly wisdom of the sovereign's proceedings.

Unfortunately no record of the trial which Murdoch, Duke of Albany, and his associates underwent is forthcoming, so that we are left in doubt as to the facts, while enough is known to present the story in that outline which appears here, although we learn in fragmentary form that he was tried *de robboria* (for robbery).*

Murdoch of Albany, and two of his sons, were beheaded on the heading-hill at Stirling in May 1425.

It is whispered that their refusal to act as hostages in England before the King's return had awakened suspicion as to their loyalty, but James I. was scarcely the man to be moved by such a mean object as revenge.

The first to suffer was Walter Stuart, the ex-Regent's

* Tytler's 'History of Scotland,' edition 1841, vol. iii. p. 191.

eldest son, whose fine presence and general dignity of demeanour had for some time attracted the poorer subjects of the Stuart dynasty, who seem to have regarded this branch of the royal family with unusual favour, and there can be little doubt that the King on this occasion generated hostility in unexpected quarters.

The spectacle of a sovereign, crowned and in the purple, dispensing this rude justice in the national forum before Stirling Castle. is illustrative of the times, and might well attract the brush of an historical artist, as it must the pen of each writer who tells this sad story of rapine, family discord, and death.

It is fair to James I. to add that notwithstanding the lack of detailed evidence regarding the crimes of Duke Murdoch and his sons, they were judged and condemned by a tribunal containing several of their own kinsmen.*

But it was in the contest which ensued with the refractory Highland chiefs that the King gathered most of the ill-will which was destined to prove fatal to him. Undoubtedly he did put down disorder cruelly, and in a summary fashion, savouring of injustice towards certain of the individuals concerned.

James had imbibed in England the opinion that public order formed the only sure foundation whereon a civilised society could build up the most ordinary prosperity. He was accustomed to say, "Let God but grant me life, and there shall not be a spot in my dominions where the key shall not keep the castle, and the furze-bush the cow, though I myself should lead the life of a dog to accomplish it." †

This design was certainly in some degree realised, but involved its author in sterner penalties than even he had anticipated. For indeed the whole of the reign, with the exception of some months spent in a futile attempt to take Roxburgh Castle from the English, was occupied in wrestling with the barons and chieftains.

First it was the Western Islanders, under Alexander Macdonald, Lord of the Isles, who felt the weight of James's sword; and then in 1431, after a victory over Lord Mar, the same hardy people dispersed, and their leaders were driven to seek refuge in Ireland. These events were followed by resolute attempts to reduce the power of the great nobles,

* Henry's 'History of Great Britain,' vol. ix. p. 312, quoting Fordun's 'Scotichron.,' bk. xvi. ch. x.
† Tytler's 'History of Scotland,' edition 1841, vol. iii. p. 174.

who, joining together from time to time, waged war on the King himself. Thus a certain amount of tranquillity was restored, and James I. then addressed himself to regulating commerce and rendering more perfect the administration of justice. He was at the same time constrained to collect taxes from the people, a measure which, in the poverty-stricken state of Scotland, rendered lukewarm a personal popularity of which, to the very last, James I. could boast.

The general discontent found vent in a plot in which one Sir Robert Graham was chief actor, as the agent of the second family of Robert II., whose representative, the Earl of Athole, claimed the throne.*

King James gave the younger family of Robert II. substantial grounds for dissatisfaction, seeing that he resumed the earldom of Strathearn because male heirs were extinct, thus rendering desperate the Grahams, one of whom had married the heiress; nor could this manifest injustice be rendered tolerable by the grant of the earldom of Menteith to Malise Graham, the representative of that family, the resentment of the Grahams being embittered by the artifices of Walter, Earl of Athole, the King's uncle, who, blinded with ambition, thought he saw his way to gaining a crown.†

Sir Robert Graham himself, a mere cadet of the Stuart family, had small concern in this matter; but, posing as the instrument whereby the King should suffer for his encroachments on the territorial aristocracy, he succeeded in surrounding himself with a band of wild and lawless men ready to follow wherever their desperate and adventurous leader desired.

Perth, or St. Johnston, as it was called in those days, is situated at the entrance to the Highlands, and the interesting events which occurred in that city might fill several volumes; but the place has undergone such changes that few monuments remain to attest its historical importance. Not the least striking incident which marked the history of the place was the ever-to-be-regretted assassination of King James I., who, heedless of the peril which threatened him—although a caution had reached him when at Roxburgh—repaired to the monastery of the Black Friars in Perth for the Christmas of 1436.‡

It was customary for the Court to quarter itself on one of the religious houses from time to time, and James I.

* Burton's 'History of Scotland,' new edition, vol. ii. p. 407.
† Ibid. ‡ Ibid.

spent the evening of February 20, 1437, at this retreat, and indulged in converse with the womankind of his household. In a garb which denoted that he felt fully at ease, when preparing to retire to rest, he discoursed with his beloved wife, and warmed himself at the fire of the room to which the ladies resorted. Suddenly, sounds familiar to Highland ears told of the approach of many armed men, and before there was time to make due preparation, three hundred wild clansmen were forcing their way into the monastery. Brave indeed were the women, for Catherine Douglas fruitlessly thrust her arm into the staples designed for the insertion of an iron bolt, while the peerless Queen never shrank before the rush of Graham's men, who—the King's bodyguard being away quartered in the town—straightway invaded the apartment. But it may be imagined that women, however brave and devoted, were powerless to stem this long-planned onslaught. The King descended into a vault which lay beneath the room, an entrance into which had, alas! been barred by his own order a day or two previously, because the ball with which he played tennis had been wont to fall therein.

The ruffians searched the whole building, and for a moment believed that their prey had escaped. By a chance, however, one of the party descended beneath the flooring, and discovered the King helpless before his enemies. It is said that in the agony of threatened separation from the Queen, he asked for mercy and was laughed at, being told that he had shown none to those of his own race.

It is moreover reported that, though short of stature, the King of Scotland nevertheless left the mark of a strong arm on the persons of his murderers. "There were sixteen stabs in his body when it was taken up." *

The resolute action of James I. in keeping order amongst his wild mountaineer subjects, and as Monarch of Scotland relegating their chiefs to subordinate positions in the State, did not injure his reputation with the people.

The popular verdict passed upon his murderers was not that hoped for and expected by the partisans of Athole, but is contained in the popular ballad, wherein it is said—

"Robert Graham
That slew our king,
God give him shame."

---

* Burton's 'History of Scotland,' new edition, vol. ii. p. 409.

Endowed with a kingly presence, strength, and good looks, James I. will be best remembered for his mental capacity. A graceful writer both of poetry and prose, wherein a comparison with Chaucer has been instituted, although his productions have been for the most part lost, those we possess are of themselves sufficient to ensure a niche in the temple of literary fame for this unfortunate sovereign.

James had a great knowledge of the Bible, which, nevertheless, did not lead to his tolerating the Wycliffites who appeared in Scotland during his reign. Otherwise this King seems to have excelled in everything to which he applied himself, and to have perpetrated few errors.*

The Abbot of Inchcolm, who was his familiar friend, tells us that the King was a proficient in eight different instruments, and of excellence in playing the harp, while his vocal skill was considerable. He also, when in the solitude of prison, invented a new style of romantic music, which, through one Carlo Gesualdo, Prince of Venosa, became popular in Italy.† Drummond of Hawthornden, in his 'History of Scotland' (pp. 24, 25), is led by his mention of the King's musical talents to record the fact that organs were first generally used in Scotland during James's reign, and to point out how scientists of various departments crowded into the realm, and that skilled artisans found employment in a state of society created by one man, but, alas! not destined to prove permanent.

Wise measures regarding trade and the coinage of the realm occupied much time during this remarkable reign, and the metal of Scotland was restored to the same weight and quality as that of England.

This sovereign is likewise said to have excelled as an athlete—in putting the stone, running, riding, and shooting with a bow‡—to such a degree, that he surpassed most of his contemporaries; so that, if this is to be believed, we may look upon him as a veritable Crichton of the fifteenth century.

But perhaps the consideration which most of all commends the reign of James to students, is the fact that, despite the imperfect machinery with which he had to deal, James taught

---

* Henry's 'History of Great Britain,' edition 1788, vol. x. p. 231.
† Ibid., p. 232.
‡ Forduu's 'Scotichron.,' bk. xvi. ch. xxviii. Fordun was a chronicler of events in Scotland at this period, whose work is valuable, but needs careful scrutiny before use.

his people to rely, more than had hitherto been customary, upon the support of Parliament, and it will be hereafter evident that resort to such natural relief became more frequent in times of national peril or disturbance. He is said to have held thirteen Parliaments in thirteen years, and the universal appreciation of his régime by posterity might well have been used as an argument by certain obsolete theorists who desired to institute such a condition of things during the nineteenth century.

Truly the memory of this monarch should ever remain prominent amongst the sovereigns of the world; while, as regards the fifteenth century, no royal competitor disputes pre-eminence in wisdom or ability with the first King James of Scotland, barbarously slain at Perth by ignorant, jealous savages, who were incapable of understanding the prescient policy whereby he hoped to restore peace to the Highlands and security to the whole country under his care.

One incident of the great King's life and experience deserves special mention, viz. the giving in marriage of his beautiful and interesting daughter Margaret to the Dauphin, afterwards Louis XI., to whom she was married on June 25, 1436. Taken prematurely from home, she was neglected abroad by her husband, and died in 1444 at Chalons before he came to the throne.

This interesting princess was a poetess and a spirited woman. Walking through the gallery of the palace and seeing Alain Chartier (the French writer) asleep, she kissed him, and, on being told of her impropriety, replied "that she did not kiss the man, but the mouth which had uttered so many fine sayings." "That kiss," says Ménage, "will immortalise her." *

Puttenham tells this pretty story † ('Eng. Poes.,' 1589) of another princess, namely Anne of Brittany, wife of Charles VIII. who succeeded Margaret's husband as King, but this is clearly an anachronism.

James I. never lived to see the sad end of this daughter, whose charms and sorrows have interested mankind ever since.

There is, unfortunately, no portrait of King James existing the fidelity of which can be relied on, inasmuch as that valuable life was cut short before artists of repute had

* Chalmers's 'Poetical Remains of the Scottish Kings,' pp. 18, 19.
† The story is discussed in 'Notes and Queries,' 7th S. viii. Sept. 21, 1889, p. 237/1.

followed the example of prominent experts in science and music, in visiting Scotland. Ideal representations, however, exist, based on the following description adopted by Drummond of Hawthornden, the substance of which is as follows :—

James I. was of middle stature, and although of a somewhat square build, possessed a graceful manner and majestic presence, while his limbs were well shaped. It is also recorded that he had auburn hair. Drummond, who was one of his greatest admirers, wrote thus regarding his hero in the first half of the seventeenth century.

Of former Scottish sovereigns and of James I. it has been well said " the nation made them kings, but this king made that people a nation." *

James I. was murdered in his forty-fourth year.

* Drummond's ' History of Scotland,' p. 50.

CHAPTER IV.

STUART, OR DOUGLAS?
James II., 1437-1460.
KING, OR NOBILITY?
James III., 1460-1488.

JAMES II. of Scotland, having originally been declared the younger of twins born at Holyrood on October 16, 1430, was only seven years of age when his father was murdered.

The two infants were knighted at the font by their father, and with them other youthful members of the aristocracy.*

Prince Alexander having died in infancy, James became the heir, and succeeded to the throne amidst a tumult of revengeful violence which had nothing akin to civilisation in its nature: nor is it possible to justify the horrors which ensued, even by urging the necessity for paralysing forces which were banded together against the Crown. Indeed, no other evidence is required to prove the prior necessity of good King James's efforts to subdue the unquiet portion of his dominions than was furnished by the confusion which ensued during the pursuit, capture, and punishment of his murderers. Robert Graham, with some of his coadjutors, suffered death at Stirling after tortures too horrible to relate; while Atholo and others paid the penalty of their crimes at Edinburgh, where the would-be monarch was tortured with a paper crown on his head, placed thereon in bitter derision.†

There is little wonder that amidst the turmoil accompanying these reprisals the young King's coronation should take place at Holyrood, instead of Scone; ‡ Perth and its environs being adjudged too close to the wild Highlands, whence had issued forth the untutored clansmen who had wrought so much ill to Scotland, aye, and to civilisation in the two kingdoms. For had King James I. survived but a few years

* Henry's 'History of Great Britain,' second edition, vol. ix. p. 317, quoting Fordun, bk. xvi. ch. xvi.
† Burton's 'History of Scotland,' new edition, vol. ii. p. 413. ‡ Ibid.

longer his broad and wide views as to domestic and foreign policy must have exercised beneficent influence far outside Scotland's realm.

A strong secular arm had been urgently needed during the last reign, inasmuch as comparative weakness in the executive, as gauged by its relative strength in other nations, had prevailed in a certain degree ever since the Stuarts came to the throne in the year 1370. Eight years later had occurred that great Schism of the West which, rending the Church asunder, removed the restraints hitherto imposed on the clergy by an authority none dared dispute. Men stood aghast to see three spiritual authorities all claiming headship and infallibility at one time, when before the Council of Constance in 1414 Gregory XII., John XXIII., and Benedict XIII., had all assumed the Papal tiara. Not until 1429, after the resignation of Clement VIII., were these divisions even nominally brought to a close; and in a country where Churchmen claimed to be so generally consulted in the conduct of affairs as in Scotland, their discipline and training, which necessarily suffered under such inexplicable conditions, had enormous influence over the lives and conduct of future generations. And to this laxity, when the healing panacea of Wyclif was refused even the barest discussion across the Tweed, may be possibly traced the deterioration of clerical morals in later reigns, bringing about the startling local changes of religious practice and opinion which ushered in the Reformation.

A minority such as began upon the death of James I., even when guided by the strongest regent, has always proved prejudicial to a feudal State depending on regular monarchical succession. It was doubly dangerous when rivals of equal influence were employed in striving to overreach one another.

One Sir William Crichton, a friend of the late King, being governor of Edinburgh Castle, detained the young prince in that stronghold; but the Queen dowager, having greater confidence in Sir Alexander Livingston, governor of Stirling, another confidant of James I., concealed her son in a bale of luggage, in order that when the article was shipped at Leith its precious contents might likewise be conveyed up the Forth near to Scotland's most central stronghold at Stirling.

Livingston having thus triumphed over his rival and secured the person of the heir, Crichton, who was Chancellor of the kingdom, seems silently if grudgingly to have acquiesced, an attitude which, in the presence of a superior in the Earl of Douglas, governor of the kingdom, was only relaxed when that nobleman died in 1439, leaving a son only seventeen years of age to succeed him.* Crichton, unrestrained by any superior genius, schemed to get the young king into his power again, and making a successful raid towards Stirling, "kidnapped" the boy when taking exercise in the royal park.

But the new Earl of Douglas, despite his youth, displayed a character which made his enemies tremble. Accepting homage from all who approached him, this haughty young noble never appeared in public without a thousand men-at-arms, and it was rumoured that he intended to set up a Parliament of his own.†

Sir Alexander Livingston, although exceedingly irritated at the King's capture and removal to Edinburgh Castle, thought it wiser to hide his resentment towards Crichton, whom, by the intermediation of the bishops of Aberdeen and Moray, he met secretly in the church of St. Giles at Edinburgh,‡ in the year 1440; the substance of the agreement then arrived at being that the King was to remain with the Chancellor in the noble castle overlooking the capital, while Livingston retained the emoluments of his place as governor of Stirling.

But the bond which allied the two conspirators together was not loyalty to the King, but dread of the Douglas power, which it was resolved forthwith to break. A Parliament having been summoned at Edinburgh during this same year 1440, nominally to adjust complaints made by numbers of the people against exactions suffered at the hands of the Douglases, two of them, Earl William and his brother David, were cajoled into accepting an invitation, couched in friendly and flattering terms, from Crichton, who set forth the mutual advantage to the King and his powerful visitors which would ensue from the proposed meeting. And so the flies were straightway entangled in the spider's web. A magnificent feast having been prepared, the young Douglases were received in the ancient castle with gracious affability by the unsuspecting King; and the scene of wassail and rejoicing went on to its settled conclusion. After a bull's head had been placed on the table, according to the method of the times, the murderous intentions of the two men who held

* Burton's 'History of Scotland,' new edition, vol. ii. p. 414.
† Ibid., p. 415.
‡ Buchanan's 'History of Scotland,' vol. ii. p. 201.

power were disclosed, and the Douglases were suddenly seized by armed retainers, who, dragging them before a mock tribunal, despatched the representatives of a line which was nevertheless yet to rise to the apex of its power.

That the young James II., at nine years of age, was as ignorant of this base and murderous breach of honour and hospitality, as we know him to have been distressed at its bloody outcome, has been attested by all writers; but he was nevertheless destined, in the capacity of King o' Scots, to spend the best years of a reign extending over twenty-three years in deciding once and for all that his family, and not that of Douglas, was to rule north of Tweed.

Two years' breathing space were secured to the oligarchy enthroned in Edinburgh; because James, the fat Earl of Douglas, elected not to disturb Crichton and Livingston in their custody of the young King. But when that phlegmatic representative of the princes of the Border died, his son William displayed all the pride and ambition of his race, combined with a statesmanlike address which did him good service.

Coming to Stirling, Douglas demanded of Livingston the right to do homage to the sovereign. The young King on that occasion, and with Livingston's acquiescence, conferred the Lieutenant-Governorship of the kingdom on the Earl, who straightway married, by Papal license, his cousin, the fair maid of Galloway, a child of eleven. This alliance immensely increased the Douglas wealth and influence.* From that moment the issue was placed before Scotland for decision, whether Stuart or Douglas should hold the national sceptre and occupy the throne of Kenneth, William the Lion, and Robert Bruce.

Space does not admit of any detailed account of the events which occurred. Suffice it to say that the King strengthened his position abroad and the hopes of his dynasty at home by a marriage with Mary, daughter of Arnold, Duke of Gueldres and Cleves, whose early family history has delighted the readers of Froissart.

By taking this beautiful woman for his consort, James II. united his family indirectly with the line of the Dukes of Burgundy, then represented by a powerful independent sovereign. The marriage took place at Holyrood in June 1449. A year later all Scotland was aflame with the violence,

* These details occur in Burton's 'History of Scotland,' new edition, vol. ii. pp. 421, 422. They are substantiated by other authorities.

murder, and rapine which the Douglas was perpetrating. In revenge for a murder punishable by ordinary law, Earl William stormed Lord Colville's castle and put every soul therein to death. Moreover the rebel tyrant executed a captive named Maclellan for the crime of loyalty to the Stuart line, holding King James's letter entreating mercy unopened in his hand while he gave the order to despatch his victim.*

But the Earl of Douglas, in common with nearly all other members of his family, stood exonerated in the eyes of the people, because the name represented the chivalry which threw a cloak over crime itself, and breathed the very spirit of the field, whether displayed in gorgeous tournament or sterner modes of strife. To use the words of the Scotch poet Home in his tragedy of 'Douglas':—

> "Douglas! a name through all the world renown'd,
> A name that rouses like a trumpet sound.
> Oft have your fathers, prodigal of life,
> A Douglas followed through the bloody strife:
> Hosts have been known at that dread sound to yield,
> And, Douglas dead, his name hath won the field!"

In the year 1449 a notable tournament was held in a hollow, called the Valley, in the Castle hill at Stirling, where James II. and the Court assembled to view the joust from a mount known as the Ladies' Hill. The rival combatants were three champions of Flanders and three of Scotland, two of the latter bearing the name of Douglas. The Earl himself witnessed the contest, which was well maintained, for one Flemish knight, Meriadet, alone prevailed over his antagonist. The Douglas escort on this occasion consisted of five thousand men.†

Such was the man who at this crisis of his fortunes made a pilgrimage to see the Papal jubilee at Rome, and gave an opportunity to those whose kinsmen he had injured at home to combine against him during his absence. Soon, however, he returned on being informed of the hostile feeling evinced in Scotland. At first Douglas appeared anxious to propitiate his justly indignant sovereign, and so underwent the formality of repentance when already committed to a course subversive of the established throne.

We have seen how, when formerly supreme on the borders,

---

* Burton's 'History of Scotland,' new edition, vol. ii. p. 424.
† Sir Walter Scott's 'Tales of a Grandfather,' edition 1880, p. 67; see also Tytler.

the Douglases had been inferior to the Stuarts in authority over the northern clansmen; since the Stuarts, by reason of their authority in Renfrew and Bute, were better able to control the wild Highlanders who lived at a distance from the Border.

Douglas now proposed to make an alliance, such as, rendering his authority supreme north of Perth and in the Isles, would give him the opportunity of assembling a force in the field superior to that of the King.

The allies who were potent enough to bring about this threatening situation for the Stuarts were Earl Crawford (the Tiger Earl, who was supreme in Perthshire, Angus, and Kincardine), while the third colleague in this triumvirate which Douglas had devised was the Earl of Ross, whose authority in the north of Scotland was undisputed.

It is not difficult to appreciate the magnitude of the dangers which beset the reigning dynasty at this moment, and James II. clearly saw that his throne was at stake. Being, however, but ill-prepared for the conflict, he took the questionable course of dissembling his dreads and doubts, giving a free-conduct under the Great Seal to Douglas and a numerous retinue, which allowed him by this means to come to Court at Stirling and presumably take counsel with his sovereign as to the national condition. Now, under ordinary circumstances, no fault could have been found with such a parley between a feudal sovereign and a dissatisfied vassal noble. But in the case under consideration William, Earl of Douglas, appeared absolutely red-handed from the slaughter of foes who were subjects of the sovereign he pretended to serve. It was impossible that any real confidence could exist between the King and Douglas under these circumstances; and mutual suspicions were doubtless uppermost when the long procession of the Border prince's retinue filed into the town of Stirling. James II. met his rival in the castle which crowns the rocky eminence overlooking Scotland's fairest plain, but the followers of Douglas were quartered in the town. There seems to have been a friendly meeting at supper, followed by an interview in another apartment where Douglas conversed with his royal master. One subject succeeding another without producing irritation, the King ventured on the delicate question of *the Band*, which, if unbroken, gave Scotland practically into Douglas's power; and the discussion seems straightway to have changed its character, each disputant becoming irritated.

At last, when he could secure no concession, James II., aflame with excitement and goaded into temporary madness, asked authoritatively that Douglas should break his agreement with the two great northern Lords, the Earl of Crawford and the Earl of Ross, and upon Douglas's refusal the King cried out, "Then this shall," and twice stabbed his guest,* whereupon an adherent of the King's, who was at hand, finished the bloody work by striking Douglas on the head with a pole-axe; and his body was thrown from the window into the court below.†

It has not been suggested that this terrible event was the outcome of any settled purpose. It was rather inspired by unbridled rage, indulgence in which might, on behalf of a private person, have been pleaded amongst half-civilised beings in condonation of bloodshed. But, even in these rude times, the sin of Cain ill fitted the monarch's *rôle*, and a deep stain remains on the name of a Stuart sovereign otherwise distinguished throughout his career for the display of better qualities.

The Douglases made a great effort to arouse the country against the King, and their retainers burnt the town of Stirling, beating in vain against its famous stronghold, which stood like a rock in mid-ocean above surging and raging billows.

It is said, moreover, that James II., for a time, meditated flight into France, aghast at the crime he had committed, as well as at the prospect of a stern conflict with so powerful a section of his subjects. For the dreaded compact, fidelity to which had cost William, Earl of Douglas, his life, had partially done its work, the north being uneasy and hostile to the crown.

* Burton's 'History of Scotland,' new edition, vol. ii. p. 425. According to Buchanan, edition 1752, vol. ii. p. 35, Douglas hesitated and was silent when the league with Crawford and Ross was named, but acquiesced as regards other matters under discussion. The King, reverting to the main object of the meeting so far as he was concerned, lost command over himself when he failed to move Douglas to reply, and hastily said, "If thou wilt not break it, I will." Hence the tragedy which ensued. Drummond, in his 'History of Scotland,' pp. 83–86, apparently endeavouring to offer some excuse for this hideous crime, gives a lengthy dialogue which the King and his rebellious subject are assumed to have carried on. No authority, however, is cited, and the account, although worth perusal, cannot be accepted as history. Drummond, as a seventeenth century chronicler, must nevertheless be accounted a generally conscientious and reliable writer, in spite of his tendency to palliate the shortcomings of the Stuarts.

† In 1797, during some alterations, a skeleton, believed to be that of William, Earl of Douglas, was found in the garden.

At this crisis, however, James II. consulted Kennedy, Bishop of St. Andrews, whom he elevated to the post of first minister. We are told that this wise counsellor asked him to break a bundle of arrows, and on this being found impossible, the Bishop suggested that the destruction should be attempted separately, a process perfectly simple and successful, which the prelate straightway applied by analogy to the rebel hosts arrayed in opposition to the Scotch King. If this be true, the worthy Bishop utilised a very old story. At any rate, the result of the policy recommended by Kennedy was that, finesse and flattery working upon the jealousy inspired by the greatness of the Douglas, a much smaller force appeared in the field against the King's retainers. For the Earl of Crawford, prostrating himself before the sovereign, craved pardon; while the Earl of Angus, himself a Douglas, withdrew from the family camp.

James, brother of the lately slain Earl of Douglas, reigned in his stead, and strengthened his financial position by marrying his brother's widow and claiming her share of the possessions held by this wonderful family. At the same time he made some sort of treaty with the Yorkists, who, in 1454, were striving to overthrow the house of Lancaster in England.

According to the chroniclers, King James raised 40,000 men and took the Douglas stronghold of Abercorn, near the Forth, in Linlithgowshire; and a battle would have been fought, had not the Hamiltons, important allies of the Douglases, withdrawn from the conflict owing to the intrigues of Kennedy, who secretly assured Hamilton of the King's forgiveness and future favour. The consequence was that, to use Sir Walter Scott's expressive words, the army of the Douglas dispersed like a melting snowball, and notwithstanding that he and his brother made a final and ineffectual stand at Arkinholme, in the valley of Esk, on May 1, 1455, it was with difficulty that the Earl escaped into England, while the head of Archibald Douglas was brought to the King at Abercorn, another brother, Hugh, Earl of Ormond, losing his life in the battle.* Thus at last this great rivalry between Stuart and Douglas for supremacy terminated in the prostration of the latter, although the several branches of the defeated and divided clan subsequently sustained leading parts in the several reigns which

* Sir W. Scott's 'Tales of a Grandfather,' edition 1880, p. 70; also Burton's 'History of Scotland,' new edition, vol. ii. p. 429.

ensued before the two kingdoms of England and Scotland were united under one crown.

James II. seems to have done all that lay within his power to improve the breathing space which the conclusion of this civil war afforded his agitated realm. Parliament was freely consulted, and laws were passed which were considered needful for the occasion; while the ablest of the clergy, with Bishop Kennedy at their head, acted as his ministers. Unfortunately his engagements with the reigning English dynasty of Lancaster involved James II. in enmity with the Yorkist party, soon to attain the throne by overthrowing Henry VI. Indeed, the key to the King o' Scots' foreign policy lies in the recognition of his overstrained fidelity to the reigning sovereign in England when events hung poised in the balance, so that it was enmity to the house of York, not to England, which impelled him, in the year 1460, to break through a truce and endeavour to seize the Border castle of Roxburgh. The castle in question was situated on an eminence where the Tweed and Teviot join their waters, and had been long held to be a bulwark of the Scotch nation. It was in English, nay, in Yorkist hands, for Neville, Lord Falconberg, who commanded there, held the place for the future King Edward IV.

James determined to proceed to regular siege, and brought into position, amongst other of the rude cannons then in vogue, a large piece of hooped ordnance, which went by the name of "the Lion," being of the same type as Mons Meg, the pride of Edinburgh Castle in our own day. But when put to the test of firing, this clumsy weapon burst, and a piece of iron broke King James's thigh-bone. He fell, never to rise again, ending prematurely, when only twenty-nine years old, a life full of promise for his country. A thorn-tree in the Duke of Roxburgh's park marks the place of his death.

This monarch did not live long enough to expiate the great crime of his life, the murder of William, Earl of Douglas, though the furious temper which prompted that lamentable deed was subdued before he died; but he imitated his illustrious father in endeavouring to consolidate the resources of Scotland, and so render her strong before the foe. To effect this, the practice of archery was enjoined, and that of golf and football—strange as it appears to us—discouraged,* lest they should occupy too exclusively popular attention. The King also reserved to himself the right of exercising eccle-

---

* A.D. 1457, "that fute ball and golfe be utterly cryit downe."

siastical patronage, although he reverenced the Holy See, and hailed with satisfaction the accession of Pius II. (the famous Æneas Silvius Piccolomini), who had resided in Scotland during part of the reign of James I.*

The person of James II. was robust and well-adapted for those warlike and knightly exercises in which he excelled, while his countenance was mild and intelligent, but disfigured by a large red mark on the cheek,† which gained for him the name of "James with the fiery face," an index, as some writers have suggested, of his fiery temper. He was interred at Holyrood, where early in the nineteenth century the royal vault was visible to every visitor who cared to pay a few pence for access thereto.

By Mary of Gueldres he left three sons, James III., Alexander, Duke of Albany, and John, Earl of Mar, and two daughters, Mary and Cecilia. The brave and able Queen Mary of Gueldres found a resting-place by her royal husband.

KING, OR NOBILITY?—JAMES III., 1460-1488.

James III., a prince of six years and seven months old, was brought to Roxburgh after his father's death, which had been concealed from the army until they had gained possession of that fortress. For, thanks to the Queen dowager's resolution, it soon fell and was dismantled. When at length the death of the King was announced, his young son and successor appeared in the camp, and received homage of his barons at Kelso.

Another minority being unavoidable, it was fortunate that the first six years of the new monarch's reign should be passed under the guidance of so wise a minister as Bishop Kennedy, who, in spite of the hospitality shown to the exiled Henry VI. of England, was successful in propitiating the Government of Edward IV., and securing a long truce on the Border. Just before Bishop Kennedy's death in 1466, he had appointed Sir Alexander Boyd, an accomplished gentleman of high family, to instruct the King in martial exercises. This new friend, together with his brother, Lord Boyd of Kilmarnock, gained, after the Bishop's death, a complete influence over the youthful James III., so that, in the face of an Act of Parliament passed in the previous reign, which declared such a deed to be treasonable, the Boyds

---

* Tytler's 'History of Scotland,' edition 1841, vol. iv. p. 130.
† Ibid., p. 155.

forcibly seized the King's person, and conveyed him to Linlithgow. This happened in the same year, 1466, wherein James lost his guardian; and the abduction was carried out under the pretence that Gilbert Kennedy, the tutor, brother of the late prelate, was too strict a disciplinarian to be entrusted with the youthful sovereign's education; so that, taking the opportunity of meeting the King on a hunting party, the Boyds turned his horse towards Edinburgh. Having thus got the royal minor into their power, they proceeded to govern Scotland in his name.

No wonder need be expressed that James III., eager to forestall the privileges of manhood and get his own way in small things, should declare before Parliament in October 1466 that he approved Lord Boyd's action, which "should never be called in question." *

Small marvel, likewise, that two years later the young King, smarting under the yoke which his new favourites imposed, should try to free himself as best he could. For the Boyds had arrogated to themselves all the power of the crown, and employed it to aggrandise their own family, facts which enemies were not slow to make manifest to the royal mind, mingling such complaints with artful suggestions that the Lord Boyd himself aspired to the crown.†

Nor did the fact that the dominant faction secured a beautiful bride for King James III. in the person of Margaret, only daughter of Christian I., King of Denmark, Sweden, and Norway, procuring at the same time the sovereignty of the Orkney and Shetland Isles for the Scotch throne, hinder their inevitable fall. Lord Boyd's son, the Earl of Arran, brought the royal lady home to Scotland, yet he was compelled to take to flight before landing his precious freight; while the sovereign called a Parliament at Edinburgh in November 1469, and summoned his late favourites to answer the accusations made against them.

Lord Boyd fled to England, where he died, but his brother, Sir Alexander, was beheaded on the Castle Hill of Edinburgh for having brought the King to that city against his will.

James was only thirteen years old when he appeared to acquiesce in conduct which he condemned and punished so severely at fifteen years of age; his youth in each case excusing an instability of character which reappeared in a different form later in life.

* Henry's 'History of Great Britain,' second edition, vol. ix. p. 371.
† Ibid., p. 375.

If, however, he really did act of his own free will in 1466 when taken from Linlithgow, his conduct deserves strong condemnation.

After the Boyds had fallen from power the royal marriage was celebrated with great public joy on June 15, 1470, the bridegroom being in his seventeenth and the bride in her sixteenth year. She charmed all with her beauty and elegance, and still more by her prudence, piety, modesty, and sweet temper.*

Temporary freedom from the trammels of his nobility by no means brought peace to James III., for his tendency to make favourites was straightway indulged amongst men of inferior rank and position, a course which, alienating the King from his two brothers, the Duke of Albany and the Earl of Mar, ultimately ranged the majority of his nobles against him.

This jealousy felt by James III. against his royal brothers, Albany in particular, was believed to have been fanned by Cochran, the King's leading favourite, in return for bribes given him by the dissatisfied nobility. On the other hand an unwonted parsimony led the monarch to prefer the increase of his gold and silver hoards to attaching powerful nobles and chieftains to the royal person by that generosity which his exalted position demanded. Add to this that James III. was looked on amongst his barons as a timorous recluse, totally out of sympathy with their warlike habits and love of martial parade, and we need look no further for the cause of those dissensions which characterised the reign.

The brothers of James III., the Duke of Albany and the Earl of Mar, possessed the very manners requisite for the sustenance of royal authority at this time. While the former was well-proportioned and of tall stature, stern in temper, and warlike in mien, the latter also shone at the tournaments and hunting and hawking parties, as well as his brother the Duke of Albany, yet gained much favour by reason of his gentle manners.

Now James III. could boast of no popular gifts, and seems very readily to have lent an ear to the reports brought to him by Cochran and others.

It was pretended that the Earl of Mar had once consulted a witch as to how the King should die, and received for answer, that in Scotland a Lion should be killed by his own

* Henry's 'History of Great Britain,' second edition, vol. ix. p. 378, quoting Ferrerius.

whelps—a prognostication freely translated into fraternal enmity—in dread of which Mar was put out of the way mysteriously in the Canongate at Edinburgh, A.D. 1477.*

Drummond, who transcribed this portion of his history from a manuscript of a contemporary writer, avers that Mar, indignant at being confined in Craigmillar Castle, fell into a fever, and that in order to be near medical aid, the King removed him to the Canongate in Edinburgh, where, to relieve the frenzy which had supervened, according to the manner then in vogue, the physicians bled him; but that the operation being performed unskilfully, the unhappy Prince sank and never rallied.†

The Duke of Albany, moved by the fate of Mar, gave rein to his indignation, and so drew on himself the hostility of those who designed his brother's imprisonment, but, being warned in time, made a romantic escape from Edinburgh Castle during 1478, ultimately reaching France, where Louis XI. procured for this fugitive prince a daughter of the Earl of Boulogne in marriage, ensuring him thereby an ample fortune.‡ Moreover, Albany was afterwards destined to give trouble to his royal brother by means of intrigues with England, acting at the same time in collusion with the discontented Scotch nobility.

Nothing but confusion seemed in store for the ill-fated James III.

The first episode in this revolutionary drama was as follows. A section of the nobility held a conclave in the church of Lauder during the year 1482 to decide whether they should obey the order of James III. to array the kingdom against Edward IV. of England, who meditated an invasion on the pretext of placing Albany on the throne of Scotland. The result of these deliberations was a resolve to deal summary justice upon Cochran and the other royal favourites before parleying with the English, the recital of a fable by Lord Gray bringing about this determination. "The mice," he said, "being much annoyed by the persecution of the cat, resolved that a bell should be hung about puss's neck to give notice when she was coming." But who was to bell the cat formed an anxious subject of discussion amongst the diminu-

* Henry's 'History of Great Britain,' vol. ix. p. 382, quoting Ferrerius and Buchanan.
† Drummond's 'History of Scotland,' p. 137.
‡ Henry's 'History of Great Britain,' vol. ix. p. 383, quoting Ferrerius and Buchanan.

tive enemies of the feline race; while an analogous difficulty presented itself to the Scotch nobility at Lauder when they contemplated the power and royal favour of Cochran and his associates. However, Archibald, Earl of Angus, a man of great strength and courage, cut the matter short directly Gray had ceased to speak, declaring that he would bell the cat; and so was called "Archibald Bell the Cat" to his dying day. Cochran, Leonard, Hommel, and Torphichen, together with Preston, a man of good birth, were forthwith hanged over the bridge of Lauder; and James III. only succeeded in saving one of his detested favourites, namely, John Ramsay of Balmain, who was spared because of his youth, being only sixteen years of age. Archibald Bell the Cat went to the borders after this tragedy, and concluded peace with England on the condition that Albany came back to Scotland, where he remained and kept on good terms with his brother James III. until, in 1484, fresh dissensions drove the duke, first to England and finally to France, where his wife resided. Albany was killed at a tournament. Albany's son was regent in the reign of James V.*

There is reason to believe that James III. was honestly desirous of living on good terms with Albany, or the King would not have elevated his rebellious brother to the Lieutenant-generalship of Scotland, after the mock siege of Edinburgh Castle in 1482 by that prince, on which occasion not a drop of blood was shed on either side, and yet the frowning stronghold yielded. As events turned out James III. regarded his brother as a deliverer, until Albany's treasonable correspondence with the Court of England, and his complicity with the enemies of the King, Archibald Bell the Cat and Andrew Lord Gray, became apparent. There was every evidence of reconciliation between the two sons of James II., who rode on one horse from the Castle of Edinburgh to Holyrood House amidst the acclamations of the people.†

It is true, as Dr. Hill Burton has observed, that very little is known for certain regarding the talents of these defunct favourites of James III.; nor is it by any means certain that the encouragement given to architecture, music, and the fine

* The above account of the deaths of the favourites of James III., and the career of Albany, we owe to Sir Walter Scott's 'Tales of a Grandfather' (edition 1880, pp. 74–76). Buchanan, Hill Burton, and the younger Tytler have also been consulted; also the general account in Henry's 'History of Great Britain,' vol. ix. pp. 382–391.

† 'Pitscottie Chronicles,' p. 82.

arts, did not tend to elevate Scotland at a moment when that country was lagging behind in the march of civilisation. But allowing for all this it is not to be wondered at that the proud untutored barons, who attended the Court, should revolt at the elevation of architects, masons, and fiddlers to a high estate unheard of at the period, their influence being regarded as by no means salutary.

The full weight of trouble did not overtake this unfortunate sovereign James III. until, for the pursuit of his architectural designs at Stirling—where he beautified the castle hall exceedingly, and built a chapel—he confiscated, about the year 1485, the revenues due to the Priory of Coldingham. Two powerful families, the Humes and Hepburns, being affected by this proceeding, swelled the confederacy of disloyal barons, and rendered futile divers efforts on the King's part to hold his own against England on the Border. In truth, the special faculties of James III., which raised him above the ordinary run of those who lived in the fifteenth century, were the cause of his ruin. The student King who takes no active part in affairs without an *alter ego* in the shape of regent to direct the policy of his government, is certain to forfeit his just influence, unless the constitutional machinery he should employ be in a fair state of regularity. The despotic monarch who takes his ease, be it of mind or body, is condemned to certain failure.

According to Buchanan,* John Ramsay, saved by James's own intervention at Lauder Bridge, who had been elevated to be master of the household, was the immediate cause of this rebellion breaking out, the favourite procuring an edict that none but he and his retinue "should wear a sword or other weapon in those places where the King lodged," while the Earl of Angus gave out that a plot of James III. to destroy the nobility had been revealed to him during the Parliament which assembled in Edinburgh at the end of January 1488.†

The King faced the storm with unexpected energy, and, after committing his son and heir to Shaw, the governor of Stirling, proceeded northward, issuing his proclamation to the Earl of Crawford, the Earls of Huntly, Erroll, Athole, Rothes, Sutherland, and Caithness, together with the Lords Forbes, Ogilvy and Fraser. Every one of these noblemen prepared to join the King; but the King's arrangements were in an incomplete state, when it was announced to James III.

---

* Edition 1752, vol. ii. pp. 88–90.   † Ibid., p. 95.

that the confederate Lords had succeeded in getting the young prince James into their hands by means of an intrigue with the above-mentioned Shaw. When, therefore, after a parley with the rebels at Blackness near Linlithgow, their head-quarters, the King arrived at his boasted stronghold, never captured since Robert the seventh Steward, as a youth, won it for the cause of King David II., he found himself excluded, and so denied the opportunity of forming a nucleus for a host sufficiently strong to cope with this dangerous rebellion.

Roughly speaking the north stood by James III., and the south by his barons. The two armies, each with the royal standard, met near a small stream called Sauchieburn, between Bannockburn and Stirling, and it soon became apparent that the borderers of the south, who were for the prince and the rebel Lords, were more than a match for the King's rudely armed Highlanders. When the King saw that the young prince's banner was opposed to him, he became sorely troubled, and, if his enemies are to be credited, showed no stomach for fighting. He was, however, mounted upon a fine grey horse given to him by the Lord Lindsay, which, when the action commenced, became unmanageable. James, being mastered by his charger, and being moreover dazed by unfamiliar and distasteful sights and sounds, was carried at full gallop across the Bannockburn, and then down hill to a house called Beaton's mill, where he was dashed to the ground in his heavy armour and much bruised. The King asked the miller's wife to tend his injuries. Placing him on the humble bed of the cottage, the good wife learnt with amazement that she was ministering to her King, who desired her to get a priest to shrive him. A passer-by declared himself to be in holy orders, and stooping down, as if to perform the sacred offices required, plunged a dagger again and again into the King's body, and when certain that his victim was dead, retired, never to be seen or heard of again.* In the meantime the royal army had been thrown into complete confusion. So died James III. of Scotland, bearing a character variously estimated, but of interest to the student even to this day. The murdered sovereign was eminently handsome, tall, athletic, and well-proportioned, his countenance combining intelligence and

---

* Buchanan, Scott, Tytler, and Burton have all been consulted for this short account of James's death, and are found to agree substantially.

sweetness, his deep brown complexion and black hair telling of his Gueldres connection with the Burgundy family rather than with that of Stuart. Such indeed are the features of that portrait in the famous Holyrood diptych, which created such a sensation at the Stuart Exhibition in London during the winter of 1888-9. It is ascribed by connoisseurs to an unknown painter of the school which Mabuse subsequently represented. Dignified, cold, and distant in manner, the King was never in touch with the nobility, whose support was necessary for his government. But what contributed more than all to make James III. unpopular in the quarter indicated, was a tendency to hoard riches rather than spend his money in supporting the rude splendour of a feudal court, such as had been associated with kingship all through the middle ages, even in semi-pauperised Scotland.

When, therefore, in his despair, just before the clash of arms at Sauchieburn, James visited the recluse warrior James Earl of Douglas, at the monastery of Lindores in Fife, and asked him to change his mode of life for a short time, receiving his sovereign's forgiveness, and striking for the crown, the Earl replied,—" Ah, sir, your grace has kept me and your black casket too long."* Douglas implied that the time when either he himself or the treasure hoarded in Edinburgh Castle could be of use, was gone for ever.

Admitting James III. to have been alienated from the Scotch aristocracy towards the close of his reign, it is probable that the feeling of the masses—could it have been elicited by their suffrages—would have been largely in his favour.† Honours were bestowed and confidence given to men of low estate whose talents attracted the King's notice, and who would have remained in obscurity under an oligarchic rule such as the Humes and Hepburns, using the young prince's name, wished to maintain. James's great fault in the eyes of men such as these seems to have been a devotion to studies and accomplishments which in this unsettled, not to say barbarous age, were held to be unworthy of one of highest rank and dignity. His real culpability, on the other hand, lay in his neglect of government, which he left to others, and those untried men.

For a considerable time it was believed that the unfortunate King still lived, and Pitscottie the Scotch chronicler

---

* Sir W. Scott's ' Tales of a Grandfather,' edition 1880, p. 76.
† Burton's ' History of Scotland,' new edition, vol. iii. p. 38.

has an account of events subsequent to Sauchieburn which is of great interest. Sir Andrew Wood, the celebrated sailor whom James III. had patronised and advanced, was waiting in the Firth of Forth with some ships of war during that battle, and sending on shore to find the King, was obliged to be contented with bringing off a few wounded loyalists in the vain hope that he might be amongst the number. Nothing could at first be heard of the missing monarch. His mangled body was, however, soon discovered, and buried at Cambuskenneth, where Queen Victoria has erected a monument to his memory, together with that of his Queen, Margaret of Denmark, also buried in that romantic Abbey, under the shadow of Stirling and near the sluggish waters of the river Forth.

CHAPTER V.

THE ANCIENT LEAGUE WITH FRANCE.

James IV., 1488-1513;
Childhood of James V., 1513-1528.

It was expected by observers of the events which brought about the destruction of James III. that the fruits of successful rebellion would be enjoyed by the Lords, who, in the fashion of feudal times, had banded against the late monarch. But the rebels reckoned without their host. Although the young king was only sixteen years old, yet he possessed much youthful ambition, and, indeed, cannot be altogether absolved from the charge of trying to supplant his father, even if we take into account the undeniable pressure put upon him by the Hume and Hepburn faction which had raised this rebellion. Soon were these men to know that, beyond a parliamentary absolution for their treason, then attainable in the single legislative chamber by each dominant party, they were to get for their pains little more than the yoke of a fresh master, whose activity and watchful energy kept them in check, while he raised his country to a commanding position by means of their enemies, counsellors of the late King.

At first, it is true, the recreant nobility who were responsible for the catastrophe at Sauchieburn were seen close to the person of James IV., whose coronation took place at Edinburgh on June 24, 1488; the Castle, hitherto hostile to the confederates, being secured and committed to the custody of Lord Hailes. But when, in the enforced seclusion of Stirling Castle, the sovereign had leisure to reflect, his sorrow and remorse for unfilial conduct towards James III. overcame any natural misgivings as to his own future; and at the instance, it is said, of the Dean of the Chapel Royal at Stirling, he wore in penitential sorrow a chain of iron about his body, and resolved to add a new link thereto year by year.*

Moreover, at this juncture, ominous expressions of dis-

* 'Pitscottie Chronicles,' p. 98.

satisfaction were heard amongst the chieftains of the north; so that had not the so-called *Healing Parliament*, held at Edinburgh on October 6, 1488, made, so to speak, things pleasant all round, scattered explosions—such as the revolts of Lord Lennox, Lord Gordon, and Lord Forbes, the last of whom carried the late King's shirt, all torn and bloody, as an ensign at the head of his forces—would have developed into a general civil war.

It is clear also that the commanding personal gifts of James IV. were such as to preclude subordination to his father's enemies, who only held their supremacy in council during the sovereign's minority by pandering to vices which were destined to blot and darken an otherwise engaging character. It is well known, for instance, that the noble family of Drummond, which had already given a Queen to the Stuart dynasty, namely, the wife of Robert III., had every right which justice and morality could urge, to see the crown set upon the head of a fair daughter of their race, whom James adored with characteristic knightly devotion, while the head of the Drummonds, presuming on James's affection for his child, rode roughshod over the laws.* This intimacy was only brought to an end by the sudden death both of the Lady Margaret and her sisters Euphemia and Sybilla, at Drummond Castle, just before the King espoused an English princess, Margaret, daughter of Henry VII. This was the most important matrimonial alliance recorded in the history of the house of Stuart.†

But the degrading influence of the cabal amongst the nobility of James III. was likewise evident in the ill blood which existed between England and Scotland throughout the succeeding reign, despite the peaceful designs of that " inscrutable " statesman Henry VII., so styled by Lord Bacon. Had the English King desired to enter into hostilities with Scotland, he might have embraced the opportunity given him in 1491 by two of the late King's adherents, John Ramsay and Sir Thomas Todd, who proposed to deliver up the new monarch to England, provided some pecuniary consideration was forthcoming, but received no definite reply from Henry VII. This plot was never revealed to public ken until Mr. Rymer, the compiler of the famous ' Fœdera,' unearthed it in 1711.‡

---

* Tytler's 'History of Scotland,' edition 1841, vol. iv. p. 297.
† Ibid., edition 1834, vol. v. p. 15.
‡ Henry's 'History of Great Britain,' second edition, vol. xi. p. 381.

As mutual distrust existed between the two sovereigns, though apparently they were on good terms, it is not to be wondered at that James encouraged and protected the impostor Perkin Warbeck, who pretended to be the Duke of York, a son of Edward IV., known to have been murdered with his brother in the Tower of London by the Duke of Gloucester. This claim, if sustained, would have transferred the crown of England from the house of Lancaster to that of York; and, strange to say, James IV., after due deliberation, endorsed this preposterous pretension, and gave Perkin Warbeck to wife the Lady Catherine Gordon, daughter of the Earl of Huntly, and granddaughter to James I., known as the White Rose of Scotland. Her sad position, after James IV. perceived the imposition foisted upon him, is almost unique in history.

Henry VII. was wise enough not to resent this provocation, but, giving good for evil, endeavoured to cement the interests of the twin countries of England and Scotland by the family union to which reference has been made. By so doing he frustrated the schemes of Ferdinand and Isabella, then reigning in Spain, who, although their only legitimate daughter Catherine was contracted to Arthur, the English Prince of Wales, endeavoured to palm off a natural daughter on James IV., as if she were really a princess of Spain and the Indies, a device which was part of the policy of the league formed to support the claims of the Church of Rome against those of France*—a quarrel which threatened to shake western Christianity to its foundation, when the Reformation supervening absorbed the attention of Europe.

It is time now to pause and discover what sort of man James IV. of Scotland was, whose individual endeavours brought Scotland to the front amongst nations. All accounts tally in recording the attractive person which the King possessed, being, according to Don Pedro de Ayala, the Spanish ambassador, "of noble stature, neither tall nor short, and as handsome in complexion and shape as a man can be." According to Stowe (edition 1603, p. 300) his beard was red. He was a finished scholar, speaking Latin, French, German, Flemish, Italian, and Spanish; besides boasting a familiarity with the Gaelic tongue spoken in the Highlands.

Like his great-grandfather, James I., the King o' Scots

---

* Burton's 'History of Scotland,' edition 1867, vol. iii. p. 217.

was well read in the Bible and in other devout books. He was also a good historian, having a retentive memory, while once at least in his life is he known to have indulged in poesy.* The "neglected Burns" of Scotland, Dunbar, received the following stanza from James IV. in answer to many petitions for a benefice. Dunbar had urged his request somewhat quaintly in the humorous character of an old grey horse. James replied—

> "According to our mandate, gar
> Bring in this grey horse, old Dunbar,
> Wha in my aucht, in service true
> To lyart changed is in hue;
> Gar house him noo, against the Yule,
> And busk him like a bishop's mule;
> For with my hand I have indost
> To pay whate'er his trappins cost." †

Add to these intellectual accomplishments the fact that James was a fine horseman, and that his power to endure fatigue seems almost incredible, and it will be understood why all Scots, high and low, rich and poor, adored him so greatly. Such was the romantic devotion of James IV. to the laws of chivalry, that he was led to adopt unwise measures of policy: as when, for instance according to the custom of the day, an appeal was made to him by some lady of high position to contest her cause against all comers; and notably when, before the fatal battle of Flodden, he yielded to the request which the crafty Anne of Brittany made, that he should become her knight and champion, and in that character advance into English territory.‡

The marriage with Margaret of England took place in 1502, and was the occasion of high festival being held in Scotland —the King advancing to meet her at Newbattle, and entertaining her with music on the clavichord and lute; while just before she entered Edinburgh he again saluted her at Dalkeith, this time displaying his horsemanship and that of his nobles by riding at full gallop, and suddenly throwing their horses on their haunches to exhibit firmness of seat.§

---

* Burton's 'History of Scotland,' edition 1867, vol. iii. p. 213, quoting Bergenroth's 'Simancas Papers,' pp. 169, 170.
† Chalmers's 'Poetical Remains of the Scottish Kings,' chapter on James IV.
‡ Tytler's 'History of Scotland,' edition 1834, vol. v. p. 59.
§ Ibid., p. 18.

Princess Margaret was married to James IV. on August 8, at Holyrood, by the Archbishop of St. Andrews. Tournaments, feasting, masques, morris dances, and dramatic entertainments went on continuously for several days, and to all appearance the much required peace between England and Scotland was at last assured.

Perhaps the most remarkable feature of James's career was his pacification of the Highlands, which he brought about by subjugating the Lord of the Isles, and rendering his sway but nominal, with the result that a balance of power was skilfully arranged amongst the Highland chiefs by which their warlike propensities were henceforth made hurtful to themselves alone; as a body they became, in the main, loyal to the crown.

On the occasion of one of his expeditions to the north, James is said to have ridden from Stirling to Elgin, a distance of 130 miles, in a single day during the winter, a feat possible, may be, nowadays, with relays of horses posted in advantageous positions for the occasion, but none the less an extraordinary evidence of hardihood and endurance. James rode unaccompanied by even a groom, with a riding-cloak around him; the first stage being from Stirling to Perth, and thence over the mountains to Aberdeen, and so to Elgin. His object was to see whether the country had been tranquillised.* With the internal portion of his dominions well in hand James turned an attention to foreign affairs which the fast rising condition of the nation necessitated. His great popularity had enabled him gradually to dispense with the services of the clique who rebelled against his father, and to prefer the wiser of those surviving counsellors who served James III. Pre-eminent amongst these stood the able sailor statesman Sir Andrew Wood of Largo, whose talents were utilised to create a navy worthy of the nation. Sir Andrew Wood, leaving his ship, had not hesitated to appear amongst the rebel Lords after the assassination of James III., and boldly charged them with treason before he returned to Leith. Nor had the loyal servant of the late King feared to rebuke James IV. by courtly imputation for the share taken in that unseemly engagement, after which Sir Andrew's old master had lost his life. Forgiving and forgetting in a spirit of loyalty and patriotism, Wood acted with the two Bartons, Sir Alexander Matheson, William Merrimonth of Leith, called "the King of the Sea,"

* Tytler's 'History of Scotland,' edition 1841, vol. v. p. 30.

and others, when endeavouring to assist James IV. to elevate the navy. Nor was personal inspection neglected by the King, who superintended each minuter detail, conversed with artisans of every country who flocked in from France, Italy, and the Low Countries; while, under the tuition of Wood and Andrew Barton, the King received lessons in navigation during the trips along the coast and to the Isles, which were from time to time indulged in for the purpose of gaining familiarity with the harbourage and general character of the sea-board.*

In the 'Pitscottie Chronicle' (pp. 257, 258) will be found an interesting account of the great leviathan vessel of those days, the *Michael*, which James IV. constructed at this period of his reign. She is said to have been 240 feet long, the hull of oak 10 feet thick. "When this ship," says the chronicler, "passed to the sea and was lying in the road, the King caused shot ane canon at her, to essay if she was wight, but the canon deered (injured) her not." Truly the counterpart of some modern trial at Portsmouth or Plymouth of the strength and invulnerability of a modern ironclad.

Nor did the vigour and energy of James IV. stop at naval preparations; for there remained no portion of his dominions wherein a wrongdoer could feel sure that his sovereign might not appear and in person demand an account of the talents committed to him; the consequence being that property had not ever been so secure across the Border as at this moment, when the geographical discoveries of the Portuguese, and the rapid introduction of the printing-press in Europe threatened to change the world altogether. Anxious to see Scotland in the van when progress such as this was in question, James IV. was never called on to make up his mind regarding any of the burning problems which resulted on the dissemination of a general reforming spirit; but the King was asked to decide whether he would or would not preserve the ancient league with France which had hitherto remained the very cornerstone of Stuart foreign policy. The necessity for "yea" or "nay" being pronounced with regard to this important matter, came about in this wise.

During the year 1507 Pope Julius II. endeavoured to entice James over to the enemies of Louis XII., but received a decided rebuff, after which confidence in the King o' Scots was never evinced at Rome; while, as years passed by, it

* Tytler's 'History of Scotland,' edition 1841, vol. iv. p. 317.

became apparent that neither family connection with England, nor offers of compensatory alliances elsewhere, were likely to divert him from the traditional alliance of his family.*

Henry VII. became conscious of this before he died in 1509, leaving his youthful son and namesake to decide whether he would accede to the solicitations of Pope Julius, which his brother of Scotland had refused two years previously, and take arms against France.

Ominous preliminary threatenings of war between Scotland and England had accompanied the silent understanding between James and Louis. Not only were there combats and disorders on the Border, but a semi-piratical expedition of Andrew Barton's, for which that brilliant sailor had taken out letters of marque against the Portuguese in the year 1511, was brought to a premature close by Sir Edward Howard, Lord Admiral of England, who surprised the two privateers in the Downs, the ships and crews being taken in triumph to London.†

Barton, who died of his wounds, is said not to have discriminated between Portuguese and English vessels, and although the survivors were sent home, the whole affair displayed a disposition to adopt high-handed conduct on the part of Henry VIII. and his counsellors, which boded ill for the hopes of peace. Little wonder then that when, a year later, Louis XII. of France did appeal to James IV. for assistance against England, although the latter employed one Andrew Forman, an accomplished Churchman, to mediate between the contending parties, the considerable power of Scotland was cast in favour of France, inasmuch as letters of naturalisation were then pending, whereby every Scotsman could claim French citizenship.‡ James, moreover, seems to have been spurred on to action by the previously mentioned wiles of Anne of Brittany, and when he knew that the forces of Henry VIII. were engaged in France, sent to that monarch a formal proclamation by herald detailing his wrongs. The English King contemptuously refused to come to terms. This defiance, however, never reached the fatuous Scotch monarch, who called his vassals around him at Morningside, near Edinburgh, and sent a fleet of thirteen ships, under the Earl

* Tytler's 'History of Scotland,' edition 1841, vol. v. p. 29.
† Ibid. p. 41.
‡ Burton's 'History of Scotland,' edition 1867, vol. iii. p. 239.

of Arran, to aid Louis; while he made no secret of his design to invade England in person. The fate of the magnificent fleet which, by means of the genius of Wood and the Bartons, James IV. had created, never was known.

The huge ship previously mentioned, the *Michael*, was afterwards said to have been sold by the Duke of Albany to the French,* but what became of the *Margaret* and *James*, together with their companion vessels, has not been discovered. We know, however, that by the appointment of the Earl of Arran, a landsman, to command the navy of Scotland, when such notable sailors stood available, a great opportunity of harassing English commerce was deliberately disregarded.

By land James IV. appeared even more unfortunate. Although his determined character, aided by the stock of ready money which had been saved by his father, enabled this monarch to present a formidable front to his foes, yet it has never been contended, despite his powers of organising and consolidating scattered resources, that he had the slightest claim to be called a general. And indeed the Spanish ambassador, Don Pedro de Ayala, had observed this, when he summed up the King's warlike pretensions in early life thus:—" He is not a good captain, because he begins to fight before he has given his orders." He acted thus on the ground that as his subjects served him at will with their persons and goods, he was bound to be " first in danger."† On this principle he went when invading England at the head of a large army, the exact number of which has not been precisely estimated. The chroniclers all speak of a hundred thousand men, a total altogether beyond any other Scotch army ever known. Dr. Hill Burton, while allowing that the personal popularity of the King would induce a larger number than usual on these occasions to join the royal standard, thinks it hardly possible that the number is correctly given.

Nor was this headstrong conduct unopposed by the wisest heads amongst James's subjects, the Queen and the aged Lord Angus joining in the chorus of disapproval which prevailed when the project became notorious.

It was at this time that these dissentients—probably

* Burton's 'History of Scotland,' edition 1867, vol. iii. p. 238.
† Ibid., new edition, vol. iii. p. 52, quoting Bergenroth's 'Simancas Papers.'

prompted by the Queen herself—attempted to play upon the well-known mysticism of James IV., so that a venerable and weird figure is said to have appeared before the King during devotion in the church of Linlithgow, and warned him to desist from his warlike purpose, avoiding also the counsel of women.* The vision of James IV. in the church at Linlithgow while at vespers is thus described by Buchanan.†

Leaning upon the chair on which the King sat was "an old Man, the Hair of his Head being Red, inclining to Yellow, and hanging down on his Shoulders his Forehead sleek thro' baldness, bare-headed, in a long Coat of a russet Colour, girt with a linen Girdle about his Loins; in the rest of his Aspect he was very venerable."

All attempts to restrain the King, however, being in vain, the army advanced to the borders, and crossing the Tweed reduced Norham and Werk Castles, the former most unexpectedly, and then encamped near Ford. Here a delay ensued during which James IV. is said to have forgotten the spectral advice vouchsafed him at Linlithgow, yielding both to the counsel and domestic influence of the Lady of that Castle, wife of the English governor, Sir William Heron, a prisoner in Scotland. This inaction became injurious to an army such as James IV. led, because the Highlanders for the first time brought from their fastnesses, were prone to desert and return home to secure the booty seized on the march—an experience repeated again and again in after ages. The delay likewise gave opportunity for Lord Surrey to concentrate his army. But the King made up, so far as personal disregard of danger could do, for this temporary inaction at Ford, and thereby tried to atone for the needlessly desperate character of the engagement which he resolved should take place. Despising any kind of tactics, he only sought to meet the foe, agreeing to fix Friday, September 9, as the day of battle. Lord Surrey only failed to tempt the King o' Scots to engage at greater disadvantage, because when asked by herald to descend into the vale of Millfield that lay between the armies, he refused to receive the communication, "because it did not become an Earl to dictate to a King."‡ And indeed it is strange to reflect that when

* The story appears at length in 'Pitscottie Chronicles,' pp. 264, 265, and is adopted by all writers on this period.
† Edition 1690, bk. xiii. p. 20.
‡ Henry's 'History of Great Britain,' second edition, vol. ix. p. 433, quoting Hall, fol. 41.

replying to the English general in this haughty fashion, he was in fact telling the elder representative of his own ancestral race—the Fitzalans—of that supremacy which the younger branch claimed as occupant of the throne of Scotland.

No account of Flodden Field will ever be read in preference to that given in glorious verse by Sir Walter Scott in 'Marmion,' and the general features not differing in the many histories dealing with the event, they will only be delineated in outline here.

James IV., before going to his doom, received an emphatic protest from the aged Bell the Cat, Earl of Angus, head of the senior branch of the Douglases, who urged that the King would serve his ally Louis XII. better by detaining Surrey and his army on the frontier, than by risking all the flower of Scotland's chivalry in a single encounter. To which argument James IV. answered, "Angus, if you are afraid, you may go home," a rebuff which that aged Border warrior took sorely to heart. In spite of his chagrin and distress he left two sons at the head of the Douglas vassals to fight for Scotland and the Stuarts, while he sorrowfully owned his body to be useless from age.*

The infatuated monarch would make but one concession to his advisers, and that was to take up position on the crest of Flodden, described by Hill Burton as "gentle rising ground strengthened by the river Till, a deep stream with broken banks." Here the King o' Scots remained with his men, while the English army under Surrey, on that memorable 9th of September, 1513, filed across the little bridge of Twisell, a difficult military operation with which James never interfered, although both artillery and skilful archers were at his disposal.

The chroniclers aver that Borthwick, the commander of artillery, begged for leave to fire on the bridge of Twisell,† and received a peremptory refusal from the King; but unless the Scots had taken up a position nearer than Flodden, this must have proved ineffectual, because the distance between James's standard and the foe (at Twisell) was four miles. But this difficulty does not excuse the King o' Scots for not advancing with all available forces, when he had his enemy at such palpable disadvantage. His object was to give the

* Tytler's 'History of Scotland,' edition 1834, vol. v, p. 74
† Burton's 'History of Scotland,' edition 1867, vol. iii. p. 244.

English a fair field, and his own countrymen no favour, and he doubtless expected to gain an easy and glorious victory.

This last great clash of arms between England and Scotland—for subsequent contests were minor in character—is famous as being the first occasion on which artillery appeared in the field during the long struggle for supremacy in the north; while it is remarkable, that after all, the skill of Lord Surrey's archers decided the day.

Sheer hard hand-to hand fighting on each flank culminated in a death-struggle around the King o' Scots himself, where, in the heart of the fray, he fell pierced with an arrow, and mortally wounded in the head with a bill, within a few yards of his fighting kinsman and antagonist the Earl of Surrey. The Highlanders had been too eager to advance under the shower of arrows which enveloped their battalions, while Sir Edward Stanley, after completing their discomfiture, turned from the pursuit and placed his column in rear of the Scottish centre, where, fighting to the last, this proud Stuart King James IV. died, in the prime of manhood, being but forty-one years of age.

Around the mangled remains of their sovereign were found the bodies of thirteen Earls and fifteen Lords or chieftains, together with many landed gentry of minor position, and in all ten thousand men. On this fatal field were stretched the Earls of Crawford, Montrose, Huntly, Lennox, Argyll, Erroll, Athole, Morton, Cassilis, Bothwell, Rothes, Caithness, and Glencairn, together with James's natural son, the Archbishop of St. Andrews, who had been educated abroad under Erasmus.* A very slight knowledge of Scotland and her historic families will be sufficient to enable a reader of the above titles to gauge the extent of this disaster. There were, indeed, few families of note in which there was not mourning for relatives after this terrible battle; and in countries where the monarchical principle was less honoured than in Scotland, the dynasty itself must have been exposed to a peril which, strange to say, did not threaten it on this occasion.

With a knowledge of the character of James IV., it cannot be desired that he should have left the field of Flodden alive, but unsuccessful. As it is, he stands out as one of the last representatives of kings who have died at the head of a nation in arms, so that the weaknesses of his character have

---

* Tytler's 'History of Scotland,' edition 1834, vol. v. p. 81.

not been much dwelt on, nor has the neglect of tactical skill which he evinced in this campaign been censured by posterity as it certainly merited. For James IV. was setting aside the best military traditions of his family, as well as ignoring the teachings of the tacticians of his own day; inasmuch as the great Bruce never joined battle with an enemy on the Border except in self-defence, or with a prospect of gaining some definite strategic advantage. Neither of these conditions affected the movements of James's army before Flodden, and therefore it is reasonable to esteem him happy, that, unlike his successor James V., after Solway Moss, he was not, as a baffled survivor, obliged to drink the bitter cup of humiliation to the very dregs.

The body of James IV. was recognised and taken by the English to Berwick, and there embalmed, and then sent to the monastery of Sheen, near Richmond, in Surrey, where it remained for some time unburied, because the late King had been excommunicated by the Pope for opposition to the holy league and consequent adherence to the King of France. Strange incident in a rapidly moving drama! The Pope relented so far as to allow his opponent to receive sepulture, which even then seems to have been withheld; for, in reference to a visit to Sheen after the dissolution of the monastery during the reign of Edward VI., Stowe, the English historian, saw "the same body so lapped in lead, close to the head and body, thrown into a wast roome amongst the olde timber, leade, and other rubble." *

Doubtless the confusion which accompanied the monastic dissolution at Sheen as elsewhere is accountable for this neglect and the decapitation of the royal corpse by some workmen. Whereupon one Young, master-glazier to Queen Elizabeth, removed the head to London, and eventually had it buried at the church of St. Michael, Wood Street.†

For a long time there was doubt as to the death of James IV. in the minds of his loyal people, and it is strange to read in a historical tract written in the Stuart interest during the reign of James II. of England and Scotland, how the Scots declared the dead body found at Flodden was that of Sir Alexander Elphinstone, who resembled their slain master in habit, stature, and figure; while it was elsewhere contended that the King had been murdered near Kelso by the Earl of Hume's retainers. Men were also found to say

---

* Stowe's 'Survey of London,' edition 1603, p. 300.   † Ibid.

that, dazed with horror at the overthrow of his arms, and the great slaughter among his nobility and gentry, James IV. had travelled as a pilgrim to Jerusalem and died there.*

Stowe's chronicle was clearly not familiar to this somewhat pliant court writer of the seventeenth century.

James IV. had four sons by his Queen: (1) James, born February 25, 1508, died July 14, 1510; (2) Arthur, born October 20, 1509, died in infancy; (3) James V., born April 5, 1512, who succeeded to the throne; (4) Alexander, a posthumous son, born April 30, 1514, died January 15, 1517.

Childhood of James V., 1513-1528.

The full measure of this disaster at Flodden cannot be gauged by the agonising distress of a high-minded and humiliated people, nor by the loss of life, destruction of national resources, and unproductive expenditure which accompanied the fourth James's chivalric but foolish adventure. Scotland may be said to have been thrown back at least a quarter of a century at a moment when its prosperity had been advancing by leaps and bounds.

The revival of learning which Walter Chepman—a servant of the fourth James's household—had initiated when he introduced north of Tweed, in 1509, the art of printing, first practised in England by Caxton, in the year 1477, was necessarily checked when confusion reigned in the councils of an impoverished and defeated State. Nor were the circumstances such as to lead men to hope for speedy recuperation from the losses incurred.

Scotland was in the first instance subjected to another long minority, the heir being only one year and five months old, and although events turned out more propitiously than had been expected, a time of intrigue and disorder was necessarily in store.

The inhabitants of Edinburgh, whose provost lay dead on Flodden Field, rose to the occasion when expecting the Earl of Surrey with his army to besiege them. For they built a wall for defence round the capital; while a steady resolve to repress private sorrow and defend their homes animated each afflicted citizen. But these preparations were never tested,

---

* 'Memories of the Family of the Stuarts and the Remarkable Providences of God towards them.' Printed at the Bishop's Head, St. Paul's Churchyard, 1683. The details therein are very curious, but not to be relied on, where the Stuarts' dynastic interests are in question.

inasmuch as, after sending a few foragers over the Tweed, Lord Surrey disbanded his victorious army, and returned to London.*

The events which occurred during the minority of James V. belong to the domain of our national history rather than that of the dynasty whose fortunes are under consideration, so the barest outline must suffice to keep the thread of the story complete.

One leading result of this overthrow on Branksome Moor by Flodden Field, was the altered nature of the Parliament, which it was necessary to call for settling the regency. Instead of the Earls and Barons killed in the lost battle whose successors were minors, a majority of Churchmen repaired to Holyrood, and it so happened that when, in a few years' time, the Reformation raised its head, ecclesiastical influence had a constitutional strength which it could not boast during the previous reign.

It is pertinent to note what a fine opportunity any new King of matured age would at this moment have had of securing himself, and perhaps also his successor, against being overwhelmed by the feudal aristocracy, which had been the fate of James III. As it was, the whole reigns of James V. and Mary were spent in battling with one or other of the great Scotch magnates. Dealing with children an adult King might have moulded them to his will. But alas! after Flodden, the King of Scotland was himself but an infant, and if he lived to reign must find that the difficulties bequeathed to him had grown with his growth.

There were three moving powers in the State, candidates for supremacy, at this juncture. One, the son of that Duke of Albany who was younger brother of James III., held a position in France, princely in character, for his mother, being a daughter of an Earl of Boulogne, inherited all the feudal possessions of that nobleman, whose immediate ancestors had exercised almost independent sovereignty, and whose wealth had descended to the son who shall be designated here as Duke Albany of Boulogne, to distinguish him from former members of the royal family who had borne the same title. Opposed to this Duke Albany of Boulogne—loth to quit the shores of his beloved France—stood the Earl of Angus, the second husband of Margaret, widow of James IV., who waited barely a year before she allied herself to the head of the

* Tytler's 'History of Scotland,' edition 1841, vol. v. p. 73.

Douglases, that family, who, having intrigued in exile during the reign of James III., returned to Scotland to take their share in the great struggle of Flodden Field, where it will be remembered the aged head of their house, after receiving a sore rebuff from the King, nevertheless left his son and grandson to represent the Douglas name. The aged Bell the Cat had passed away in nature's due course, while his son and heir lay buried beyond the Tweed. The grandson whose career is under consideration not only covered himself with honour on that dread 9th of September, 1513, but in August 1514 was allied to the Queen Margaret, sister of Henry VIII. The child of this marriage, Lady Margaret Douglas, became Countess of Lennox, and was mother of Henry, Lord Darnley. The third prominent interest in Scotch affairs was that of the Earl of Arran, son of Lady Margaret Stuart, daughter of James II., sister of James III., and therefore next in succession to the throne if direct heirs of James IV. failed, and Duke Albany of Boulogne remained childless.

But the Parliament resolved to elevate Albany to the Regency.* Admiral of France, and the owner of many acres in that fair country, some hesitation ensued before he accepted the duty thrust upon him, and he did not reach Dumbarton, escorted by a fleet suitable to the occasion, until May 18, 1515. Before starting he had stipulated that his father's confiscated honours and estates should be restored; and as security for the performance of these conditions, the Castle of Dunbar was surrendered to Beauté, the new regent's ambassador; † so it is possible that the experiences of the French general, Sir John de Vienne, when allied with the Scots, may have reminded Duke Albany of Boulogne that he was about to undertake perilous and thankless duties. The Regent seems to have evinced quite as much capability to rule as any foreigner could hope to display when ignorant of the people he was called on to govern. He was perforce recognised as the representative of the French party, and so opposed to that of England, which Queen Margaret and her husband championed north of Tweed. In this capacity he found himself confronted by Henry VIII. and his great minister Cardinal Wolsey, who looked on Duke Albany's acceptance of the regency as an act of hostility to English interests, and affected to feel great anxiety as to the safe custody of James V. In the course of the year 1516 these

* Henry's 'History of Great Britain,' vol. xi. p. 445.
† Drummond's 'History of Scotland,' p. 242.

sentiments were placed formally before the Scots Parliament, wherein existed a majority favourable to the French party of Albany; and the legislature consequently testified their belief in the Regent's probity and honour, and vouched for his tender care of the young King.

It was in the nature of things that the Estates should look askance upon the English King's project of marrying James V. to his daughter Mary, as threatening the national independence, although Henry VIII. and Wolsey were bent on a statesmanlike project, the realisation of which might have advanced Scotland fifty years, besides saving the two Kingdoms several wars, and possibly averting more than one revolution.

At this time (according to Buchanan) the infant James V. remained in Stirling Castle. His mother, however, had fled across the Border to Harbotle Castle, whence, after the birth of Lady Margaret Douglas on October 7, 1515,[*] she had proceeded to London. Henry VIII. and her sister, the Queen Dowager of France, received her with open arms.[†] Margaret originally had induced Henry VIII. to distrust Duke Albany of Boulogne, and now fanned the flame anew, averring her own belief in the danger to which the King of Scotland was subjected; and although a visit from the Regent's envoy, Count de Fayette, allayed these anxieties in some degree, and appeared to satisfy the prescient Wolsey, yet the truce which ensued left the elements of disturbance ready to burst forth again on the least provocation. For Scotland was internally in a dreadful state of anarchy, no longer restrained by the strong hand of James IV. The chieftains acknowledged no law; and notwithstanding that Robertson of Struan, a Highland leader of great repute, and the potent Lord Hume, warden of the marches, and the most distinguished survivor of Flodden, were successively beheaded as the result of turbulent conduct on the part of themselves and their followers, the difficulties of government were rather increased than diminished by the tempestuous desire for vengeance, which animated the friends of the powerful Hume family.[‡] And this sentiment of indignation was not diminished when the Humes reflected how the late Lord had contributed to place the Regent in his seat of power. Albany, weary of a contest which seemed endless, and anxious to return to France, persuaded the Parliament to let him

[*] Henry's 'History of Great Britain,' vol. xi. p. 452.   [†] Ibid., p. 456.
[‡] Ibid., p. 459.

negotiate in person with Francis I. a renewal of the ancient league which that monarch solicited in the spring of 1517. During Albany's absence, the Queen Margaret returned, and displayed an animosity towards Angus her husband for deserting her at Harbotle Castle, which in the year 1526 resulted in a divorce;* while a feud commenced between the Douglases and Hamiltons, which, combined with utter relaxation of authority in the Highlands, rendered life and property alike insecure,† the two great powers of England and France being far too busy with their own rivalries to find time for composing the internal quarrels of this distressed country.

Before leaving Scotland, the Regent, bent on establishing his authority, found himself face to face with the necessity of investing Hamilton Castle, and did so with the resolve to raze it to the ground, when he was confronted by a defender more powerful than men at arms or artillery, in the person of his own venerable aunt, Lady Mary, Dowager Countess of Arran, daughter of James II., sister of James III., and aunt of James IV. No Stuart general could ignore the pleadings of one claiming such kinship with the dynasty, nor did the Regent leave without promising to pardon the Earl of Arran, her son, provided that he made formal submission.‡

This incident shows how complicated was the task which the temporary governor of Scotland had undertaken. He maintained after this a nominal regency, while enjoying the delights of Paris, overlooking his estates in France, and negotiating with Francis I. as to renewal of the ancient league; but the murder of his deputy, La Bastie, in 1517, soon after his departure, and the general confusion which prevailed, convinced Albany that absentee rulership was impossible in oligarchic Scotland. And this, although immediate danger of war was averted, while Henry VIII. and Francis I. were fast allies. For when their meeting at the Field of the Cloth of Gold took place in 1520, the Douglases and Hamiltons were in open feud, fighting a pitched battle near Kelso, in which the latter were worsted, and carrying their bloodshed into the capital itself, where Arran escaped with the loss of seventy followers, and of his brother, Sir Patrick Hamilton, whom Angus himself slew.§

At last, in the autumn of 1521, events conspired to make

* Henry's 'History of Great Britain,' vol. xi. p. 490.
† Ibid., p. 464.   ‡ Ibid., p. 454.
§ Burton's 'History of Scotland,' new edition, vol. iii. p. 95.

Albany hazard a great stake on his return to Scotland, whence he had absented himself nearly five years on four months' leave from Parliament; but the imminence of renewed conflict between England and France rendered the Regent's presence a necessity if Henry VIII. and England were not to triumph across the Tweed. For Angus and the Douglases, obeying Henry's behest, stood ready to champion the cause of the Tudor monarch, who straightway demanded that Albany should be driven from his post, and so involved Scotland in the European war which was just beginning.*

The Regent reached Scotland in November 1521, and after dismissing all the officers and magistrates of Angus's party, prepared to face the inevitable, and make ready for the threatened campaign.

The two expeditions conducted by Duke Albany of Boulogne on the borders have been variously judged from a military point of view, but later historians cognisant of the facts have allowed that the numerous army which encamped on the banks of the river Esk, near Carlisle, in September 1522, was prevented from advancing into England by the hesitation of the Scotch chieftains, combined with the diplomatic ingenuity of Lord Dacre, the English warden.

Flodden had occurred but nine years previously, and its lessons were full of warning; enjoining a defence of the frontier, rather than an aggressive movement into England; nor had the conditions of later warfare so changed the aspect of military science that the tactics of Robert Bruce could be with safety set aside.

Instead of prolonging the conflict, Albany allowed the Queen Margaret to mediate, but these pacific attempts failed.

When Francis I. made peace with England, Scotland was not included in the English terms of agreement.† The Regent set out, therefore, again for France, to obtain auxiliaries from that warlike ally. And although a truce was morally existent, England having waived her demand that Albany should be sent across the seas, when the Scots dispersed; yet during the Regent's voluntary absence which ensued, the Lord Dacre, at the head of ten thousand men, harried Jedburgh and the country around—a notable breach of faith, even if defended by the technical excuse that a

---

* Burton describes this as a diplomatic revolution, when England united suddenly with Spain and the Pope against France.

† Henry's 'History of Great Britain,' second edition, vol. xi. p. 473, quoting Lesly.

military leader had no power to treat about the renewal of truces.*

At Albany's instance, French troops, to the number of three thousand infantry and a thousand men at arms, were provided with great despatch. The admiral of the English fleet, Sir William Fitzwilliam, seeing no accumulation of shipping in any of the French harbours, concluded that the expedition had been given up. According to Buchanan, Albany, however, had appointed Brest for a rendezvous of fifty sail, and forthwith embarked the troops on September 21, 1523, and reached the Clyde before the close of that month.

There was division in the Parliament at Edinburgh when the question was raised as to a fresh campaign against England. On overcoming this opposition and marching to Melrose, Albany found the most powerful chieftains were again unwilling to cross the frontier, deprecating an offensive war, when by their presence near the Tweed they could protect their own country from invasion. Albany was on this occasion constrained to limit his efforts to a regular siege of Werk Castle, opposite to Coldstream, a fortress of great strength in those days. Of these ineffectual operations George Buchanan, the scholar, poet, and writer, was witness, and his account remains one of the most interesting on record of such an attack.†

Suffice it here to say that although a breach was effected in the walls, a retreat had to be made by the French, who, with the few Scots accompanying them, were in danger of being cut off from the main army by a swelling of the Tweed, consequent upon heavy rain. This failure convinced the Regent that he could do nothing with an army that was not really under his command, so that, marching to Lauder, he dismissed his troops on November 29, 1523, and went to Stirling. There he gave such advice to the youthful James V. as a boy in his thirteenth year was capable of understanding, and, directing the Council to make no peace with England, sailed on May 19, 1524, for France, whence he never more returned.

It may be imagined that with the regency vacant, intrigue became rampant in Scotland. Angus, an exile in France, was adopted by Henry VIII. and Wolsey as a tool whereby

* Burton's 'History of Scotland,' new edition, vol. iii. p. 103.

† Tytler's 'History of Scotland,' edition 1841, vol. v. p. 141, quoting Buchanan.

to gain supremacy in the councils of Scotland; and after many evil discords, during which the Queen mother conducted the King to Holyrood and declared him capable of exercising the royal functions,* the poor boy fell into the hands of Angus and the Douglas faction, so that from October 1525 to the summer of 1528 James V. was subjected to this evil tutelage. Like his father James IV., seduced into wild courses by dominant nobles, the young King was indulged in the exercise of baser passions by his captors, and a naturally fine character was in a great degree ruined in order that the Douglas faction might perpetuate their infamous sway. But even their thus pandering to evil did not prevent the youth from writhing under a captivity which seemed as hopeless as inexorable when his own mother concurred therein. For the widowed Queen Margaret, after her divorce from Angus, had married the young Henry Stewart, brother of Lord Evandale, who, surrendering Edinburgh Castle, made common cause with the triumphant house of Douglas.

The most important demonstration made by the enemies of Douglas in order to rescue the King was that designed in 1527 by the Earl of Glencairn, Chancellor Beaton, and other noblemen acting with the Earl of Lennox; the last-named Earl resolving to attain the King's release by personal effort, having before confided his designs to the Buccleuch family. Assembling no less than ten thousand men, he advanced on Edinburgh from Stirling. James, forced to take horse and apparently champion the Douglas cause, became aware outside Corstorphine village that he was nearing the battle at Manuel,† so soon to be decided adversely to his real interest. Refusing to hurry forward when expecting aid from the Hamiltons, he was told by George Douglas, his immediate attendant, " Sir, rather than our enemies should take you from us, we will lay hold on your body, and if it be rent in pieces we will be sure to take one part of it." ‡ It is said that James V. never forgave this.

The hour of release was nevertheless approaching, although the bold Buccleuch and the King's dear friend and cousin, John, Earl of Lennox, had failed to gain their sovereign's release by force of arms, Lennox being stabbed treacherously

---

* This occurred in 1524, and is known historically as the "erection of the King."

† About three miles west of Linlithgow, and fifteen miles west of Corstorphine.

‡ Buchanan, edition 1752, vol. ii. p. 155.

by a natural son of Arran's in the battle just alluded to. Escaping from Falkland by stratagem, under colour of preparing for a hunting party, James V. secured a swift horse and rode into Stirling Castle at the end of May 1528,* calling —by couriers sent in every direction—on the barons and gentlemen to attend with their followers, who straightway assembled in such numbers as enabled the King to defy the baffled Douglas, posted amongst his lieges at Linlithgow, and in despair at the turn events had taken. And, in truth, the sun of loyalty was rising to brighten the otherwise dark horizon of Scotland's hopes.

* Tytler's 'History of Scotland,' edition 1834, vol. v. p. 219.

CHAPTER VI.

THE CHURCH AT BAY.

1528-1560.

James V. King in Fact, 1528-1542;
Minority of Mary Stuart, 1542-1560.

THE early education of James V. had not been entirely neglected during the internal broils which disturbed the nation Gawyn Dunbar, prior of Whithorn, a man of learning, afterwards Archbishop of Glasgow, was mainly responsible for the young King's instruction ; while John Bellenden, Archdeacon of Moray, and Sir David Lyndsay, who rose to be Lion King at Arms, were amongst the pages in whose society the future ruler of Scotland lived.*
The deliverance of this sovereign from the Douglas domination could never have been effected but for the secret connivance of leading members of the nobility, Argyll amongst the number, while James Beaton, Chancellor of Scotland, and uncle to the famous minister of the Guises during Queen Mary's minority, gave silent consent.†
James V., rejoicing in the glorious sense of freedom which succeeded to this imprisonment of several years, developed a strength of character quite amazing to those who believed his better instincts to have been swamped by enervating indulgence, provided as a salve for loss of personal liberty. Inexorable towards the Douglases, he raised an army and besieged his late gaoler Angus in his stronghold of Tantallon, magnificent even in its present shattered condition, and still familiar to visitors on the coast whereon North Berwick is the chief attraction.
Although James V. was unable to gain his purpose forthwith, the opposition he received served only to make him

* Chalmers's 'Poetical Remains of the Scottish Kings,' edition 1824, p. 122.
† Tytler's 'History of Scotland,' edition 1834, vol. v. p. 216.

more determined to drive Angus out of the kingdom, a resolution which was accomplished before the year 1528 closed. Arresting certain recusant earls and barons with the connivance of Parliament, James V. then swooped down on the disturbed borderland with eight thousand men, and, to the astonishment of the scattered feudalities there established, hanged Armstrong, the most powerful freebooter of all, together with forty-eight retainers. During the following year, 1529, measures were taken to conciliate the Western Islanders, who had been at variance with their chief, Argyll; while elsewhere stern justice was executed on the persons of law-breakers, such as those who murdered the Abbot of Kilross—these necessarily rigorous means of pacification being accompanied by acts of clemency, for which the King received little credit.*

The events of after years show that on the whole James V. made more enemies than friends by this necessary severity; but amongst his subjects generally, and especially the poorer portion of them, the young King soon became popular. Inheriting the striking person which had been bestowed by nature upon most of his predecessors, James V. rivalled his father in courage and endurance, penetrating on foot into the most distant portions of his kingdom; and when bent on adventure he would roam in disguise and associate with gipsies and Highland servants, travelling incognito as Goodman (that is, "tenant") of Ballengiech, a steep pass behind the hill of Stirling, while the title "King of the Commons" clung to him as a favourite name long after his death.

Like his grandfather James III., he was looked upon as being no friend to the nobility, while he shared also with that hapless ancestor a reputation for the love of gold. Avarice, as such, cannot, however, be justly charged against a monarch whose empty treasury impressed upon him the necessity for excessive thrift. For Buchanan says that such were the needs of those directing the late regency that the young King found his palace stripped of upholstery. Nor had the national resources recovered from the strain placed upon them in order to equip the army lost at Flodden.†

The late Dr. Hill Burton was of opinion that popular familiarity with his meaner subjects had led to the traditional belief that James V. was author of 'Christ's Kirk on the

* Tytler's 'History of Scotland,' edition 1834, vol. v. pp. 234, 235.
† Buchanan's 'History of Scotland,' edition 1752, vol. ii. p. 184.

Green,' and 'The Gaberlunzie Man,' poetical compositions full of Scotch humour; but no existing evidence beyond that of tradition seems to connect these productions with Mary Stuart's father.*

But King James sometimes displayed his handsome face and figure amongst society of a different type; and in the year 1533, he had the wisdom to accede to the request of his kinsman, the Earl of Athole, that he might entertain his sovereign during a summer tour amongst the noble mountains around Blair Athole. Those conversant with the plateau in front of the castle, making an arena fit for any Highland pastime, will realise what a beautiful and romantic scene was presented, when a rural palace of green timber appeared, a high tower crowning each angle of the edifice, the windows of which were of coloured glass, and its chambers daintily decorated by tapestry of silk and gold. Here, James V. learned the delights of his Highland dominions, alternately fishing, feasting, and hunting—the latter amusement being especially to the King's fancy, so that he constantly relieved the tedium of progresses through the kingdom by the chase. On this occasion the Queen mother and the Papal ambassador were with the Court; and when the royal procession filed away southwards, Athole gave this fairy dwelling to the flames, vowing that it should never henceforth shelter any person not of royal rank.†

The condition of Scotland was nominally peaceable, when, in 1534, the definitive decision of the Curia against Henry in the matter of his divorce suit brought about a complete alienation of England from Rome, the details of which are well known to readers of history. From that date the relations between Henry VIII. and his nephew the Scotch King became strained.

* Drummond of Hawthornden, the poet and historian, 1585-1649, spoke of James V. as given to " poesie; as many of his works yet extant testifie," but did not name the pieces upon which this reputation is founded. Moreover Bellenden, Archdeacon of Moray, a friend of the King in his childhood, speaks of James V. as singing
" With notes sweet and song melodious;"
while Sir David Lyndsay, also a contemporary, concurs. But they say nothing about either 'The Gaberlunzie Man,' or 'Christ's Kirk on the Green,' which many attribute to James I. Sibbald, the poetical chronologist, on the other hand, agrees with Chalmers in ascribing these works to James V., on account of the style not being that of his great ancestor, James I.— Chalmers's ' Poetical Remains of the Scottish Kings,' pp. 126-7.

† Tytler's 'History of Scotland,' edition 1834, vol. v. p. 243.

James V., acting on the advice of his Council, refused to receive a treatise on the Reformation, described as 'The Doctrine of a Christian Man,' sent by the English King; and a proposed conference between the sovereigns, which Queen Margaret had devised, fell through. This was a grievous disappointment to Henry VIII., whom seems to have thought that in the last resort he might hope to carry his nephew with him. But it was not so ordained, inasmuch as after offers of matrimonial alliances from Charles V., who proposed three of his relations, viz. the Queen Dowager of Hungary, his sister, and his nieces, Mary of Portugal, and Mary of England, James V. nevertheless turned finally towards France. He first guarded himself from any fear of offending Charles V. by asking Isabella of Denmark, another of his nieces, in marriage. Buchanan, however, says that the princess had been already contracted to the Elector Palatine, and that James was not ignorant of the fact.*

Henceforth there remained no obstacle to the alliance with France which the King had always personally preferred.

It is worthy of remark that although James V. never closely examined the controversy engendered by Luther, which was convulsing Scotland, he professed himself at one time favourable to the reformation of manners amongst the clergy;† and yet, either persuaded by those in his Council who belonged to that sacred order, or moved to such decision by the overbearing conduct of his uncle, the King was finally led into the position of championing the ancient faith, with all its accompaniments good and bad.

The first intimation of this which the world received was owing to the King choosing a French princess for his wife, Mary of Bourbon being recommended by David Beaton, who

* Henry's 'History of Great Britain,' second edition, vol. xi. p. 506, quoting Buchanan, who (edition 1821, vol. ii. p. 428) confirms this statement generally, but does not name the Elector Palatine. A work has appeared lately by Edmond Bapst, Secretary to the Embassy at Paris, which tells of some curious, not to say tortuous, intrigues for the hand of the youthful James V. during his captivity amongst the Douglases. The Princess Louise, daughter of Francis I., was proposed in 1516, being superseded in the matrimonial market a year later by her sister Charlotte, while another sister Madeleine, was also taken into consideration. All these projects, however, fell through, though Madeleine eventually, after an interval of several years, became James's Queen. In 1524 and 1525 a marriage with a Danish princess was on the tapis, so James V. only reverted ten years later to a former proposition, although we do not learn that the Danish princess first mentioned was niece of Charles V. (See *Athenæum*, Aug. 31, 1889, p. 285.)

† 'Life of John Knox,' vol. i. p. 50.

had been despatched to France for the purpose of advising with Francis I. on the subject. Rejecting the proffered friendship of his uncle, the King of England, James, after pacifying such portions of his dominions as required assertion of the royal authority, made an ineffectual attempt to accomplish the projected voyage to France, journeying as a private individual. Sailing from Leith, in July 1536, he went round the north of Scotland, to avoid the English cruisers, and then unfortunately was driven back into the Clyde by a storm. On September 1, in this same year 1536, he recommenced the journey in a different manner altogether, sailing from Kirkaldy in Fifeshire with six ships—one of 700 tons—and taking with him about 500 people in all.* The spectacle of this passing naval cortége seems to have interested the good people of Berwick, and we learn that, after eluding the English ships of war, on the tenth day James safely reached Dieppe.† At Paris the royal visitor received a cordial greeting, being introduced to Francis I. by the Dauphin, who had hastened to meet his father's guest.

James lost no time in seeking his proposed bride, and went to a fête at the Duc de Vendôme's, where, himself in disguise, he saw Mary of Bourbon, who recognised him from a miniature he had sent her from Scotland, and was duly captivated by his attractive person. The King, nevertheless, for some unexplained reason, did not reciprocate the sentiment, but set his affections upon the Princess Madeleine (Magdalen), daughter of Francis I., who, alas! with all her attractions, was known to be a prey to the terrible disease consumption. Her melancholy style of beauty—combining as it did great refinement of feature with a cheerful and, so far as James was concerned, an affectionate demeanour—settled the question; for indeed the Scots monarch was in love. Francis, on the other hand, made no abiding objection, although he urged the delicacy of his daugher's constitution as an obstacle, which certainly should have been considered fatal to the match when the transplanting of this fair flower into cold Scotland was in question.

But the young people's affections were deeply engaged, and it is curious to hear of James V. rushing from shop to shop, in the streets of Paris—as many a bridegroom has done, year by year, during the three centuries and more than a half which

* Burton's 'History of Scotland,' new edition, vol. iii. p. 164.
† Tytler (edition 1841, vol. v. p. 212), who is alone precise on this point, s the authority followed.

have passed since that time,*—bent on finding some tasteful gift for the lady soon to be his bride. James, on these expeditions, was recognised by the Parisian loungers of that day, every carter pointing with his finger at "le Roi d'Escoisse."†

After a magnificent religious ceremony at Notre Dame, on January 1, 1537, and at the expiration of a happy eight months' sojourn in Paris, James took his wife home by the long sea voyage, a safe-conduct through England having been unceremoniously refused by the King's irate uncle, Henry of England, notwithstanding that Francis acted as mediator.

So this tender flower, which, to do him credit, James prized highly, was subjected to the caprices of winds and waves. She reached Leith on May 19, 1537. On descending from the ship, Magdalen knelt upon the beach, and taking up some portion of the sand, kissed it, and asked a blessing upon her new country, where she was received with great popular enthusiasm. But alas! she speedily sickened, and died on July 7, not two months after the incidents just recorded.

Royal hearts had no time allowed them to break in Scotland at this period, and the susceptible King seems to have roused himself from his sorrow, and allowed a mission, with David Beaton at its head, to proceed straightway to France and demand the hand of the widowed Mary of Lorraine, Duchess de Longueville, and daughter of the Duke of Guise, head of the Catholic party in France. James V. is said to have been captivated by the fine figure, bordering upon *embonpoint*, which characterised his second wife. A description of her comely proportions had previously fired the ardour of no less a personage than Henry VIII., who contemplated becoming a suitor for her hand, but was deterred by considerations of policy. At a juncture when the Reformation doctrines were patronised by Henry VIII., his nephew's alliance with the house of Guise meant war with England, not long to be deferred. Nevertheless, the alliance with Mary of Lorraine was celebrated in the cathedral of St. Andrews in June 1538, the clear year of mourning for the lost Magdalen not having expired.

Meantime other events happened in Scotland which it is necessary to mention. The impression of the Court of Stirling (whence James V. took his poetic name, "Snowdoun's

---

* Pinkerton's 'History of Scotland,' vol. ii. pp. 490-494.
† Ibid.

graceful Knight"*) conveyed by Sir Walter Scott's 'Lady of the Lake,' is doubtless correct. In this charming poem we are made familiar with "banner and pageant, pipe and drum," while the popular sovereign nods approvingly in answer to the salutations of the crowd,

> " Who rend the heavens with their acclaims,
> Long live the Commons' King, King James!"

But alas! it is for the historian, admitting the wonderful grasp of the general features of life prevalent in Scotland during this reign as delineated by the Wizard of the North, to present the other side of the shield. Thereon it is necessary to inscribe the fact that James V. lacked the paramount virtue of mercy when the upper classes of his subjects were concerned. We allude to the execution of Lord Forbes's son, a mere youth, convicted by the Council on insufficient evidence of an intention to kill the King early in the year 1538, and also to the burning of Lady Glamys, a hated Douglas, sister of the Earl of Angus, five days afterwards, that lady being vaguely accused of an intention to poison her sovereign,† who in each of these cases might have shown clemency to the accused, although responsibility nominally remained with his advisers. But a Nemesis awaited the kingdom wherein such cruelties were enacted.

Renewed persecution of the Reformers soon persuaded Henry of England and his astute ambassador, Sir Ralph Sadler, that Scotland's government was hostile to the Protestant cause, and they took their measures accordingly, urging on James the necessity, if amity were to be preserved, of the uncle and nephew meeting to consider the condition of affairs. This idea, proposed in 1539, was then rendered somewhat palatable to James by the hope of his own succession to the English crown, as it was not improbable that Prince Edward, Henry's only son, would die young. But the consideration asked for in return the Stuart Prince refused to give. He would not dissolve the monasteries, nor abjure the religion of his fathers.‡

Three years of delay occurred, during which Archbishop

---

* William of Worcester, who wrote about the middle of the fifteenth century, calls Stirling Castle "Snowdoun."

† Drummond's 'History of Scotland,' pp. 313-315—a courtly historian who credited neither accusation.

‡ Tytler's 'History of Scotland,' edition 1834, vol. v. p. 275; also Sadler's 'State Papers,' vol. i. pp. 29, 30.

David Beaton was James's minister, and did not refrain from any measure, secret or public, which seemed likely to bring on this threatened religious war. This, on the other hand, is known as the period wherein James V. performed some of his more remarkable progresses through his dominions; while, by strong reprisals whenever conspiracies against his own person, or designs threatening law and order were concerned, he lost popularity amongst his nobility. Nor were they mollified by the fact that James Stuart was bent on introducing into his own dominions the centralisation he had admired in France.

In 1541 two sons, borne to him by Mary of Guise, who had been the hope of their nation, were suddenly cut off, James, the heir, a year old, at St. Andrews, and Arthur, an infant, at Stirling. Thus the Hamiltons, Arran in particular, were left next in the succession to the throne, so long as James should have no more children.

At this crisis Henry VIII. almost demanded that his nephew should meet him at York, scouting the alternative of Newcastle as a rendezvous, put forward on behalf of the Stuart sovereign by his lay advisers, who allowed James to agree to the proposal provided that he had safe-conduct. But the ecclesiastical majority who dominated the Council would not let their King leave for performance of this promise, so that his indignant uncle, already full of anger against all things Scottish, waited in vain at York for James's arrival. Henry returned to London in high dudgeon, and hearing soon after that a skirmish across the Border at Halydon Rigg had ended adversely to the English, prepared for war in real earnest.*

James V., with no means of raising an army but that of summoning the nobles and heads of clans, mustered his men on the Boroughmuir, near Edinburgh, now known as Morningside. On reaching Fala Muir, a plain beneath the western limits of the Lammermuir Hills, he halted and held a council of war, whereat it transpired that the Duke of Norfolk, commanding the English, had indulged in a Border foray, and was in retreat. In this expedition, to quote Mr. Froude's words, "the harvest (newly gathered in) was reduced to ashes, and farms, villages, towns, abbeys, went down in blazing ruins." † Finding, however, that the requisite commissariat had not been lodged in Berwick, as had been expected, Norfolk left a

---

* Froude's 'History of England,' edition 1858, vol. iv. p. 178.   † Ibid., p. 185.

garrison for the winter in each available spot, and halted awhile, before retracing his steps to York with the main body of his army.

James V., thinking the moment had arrived for avenging his father's death at Flodden, called on his lieges to cross the Border with him and advance into England, but was met most unexpectedly with sullen refusal. Some present doubtless had not forgotten Flodden Field, and some, being well affected towards the reforming doctrines, did not care to forward the Catholic cause; while others, and they not the least numerous, were dissatisfied with the high-handed rule exercised over themselves ever since the King escaped from the tutelage of Angus and the Douglases, whose own kinsmen were doubtless represented amongst the dissentients. "Deaf," says Mr. Froude, "to entreaties and indifferent to taunts," they watched the English until they were across the Tweed, and then dispersed to their homes. James retired sadly to Edinburgh, where, after consultation with Cardinal Beaton, a fresh enterprise was entered upon. The gathering was fixed to be at Lochmaben, on the night of November 24, and 10,000 men did meet there without any preliminary preparation; the most extraordinary part of the matter being that James himself was to remain in Caerlaverock Castle, while Maxwell, Warden of the Marches, conducted the men across the Esk, as if to capture Carlisle. No leader of recognised authority appeared amongst this semblance of an army until they had struggled across the river, when they were confronted by the spectacle of an obscure favourite of James, one Oliver Sinclair, displaying his commission as General, and being elevated by the soldiers and supported by two spears.

Straying on to the Solway Moss in a disintegrated condition, the Scots were suddenly surprised by the arrival of 300 English cavalry under Dacre and Musgrave, two stout moss-troopers, who, observing the disorderly character of the Scots' advance, dashed amongst them with a confidence which presumed the advent of more numerous battalions. The rout was instantaneous, and the Scots fled, one-tenth of their number being taken prisoners. When intelligence reached James V. of this disgraceful disaster, it is said that he fell into a deep gloom from which he never recovered; but the mystery surrounding his illness is probably subject to the explanation that the King was stricken with some recognised malady before he ever let loose the dogs of war, for in spite of many shortcomings—and they have not been shrouded here—James was one of the bravest men who ever governed Scotland, and would never have consented to levy forces in his own name and then stand aside in the hour of danger, had not physical weakness forced him so to do.

Retiring to Falkland Palace in Fife, when admittedly suffering from fever, James, so to speak, slept his life away, arousing himself but slightly when told that Mary of Guise had given birth to a daughter. Upon hearing this he is said to have murmured the words, "It came with a lass, and it will go with a lass," meaning that as the dynasty was created by means of the marriage with Marjory Bruce, so would it then end by the birth of Mary Stuart.

Little happened in this reign to advance the Scots morally. Although the fact that they were not yet prepared for the Reformation and its liberating influences can scarcely be charged against the King, whom Scott regards as a good economist, who encouraged science and the fine arts, it is certain that he, like his father James IV., had been tainted by the lax morality of those clerics whose advice he sought, and whose habits he copied. A careless disregard of the marriage tie increased the difficulties of his unfortunate successor, for one lady at least, who had received the attentions of James V., but who held no position at Court, considered that she ought to wear the crown. M. Edm. Bapst (see *Spectator*, Sept. 14, 1889) says that James V. asked the Pope to dissolve Margaret Erskine's marriage with Douglas of Lochleven, and give her a dispensation to marry himself (the King).

Minority of Mary Stuart, 1542—1560.

James V. was laid in the grave at Holyrood, at the age of thirty years, by the side of his first wife, the fair Magdalen, and with him was buried all hope of present unity in his dominions. Allegiance to a female child of eight days could in the first instance be but nominal, and the possession of power could but become the sport of faction.

Henry VIII. of England perceived this, and made no secret of his determination to secure custody of the infant Queen.* By too hastily proceeding in this design he gave a leverage to Cardinal Beaton and the Queen mother, who,

* Froude's 'History of England,' edition 1858, vol. iv. p. 204.

although they had not yet realised the strength of the reformation in religion which was in progress south of Tweed, yet gladly seized the opportunity which Henry VIII. gave them of arousing national feeling against his projects. Besides the Douglases—still in the English interest—an unexpected ally appeared to aid Henry's cause in the shape of Matthew, Earl of Lennox, a Stuart of high degree, and the brother of John, Lord D'Aubigny, whose French title dated from the battle of Beauge, fought in 1421. Lennox, whose sympathies were supposed to be French and Catholic, had possession of the Castle of Dumbarton, and when a French fleet appeared off that stronghold with a large sum of money for the Catholic cause, he calmly retained the money and shut the gates against his French friends. Ultimately forced to retreat to England, Lennox returned from thence after fitting up an expedition in Bristol, and took possession of the old Stuart country around Renfrew and Paisley. Unable, however, to hold his own at home, he again took refuge in England, where Henry VIII. had given him his niece, Lady Margaret Douglas, in marriage, the eldest child of the union being Henry, Lord Darnley.

Elsewhere Henry VIII. made the most of his opportunities, and prevailed upon several of the noblemen he had taken prisoners at Solway Moss to act as his agents in Scotland provided he gave them liberty. As their lot in England had been hard, subjected as they were to popular contempt when dragged through the streets of London, while they were subsequently imprisoned in the Tower, this unpatriotic submission is not altogether to be marvelled at.

Arran, head of the Hamiltons and next heir to the throne after the infant Queen Mary, was not to be relied on by either side, and his infirmity of purpose became a byword. When, in the capacity of Regent, he temporised during the diplomatic duel between Cardinal Beaton and Sir Ralph Sadler, emissary of Henry VIII., the unstable character of this nobleman militated against a peaceful issue to the contest. For owing to Arran's optimism, real or assumed, Beaton was at a critical moment permitted to return from confinement at Blackness to St. Andrews, and shut himself up in his own stronghold there; while Sir Ralph, instead of getting possession of the infant Queen Mary, had to content himself with the best compromise available, out of the inconvenient consequences of which the wily Cardinal intended to escape.

David Beaton, a prince of the Catholic Church, and Mary of Lorraine's most able minister, had, it is said, strained a point to gain the Regency of Scotland, " guiding the hand of James V. in the moment of departure," and had thus obtained a royal endorsement of his claim to supremacy.* But his proclamation at the market cross of Edinburgh was repudiated when men learned the means whereby the late King's signature had been secured, and the election of Arran as Regent followed. Beaton, moreover, was immediately arrested and imprisoned in Blackness Castle, where he nevertheless remained cognisant of the course of events, and the arbiter of Catholic counsels in Scotland. Sir Ralph Sadler, on the other hand, had so far justified the confidence of Henry VIII. in his diplomatic skill, as to get it stated in treaty form, and the document signed by the Regent Arran, that Mary Stuart was to be affianced to Prince Edward of England, and that, after the lapse of ten years, the bride should be brought to Berwick, and rendered up to the English, a ceremony of marriage being then performed. † Beaton, however, skilfully posing as the preserver of Scotch independence, schemed to get the agreement laid aside on technical grounds, and it was never ratified. When it became apparent that Beaton had really thwarted his design of uniting the crowns, Henry VIII. wreaked his vengeance on the sister realm so cruelly and relentlessly that he rendered the future difficulties of the Protestant and English parties in Scotland greater than before.

Lord Hertford came into the Firth of Forth with 200 vessels at the end of April 1544, and, landing at Leith, burnt the shipping there. Edinburgh made some resistance but succumbed before superior force, the Palace of Holyrood suffering terribly from fire, wooden houses also, around the impenetrable castle, blazing for three days and nights.

Again the English fleet ravaged the coast of the Forth, destroying every trace of fortification there, and sparing only Dalkeith, as belonging to a Douglas ; until, when no more punishment could be inflicted in this naval raid, Henry's forces withdrew, shortly to recommence their attacks elsewhere.‡

A Border defeat at Ancrum having irritated the baffled English monarch, he sent Lord Hertford to desolate the

---

* Froude's 'History of England,' edition 1858, vol. iv. p. 200.
† Burton's 'History of Scotland,' new edition, vol. iii. p. 202.
‡ Froude's 'History of England,' edition 1858, vol. iv. p. 323.

country about the Tweed, and repeat the process just mentioned on this portion of the infant Queen Mary's dominions. Ruined "monasteries and friar-houses" at Kelso, Melrose, Dryburgh, Roxburgh, and Coldingham, * all remain to attest the terrible vengeance taken on this occasion, at a moment when that coveted child, the Queen o' Scots, was in Stirling Castle, out of danger of attack from external foes. The well-known train of events follows naturally on this inflamed situation. The reformed doctrines gaining ground amongst the people of Scotland, Beaton and his coadjutors burnt the high-minded enthusiast, George Wishart, in 1545; and a year had not passed before Norman Leslie, son of Lord Rothes, gaining admittance into the Castle of St. Andrews, stabbed Cardinal Beaton, exposing his body over the wall, so that passers-by might see that the direst foe of Protestantism could vex the world no more.

Here in St. Andrews. Castle a Protestant garrison soon assembled, and defied the Government of Arran to dislodge them. Fired by the admonitions of John Knox, for fourteen months they held the place, until at last, in August 1547, Leo Strozzi, with a French force, attacking them simultaneously by land and sea, the castle surrendered. Knox being taken prisoner, and condemned to work an oar in the French galleys, lay tossing, sick to death, off this very bay of St. Andrews,† and when aroused, recognised, as he said, "the steeple of that place where God first in public opened my mouth to His glory;" while he remained convinced, in spite of adverse appearances, that he should not die until his tongue glorified God's name in the same locality. Faith such as this in the hour of distress, combined with inflexibility of purpose, when the opportunity arrived, was destined to reap its reward in the gradual permeation of Knox's opinions throughout Scotland, and, after the lapse of eleven years, there was a general acknowledgment that he was the mainspring of the Reformation in that land. He was in Scotland for a short time in 1555, but the date of 1559 may be taken as that when Knox became conspicuous.

Meantime, the death of Henry VIII. on January 29, 1547, had not altered the policy of England towards Scotland, whose army was crushed by the Protector Somerset at Pinkie,

---

* Froude's 'History of England,' edition 1858, vol. iv. p. 248. I am indebted to the late Dr. Hill Burton for the facts on which I base these later statements.

† Skelton's 'Maitland of Lethington,' vol. i. p. 211.

near Musselburgh, in September of the same year. The defeated nation, with no other resources left, rallied round the crown represented by the child of six years, who, after a sojourn on the island of Inchmahome on Lake Monteith, was spirited off to France under convoy of a French squadron, and landed safely at Brest, on August 30, 1548. With the Queen of Scotland on this occasion travelled her illegitimate half-brother Lord James Stuart, son of James V. by a daughter of Lord Erskine. Brought up with his sister, this youth, age seventeen years, was just old enough to discover the anomalies of his own position; and it is not wonderful to read of his being hereafter, as Earl of Murray, suspected by his enemies of a desire to wear Mary Stuart's surrendered crown. An ambition this, represented to him as a right, for his mother always averred that she was the lawful wife of James V.

The character of the Queen's half-brother, best known in history as " Murray," remains one of the enigmas most difficult to solve in Stuart history. The stern sense of morality inherent in the man was never known to be infringed in practice, and in this particular he eclipses the ecclesiastical rivals who so long had held sway in Scotland, setting examples of profligate living in high places. Nor is it possible to deny that Mary Stuart's brother acted with an honest preference for Protestantism over the older faith, the spiritual efficacy of which he had been probably led to question when he found it allied in France with the political wiles of the Guises.

And yet, when these facts are recorded, it is impossible to say that in Murray's relations with his royal sister he sustained the same high level of rectitude which characterised his dealings in private life, and which, combined with remarkable sagacity in the conduct of government, was destined to earn for him the title of " the good Regent."

Details concerning Mary Stuart's infancy are few, although we know that within the lofty walls of Stirling did the Lords Erskine and Livingston for the most part elect to keep their precious charge.

When the thunder of Hertford's artillery resounded even to the gates of Linlithgow, it was to the Stirlingshire stronghold that the guardians hied with their youthful sovereign; while, until the Priory of Inchmahome on Loch Monteith was chosen as an island retreat, the Scots never felt certain as to the safety of the royal person, unless she dwelt in the keep of that rock-seated castle. And when at last the Council, in something akin to despair, allowed the rightful Queen to leave her country and become naturalised in France, men knew that the hopes of any abiding union with England were at an end, so long as the Scottish Queen remained free to choose a husband, a fact realised tardily but decidedly by Henry VIII. before he died, so that he passed the Scotch line over when apportioning succession to the British throne in his famous will.* It is at the period of her departure for France in July 1548, that we first hear of Mary Stuart in connection with the four young ladies of high degree, who have become famous as " the Queen's Maries," their surnames being Livingston, Fleming (married in after years to Maitland of Lethington), Seton, and Beaton. They were the playfellows of Mary's youth, as well as the companions of her older and darker days; and we now get a passing glimpse of them on board the vessel which was to bear the Scottish Queen to the shores of France. Mary, when she reached that country, was sent at first to be educated at a convent,† while her brother, the Lord James Stuart, returning to Scotland, was soon chosen amongst the leading Lords of Congregation when it was known that he favoured the Protestant cause.

In Scotland, the Earl of Arran had resigned the Regency to the Queen mother, in 1554, the dukedom of Chatelherault in France consoling the feeble and flexible Hamilton for loss of dignity and power at home.‡

Four years later, on April 24, 1558, the Scottish Queen married the Dauphin of France, who was destined in a few months' time to become Francis II.

Henry II. being accidentally wounded in a tournament in July 1559 by the Count de Montgomery, died in a few days, and consequently Francis and Mary were hailed King and Queen of France.

Fatal prospect apparently for those who hoped for unity of the English and Scotch crowns, and the peaceful establishment of Protestantism in those countries!

Mary, acting under the prompting of her uncles the Guises—one of whom, the Cardinal of Lorraine, became First Minister, and his brother, the Duke of Guise, Commander-in-Chief—took the fatal step of quartering the arms of

* Froude's 'History of England,' edition 1858, vol. iv. p. 528.
† Ellis's 'Original Letters,' 1st series, vol. ii. p. 252.
‡ Burke's 'Peerage,' p. ii.

England with her own, by which means the jealousy of Elizabeth and enmity of English statesmen were speedily to be aroused; as, although France had won the long struggle for Mary's hand, her ministers must have expected sooner or later to reckon with the might of England. And this because there were potent signs which led to the belief that the Marian persecutions in England were not fated to issue in the final establishment of Roman Catholicism in that country, so that when Mary Tudor died in November 1558, and Elizabeth came to the throne, the young couple soon to become sovereigns of France found themselves face to face with a difficult political situation.

On the other hand, throughout Scotland the reformed doctrines gained ground speedily, in spite of divers prosecutions for heresy, and the burning of Walter Mill at eighty years of age, which disgraced that same year, 1558.

How it came to pass that hands were not laid on John Knox himself one wonders when perusing the histories of the time; but the eloquent zealot went on defying the Regent, Mary of Lorraine, in his own rough way, until, in 1559, after a sermon at Perth, the crowd rose against the priests and destroyed the famous Carthusian monastery there, as well as that of the Black Friars, where James I. had been entertained before being so cruelly murdered. These disturbances were soon repeated on the same scale at St. Andrews. John Knox urges that these acts were those "of the rascal multitude," but in the inflamed state of the public mind no other result would be likely to follow exciting, not to say iconoclastic, preaching such as his.*

Before leaving Perth for Edinburgh, the Calvinist Lords of the Congregation, animated as before by Knox, sacked the Abbey and Palace of Scone, with its monarchical monuments, and passing by Stirling, wrecked its monasteries, a fate which overtook kindred institutions in the romantic capital itself. A graphic description of these events will be found in Mr. Skelton's 'Maitland of Lethington,' vol. i. pp. 234, 235.

At this crisis the Regent, Mary of Lorraine, forced to take offensive measures which she deplored, fortified Leith and garrisoned that town with the few French soldiers who alone supported her cause. For had not the wily Maitland of Lethington, supreme in council, followed Chatelherault—

* Knox's 'History,' p. 128.

unstable it may be, but by family position head of the Scotch nobility—into the camp of Knox and the Congregation?

Elizabeth, the Queen of England, but lately installed on her father's throne, after some deliberation hearkened to the prayer of the Protestant Lords for assistance, and ships of war and men at arms besieged the devoted town of Leith, which, in spite of an ever memorable defence,* was starved into submission, not, however, before the Queen-regent sank to her rest in the Castle of Edinburgh on June 10, 1560, the victim of bodily weariness and mental disappointment.

The evil odour wherein the house of Guise has been justly held for lighting the torch of religious persecution in France, and endeavouring to waft its flames over Europe, long obscured the mild virtues of Mary, widow of James V., but it is certain that the Regency was conducted during her sway with a desire to minimise bloodshed and persecution so long as a contrary policy was not forced on her by the two brothers who ruled the family conclave in France. That she finally yielded to their behest, and did not altogether surrender to the Calvinist Lords of the Congregation, may seem reprehensible to those who can see no foe but the Church of Rome, but does not give just cause for historical condemnation.

The opportune moment for embracing the Knoxean reformation in its full development was scarcely as yet discerned by Maitland of Lethington, or even by the Lord James Stuart, and it is not reasonable to expect submission to Protestantism from a French princess brought up in the faith of ancient Catholicism.†

With the Queen-regent's death, and the departure of the French troops for their own country after Leith surrendered, the ancient league may be said to have spent its active force. Some community of interest remained between France and Scotland, and appears in the expressions of sympathetic diplomacy which from time to time were evoked, but active interference north of the Tweed was never again attempted

* The English government had undertaken a tougher task than they bargained for. " We think you do well to comfort Winter (the admiral stationed in the Forth) and such as serve there, for they have a sore and painful time." Privy Council to the Duke of Norfolk.—' Hatfield Calendar,' part i. p. 189.

† " She (Mary of Lorraine) appears to have been sincerely anxious to promote a moderate policy, to conciliate public opinion, to reconcile the contending factions, to bring about an accord. She failed—as she was bound to fail."—Skelton's ' Maitland of Lethington,' vol. i. p. 214.

by the house of Valois or their Bourbon successors. It is true that during the first half of the eighteenth century, the then exiled Stuarts made four distinct attempts to regain the British throne, three of them, directed by French advisers, being organised in France itself, Scotland on each occasion being the field of operation, while in 1719 a handful of Spaniards were taken prisoners in Glenshiel. But neither in 1708 nor 1715 did a French force land to succour the Jacobites. The few Frenchmen who accompanied the Scotch and Irish under Lord John Drummond to Montrose in the '45, when Charles Edward was at Derby, exercised little influence upon the Stuart fortunes. Dutch troops, on the other hand, to the number of 3,000, reinforced Argyll's army in 1715, a similar number remaining in England.

Francis II. of France and his wife Mary Queen o' Scots directed, as a result of the surrender at Leith, that a Council of Government should be chosen by Parliament in Edinburgh, and the office of Regent remain in abeyance, a measure which gave full power to the reforming party of Knox and the Congregation. One clause in the treaty bound Francis and Mary to desist from using the arms of England, and another acknowledged Elizabeth's title as Queen of England.

Mary's claim to succeed Elizabeth, if the latter remained childless, was also said to be sacrificed in this surrender after Leith fell; but the Scottish Queen repudiated such a clause altogether, and never, therefore, ratified the Treaty of Edinburgh. Cecil had himself been present and contrived the far-reaching clause which struck at Mary Stuart's future title.

The whole proceeding may now be traced in the 'Hatfield Calendar,' Part I., of Lord Salisbury's family papers dealing with the years 1560 and 1561. On page 246 appears Cecil's statement that the original articles of the treaty were altered and enlarged. Also the draft clause providing for the obliteration and defacement of the English arms wherever they existed in the realm of France, so strongly did Cecil and Elizabeth resent the action of Francis and Mary in adopting the royal style of England.

The triumph of the Protestant cause was actively followed up in Scotland, where Episcopacy was straightway abolished, and the Presbytery erected in its stead. With this portentous event closed the era we have designated as that of the Church at Bay.

During the minority of Mary Stuart the feudal nobility of Scotland were enjoying almost absolute rule in their several mountainous territories, and the Regent had neither time nor strength to curb their power. A number of these nobles imbibed an intellectual conviction of the truths which Protestantism enforced, heart and mind alike owning a fresh motive force which aroused them to enthusiasm; while Knox, working on the natural cupidity of half-civilised mankind, proposed, when establishing the Presbytery, to endow it out of the revenues of the discarded Church, whose pillaged coffers were likewise laid under contribution for the benefit of doubting feudal adherents.*

The Reformation, as its great apostle north of Tweed well knew, never could have been so swiftly consummated in Scotland but for the preponderance of support accorded it by the barons, so that a minority of the nobility and a minority of the people alone remained to champion the Catholic cause.

Against these religious changes, however, a powerful section of the nobility was arrayed, and it was questionable how far their leading northern representative, the Earl of Huntly, owning princely sway in the north-east, was prepared to go in defence of his faith. For this conservative section of society in the Highlands never concluded an offensive and defensive alliance with France when that country was under the Guise influence, else the small French force which defended Leith must have been succoured by reinforcements from their own country.

Had the life of Francis II. been prolonged, there is every reason to believe that Scotland would have become the theatre of a sanguinary religious war; but the early death of Mary Stuart's first husband, in December 1560, relegated the Cardinal of Lorraine and the Duke of Guise to subordinate positions, their enemy, Catherine de Medici, becoming Regent of France during the early years of the reign of Charles IX.

That these dissensions in France enabled Elizabeth and Cecil to sustain the Protestant party in Scotland the course of events will show.

Such, then, were the several conditions under which the beautiful and attractive daughter of James V. commenced her reign over faction-torn Scotland.

* "The reformed preachers did their part fairly well; but if the title of the aristocracy to the patrimony of the Church of Rome had not been identified with Protestantism, it is probable that the church of Knox would have been short lived."—Skelton's 'Maitland of Lethington,' vol. i. p. 202.

CHAPTER VII.

MARY QUEEN OF SCOTS. HER REIGN.

1560–1567.

This reign has been taken out of its historical context, its leading events recounted, commented on, and disputed over, until every one knows the main features of the story. It is strange, however, to reflect that the one piece of modern history which attracts mankind generally by its personal romance and by the sensational interest which it excites in the inquirer's heart, should remain so obscure in spite of the elucidatory efforts made by three generations of antiquaries, and the diligent researches of many recent writers.

The reign itself proved a sad and irreparable failure; and, indeed, with a knowledge of the circumstances, little else could have been anticipated for the female successor of James V. The difficulties in store for her were foreshadowed by the experience which Mary of Lorraine had gathered when exercising the Regency of Scotland which closed with the Treaty of Edinburgh in the summer of 1560.

A few short months after England and its Queen had registered their triumph over the houses of Valois and Stuart by the capture of Leith, King Francis II. died, and left his widow with no position in France suitable to her condition. Queen of Scotland she remained by right, and she proceeded to entitle herself to the Scottish throne by the strong argument of possession. It is said that the well-known romantic voyage to her northern dominions was undertaken in the teeth of adverse advice given by the astute Maitland of Lethington and others capable of discerning the course of events in Scotland. We read:—

"I have shown your honour's letter unto the Lord James, Lord Morton, Lord Lethington;* they wish, as your honour doth, that she might be stayed yet for a space, and if it were

---
* Maitland of Lethington, the Secretary.

not for their obedience sake, some of them care not though they never saw her face."*

Anyhow, the enmity of England's Protestantism was certain to assail the sovereign who was regarded by mankind as a pivot of the coming Catholic League which was to extirpate heresy throughout Europe. Mary's position as a representative of the house of Guise insured this, notwithstanding her own well-known desire to exercise toleration towards those differing from her in religion. That she made a promise of this description to her subjects, and kept it faithfully, was probably the cause of her ultimate destruction; for it has been discovered of late years that although Mary remained the centre of Catholic intrigue to her death, yet she never signed the famous League of 1565, which ultimately led to the Huguenot massacres in France and the attempts of Philip II. to invade England; and herein we discern the key to various unsettled questions regarding Mary's foreign policy, the events connected with which have been both distorted and misunderstood.

Professor Wiesener, in a small work published in Germany, has shown that the assertion of Randolph that Mary signed the League declaration is altogether mistaken. The reference given is to the 'Archives de Medici,' from which we find that, on March 16, 1567, the Bishop of Mondovi, Papal Legate to Scotland, wrote as follows:—

"If the Queen had done as was proposed, and urged on her (in regard to the League) with the promise of all succour necessary for her objects, she would at this time have found herself mistress of her kingdom, in a position to establish fully the Holy Catholic faith. But she would never listen to it, though the Bshop of Dunblane and Father Edmond (a Jesuit) were sent to determine her to embrace this most wise enterprise." Mary Stuart would not break faith with the people to whom she had promised free exercise of religion.†

If, instead of honestly attempting to satisfy the Calvinist oligarchy of Knox and Murray, Mary had frankly turned towards Spain, in the first hours of her reign, Scotland would possibly have been in alliance with Philip II. when the Armada appeared on the coast of Caledonia seven-and-twenty years afterwards, but whether with a result advantageous to England may justly remain open to question.

* Randolph to Cecil, Aug. 9, 1561. Ten days before Mary Stuart landed at Leith.
† Caird's 'Mary Stuart,' pp. 36, 37.

That the Queen of Scots tried to carry out an almost hopeless compromise at home is proved by a simple relation of events, and her toleration should be placed to the credit of her assailed character.

It is difficult to say why the popular sympathy with the fair Queen of Scotland has increased in succeeding generations, in spite of the adverse verdict registered against her character by powerful writers both contemporary with and later than herself. When Knox and Buchanan are found in agreement with Hume, Malcolm Laing, and Robertson, who in their turn are supported by Mignet, Lamartine, Froude, and Hill Burton, good evidence would be required to prove these men mistaken. Yet the *vox populi*, disregarding what may be called the bird's-eye or external view of Queen Mary's conduct and rule, seems to be more in accord with modern scientific historical criticism than the conclusions of those eminent writers whose names have just been mentioned.

So desperate did the case of Scotland's hapless Queen appear to our ancestors who were subjects of Elizabeth, aye! and of the later Stuarts also, that had not a notable reaction set in during the eighteenth century, when men could afford to look calmly on the past and its constitutional perils, Mary Queen of Scots would either have sunk into oblivion, together with other beautiful, clever, and unfortunate characters who have figured in our national story, or possibly have been doomed to infamy as ineradicable as that which, with some taint of injustice, still clings to the popular conception of Mary Tudor. One thing, however, is certain, that if Mary Stuart had not fascinated those of her contemporaries with whom she came in contact in France, Scotland, and England, so as by the interest excited to insure a thorough investigation of facts, her literary condemnation would have ensued as certainly as her failure to govern the oligarchic factions in Scotland followed her return to that land of hill and heather.

One of the earliest recorded illustrations of her power thus to attract mankind is to be found in Camden's 'History,' indited by that learned antiquary at the behest of James I. as an antidote to the poisonous untruth disseminated by Buchanan in his 'Detection,' a work discredited in important particulars even by the most unfriendly narrators of Mary's career. Camden had in the first instance to show that the Queen was not by nature the bitter, revengeful, intemperate woman represented by Knox and Buchanan, and he remarks how, after some years of cloister life spent in devotional and industrial habits, Mary captivated Henry II. of France, who desired to marry her to the Dauphin. He draws a picture for the purpose of explaining how this came about, and gives us a glimpse of a beautiful girl, fond of poetry, and thereby attracting the poet Ronsard, having good taste for music, dancing well, and riding as if to the manner born; while such was her skill in Latin, that she spoke an oration of her own composing, in the great guardroom of the Louvre, before the royal family and nobility of France.*

The fame of this beauty and fascination was wafted over the Scotch moors long before she came as queen to govern the hardy but lawless Highlanders who peopled that region. The hold thereby gained on national sympathies can scarcely have been rendered less secure by the possession of that national accent lisped in childhood which a youth spent in France had not obliterated.

Writing during Mary Stuart's imprisonment in England, one of Cecil's correspondents says that he has been to Tutbury and seen the Scottish queen, and advises that very few should have access to or conference with this lady. " For besides that she is a goodly personage, she hath withal an alluring grace, *a pretty Scottish speech*, and a searching wit, clouded with mildness." †

We have spoken of Mary Queen of Scots as engaged in an impossible task when seeking to govern Scotland as a zealous Catholic upon Calvinist lines, giving at the same time to others the religious toleration she asked for herself and desired for her co-religionists.

Relying upon the counsels of her illegitimate half-brother —whom she elevated to be successively Earl of Mar and of Murray—and also on the unrivalled wisdom of William Maitland of Lethington, an attempt to revert to the compromise so long prevalent under Mary of Lorraine's regency met with temporary success.

Knox, however, on the one hand, and the Earl of Huntly on the other, did their very best to render a continuance of religious peace impossible, the former not seeking to hide his distrust of the sovereign whose kindly courtesy was straightway perverted into veiled hostility towards the Reformers. Knox writes :—

* Camden's 'History,' p. 60.
† N. White to Sir William Cecil, Feb. 26, 1568-9, 'Hatfield MSS.,' part i. p. 400.

"Some of no small estimation have said wt open mouht; The quen neyther is, ncyther shallbe of o' opinion, and in verrey dead her hole proceadinges do declayr that the cardinalles lessons are so deaplie prented in her hart that the substaunce and the qualitie ar liek to perrishe togetther. I wold be glaid to be deceaved, but I fear I shall not; in communication w' her I espyed such craft as I have not found in such aige; since hath the court bein dead to me and I to it."*

The head of the Gordons, a rigid and disappointed Catholic, attracted to his cause a powerful party which James Stuart deemed dangerous to the peace of Scotland.

Urged by this able but ambitious brother to overawe the northern dissentients and lean towards the Calvinists for the nonce, Mary accompanied her army to Inverness, and afterwards to Aberdeenshire, where, in an otherwise indecisive engagement at Corrichie, Huntly fell from his horse and was killed. It is said that on this occasion James Stuart made good his questioned title to certain lands of the Gordons within the Earldom of Murray, gaining that title at the same time, thereby earning the endless hostility of the powerful clan who disputed the ownership with him. But the Queen found, on returning to Edinburgh, that her victory over Huntly had not in the slightest degree appeased the acid malignity of Knox and those ministers whose Pope he claimed to be. The great Calvinist divine himself did not refrain from using hard words bordering on insult when admitted to the royal presence, and although foiled by a fine wit, and for the moment conciliated by a placid temper which enabled the Queen to deliver the most searching rebuke with dignity, yet Knox's hostility remained unappeased and unappeasable; while—strange to add—he extended his disapproval of Mary and all her works to the unconscious womankind who waited outside the Queen's chamber at Holyrood, telling them sarcastically and sententiously not to "target their tails." †

The great reformer would fain have placed a veto on the latest Parisian taste in dress, just as he had succeeded, when waging war with Popery, in banishing æstheticism from the churches and cathedrals of his native land.

Nor were the difficulties of this widowed Queen lessened by reason of the numerous suitors who sought her hand,

* John Knox to Sir William Cecil, 'Hatfield MSS.,' part i. p. 262.
† Burton's 'History of Scotland,' edition 1867, vol. iv. p. 226.

none of the earlier applicants receiving the slightest favour; while the unhappy Chastelard suffered the death awarded for high treason, because, lost in admiration of Mary's accomplishments, he revealed to unsympathising onlookers that he "loved, not wisely, but too well."

The sad tragedy of Chastelard having been enacted, another foreign figure occupies the stage in the shape of David Rizio, said by Mary's foes, Knox among the number, to have been her lover—an assertion rejected by the most unsympathetic of the Stuart Queen's critics.* In reality, the musical Italian seems to have conducted the foreign correspondence during the time of his sojourn at Court, the need for such an official being patent amongst courtiers whose gift of tongues was more often than not limited to Gaelic, and many of whom had never crossed the seas.

At length a natural disposition towards the fine person and presence of Lord Darnley, whom Mary met first at Wemyss Castle, in Fife, was followed by a resolve on the Queen's part to accept this youthful Stuart as her husband. This decision entailed a semblance of displeasure by Queen Elizabeth, and the actual hostility of the Protestant Murray, who went to Glasgow and gathered forces to act in rebellion against his sister because she was about to ally herself with a Roman Catholic family.

Mr. Skelton † shows that Elizabeth and her Council secretly desired the alliance of Darnley and Mary Stuart, notwithstanding the English Queen's conduct in recalling the former to England, as if in wrath, and sending Sir Nicholas Throckmorton to protest against the marriage. Buchanan, Knox, Randolph, and Darnley's mother, Lady Lennox, all suspected this secret acquiescence, but Sir Nicholas Throckmorton sets the matter at rest when writing to Cecil from Scotland as follows:—

"I shall be sorry if any one coming out of England should be able to give this Queen (Mary) intelligence that her proceedings with Lord Darnley are not so ill taken there by her Majesty and her Council, as in all my negotiations I *pretended*, for that would hinder the purpose the Queen (Elizabeth) would be at." ‡

---

* The late Dr. Hill Burton denounced this calumny as totally unfounded. See his 'History,' new edition, vol. iv. p. 141.

† 'Maitland of Lethington,' vol. ii. pp. 131, 132.

‡ Throckmorton to Cecil, May 21, 1565.

The Scottish Queen's combined ability and popularity were such, however, at this crisis, that following close on Murray's heels in his retreat with his ill-organised levies, Mary drove her rebellious brother into well-deserved exile in England, where he scarcely met with the open encouragement that Elizabeth's secret support had led him to hope for. This rebellion was known as the "Runabout Raid," so active in retreat were Mary's foes before her vigorous and energetic advance. Anyhow, at home and in her capital more especially, Mary Stuart stood triumphant. All might have continued well with the monarchy at Holyrood, if only Darnley had filled his exalted position with adequate dignity, and shielded the royal lady whose affections he had so deeply engaged, as a husband and King Consort should have done at all hazards. Instead of this marital care which she naturally craved for, Mary found herself allied to a dissipated, frivolous, vain boy, with more than average scholarship, but at twenty years of age naturally possessing no pretensions to knowledge of public affairs, into the management of which he nevertheless endeavoured to plunge. In so doing Darnley found himself confronted by his own friend and ally Rizio, who urged the impolicy of a cause of offence being given to the powerful family of Hamilton, heirs to the throne provided Mary had no issue, who would necessarily scheme to prevent the King from gaining "the crown matrimonial" so urgently desired by him at this time; because thereby their claims would rank second to those of any child born to Darnley by a future marriage. The King Consort, however, heedless in pursuit of his object, and urging that his predecessor Francis II. had enjoyed the coveted honour in question, turned savagely upon Rizio, and was weak enough to enter into a "band" with certain nobles for the purpose of destroying the protesting Italian, whose influence in affairs of State was pre-eminent, and of smoothing down other difficulties which might then appear.

Darnley, on the other hand, was to use his influence as King to shield these conspirators from the consequence of their murderous conduct. Hence, on March 9, 1566, occurred the famous tragedy at Holyrood, when Mary, supping with her illegitimate half-sister the Countess of Argyll, and several others, in the little cabinet familiar to all who have explored Holyrood Palace, saw Rizio dragged from her presence, and soon knew that he had been murdered by Darnley's associates, amongst whom she had recognised the ghastly features of the invalid Ruthven, and declared that she had been endangered by the threatened violence of Ker of Faudonside.

It is not generally realised that, as a result of Rizio's murder, the Queen became virtually a prisoner in the hands of her insurgent subjects, and that if Darnley had not recognised this and escaped with her from Holyrood Palace, and met the assembled loyalists at Dunbar, she would have been confined in Stirling Castle and forced either to abdicate or embrace the Protestant faith.*

The King Consort, however, had sealed his own fate; for, by reason of his duplicity, he became the enemy of irreconcilable and dominant members of the oligarchy who had combined with him to trammel Mary in the exercise of her power. Morton, Lindsay, Ruthven, banished on account of their share in Rizio's murder, were on the watch to revenge themselves, and treachery such as Darnley's could but meet with one reward, when by his unstable conduct he literally laid his breast open to the striker. For on the Queen's return in apparent triumph to Edinburgh, the King Consort resumed his insolent conduct towards the nobles, while he lacked the sense to preserve his proper position as Mary's husband. Moreover, at this time, the breach between husband and wife was increased by Mary's discovery of Darnley's share in the conspiracy against her which culminated in Rizio's destruction.

His fellow conspirators, when deserted by the King Consort, had taken the earliest opportunity to reveal that the doomed youth had been lately guilty of treachery towards the Queen herself. On realising this she had desired nothing more than to retire to France, and leave the affairs of the kingdom to the various factions who had resolved to make government dependent on their ambitions and intrigues. Had not the hostility of the Queen-mother, Catherine de Medici, proved insuperable, it seems probable that Mary would at this time have fled the kingdom.†

The rejoicings were general throughout the realm when at length a Prince was born on June 19, 1566, and for a time the Queen's domestic happiness seems to have returned.

This epoch marks a portentous crisis in the Stuart fortunes.

* Tytler's 'History of Scotland,' edition 1834, vol. vii. p. 33.
† Hosack's 'Mary Queen of Scots and her accusers,' vol. i. p. 160.

Such was the general distrust and suspicion abroad * that the Privy Council declined to allow the Queen to remain at Holyrood during her confinement, but entrusted their Sovereign to the care of the Earl of Mar, governor of that then impenetrable stronghold, Edinburgh Castle.

Of the joyful event which occurred on June 19, 1566, we have various accounts, but most valuable of all that of Darnley himself, written from the actual scene. And this because such was the King Consort's state of mind that men feared lest jealousy and injured pride should lead him to deny a paternal interest in Mary's offspring.

And as, with every temptation to create a party for himself, and thus to rise above the neglect of his wife and the contemptuous enmity of her nobility, Darnley thus wrote, it will not be amiss, considering the prevalence of wild rumours even in our own times,† to reprint here this brief but historic epistle.

King Henry Darnley to Monsieur the Cardinal de Guise.

"From the Castle of Edinburgh, this 19th day of June, 1566, in great haste.

"Sir, my uncle, having so favourable an opportunity of writing to you by this gentleman, who is on the point of setting off, I would not omit to inform you that the queen, my wife, has just been delivered of a son, which circumstance, I am sure, will not cause you less joy than ourselves; and also to inform you how, on this occasion, I have, on my part, as the queen, my said wife, has also on hers, written to the king,‡ begging him to be pleased to oblige and honour us by standing sponsor for him, by which means he will increase the debt of gratitude I owe him for all his favours to me, for which I shall always be ready to make every return in my power.

"So having nothing more agreeable to inform you of at present, I conclude, praying God, monsieur my uncle, to have you always in His holy and worthy keeping.

"Your very humble and very obedient nephew,

"HENRY R."§

---

* Burton's 'History of Scotland,' vol. iv. p. 160.
† See Appendix II.   ‡ Of France.
§ 'Letters of Mary Queen of Scots, and Documents connected with her Personal History.' Edited by Miss Strickland, edition 1842, vol. i. p. 21.

The King wrote this letter during a brief return of that domestic happiness which had been originally so shortlived, and in the first blush of parental joy probably intended to repent of his shortcomings and amend his conduct.

But Darnley, unfortunately, had made enemies of nearly all the influential men in Scotland, and he now accentuated this disability by demanding Secretary Lethington's dismissal in favour of Leslie, Bishop of Ross, so that, had the King Consort had his own way, the wisest statesman at Court would have received a rebuff when Mary most desired his assistance.* Indeed, Lethington abandoned the Court for some time, and lived with Athole in Perthshire.

Whatever may have been the relations between Darnley and the Queen at this precise part of the year 1566, a deadlock in the progress of public affairs appeared imminent if Darnley, dissolute, irresponsible, and headstrong, were to retain his commanding position unchecked and to gather a party around him. Darnley, we know from Melville's 'Memoirs,' was so conspicuously neglected by his wife during the baptismal ceremony at Stirling in the autumn of 1566, that the Earl of Bedford, the English representative, expressed to Sir James Melville his regret at such an estrangement.† It is, however, questionable whether Darnley himself was not partly responsible for the strained situation then existing; inasmuch as he not unnaturally deprecated Morton's pending return from exile, to which the Queen agreed at the instance of the French ambassador, Le Croc.‡ Nor is it possible to deny that the unfortunate King had ample reason for distrusting the confederate he had himself betrayed. It is difficult to say whether Mary's despair at her husband's dissipations, or the Lords' conviction that his unwisdom threatened the stability of Scotland, brought about the conference of December 1566, at Craigmillar Castle, near Edinburgh, where and when the Queen fell into the first of those startling errors which her enemies have not unnaturally, and with much plausibility, represented as crimes. The assembled Lords, the leading spirits being Murray, Lethington, and Bothwell, desired that Morton might be recalled from exile in England, and pardoned for his conspicuous share in Rizio's murder. To effect this object it was suggested that perhaps the Queen might look with

---

* Skelton's 'Maitland of Lethington,' vol. ii. p. 185.
† Sir James Melville's 'Memoirs,' edition 1683, p. 77.
‡ Hosack's 'Mary Queen of Scots. A brief Statement,' p. 15.

favour on Morton's return, if it was coincident with a divorce or separation from her troublesome husband, whose conduct threatened to embarrass affairs of state, while, though his own life was loose and disorderly, he was jealous of every one who approached Mary's presence.

At this winter's gathering in Craigmillar Castle five of the most influential noblemen in Scotland were present—viz. Murray, Maitland of Lethington, Argyll, Huntly, and Bothwell—the Queen being unwise enough to grant them an audience, and to listen patiently when they talked to her of her husband's faults and the desirability of a separation being effected. Maitland of Lethington acted as spokesman on this occasion.

"Madam," said he, "fancy ye not we are here of the principal of y^r grace's nobility and Council that shall find the means that y^r Majesty shall be quit of him without prejudice of y^r son, albeit that my Lord of Murray here present be little less scrupulous for a Protestant than y^r Grace is for a Papist. I am assured he will look through his fingers thereto, and will behold our doings, saying nothing to the same."

The Queen answered,

"I will that ye do nothing where through any spot may be laid to my honour or conscience, and therefore I pray you rather let the matter be in the estate as it is."

"Madam," said Lethington, winding up the conference, "let us guide the matter among us, and your Grace shall see nothing but good and approved by Parliament."*

From that moment, notwithstanding the qualifications which Mary insisted on, while forbearing to chide the nobility for such insolent interference, she had placed a weapon in the hands of her detractors which will, alas! be available for all time. For this Craigmillar conference of December 1566 was destined to be followed little more than two months after by the tragedy of February 10, 1567, when that house in Kirk o' Field, where the King had been taken during convalescence after the small-pox, was blown into the air, his dead but unmutilated body being found in an adjoining orchard.

The idea of most modern writers seems to be that the King, aroused by some suspicion, went out of the house with his attendant but met some of those forming a murderous cordon around the Kirk o' Field, and was strangled, the bodies

---

* Caird's 'Mary Stuart,' pp. 189, 190.

of master and servant being thrown into the orchard. Blown into the air by gunpowder they could scarcely have been, and their bodies remain recognisable.

There are various rumours and theories concerning the manner in which Darnley's murder was carried out, while the individuals concerned therein have been multiplied amazingly if surmise is to be taken into consideration. Several rest under suspicion, but the only two noblemen *proved* to have been privy to the design are Bothwell, the chief actor, who confessed on his deathbed, and Morton, who acknowledged that he knew the King was to be killed, and took no measures to prevent it.

Although it may be shown that at the time Darnley, after leaving Stirling (where he had been to see his wife and child) was stricken, as has been said, with that hideous disease small-pox, held in horror scarcely imaginable during the sixteenth century, Mary came to Glasgow and treated him with due affection and that her conduct to him within an hour of the catastrophe was that of a loving wife; yet the glaring fact of her unfortunate parley at Craigmillar with the Lords who were conspiring to rid her of Darnley, has discredited the Queen's case at the very outset, and inclined many people ignorant of all the facts to give a hasty but plausible verdict against her.

The leading spirit amongst those guilty of this terrible crime seems undoubtedly to have been the Earl of Bothwell, who was probably engaged in carrying out the sentence pronounced on the erring King at, or soon after, Craigmillar. Several names have been mentioned as being associated with him on this occasion, and rumour speaks of a " band" having been signed to bring about Darnley's death, just as Rizio's fate had been decided by a similar tribunal.* But for travel into the region of rumour and surmise there is no scope here, and it remains but to repeat that Morton, judging by his own subsequent statement, was privy to the design which Bothwell carried out, this view being corroborated by the confessions of servants concerned in Darnley's murder, not to mention an alleged statement made on the fugitive Duke of Orkney's (for this title Mary conferred on her third husband) own death-bed.†

* Malcolm Laing's 'History of Scotland,' vol. i. p. 21, quoting Paris's deposition.
† For this alleged confession of Bothwell's, and a rambling inaccurate deposition taken down when in health, see ' Letters of Mary Queen of Scots, and

That the associates of these two noblemen on this terrible occasion were for the most part members of the extreme Protestant party, may be explained by the fact that Darnley, when lightly regarded by his wife and shunned by her nobility, had the craft so far to mingle method with his madness as to pose in the character of Roman Catholic leader.*

King Consort of Scotland, Darnley's elevated position rendered it possible that the Catholic nations of Europe might see their opportunity arise when he was willing to cast his influence on their behalf into the then trembling scale.

However, the unfortunate husband of Mary Stuart seems to have lacked the stability to carry out any settled course of policy, and the present instance proved no exception to the rest. Indeed he succeeded in making enemies more numerous and bitter as time passed on. It is certain that, having shrewdness enough to recognise this, he once meditated a retreat into France.

The character of James Hepburn, Earl of Bothwell, has been analysed by numerous writers, many of them eager to soften the adverse verdict clinging to his name, but neither in sober narrative nor attractive fiction has it been found possible to adhere to truth even in its barest outline, without presenting the reader with a character destitute alike of virtue and refinement. It must, however, be allowed that in the backward condition in which James V. had left Scotland, there was both need and scope for the rude talents of a resolute Border soldier such as Bothwell. His adherence in early life to the Regent Mary of Lorraine, when the Protestant Lords deserted her, gave Mary Stuart reasonable cause for welcoming the Earl to Court, and relying on his sword in time of peril. According to Knox and Buchanan she conceived an affection for this nobleman some time before Darnley's death, and the two histories written by these prominent contemporary actors on the stage of Scotland's Reformation, speak openly on the subject. On the other hand

---

Documents connected with her Personal History.' Edited by Miss Strickland, vol. i. pp. 218–256.

* Robertson's 'History of Scotland,' edition 1794, vol. i. p. 386. First and last Bothwell declared Murray to be designer of Darnley's murder. When dying, however, the unscrupulous Hepburn added the name of Morton, and then, despite former asseverations of innocence, acknowledged his own guilt. No reliance can of course be placed on his statements.

their averments are unsupported by any proofs ; nor do we elsewhere hear of such calumnies being so early repeated even by the divers bitter enemies who surrounded the Scottish Queen. The course of events nevertheless conspired to make such statements—in appearance at least—well founded. Chalmers, in his voluminous Life of Mary Queen of Scots, avers that so early as 1561 Bothwell had matured a plan to carry the Queen off to Dumbarton Castle, a design doubtless utterly unknown to Mary herself, while after June 19, 1566 this bold adventurer's efforts to seize the young Prince of Scotland were notorious.

In October 1566, two months before the Craigmillar conference, Mary had been holding a Court of Justice at Jedburgh, whither Murray went with her. While she was there, Bothwell, acting as Warden of the Marches, was wounded in the hand near Hermitage Castle in a Border fray with one of the Elliots. The tidings reached Mary Stuart, who, with her brother and others of the suite, galloped across country to the scene of the late skirmish and consoled Bothwell by an unexpected royal visit of sympathy, returning as she came, to Jedburgh. The distance (twenty miles each way) has been spoken of as if the Queen had not been—like her father and grandfather, James IV. and V.—accustomed to similar equestrian efforts, and though at one time no such exercise, however violent or prolonged, seemed to fatigue her ; while Murray's presence would surely have been dispensed with, had the occasion deserved the description which enemies spread concerning it. Nor was the persistency of the calumny directed against the Queen the least diminished when it became known that, as the result of this fatigue acting on a lately developed affection of the side, Mary Stuart lay sick at Jedburgh of a dangerous fever ; while Darnley, who at that time was in the west with his father, Lord Lennox, did not arrive until his wife was convalescent, and then received a by no means cordial greeting.*

An evidence this of manifest ill-feeling between Mary and her husband which gave their enemies further opportunity for spreading evil reports concerning them. Mary, they did not hesitate to assert, was enamoured of Bothwell. This accusation, whispered maybe by jealous courtiers, never received serious attention until the popular voice, calling for Bothwell's trial after Darnley's murder, was at last guided

* Robertson's 'History of Scotland,' vol. i. p. 390.

to charge the Queen with lukewarm conduct in bringing the case to legal issue. It cannot be denied that Mary allowed Bothwell's acquittal to be gained under circumstances favourable to the accused. The Earl of Lennox, Darnley's father, hesitating to approach a Court filled with Bothwell's retainers, did not appear in person to urge the cause, and failed to substantiate his accusation. But Lennox had nevertheless written to the Queen begging that the day of trial might be postponed, due leisure and deliberation being thereby secured in order that the truth might prevail in a matter of such supreme moment.*

It is clear that Mary Stuart, either by reason of the despair which had seized upon her when, torn with conflicting passions, she learnt her husband's cruel death, or perhaps distrusting Lennox's partisanship against Bothwell, made no reply to the father pleading against the murderer of his son, although that son had once been nearest and dearest to herself. This conduct of course necessarily laid her open to suspicion. That the moment of Bothwell's acquittal by default should have been chosen by twenty of the leading nobles of Scotland for accepting his invitation to Ainslie's Tavern in Edinburgh, April 9, 1567, where he had the assurance to recommend himself—a married man—as the Queen's husband, passes comprehension, and yet it is true; while—even more astonishing though it be—the collected nobles appear to have raised no objection, but signed the written proposal which Bothwell produced. The list of names was headed by that of Murray, who must have signed by deputy, he being absent in France; while among those who recommended a marriage so fatal to the Queen's honour, and injurious to the realm, appeared Argyll, Huntly, Sutherland, Glencairn, and Morton—men who, taken together with those signing afterwards, could furnish retainers sufficient to ensure the success of any domestic policy they favoured. Cassilis, Rothes, Caithness, Boyd, Seton, Sinclair, Semple, Oliphant, Ogilvy, Rosse Hecat, Carlyle, Herries, Hume, and Invermeith complete the list. "Eglington subscribed not, but slipped away."†

Four days later, Bothwell, thus fortified, seized the Queen at Fountainbridge, to the west of Edinburgh old town, on her return from a visit to her child at Stirling. Surrounded

* Hume's 'History of England,' edition 1782, vol. v. p. 108, quoting Keith, p. 375.
† Cotton MSS., Caligula, Brit. Mus., c. i. p. 50.

by a thousand of his horsemen she had small chance of escape, and was carried to Dunbar in company with Sir James Melville, the Secretary Maitland, and the Earl of Huntly.* There, at Dunbar, after undergoing something akin to violence—Melville ('Memoirs,' p. 80) believes acting under absolute compulsion—Mary Stuart consented to a marriage which enabled the party hostile to her rule—that of Murray and Morton—to appear in arms with some public approval; while the news of it spread dismay amongst those of her relatives in France who watched events in Scotland, hoping that the course taken might tend to the advantage of Catholic principles. Therefore, when Morton, Athole, and Argyll were found combining with Maitland (driven from Mary Stuart's presence by Bothwell's violence), and also with Kirkaldy of Grange, the soul of Scotch chivalry, men felt that there was no specious pretence in the declaration that these measures were taken to free the sovereign from durance vile. Hence the proclamation issued by the Privy Council, June 6, 1567, which, having averred that the Queen had for a long space been detained "in captivity and thraldom," goes on to declare that the nobility have assembled to deliver her from her abductor's clutches.†

It was all too true that this unjust and unnatural marriage had not only lost Mary Stuart the hearts of her people, but rendered life a burden to the ensnared Queen herself.

Le Croc, the French ambassador, told Catherine de Medici that he saw the beautiful ruler of Scotland on her wedding-day—if such the wretched occasion can be termed—and perceived, when he came into her presence, "an estranged demeanour between her and her husband." "If I saw her sad (added Le Croc) it was because she could not rejoice, for she did nothing but wish for death." "Yesterday being shut up in her cabinet with Bothwell, she screamed aloud and then sought for a knife to stab herself."‡ Sir James Melville, moreover, in his 'Memoirs' (p. 81), recounts how the wretched Queen at this time seriously entertained the idea of courting death by steel or drowning.

Pitiful outcome of a train of events, as inexplicable as unexampled!

Not against Mary Stuart's personal rule then, but to sunder

* Sir James Melville's 'Memoirs,' edition 1683, p. 80.
† 'Privy Council Register,' vol. i. p. 519.
‡ 'Letters of Mary Queen of Scots, and Documents connected with her Personal History.' Edited by Miss Strickland, vol. iii. p. 19.

her connection with Bothwell, did the Lords collectively strike, when nearly surprising the Queen and Bothwell at Borthwick Castle, they drove them in hasty flight to Dunbar, where the unhappy lady, who was Queen of Scotland, appeared disguised as a page.*

The Confederated Lords now marched their forces towards the retreat of Mary and Bothwell, resolved that matters should be brought to an issue before any friendly forces could reinforce the Queen's little army which speedily advanced to meet their opponents. It is said that the Hamiltons were on the march to rescue her, and that they were in force. The two rival armies confronted one another at Carberry Hill, near Musselburgh, June 16, 1567. Bothwell having offered to prove his innocence by single combat, successively took exception to Kirkaldy of Grange, Morton, Murray of Tullibardine, and Lord Lindsay, as opponents. The Queen, it is asserted, restrained him from submitting his case to this test. But a process of disintegration was at work amongst Mary Stuart's soldiery, whom their officers dared not lead to the charge so long as Bothwell remained with them. This condition of things very shortly resulted in the Lords gaining their avowed object, by separating Mary from this violent schemer. He, aware that safety was only to be gained either for his wife or himself by flight, adopted this course with the Queen's leave, if not at her suggestion.†

The scenes which followed this collapse of Bothwell's power are familiar to us all, but none the less terribly dramatic in their sad intensity. Surrendering to the highminded Kirkaldy, who undertook to guard her person from immediate peril, Mary Stuart was taken to Edinburgh by the triumphant Lords, and conducted in solemn procession through the streets. In front of her marched the Earls of Morton and Athole, while near to them was carried a flag whereupon the late King Consort's recumbent corpse appeared under a tree, while the infant Prince was represented engaged in prayer, with the inscription " *Judge and avenge my cause, O Lord !* "

Wearied and humiliated, disordered in her person, and dazed with the shame of the insults heaped upon her and approved by the dregs of the people, the unhappy Queen

* Sir Walter Scott's 'Tales of a Grandfather,' edition 1880, p. 118.
† Robertson's 'History of Scotland,' vol. i. p. 444 ; also Froude's ' History of England,' edition 1866, vol. ix. p. 92.

reached the Provost's house at Edinburgh, virtually a prisoner, without a friend to advise her, or any well-known voice to cheer her. Such a sight as this was certain to bring about a reaction amongst the people of the beautiful city wherein such terrible scenes had been recently enacted; and crowds surrounded the house of Mary's captivity expressing their pity and compassion. Morton and his associates were straightway forced to announce that they did not meditate putting any constraint upon their sovereign, and she was sent to the seclusion of her own palace at Holyrood, where the popular sympathy would be less likely to interfere with the fulfilment of what it is manifest was a settled plan.

Hurriedly holding an assembly to consider some immediate action, which the changed popular attitude rendered necessary,* the Scottish Lords who had captured Mary Stuart justified their severity towards her on the ground of her continued fidelity to Bothwell. Some such profession was necessary to satisfy the scruples of Kirkaldy, a high-minded and honourable man, who had been drawn into the toils of Morton and his friends, and to whom, on condition of a safe-conduct, the Queen had surrendered. The statement that Mary tried at this juncture to communicate with her fugitive lover rests on personal evidence given by the protesting and triumphant Lords themselves, and the Queen may or may not have refused to repudiate the connection with Bothwell at a moment when uncertainty prevailed whether the marriage was to exercise future influence over the dynasty she represented and whose name she bore.

Had Mary (as she believed was probable) borne a child by her third marriage, the question would have cropped up whether Bothwell could legally have gained a divorce from his former wife, the earl of Huntly's sister, a Papal dispensation for that marriage being in existence.

At all events, the story that Mary wrote in terms of affection to Bothwell at this crisis is unsupported by evidence, if not absolutely disproved. Sir James Melville, indeed, says that some such writing was produced to silence Kirkaldy of Grange's scruples; but when Queen Elizabeth called on the ruling oligarchy in Scotland to justify the extreme measures taken at this period, no allusion to any such epistolary evidence was made, the Lords' reply being placed in literary form three weeks after Carberry Hill.†

* Calderwood, vol. ii. p. 37 ; Spotiswood, vol. ii. p. 63.
† Skelton's 'Maitland of Lethington,' vol. ii. pp. 244, 245.

But the report that Mary Stuart remained obdurate as regards Bothwell, and had signified the same in writing, gave a specious excuse for conveying her by night to Lochleven, where Morton committed his charge to the care of Murray's mother, wife to Douglas of Lochleven. As this lady declared that James V. had been her lawful husband, and therefore believed that her son was born King o' Scots (see p. 89 of this volume), it is easy to see into what unfriendly hands the helpless interloper had fallen, whose existence had dissipated such delusive hopes.*

The insurgent Lords then undertook the management of State affairs. They tardily allowed Kirkaldy of Grange to pursue Bothwell, several of their number being interested in his safe escape beyond seas, inasmuch as neither Morton nor the coming Regent of Scotland, Murray, would have cared to encounter the blunt and unscrupulous Hepburn at the bar of a Court of Justice. Inconvenient memories of Kirk o' Field might oppress the one, while thoughts of what happened after Craigmillar and its conference might shake the faith in his own star which the other steadily held until the epithet "Good" was assigned him by admiring co-religionists. Meantime, Mary Stuart spent her weary days and nights in a small tower which rises upon one of the islands which stud Lochleven's placid breast. The alleged scene of her miserable and unnecessarily cramped imprisonment may still be viewed by the passing traveller. Nor was Mary's wretchedness relieved by the advent of her half-brother Murray, who, according to a well-rehearsed plan, appeared in Scotland, when his sister had been forced to abdicate in favour of her son, and also to make Murray himself Regent. We are told that after the sceptre had been thus wrested out of her hands, Murray came to his mother's house on Lochleven and rated the unfortunate sister to whom he owed title and fortune so unmercifully, that she burst into tears, and abandoned herself to d spair.† Possibly at this moment the "Good Regent" may have remembered how—inadvertently, it may be, but still without subsequent withdrawal—he had allowed his name to head the list of twenty nobles who recommended Bothwell as a fit husband for the Queen whose sins (on ac-

* Hume's 'History of England,' edition 1782, vol. v. p. 120.
† Robertson's 'History of Scotland,' edition 1794, vol. i. p. 462, quoting Keith, pp. 445, 446. The injuries were such, says Sir James Melville, speaking of Murray's visit to Lochleven ('Memoirs,' edition 1683, p. 87), "that they cut the thread of love and credit betwixt the Queen and him for ever."

count of which he upbraided her) began at Craigmillar, when he himself had conferred with her how best to rid the Court of Darnley by such means as should not sully the family honour. Thus closed, in personal durance, and exposed to shameful suspicion, the reign of the most unfortunate occupant of the throne of the Stuarts. Although Robert II., the first monarch of that race, is the only one of Mary's predecessors who can be said to have ended his career in perfect peace —for Robert III. sank to the grave bitterly grieving over the captivity of his son and heir—yet Mary's enforced resignation is sadder than any death-scene. Better, indeed, the last struggle of James I. with Robert Graham, in 1437, under the Black Friars Abbey, the mortal wound and untimely death of James II. at Roxburgh in 1460, or the weird assassination of James III. after Sauchieburn, twenty-eight years later; aye! even the self-obliteration of James IV. when courting national disaster at Flodden in 1513, or the despairing sickness which laid James V. low after Solway Moss in 1542,—all seem less pitiable than the case of the last-named King's beautiful daughter, deprived of her crown and immured at Lochleven.

CHAPTER VIII.

MARY STUART'S CAPTIVITY AND DEATH.
1567–1587.

Although Murray, the new Regent of Scotland, and his associates had triumphed, they were called on immediately to deal with Queen Elizabeth in a mood of real compassion for Mary Stuart. Sir Nicholas Throckmorton had been sent on a friendly mission to Lochleven, and, but for Cecil's influence, the Lords of the Congregation might not impossibly have found themselves confronted with the power of England.* Thus encouraged, Mary employed all her wiles to regain freedom and strike a blow for her crown. It is even said that she held out hopes of marriage to her deliverer, George Douglas, whose connivance made the romantic escape from Lochleven possible.† The plan formed by this ardent esquire was carried out on May 2; a youthful kinsman, William by name, conducting Mary's escape from the castle and rowing her to the shore, while Lord Seton, with a body of the Hamiltons, waited near the bank, and hurried the Queen off to Niddry in West Lothian, and thence to Hamilton on the following day.

At this crisis of her reviving fortunes Mary Stuart's name served as a talisman to attract loyal supporters to her side, nine Earls, nine Bishops, and eighteen Lords being amongst the powerful confederacy of those who, forgetting their sovereign's errors, were resolved to support her rights.‡ But, unfortunately for Mary Stuart, the military talent of Murray, Morton, and Kirkaldy far overbalanced that which was found in her army.

Hastily endeavouring to gain the shelter of Dumbarton Castle, Mary lost all at Langside, two miles from Glasgow, which in her progress it was necessary to skirt, on May 13, 1568. Her adherents were boldly pressing towards the village from which the battle took its name, when they were

---

* Hosack's 'Mary Queen of Scots. A brief Statement,' p. 30.
† Robertson's 'History of Scotland,' edition 1794, vol. i. p. 468; also Burton's 'History of Scotland,' new edition, vol. iv. p. 364.
‡ Sir Walter Scott's 'Tales of a Grandfather,' edition 1880, p. 120.

attacked, and after a feeble resistance dispersed,* their direct passage being barred by outposts placed in position at Kirkaldy's instance.

Escorted by that faithful and true subject Lord Herries, with a few supporters, the fugitive Queen rode sixty miles before resting at Sanquhar, and thence went forward thirty miles farther to Terregles, Lord Herries's home, close to Dumfries. Resting there a few days, Mary Stuart is said to have gone west to a place on the coast near the abbey of Dundrennan, in Galloway. Hastily deciding not to take ship to France, Mary, attracted by the sympathy shown her by Elizabeth at Lochleven, took the fatal step of crossing into that sovereign's dominions.† Nor is there reason to doubt that Elizabeth had been sincere in her previous advocacy of Mary's cause; but Cecil and the English Ministers were so convinced of the danger to England which existed so long as the fair Stuart lived, that they considered Mary's destruction a matter of necessity for their country, and therefore, so to speak, loaded the dice against her all round. In England, moreover, Mary's presence was specially distasteful to statesmen who, aware of the doubt thrown on Elizabeth's legitimacy, owing to the disputed validity of her father's marriage with Anne Boleyn, knew also that the northern portion at least of the Tudor Queen's dominions leaned decidedly towards Roman Catholicism, in which its inhabitants recognised the faith of their forefathers, and, as they believed, the true religion.

At this most critical position of affairs Murray announced that Morton had furnished him with documentary evidence in his sister's own handwriting, showing beyond all doubt that she had been guilty of adulterous connection with Bothwell before Darnley met the violent death which she had hastened by luring the victim from a sick-bed to the scene of his destruction. This mass of papers, branding the captive Queen of Scots as an adulteress and her husband's murderess, is known in history as the "Casket Letters,"

* Sir James Melville's 'Memoirs' are followed, as they agree with the account in Burton's 'History of Scotland,' vol. iv. p. 373.
† Burton's 'History of Scotland,' vol. iv. p. 375. Froude's 'History of England,' vol. ix. pp. 228-9. Dr. Hill Burton, while stating the prevalent belief, judiciously leaves the place of departure for England uncertain. Burton refers to, but declines to accept as a trustworthy authority, the author of Lord Herries's 'Memoirs,' who says "she embarked at a creek near Dundrennen . . . and landed at Cockermouth." Cecil, who was probably well informed, makes her land at Workington. Was the creek Port Mary?

because they were said to be discovered in "a casket about a foot long, decorated with silver over gilt, and bearing the crown of France and the initials of Francis II.," * Mary Stuart's first husband. The history of these "Casket Letters" is very curious. According to a copy of Morton's deposition accepted before the inquirers at Westminster and given to Cecil, December 8, 1568,† Bothwell, on his flight to Dunbar, left behind him, in Edinburgh Castle, a silver casket, containing certain love-letters from the Queen to himself, and also sonnets of a similar character. The Earl of Morton's written statement was apparently not denied at the time by any of those said to have been present when the casket was opened, viz. the Earl of Athole, leader of the Catholic nobility in Scotland and by birth a Stuart, the Earls of Mar and Glencairn, Lords Home (Hume), Semple, and Sanquhar, Maitland of Lethington, the Laird of Tullibardine, the Master of Graham, and Mr. Andrew Douglas.

It appears that, anxious to recover this precious possession, Bothwell sent his servant, one George Dalgleish, into Edinburgh Castle to demand of the Governor, Sir James Balfour, the restoration of the casket; this same Sir James Balfour, who is said to have acknowledged his own complicity in Darnley's murder to a correspondent of De Silva, the Spanish ambassador,‡ accompanying the narrative with vague and unsupported accusations against Mary herself. Apparently, he would not have parted from the casket without gaining some knowledge of what it then contained; and, indeed, in such custody, the casket may well have undergone a preliminary purgation from any matter inconvenient to those who had conspired against the murdered King.

Bothwell's servant, Dalgleish, was arrested, at Sir James Balfour's instance, at a lodging in the Potter Row, Edinburgh, where the casket had been left under a bed, and appears, under torture or threat of torture, to have revealed the fact, and ultimately to have produced the casket.

Morton kept his prize from eight at night on June 20, 1567, until the following morning, when the above-named noblemen and gentlemen joined in what could have been but a cursory inspection of such momentous documents, if, as appears probable, the task was concluded in a single sitting.

---

* Burton's 'History of Scotland,' new edition, vol. iv. p. 252.
† Additional MSS., Brit. Mus., Folio 216, No. 32,091, quoted in Henderson's 'Casket Letters,' 1889, Appendix A, pp. 113-116.
‡ Froude's 'History of England,' edition 1866, vol. iii. p. 115.

"Sichted" is the word used in Morton's declaration, and Mr. Henderson tells us that the word technically implies "to view narrowly, to inspect." But no pains were taken to secure Dalgleish's own written statement of the circumstances in which he came to remove this wondrous box from Edinburgh Castle to the Potter Row, filled, as it must have been, with documentary evidence certain, if disclosed, to ruin Bothwell.

We know only that it was under the pain or dread of torture that Dalgleish revealed his story; while, almost incredible though it be, notwithstanding that he was forthwith executed as an accomplice in Darnley's murder, yet the Lords and gentlemen who examined the papers thus discovered never took down his statement concerning them— although he did make a deposition concerning other matters before he died; nor is it possible to regard as in any way sufficient the excuse given for this omission, viz. that the confederates were at first anxious not totally to alienate certain of Mary's supporters, while they afterwards desired to hold the letters as a means of extorting a resignation of the crown.*

The discovery of Morton's deposition does certainly throw fresh light on this mysterious historical incident, because not only is the date of the Casket Letters falling into Morton's hands made clear, but their genuineness is found to have been vouched for by responsible men of light and leading, but who were one and all hostile to the Queen some time before December 1568, although it is not known that any of them had been banded against Darnley. For instance, the warrant for Mary's imprisonment in Lochleven had been signed by Athole, Glencairn, Graham, Sanquhar, Morton, Mar, and Semple, while Andrew Douglas was Morton's cousin. The fact is alluded to in the *Athenæum*, July 13, 1889.

The term "Associated Lords" arose not from the "band" formed against Darnley, but originated about three weeks after Mary had called her subjects to arms at Melrose. It was believed that Bothwell, with the consent of the Queen, intended to carry off the young Prince from Stirling. To prevent this, an association was formed, which included Athole, Mar, Morton, Glencairn, Semple, Sanquhar, the Lairds of Tullibardine, Grange, and Lethington, as well as the Lords Hume, Ruthven, Lindsay, and Boyd. The Earl of Argyll

---

* Laing's 'History of Scotland,' edition 1804, vol. i. p. 121.

was an original member of this association, but he and Lord Boyd went over to the Court and betrayed their confederates. Nine of these men were present when the casket was opened on June 21, 1567, and can scarcely be considered unbiassed witnesses.*

Now whereas all these men present at the "sichting" of the Casket Letters had previously become subject to arraignment for treason whenever the Scottish Queen should recover her power, they can scarcely have approached the inspection in question with judicial minds, even if they had not prejudged the matter altogether. For the rest we have only Morton's word to prove that, during a full year he had kept the Casket Letters without alteration,† an assertion which, being made by one cognisant of the conspiracy against the late King's life, may or may not be true.

There are over likely to remain two schools of opinion regarding these letters, each side finding support from champions of diverse methods in controversial combat. Some, like Mr. Froude and the late Dr. Hill Burton, will not pause to thread the labyrinth concealing the truth, but take their stand on the assumption that Christendom believed in the charges brought against Mary Stuart by the then responsible Government of Scotland, merely because the Pope and the Kings of France and Spain did not simultaneously take up her cause. As Mr. Froude, however, himself previously admits, the internal differences of the Catholic party in Europe had saved Queen Elizabeth from a coalition being formed against her.‡ Similar reasons probably determined the counsels of these potentates, when they saw a Roman Catholic Queen traduced in character and deprived of her crown, especially in a country where the Protestant opinions were predominant, and where she had herself declared for Liberty of Conscience in Religion.

Closer examinations conducted by other unfriendly critics, such as Malcolm Laing and Robertson, have failed to accomplish an analysis of the Casket Letters, and prove Mary Stuart's guilt without leaving many points so uncertain, and others so inexplicable, that when Mr. Hosack appeared on the scene as Queen Mary's able defender, his course was rendered clearer, and his readers enticed to listen, by a simple recital of anomalies surrounding the situation. It is with the

* Laing's 'History of Scotland,' edition 1804, vol. i. p. 96.
† Henderson's 'Casket Letters,' 1889, Appendix A, p. 115.
‡ Froude's 'History of England,' edition 1866, vol. iv. p. 1.

latter writer that we would associate the second and more modern school of opinion. The late Mr. Hosack, and also Mr. Skelton, have both utilised and improved upon the researches of Goodall and the elder Tytler in showing the great probability that "in the Casket genuine letters—but letters really sent to Darnley—were placed alongside of forged ones."*

Now, the discovery of Morton's deposition, although it diminishes the probability of any such fraud having been committed between June 21, 1567, and December 8, 1568, yet leaves it very uncertain whether Mary's arch-foe Morton, and his associates, did not carry out some such process before the letters were rendered up to Murray, at the expiration of a year's time.

The peculiar nature of the tribunal before which these charges against Queen Mary were sifted, has caused the verdict to remain practically undetermined to this day. A jury which examined the Casket Letters exhaustively and judicially, named by Queen Elizabeth, and composed of such Englishmen as Sir Nicholas Bacon, Norfolk, the Lords Arundel, Sussex, Leicester, Clinton and Saye, Cecil (Lord Burleigh), and Sir Ralph Sadler, together with nine acute Scotch colleagues representing Mary Stuart, such as Leslie, the Bishop of Ross, Lords Livingston, Boyd, and Herries, Gavin Hamilton the Commendator of Kilwinning, Gordon of Lochinvar, and Sir James Cockburn of Skirling†—would have speedily got to the root of the matter, satisfying intellectual doubters, and registering something more than a mere compromise. Mary Stuart's Commissioners were at a disadvantage, according to Sir James Melville, who in his 'Memoirs' (edition 1683, p. 93), writes as follows:—"For those who were the Queen's Lords, who came there to defend the Queen's part, had no credit or familiarity with the chief faction in England concerning the Title, nor durst open their minds but to such as by long acquaintance they were well assured of their honour and secrecy." Murray and his following, on the other hand, had long been acquainted with the men employed in the conduct of Queen Elizabeth's Government. Again, the English and Scotch Commissioners did not prosecute their inquiries in open court, while each individual must have felt that he attended rather in the character of advocate for his own sovereign, not to say partisan of his own country, than in that of unbiassed adjusters of rival accusations which must have required no

* Skelton's 'Maitland of Lethington,' vol. ii. p. 335.
† For these names see Burton's 'History of Scotland,' vol. iv. pp. 415, 431.

little patience and skill to fathom. For Queen Mary's Commissioners boldly accused Murray and others, his adherents, as authors of Darnley's murder; and although the charge against Mary's half-brother has never been supported but by specious gossip, akin in character to much of that directed against the Scottish Queen's character as a woman and honour as a wife, yet the accusation had to be dealt with by the selected tribunal, which got rid of the difficulty by dismissing the charges against both Mary and her brother, as practically unproven.

That the case was never fairly and exhaustively tried either at York or at Westminster, when Murray produced what he declared to be the original letters and sonnets, but declined to allow the accused party a sight, or even a copy, of them,* must be patent to everyone cognisant of the most ordinary paths of public justice. On the other hand, as has been stated, the nature of the tribunal, and its unwonted secrecy, detract from the value of the verdict which technically relieved Mary from the suspicions under which she laboured. Indeed, hostile critics altogether disregarded this justification on the ground that Elizabeth and Cecil never intended to pronounce their adversary guilty. The Duke of Norfolk addressed the Regent Murray before the inquiry commenced at York in the following terms:—" I am sent to hear your accusation, but neither will I nor the Queen my mistress give any sentence upon your accusation."† Be that as it may, the official verdict was to this effect, " That there had been nothing produced or shown whereby the Queen of England should conceive or take any evil opinion of the Queen, her good sister, for anything yet seen." Nevertheless, a powerful band of historians calmly continue to declare their implicit belief in the contents of Murray's casket, which he carried off to Scotland forthwith, together with 5000*l*. as a douceur from England, pausing only in the north to conduct an intrigue with the Duke of Norfolk regarding his marriage with that sister who had just been charged with such criminal conduct.‡ The silver casket and what it contained presents food for much discussion in the future, as it has done in the past, and the subject is practically inexhaustible. As it is certain that the attention attracted by Mr. Henderson to Morton's declaration will quicken this controversy, it is

* Goodall, vol. ii. p. 297.
† Sir James Melville's ' Memoirs,' edition 1683, p. 95.
‡ Hosack's ' Mary Queen of Scots. A brief Statement,' pp. 55–56. The fact is undoubted.

fair to emphasise the fact already mentioned that the signatories were opposed to Mary Stuart long before the Casket Letters fell into Morton's hands. Again, the adherence of Athole—a leading member of the Roman Catholic party—has scarcely the significance Mr. Henderson would attribute to it,* not only because the Lord of Blair Athole had played a conspicuous part of antagonism to his sovereign after Carberry Hill, heading the subsequent procession into Edinburgh *pari passu* with Morton, but because relationship to Darnley had led the Catholic Earl into such strong partisanship against Bothwell, as soon induced him—a proud Stuart noble—to fly to arms.† Among the Associated Lords, none was more enthusiastic than Athole in defending Mary's child from the assumed machinations of the dreaded Hepburn,‡ and, having been a main supporter of the match between Mary and Darnley, he was in no philosophical mood, when, three days after the Queen went to Lochleven, the historic "sichting" of the letters took place in Edinburgh. John, fourth Earl of Athole, a descendant of Jane, the widow of James I. (James Stuart, the Black Knight of Lorn, being her second husband), was in the first instance a zealous foe to the Reformation, and doubtless looked askance upon the politic tolerance which Mary adopted towards the disciples of Knox and Buchanan. Again, Darnley's violent and mysterious death had thrown Mary Stuart into the arms of the scoffer Bothwell, who had been wont to pose as a Protestant. If, however, it could be shown conclusively that the high-minded Athole had judicially examined the Casket Letters, Mr. Henderson's argument, forcible as it stands, might have had still greater strength. Considering that a rooted distrust of Morton and all his works was subsequently displayed by Athole, his mere presence at the alleged opening of the casket cannot fairly be held to indicate his real estimate of the letters.

Again, the loyal adherence of Mar could scarcely be consistently counted on for Mary Stuart, since he was ready, just before he died, to bargain with Queen Elizabeth for the power to destroy her captive, the deposed Queen of Scotland.

Lord Semple, notwithstanding his Catholicism, was the partisan author of certain anti-Marian ballads, full of Murray's praises, which are said to be more curious than trustworthy. On authority such as this, it is vain then to

---

* Henderson's 'Casket Letters,' 1889, p. 94.
† Skelton's 'Maitland of Lethington,' vol. ii. p. 225.
‡ Douglas's 'Peerage,' vol. i. p. 141.

depend for an accurate statement as to the contents of the casket. These documents are officially declared to be both holograph and signed, but are not proved to be either. They rest likewise under grave suspicion of being tampered with during the twelve months they remained under Morton's care, having been afterwards presented to the Commissioners at York as Scotch, and at Westminster in French. The avowed originals have never been seen since the latter conference, and so the extant versions are not unnaturally declared, by the best critical experts which England can produce towards the close of the nineteenth century,[*] to be useless for historical purposes.

Sir James Melville of Halhill, in Fife, was a courtier of Mary Stuart's during her active sovereignty, although he embraced the cause of her son, James VI., when the Queen seemed to be hopelessly imprisoned in England. He both spoke plainly and gave good advice to Rizio, Darnley, and Murray, as well as to the Queen.

It is remarkable that, despite his adherence to James VI. after Mary's enforced abdication, he expresses no belief in the Casket Letters, nor indeed any knowledge of their existence, but only a regret, several times repeated, that at the instance of "the least honest" and "most ambitious" of those "banded together to assist each other whereby to advance themselves," the Regent should have been persuaded to accuse his Sovereign.[†]

Upon the genuineness or spuriousness of these letters depends the verdict as to Mary's innocence or guilt; because the story of Bothwell's page, French Paris, told under the threat of torture, and never subsequently confirmed—inasmuch as, like Dalgleish, he was promptly hanged—was absolutely incredible. Who, for instance, believes Mary Stuart foolish enough to adopt funereal black curtains for her bed a few hours after Darnley's violent death, when the terrified youth was brought to declare he had seen her leisurely eating an egg?[‡] No! she stands or falls with the incredibility or genuineness of the Casket Letters[§]

Into the internal evidence which has been adduced regarding the assumed credibility or incredibility of the Casket Letters we shall not be expected to enter exhaustively

---

[*] See article on Buchanan, 'Dictionary of National Biography.'
[†] Sir James Melville's 'Memoirs,' edition 1683, p. 93.
[‡] Froude's 'History of England,' edition 1866, vol. ix. p. 5.
[§] See Appendix III.

here, because to do so with effect, and not present a mere *ex parte* statement, would involve a treatise nearly as long as this whole volume; but, allowing for the discovery of Morton's deposition, it must be allowed that later scientific opinion regards these mysterious productions with increased suspicion, while Mr. Hosack's before-mentioned theory gains credence steadily now that it has become known that Darnley knew sufficient French to read the letters (admitted to have been written in that language), which Mary's able and most successful advocate believed were addressed to Darnley, and not to Bothwell. Darnley's early proficiency in Latin and French is attested in a letter of the Rev. John Elder to Lord Robert Stuart, Bishop of Caithness, January 1555:—" I have sent also unto your Lordship certain verses and adages written by Henry Stuart, Lord Darnley, your nephew, which he wrote this time twelvemonth, I being with him at Temple Newcome, in Yorkshire, he being not yet full nine years." Mr. Elder adds " that he was good in French and Latin."*

As regards the statements in the present chapter, derived from the best authorities available, they have led to no more scientific view than that of Dr. Johnson when he read the evidence collected by the elder Tytler during the last century, and expressed an opinion that posterity would not attribute the Casket Letters to Mary Stuart, because she, the arraigned Queen, was neither allowed to see originals or copies of the letters she was accused of writing. Here, moreover, morally and legally, the defence stands on firm ground.

The untrustworthiness of these documents does not, however, in the writer's opinion, exonerate Mary Stuart from blame for her fatal interview with the Lords at Craigmillar, when they were bent on freeing her from Darnley; so that, in spite of the deprecatory language which Mary certainly did use regarding anything contrary to her honour being devised on this occasion, unfriendly critics will always recur to that unfortunate December day in 1566, the apparent precursor of the Kirk o' Field. If this impression prevails in our own time among writers such as Mr. Froude, impregnated with knowledge of sixteenth century history, how much more may the natural doubts of her own contemporaries, even of her attached adherents, stand excused, who, of course, wrote

* See *Athenæum*, Aug. 10, 1889, pp. 193-194.

and spoke without the light of nineteenth century research and criticism.

Hence the Bishop of Ross, when driven into a corner by one of Cecil's agents, and without the means of demonstrating the anomalies contained in the Casket Letters, once unguardedly took his stand on the inviolability of sovereigns even if they had committed crimes; while Sir James Melville, deprecating Murray's course, and deploring the conduct of the interested men who urged an accusation of their Queen, expressed his wonder that Murray should take part in such a prosecution, " for albeit she had done, or suffered harm to be done to the King her husband, yet there was respect to be had to the Prince her son."*

But if Mary Stuart's grave error, when she allowed the subject of her husband's conduct and the manner of separation from him to be mooted at the audience she gave the Lords at Craigmillar, placed a weapon in her detractors' hands, to be serviceable for all time; so must Murray, the brother who usurped that royal authority which gradually drifted away from the Queen when men learnt what had happened on this occasion, fall under similar aspersion. By this we mean that, although nothing has been brought home to Murray, connecting his name with Darnley's murder—and the gossip we reject;—yet, in company with his unfortunate sister, he remains under the cloud of doubt which envelops the memory of those who were present at Craigmillar on that unhappy occasion.

The verdict of acquittal which was registered in Mary's favour by the Commissioners at Westminster, who were unable to endorse Murray's and Morton's view of the Casket Letters, was practically useless to the unfortunate captive. Faithful as we believe her, in the first instance, to have been to Elizabeth's friendship, and guiltless of conspiring with England's foes, the moment was soon to arrive when despair of ever gaining her liberty led Mary Stuart to change her line of conduct.

Self-preservation stands high amongst the arts which all mankind find it necessary to cultivate, and when the prison-door seemed likely to open only to disclose the tomb, Mary Stuart naturally seized on every opportunity which might lead to her becoming once more a free woman, even though in so doing she were to appear before the world as head of the Catholic party in Great Britain.

* See James Melville's 'Memoirs,' edition 1683, p. 95.

The difficulties and dangers of the dethroned Queen were enhanced by several events which occurred during her captivity. (1) The Papal Bull launched by Pius V. against Queen Elizabeth on February 25, 1569,* wherein were reiterated the thunders and anathemas with which Paul IV. had greeted the English Queen's accession in 1558. (2) The rising of the Earls of Northumberland and Westmoreland in the north of England, and the succeeding rebellion of Leonard Dacre's which ushered in the year 1570. (3) The assassination of the Regent Murray in the streets of Linlithgow, on January 23, 1570, by Hamilton of Bothwellhaugh, to whom Mary Stuart granted a pension out of her French dowry, thus subjecting herself to a grave charge—the only distinct one,—which her enemies have but too completely proved.†

The Regent Murray is regarded with very different eyes by two opposing schools of historians, neither of which can discern any *via media* between the crown of martyrdom which Mr. Froude would confer,‡ and the ignominy to which Messrs. Hosack and Skelton consign his memory. Sir James Melville, however, who probably knew Murray better than most of his contemporaries, believed that fidelity to the Protestant faith was the mainspring of his early conduct, however mistaken.

Sir James's own words are worth recording:—"Himself was at the first of a gentle nature, well inclined, good, wise, stout. In his first uprising his hap was to light upon the best sort of company; his beginning was full of adversity; true honest men stuck by him because he was religiously educated and devoutly inclined. But when he became Regent flatterers for their profit drew near him, and put him up into too good an opinion of himself. His old true friends, who would reprove and admonish him, thereby lost his favour. I would sometimes say to him that he was like an unskilful player in a tennis court, running ever after the ball, whereas an expert player will discern where the ball will light, or where it will rebound, and with small travel will let it fall on his hand or racquet."§ An apt simile, which will be appreciated by some who read these pages. The study of Murray's character raises the interesting question whether one so spoilt

---

* 'Hatfield Calendar,' part i. p. 400.
† Hosack's 'Mary Queen of Scots. A brief Statement,' p. 60.
‡ Froude's 'History of England,' edition 1866, vol. ix. p. 581.
§ Sir James Melville's 'Memoirs,' edition 1683, p. 103.

by success, and so easily deceived by flatterers, may not have been himself taken in by those who tampered with his sister's correspondence, forging part of the Casket Letters and adapting genuine documents to their abominable purpose. But the death feud between Mary Stuart and her brother is a terrible fact to contemplate.

Murray himself, strange to say, was engaged at the time of his violent death, in negotiating with Elizabeth for Mary Stuart's surrender; and indeed two out of three consecutive Regents of Scotland, namely Murray and Mar—Lennox, who came between them, not being similarly tempted—died just as their Queen was about to be delivered up to destruction; while to the grasping Morton, the next Regent, Elizabeth's offers appeared insufficient, prepared as he was to betray his lawful monarch to her enemy, provided it were made worth his while so to do. We read:—

"It is found that the continuance of the Queen of Scots here is so dangerous, both for the Queen's Majesty and the realm, that nothing presently is more necessary than that the realm might be delivered of her. For certain respects it seems better that she might be sent into Scotland to be delivered to the Regent and party, if it might be wrought that they themselves would secretly require it, with good assurance to deal with her, by way of justice, that she should receive that she hath deserved, whereby no further peril should ensue by her escaping or by setting her up again."*

The fourth event which helped to shut Mary Stuart's prison-door closer than ever was the discovery of Norfolk's connection with Rudolphi, a Florentine adventurer, who had been conspiring to bring about an invasion of England by the Duke of Alva; this disclosure occurring when a projected marriage between Mary Stuart and Norfolk was under consideration, and giving point to Queen Elizabeth's freely expressed displeasure thereat.

The fifth, and probably determining, cause of the Scottish Queen's prolonged and embittered imprisonment is found in the Civil War which raged throughout France between Catholics and Protestants, culminating in the massacre of St. Bartholomew on August 28, 1572, after which religious partisans took it for granted that the royal captive was acting in unison with her French relatives the Guises. So general, indeed, became this conviction, that when the

* 'Secret instructions to H. Killigrew' (Burleigh's nephew), Sept. 10, 1572, 'Hatfield Calendar,' part ii. p. 23.

Catholic League of 1577 sprang into being, as a set-off against the tolerant tactics of Henry III. when dealing with the Huguenots, Queen Mary was believed to be an active party to the compact framed by her uncles, the Duke of Guise and the Cardinal of Lorraine, and suffered accordingly in her English imprisonment, which became more and more rigorous.

The frequent internal conspiracies against the Government of Elizabeth gave a political pretext to justify this severity, while at length the clouds gathering over England betokened that force would decide the question at issue between the two branches of the Christian Church represented by Spain and England.

The destruction of Mary Stuart has been truthfully represented as a natural outcome of this struggle, but her detention by Cecil and Elizabeth, after the letters were discredited at Westminster, remains without moral or legal justification. One of the strongest pieces of evidence in her favour consists in the fact that her mother-in-law, Lady Lennox, who, like other contemporaries, at first believed in Mary's guilt, quite changed her view about the year 1575, then writing to her daughter-in-law, and advising her to trust in God and that all would yet be well, adding, "the treachery of the traitors who accused you being now better known than before."*

Notwithstanding the maternal instinct, strong in the heart of Darnley's mother, yet the progress of events removed the scales from her eyes, so that she held the assassins of her son responsible for their guilt, without enveloping in their deserved infamy the helpless woman who at once claimed sympathy and demanded justice.

It is impossible to scan the Cecil Manuscripts without seeing that whether Mary Stuart did or did not aid Babington in his treason, the act would be but an incident in the weary passage which, with more or less devious course, was destined to end at Fotheringay. One ray of hope seemed to brighten the last few years of the exile's life. Mary's son, the King of Scotland, was approaching manhood, and had it in his power to offer an alliance to Spain, so that the harbours of the Northern Kingdom might have sheltered some of the Spaniards from those tempestuous winds which destroyed them. In McCrie's 'Life of Andrew Melville' there is a striking picture of a representative Don, who commanded

---

* Skelton's 'Maitland of Lethington,' vol. ii. p. 333.

one of the Spanish men-of-war, after the Armada's defeat, coming ashore with his crew into the little Fifeshire town of Anstruther, and asking for food and shelter. It was granted by the people there, not, as the Spaniard suggested, to an ally, but in the interests of humanity.

But during the regency of Morton, Mary Stuart's party in Scotland had been broken in twain by the defection of Huntly and the Hamiltons; while the surrender of Edinburgh Castle in 1573, together with the subsequent deaths of Kirkaldy and Lethington—who spent the close of their lives loyally striving to restore the Queen—had placed all Scotland at the Regent's feet. This collapse of Mary Stuart's interest in Scotland had been brought about by several causes. First, Morton's craft in detaching Chatelherault and Huntly from his opponents, and next the realisation by those noblemen of the probability that the massacre of St. Bartholomew, by uniting the Protestants, had hindered and not advanced the prospect of French troops appearing to succour Edinburgh Castle, which the English confidently advanced to attack. A third reason seems to have been Queen Elizabeth's resolution to send Killigrew northwards to divide Mary Stuart's party, and to discourage the French from venturing into Scotland.*

Whatever verdict may be pronounced on Morton's regency there was genuine peace between England and Scotland during his sway, while the formerly perpetual Border warfare practically ceased for ever.

In a former chapter it has been told how Walter Chepman introduced printing into Scotland in the year 1509, and how, with other symptoms of national advance, this great discovery languished in consequence of the sad waste of wealth and other resources which accompanied the destruction of human life at Flodden Field. We have likewise, when describing the subsequent rivalry between the two branches of the Church in Western Europe, not refrained from indicating how the purest theological aims constantly failed to inspire their advocates, whether Catholic or Protestant, with a corresponding rectitude in the several relations of life. Without particularising individual instances, it is enough to say that the writer, coming to these researches with a strong faith in the truth and power of the Reformation, has stood aghast at some actions performed by advocates of its prin-

* Robertson's 'History of Scotland,' edition 1794, vol. ii. pp. 46-49.

ciples who are highly spoken of in history. Prominent among these appear Murray and Morton, whose careers present anomalies and contradictions likely to remain a marvel for future students in all time. But that the régime of Morton, conceived as its instincts were in the very spirit of Calvinistic Protestantism, tended to advance Scotland in the sciences, as well as preserve peace with England, can never be denied with truth. Take for instance the revival of intellectual activity which at this time animated our neighbours across the Tweed.

For example, though copies of the English Bible had found their way into Scotland, there was but a meagre number in that kingdom during Queen Mary's reign, or the regencies of Murray, Lennox, and Mar. When Morton, however, became head of the Government, a burgess of Edinburgh, who possessed a printing-office, brought out an edition of the Scriptures, the undertaking being favoured by the Regent, and encouraged by the spiritual authorities.* It would be inconsistent with truth not to admit the benevolent character of a policy such as this.

The career of this prominent statesman must therefore be considered as a whole; and although his foreknowledge of Darnley's murder and his complicity in Rizio's destruction, not to speak of his harsh disloyalty towards Mary Stuart, prove him to have participated freely in the iniquities which disgraced his times, yet much remained to redeem his character from absolute ignominy.

It would seem that the love of gold was at the root of his more manifest weaknesses. When, for instance, Sir James Melville was endeavouring to unite the factions of the Queen and of her son, the King, previous to the fall of the Castle and obliteration of Mary's hopes in 1573, Morton argued thus: Very much did he desire to promote national unity, but there had, he said, been crimes committed in Scotland which must, nominally at least, be punished; and added, "I would rather that the crimes should be laid upon the Hamiltons, the Earl of Huntly and their adherents than upon your friends, and by their wrack (the Hamiltons, &c.) I will get more profit than by those in the Castle that have neither so great lands to escheat to us, as the reward of our labours."† Morton was beheaded in 1581, as accessory to Darnley's murder.

* Chalmers's 'Domestic Annals of Scotland,' vol. i. p. 100.
† Sir James Melville's 'Memoirs,' edition 1683, p. 119.

James VI. of Scotland had been entrusted during early youth to the care of Annabella, Countess of Mar, widow of the Regent, whose execution of her duties was unexceptionable; and directly the child was old enough to enter the school-room, George Buchanan superintended the mental studies of the future King, whose bodily exercises were overlooked by David and Adam Erskine, Commendators of Dryburgh and Cambuskenneth. Buchanan had an assistant in Peter Young, a preceptor whose episcopal opinions were more palatable to his royal charge than the Presbyterian tenets enjoined upon him by the celebrated scholar responsible for the results of this two-edged religious education. The fact is, James never liked Buchanan; finding his old-fashioned severity as repellant as the peculiar cast of his opinions.* Under these circumstances Young, whose code of education was less severe and strict, gained great favour at Court, and profited thereby in after years. The effect of this education on James VI. was to encourage a tendency to balance religious opinions in his mind, an intellectual process wherein the Presbyterian faith fared ill. With all the address displayed by the King—and it seems to have been considerable—he could neither conceal his personal dislike to Buchanan, nor his distaste for ministerial superiority as evinced in the General Assembly. In later times, as Moderator, the King positively argued with and lectured the reverend members of that august body.

The same instability of opinion led the young sovereign to take refuge in the counsels of favourites such as Lennox and Arran, so that, although the whole realm of Scotland had been torn in twain by the two factions of King's men and Queen's men, yet the head of the State himself held doctrines which, pressed to their logical conclusion, should have made this Prince forthwith surrender the crown to his captive mother. Hence arose the project of a joint government by Mary Stuart and her son, devised, it is said, by Arran, which, although it fell to the ground, left men in Scotland with the impression that James looked on the teachings of his youth as dangerous to monarchy, and believed that no good subject could approve the conduct either of Knox, Murray, or Buchanan. †
There is, then, little wonder that anxiety was evinced to learn how James would act when he knew his mother's life to be really in danger. On the whole, it must be allowed

---

* McCrie's 'Life of Andrew Melville,' vol. i. p. 255.   † Ibid., vol. ii. p. 312.

that James temporised; although the plea put forward on his behalf in 1580, when soliciting from the King of France aid of both men and money to secure Mary's deliverance, cannot be denied, i. e. that, young and under age, he was not obeyed by his subjects, the greater part of whom—as he phrased it—were heretics and partisans.*

We find, therefore, that a year before Morton's death—when Darnley's own cousin, Esmé Stuart of Aubigny, created Duke of Lennox, and Captain James Stewart of the Ochiltree family, created Earl of Arran (the Hamiltons having temporarily forfeited their titles and estates, 1579-1585), were the advisers of James VI.—that he was negotiating with France, on the assumption that Catholic principles were to his taste, for an offensive alliance.

On the other hand it is notorious, in spite of Morton's execution on June 2, 1581, as one cognisant at least of Darnley's murder, that the tide of Protestant opinion ran with resistless force in Scotland, and that three-fourths at least of the nation would have revolted from a sovereign allied to France or Spain.

The Ministers in Edinburgh, fantastic and violent as their Calvinist tenets appeared even to many who had rejected the Roman Catholic opinions, not only represented the traditions of Knox—gone to his rest in 1572, a few months before Mary Stuart's adherents laid down their arms—but also reflected the current religious views of their countrymen. If then, before the Spanish Armada came to invade England in 1588, James had thrown in his lot with Philip II., there is reason to think that his own power would have departed forthwith. Conscious of this disability, James, although really scandalised and grieved at his mother's harsh treatment, and still more at the fatal contingency involved, was at a loss how to act; and thus both the inconsistencies of his conduct and the inadequacy of his resentment are explained, even if the excuse seem insufficient to chivalrous minds.

James despatched Sir William Keith, and afterwards the Master of Gray, to intercede with Elizabeth, and to use threats, if necessary, to preserve his mother's life. One Alexander Stewart, in the Master of Gray's retinue, is said to have held the opinion, and made no secret thereof, even to the English Queen, that were Mary dead they might

* 'Hatfield Calendar,' part ii. p. 372, A.D. 1580. This memorandum confirms James's intrigues with the Catholics, and is of the greatest historical importance.

easily satisfy James by sending him dogs and deer. This, according to de Courcelles, the French ambassador, was reported to the Scotch King, who swore that if Stewart came home he would hang him before he took off his boots. Nevertheless, this babbling diplomatist seems to have made his peace at Court.* It must be borne in mind that James did not remember his mother, who, in turn, had never beheld her child since the day she was carried of by Bothwell in 1567, while she had been represented to the inheritor of her rights as a bad woman.

In Scotland the King did enforce on the unwilling Presbyterian ministers the duty of praying for his mother when under sentence of death; yet even this insistance upon the discharge of a simple Christian duty was resented, as involving partisanship on her behalf.†

Elizabeth and Cecil—now Lord Burleigh—were perfectly aware of the paralysis in the counsels of James VI., as well as of his somewhat boastful character, and surveying the European situation, knew that the moment was ripe for the *dénouement* of Fotheringay.

Even if Mary Stuart was technically guilty in desiring to destroy her rival by Babington's aid during the year 1586, there is no doubt that the strife between the Queens had reached its crisis, and that unless one of them left the political sphere, Christendom must have been convulsed by a religious war.

The time has fortunately arrived when an Englishman and a Protestant may retain his patriotic feelings intact, and yet speak with sorrow of the tragedy at Fotheringay, while commending the lion-hearted courage which enabled Mary Stuart to meet death with such manifest nobility. It has been objected that so perfect was Mary's conduct on this terrible occasion, that her departure from the world partook of a theatrical character—the objector apparently being unconverted to Shakespeare's view that "All the world's a stage, and all the men and women merely players." That the Queen of Scotland made her exit from life's stage in such fashion as—simply recorded—will entrance human nature for all time is undeniable. The very rites of the religion in which she believed were refused her when standing on the

* See Extracts from Mons. de Courcelles's Negotiations in Scotland, from October 4, 1586, to September 28, 1587. Cotton MSS., Caligula, Brit. Mus., c. ix. p. 233.

† McCrie's 'Life of Andrew Melville,' vol. i. p. 284.

brink of the grave, and yet, strong in faith, she maintained the same even tenor of conduct which she had shown in the hour of mortal peril at Jedburgh, twenty years before.

It was clearly no unnatural calm which Mary Stuart presented on this terrible occasion, February 8, 1587. After making her will, and distributing such effects as she possessed among the devoted attendants who were present, the Scottish Queen slept her last sleep on earth. In the morning she desired to see her faithful Master of the Household, Sir Andrew Melville, who, losing command over himself, wept aloud in grief for the fate of his beloved mistress. Tenderly, but firmly, she sought to check his emotion with words of pathetic dignity: " Weep not for me, my good Melville, but rather rejoice, for thou shalt this day see Mary Stuart relieved from all her sorrows."

CHAPTER IX.

FEUDALISM ON THE WANE.

1587—1649.

James VI. of Scotland, 1567-1603; also James I. of Great Britain, 1603-1625.
Charles I., 1625-1649.

WHATEVER may be the verdict of posterity as to Mary Stuart's character, the brilliancy of her personality will more or less eclipse the remembrance of that successor who held her sceptre and wore her crown.

The strange form of Sully's "wisest fool in Christendom" rises up before us whenever this epoch is mentioned, and Sir Walter Scott's "bold assertor of his rights in words" is seen striving for victory in periods more or less spasmodic owing to his tongue being too large for his mouth. Indeed, gazers at the several presentments of this monarch at the Stuart Gallery in the winter of 1888-9 were amazed to see such lack of refinement in the child of Mary Stuart and Darnley—two of the most beautiful people of their time. It was, however, curious to observe how precisely like his father at the same age was the infantile representation of King James VI.

This pedantic monarch had inherited nothing courtly or chivalric. That he lived in an unsettled age when the old order was yielding to the new, and had endeavoured vainly to balance religious opinion in his Court and nation, are the considerations most impressed on the mind when striving to discover how far events were shaped by his guidance, and what excuses can be framed for the shortcomings of a reign which, sorely lacking nobility, was only saved from ignominy by that union of crowns which seated the Stuarts at St. James's.

Although the Knoxean Reformation had gained fast hold on the Scotch mind, various degrees and divisions existed in the ranks of that Protestantism which flourished in the northern kingdom.

Men there were of light and leading who, unanimously

rejecting the doctrines taught at Rome, yet remained conscientious votaries of an Episcopalian form of government. Among these, we know, stood prominent the King himself, who silently elaborated the idea that the downfall of the Mitre involved danger to the Crown. It is therefore destructive of all faith in James's sincerity of purpose to find him, after Anne of Denmark's coronation in 1590, delivering a panegyric on the Presbyterian Church of Scotland, and thanking God that he was King in the purest Kirk in the world, while he spoke of English ritual with passing contempt as wanting "nothing of the mass but the liftings."*

It is true, as the previous chapter has shown, that this royal trimmer had been educated by persons holding divers theological doctrines, and instead of any preference for definite forms of belief being thereby implanted in his breast, James learnt to dissemble all round within the limits of Christianity as presented to his view.

When securely established in the seat of authority, this King did not hesitate to reveal that the prejudices of his heart were opposed to the Presbyterian form of Church government, and by inculcating the same into his children's minds, and particularly into that of his son Charles I., he alienated Scotland from the royal cause when monarchy was at stake in the United Kingdom. In justice, however, to James I. of England and VI. of Scotland, it must be admitted that his experience in the latter kingdom was altogether such as to excuse this distrust of the Presbytery. When a youth of fourteen years, James had received practical warning that the religious changes in Scotland had not eliminated the oligarchic elements which had baffled so many of his predecessors when striving to make their rule acknowledged. The family of Ruthven, warmly inclining to Calvinistic tenets, did not hesitate to collect around their chieftain, the Earl of Gowrie, an insurgent faction of Protestant Lords, who usurped the Government and put James under restraint from August 1582 to June of the following year; a measure so palatable to the Presbyterians in Edinburgh, that they never forgave Gowrie's execution, and avowed this as a reason for disbelieving the King when he was murderously attacked at Perth, seventeen years later, by the late Earl's son, and claimed in vain the official sympathy of his clerical subjects.†

* Calderwood, vol. iv. pp. 198, 204.
† McCrie's 'Life of Andrew Melville,' vol. ii. ch. vii.

A perusal of the evidence given at this man's trial should convince any fair-minded reader that Lord Gowrie and his brother did commit high treason against James VI. in 1599, and would probably have taken his life but for timely intervention. Anne of Denmark is said to have championed the cause of the Ruthvens in consequence of her friendship for Beatrice, sister of Lord Gowrie and Alexander Ruthven, and to have shown scant sympathy for her royal husband when, after escaping from the tower in Gowrie House at Perth, he returned to Falkland and recounted the tragedy wherein Beatrice Ruthven's brothers had fallen.

It is refreshing to turn from this portrait of one lacking the Stuart presence and daring, while wont to keep silent counsel even amongst avowed friends, to that of an eager lover, ready to brave the dangers of a stormy sea and the discomforts of a wild and inhospitable coast, for the sake of the lady chosen to share his throne. Such a man was James VI. of Scotland when, in 1589, unknown to his Minister, John Maitland—brother to the more famous Lethington—he set out in quest of Anne, daughter of Frederic II., King of Denmark, who, after an attempt to reach Scottish shores, had been detained at Upslo, on the coast of Norway.* It was at this site of the modern Christiania, now capital of the Norwegian kingdom, that James VI. espoused the Princess Anne, crossing the mountains that separate Sweden from Norway, in the midst of winter, and being subject to many hardships thereby, both by reason of the inhospitable nature of the country and the assumed unfriendly attitude of the Swedish King, over part of whose territories it was necessary to pass. Unwilling to subject his bride to a single danger from which it was possible to protect her, James previously travelled the country alone, and sent an agent in Captain William Murray to gain a safe-conduct for the Queen. In reply there arrived four hundred troopers, who escorted the young people across the Swedish territory after James had rejoined his bride. Seven children were born of this romantic marriage, three of whose names are as household words among the inhabitants of the United Kingdom—viz. (1) Henry, Prince of Wales, who first saw light on February 19, 1595 (New Style), being named after his grandfather, Henry, Lord Darnley. (2) Elizabeth, the unfortunate and romantic Queen of Bohemia, born in

* For an interesting and condensed account of this wedding, see Miss Strickland's 'Queens of England,' edition 1880, vol. iv. pp. 10–23.

1596, who was progenitrix of the English Guelphs. (3) Charles, of honourable memory, by some styled Martyr, who came into the world destined to use him so roughly on November 19, 1600. Called after his royal father—whose real name seems to have been Charles James—Charles Stuart shares with his grandmother, Queen Mary, the unenviable supremacy of attracting by misfortune, and this although the Stuart traditions were those of death by sword or dagger overtaking men who were but in life's prime.

We are approaching the time when, the Union of the Crowns having been accomplished, and the life-long project of Lethington thus brought to a successful issue, it behoves a chronicler of these lives to consider why, despite this happy conjuncture, the name of Stuart does not on the whole commend itself to those who essay to pronounce on the actions of kings. A more favourable verdict can scarcely fail to result from a philosophic contemplation of those successors of Robert Bruce who inherited the crown of Scotland through the female line, and claim Marjory Bruce as ancestress. On the whole these sovereigns reflect alike the virtue, the valour, and the rude habits of their countrymen in successive ages, when the population increased but slowly, owing to the blood feuds and Border conflicts which decimated the Scotch manhood, and left but 600,000 inhabitants to say Yea or Nay when the Reformation demanded their assent.

Now, although the Stuart Kings were perhaps in advance of their times, it is idle to deny that the greater movements of European society reached the northern kingdom with slower steps than those with which they advanced in England, and that one indication of this intellectual tardiness was the profligacy of those Churchmen whom lay contemporaries were obliged to own as guides in things temporal as well as spiritual.

For two centuries the Stuart sovereigns were more or less guided in youth by these men, and as a consequence several partook of the lax morality prevalent, so that in some instances, which have not been hidden from view in this work, a loose style of education had its natural outcome in a life such as James I. of Scotland or Charles I. of England would severally have condemned. This was specially true of James IV. and James V., who, when very young, were imprisoned by a portion of their nobility, and allowed, nay even *encouraged*, to live recklessly in order that they might rest content in ignorance of political affairs of which it was not desired that they should be cognisant. Otherwise it may be contended, without fear of denial, that the Stuart dynasty, between its commencement in 1370 and the religious reformation which gained a footing two hundred years after, served Scotland well.

Putting aside the rule of Queen Mary, which must, it is to be feared, ever present matter for contention so long as Christendom in Western Europe remains disunited, there are left but the later reigns whereon to pronounce a verdict.

Of James VI. it may be said that if he had lived in the nineteenth century, and been born in a humble station, his name would probably have become familiar to frequenters of Parliament, while more than one article in the *Athenæum* might have attested the value of his literary labours. For, while we may dissent from many propositions in the "Basilicon Doron," we may yet admit that a deep, comprehensive work was written by this royal author for the guidance of his distinguished son, Henry, Prince of Wales. But to assert that the good-natured rhetorician, with awkward gait and uncouth presence, was really a great King, is no more true than his favourite propositions, that the right of kings is divine, all resistance to monarchical tyranny illegal, and that "No bishop" necessarily meant "No king." That he evolved these theories when feudalism was decaying around the throne in Scotland, and at a moment when he descried future troubles brewing in semi-Puritan England, is more creditable to James's knowledge and forethought than was his manner of dealing with these difficulties as they gradually arose.

When James I. came to England the general welcome he received did not render it probable that the horizon would speedily be overcast, and that two conspiracies would follow one another in successive years, so that the monarch whose life had formerly been attempted by Gowrie and Alexander Ruthven should find himself face to face with a mysterious scheme for altering the succession in favour of his first cousin, Arabella Stuart, in 1603; while some two years afterwards some eighty Roman Catholics, instigated by one Catesby, and using Guy Fawkes as their agent, were prepared to blow King, Lords, and Commons into the air by gunpowder. These desperate fanatics also intended to murder the young Duke of York, afterwards Charles I., and, seizing the young Princess Elizabeth, to proclaim her Queen.*

* Hume's 'History of England,' edition 1782, vol. vi. p. 33.

Supposing that success should unfortunately have attended this murderous plot, it is scarcely possible that Great Britain would have calmly assented to such a dynastic settlement; and it is possible to conceive a rival programme wherein the surviving captive, Arabella Stuart, might have played a leading part as putative Queen, since the remaining female representative of the direct line had been brought up in a religion distasteful to the English people. In fact the events of 1688 would have been enacted more than eight decades earlier. In any case, it is strange to read how to Elizabeth of Bohemia, from whom sprang the Protestant Brunswick line, was thus assigned a course in life of a distinctly opposite character. With regard to the other unfortunate princess, whose claims to the throne could have no hereditary basis so long as a child of James I. remained alive, it has never been explained why, to the reproach of Englishmen, she was allowed to pine in prison, whence she had attempted to escape with her husband, William Seymour, until she died in the year 1615, bereft of reason.*

The only rational motive assigned for the undue severity exercised against poor Arabella Stuart, so cruelly treated as a captive in the Tower by the governor, Sir William Wade,† was that she had allowed herself to be put forward as a claimant for the British throne, Sir Walter Raleigh standing responsible for inciting her to adopt such a line of conduct. This plot is excusable only on the ground that no securities for constitutional conduct had been required from or offered by James I. when he accepted the crown,‡ while it was possible to wring them from this unfortunate princess.

The attempt of Catesby, Sir Everard Digby, and Guy Fawkes to destroy the flower of English nobility and the chosen representatives of the people, at the same time that the royal family were to be sent to their last account, has always been attributed to the Roman Catholic Church, and yet the plot in question was only known to eighty persons, who were sworn to secrecy.§ Nevertheless the popular view of November 5, 1605, is so far correct that the "Gunpowder Treason" reflected a sentiment of enmity, which, together with a desire for revenge, animated the Roman Catholics after James I. became King of Great Britain. Nor is it

* Somers's 'Tracts,' edition 1809, vol. ii. p. 283.
† Ibid.
‡ Rapin's 'History of England,' edition 1758, vol. viii. p. 15, note x.
§ Hume's 'History of England,' edition 1782, vol. vi. p. 36.

possible to doubt that he had—previous to his assumption of that office—encouraged members of their Church to expect complete toleration, and afterwards disappointed them.

We have spoken of this King as addicted to showing undue preference for favourites, and, unfortunately, under the influence of the brilliant and profligate Villiers, Duke of Buckingham, he was not only encouraged in untimely assertion of those prerogatives which the Parliament assailed, but also failed to show a statesmanlike interest in the conduct of affairs in Continental Europe, such as the people of England desired, and for seeking to preserve which they had forgiven Queen Elizabeth much domestic autocracy.

Hesitating to succour his daughter the Princess Palatine in 1621, when Parliament was aflame with zeal for the honour of England and the defence of the Protestant cause, James let a great opportunity pass,* but lived to see an untimely quarrel with Spain at the moment when, in a half-hearted way, he was trying to save his son-in-law's territories. Little wonder that the expedition in question was fruitless, and that the last hours of James I. were embittered by this failure when, in March 1625, he sank to rest. Attacked with ague early in the year, and told that in the spring such an ailment was health for a king, James replied "For a young king," † and, never rallying, sent for the Prince of Wales, committing religion, as embodied in the Church of England, to his care, and also the unhappy family of Elizabeth of Bohemia.‡

The new King fell naturally under the influence of his father's friend and favourite Buckingham, and construed parliamentary hostility to that Minister's measures as directed against himself. The romantic journey to Spain, for the purpose of uniting Charles and the Infanta, and the mysterious breaking-off of negotiations at Buckingham's instance, are as familiar to Englishmen as the fact that a Spanish matrimonial engagement being discarded, led to the subsequent marriage in 1627 with Henrietta Maria, daughter of Henry IV. of France.

Again do great events group around the brilliant figure of Buckingham, alternately caressed and loathed by the people, and ever supported by his sovereign. As a statesman the Duke can scarcely be regarded, when foresight is considered as a part of the panoply wherewith a Minister should be furnished; and, indeed, this fact became painfully apparent

* Hume's 'History of England,' edition 1782, vol. vi. p. 113.
† Ibid., p. 152.   ‡ Ibid., p. 153.

during the rivalry between Richelieu, the ruling spirit of Europe, and the proud favourite of James I. and Charles I., destined to fall at Portsmouth in August 1628, by the knife of the assassin Felton.

Indeed, in an epoch illumined by the genius of Bacon, the lack of forethought in the administration of public affairs strikes the most ordinary beholder; for not one single actor on the public stage of England, except James himself, seems to have discerned the real nature of the ferment which animated the nation when it first rose against an undue stretch of kingly prerogative; for, though it is difficult to believe that Robert Cecil, Earl of Salisbury, was entirely ignorant as to the depth and intensity of the national resolve, he had been too courtly a Minister to advise timely concession.

After several years of controversy, grievous to be narrated, in which brother found himself opposed to brother, knowing that the time might come when no arbitrament but the sword would remain, matters had reached such a climax that Strafford's resolution to protect and preserve the monarchy intact in its assumed prerogatives—which, as Sir Thomas Wentworth, it had been previously his aim to minimise, if not even to destroy—was encountered by stern refusal, betokening ill to such as obstructed the parliamentary will. And when the crisis came in that terrible year 1641, and the brave Minister, deserted by the King, perished in the strife, monarchical government, bereft of its greatest champion, tottered to its fall.

How much better the Stuart cause might have fared had matters reached a climax *before* Strafford's execution! But the sacrifice of his Minister—so degrading to the King who made it, albeit for the sake of peace—was made in vain, and proved insufficient to avert the calamity with which England was threatened, that of civil war. Little more than a year from the time when Strafford perished and Laud entered upon the three years' imprisonment which ended tragically on Tower Hill in January 1645, Charles I. and his two sons, the Prince of Wales and Duke of York, afterwards Charles II. and James II.—the "Grand Remonstrance" against the King's policy having been carried in the House of Commons by a majority of eleven, and the King having failed in his attempt to seize "the five members"—were on their way to York in full preparation for war.*

* Hume's 'History of England,' edition 1782, vol. vi. p. 484.

Although these pages are occupied almost exclusively with a dynastic history, it is just to record that during these civil dissensions three reputations stand out pre-eminently. John Pym, called by Professor Gardiner " the originator of constitutional government," and by the late Professor Green " the King of the Commons," shares with the illustrious and self-sacrificing patriot, John Hampden, the honours which men have also generally agreed to confer on the high-minded and able Falkland, who embraced the losing side.

After the battle of Edgehill, fought in October 1642, the King's army was able to press on towards London, and so, despite the utter rout of their foot, had gathered those sparse fruits of combat which were within reach.* But Essex, the Parliamentary general, brought to London the relics of his forces, outstripping Charles and Prince Rupert, who were seemingly triumphant through the capture of Banbury. And when the royal army was concentrated around Turnham Green for an assault on Brentford, they at last became aware what power was inherent in a brave and hardy people who deliberately took arms in defence of what they deemed their rights. Six thousand new levies stood side by side with the soldiers of Edgehill to bar the sovereign's further advance on his capital.†

No wonder that well-wishers of England should agree to a conference, though with small hope, when such elements were perceived in the rival camps as the first conflict at Edgehill disclosed. But the Parliamentary leaders were men of thought, and inferring from the latter events of this short campaign that the *vivida vis* was really on their side, declined the terms of accommodation to which Charles's pride could allow him to accede. As Professor Rawson Gardiner has aptly said, Turnham Green proved to be " the Valmy " of the King's cause. Henceforth, thinking men, whatever their opinion might be as to the matters of principle at issue, felt that mere Cavalier dash was at least not likely to settle this long dispute off-hand.

Regarding the events which ensued, it is difficult, after the lapse of nearly two centuries and a half, to think or read of them without distress when it is realised how much was staked by every portion of the community which engaged in that deplorable Civil War. Never in modern history were masses of men moved to exertion by nobler sentiments, or

* Gardiner's ' Fall of the Monarchy,' vol. iii. p. 59.   † Ibid., p. 63.

attached to their chosen cause of King or Parliament by more conscientious motives. Hence it is that the historian anxiously strives to discover whether the materials for a national settlement had existed during the reign of James I. It is conceivable, for instance, that it might have been well for the united realm of Great Britain had Henry, Prince of Wales, grown into manhood, retaining the sterling qualities and developing the singular abilities which attracted men to him. Steeled by the manliness of his nature against any pusillanimous course, and conversant with the use of arms, there is good reason to believe that under his sway a policy based on the maintenance of national strength and dignity would have been substituted for that of dependence on France, which so sadly soiled the Stuarts' escutcheon during their rule at St. James's.

On the other hand, it will ever be remembered that this prescient prince avowed an intention of reconciling the Puritans to the Church of England, should he live to occupy the throne.* As, therefore, he promised to become a man of wide intelligence and thoughtful zeal, it seems not altogether impossible that for a time, at least, the pending storm might have been dissipated at the accession of Henry IX., even if the dispersion could scarcely have proved final.

James VI. of Scotland and I. of England deserves considerable praise for the successful education which Henry, Prince of Wales, received in early youth under the Erskine family at Stirling. Anne of Denmark had remonstrated sorely with her royal spouse when the Prince was thus subjected to a tutelage that separated her from her first-born, and the mother's natural protest could have been met by no adequate reply if domestic considerations had not sunk into comparative insignificance, when contrasted with the danger which James descried in the turbulence of his nobles. Like James IV. and James V., and Prince Henry's own father, James VI., the heir remained in some peril lest a successful raid should place him in the position of hostage to some unscrupulous leader of faction.

That Prince Henry's youth was so tenderly watched over is therefore creditable alike to his royal father's forethought and to the care bestowed on the Prince's education by Lady Mar, his preceptress.

Of the reign of James I. as monarch over the three

* Rapin's 'History of England,' vol. viii. p. 93.

kingdoms, it must be regretfully recorded that in this later part of his career, the methods of rule adopted, hastened rather than otherwise the dreaded convulsion which overwhelmed Charles I.

That unfortunate monarch should then be judged in the lenient spirit which has happily supplanted the partisanship of former days, thanks in great measure to Professor Gardiner in his admirable history, as well as in the succinct but comprehensive biography of the unfortunate Charles, which he has contributed to Mr. Leslie Stephen's 'Dictionary of National Biography.' The portrait therein delineated is that of a well-intentioned, high-minded man, whose "lack of imagination" and limited vision when difficulties pressed around him rendered the adoption of a wise and politic line of conduct almost impossible.

Promising hastily, because a natural shyness induced him to avoid discussion at the outset, he was unfortunately apt to fulfil a promise in such a way as altered circumstances might make convenient, although he fully intended faithfully to perform his part in every covenant he entered into. To use Professor Gardiner's words, "Honestly anxious to take the right path, he would never for expediency's sake pursue that which he believed to be wrong, but there was in him no mental growth, no geniality of temperament leading him to modify his own opinions through intercourse with his fellow men."* Many think they descry these qualities, which Charles I. lacked, in his elder brother Henry, while so few faults of character appeared during that prince's youth, that his early death was much to be regretted. On the other hand, the memory of Charles I. will very properly be dearly cherished wherever the principle of monarchy is considered favourable to national dignity, wealth, and importance: for most assuredly, by the lofty resolution with which he met misfortune, and the courage with which he faced death, he did much to elevate the kingly office in the minds of men, and secure for it abiding respect and honour.

So much for the purely personal influence of this King over the times in which he lived. His attitude in relation to the two main constitutional questions at issue stands on an altogether different footing, because it combined two distinct sources of unpopularity, which in conjunction caused his ruin. On the one hand, his adoption of various forms

---

* Leslie Stephen's 'Dictionary of National Biography,' vol. x. p. 68.

of taxation without parliamentary sanction was part of the heritage which James I. bequeathed to his son; on the other hand, the strengthening of Episcopacy, under the shadow of Anglican forms and traditions, was soon superadded, just at the moment when the Puritan community became numerous and dissatisfied. The separation of these two causes of offence is important, because, in spite of the gallant stand made by the Puritans subsequent to the battle of Edgehill, the purely civil questions at issue must have been settled by the sword in a manner adverse to the Parliamentary cause, but for Archbishop Laud's untoward resolve, in which the King concurred, *to restore Episcopacy in Scotland.*

It is very well known, as a result of later research, how desperate became Parliamentary affairs early in the year 1643, and how completely Scotch adhesion to the popular side turned the scale at Marston Moor on July 3 of the following year, albeit the Parliamentary wing on which the Scots were posted gave way before the charge of the King's horse opposed to them. How Charles I. ever could have believed it possible to succeed in the "rash and fatal experiment" of July 23, 1637, passes comprehension, when we know that he was not unlearned in his national or family traditions, and must have been familiar with the history of his great-grandmother Mary of Lorraine's regency in Scotland, not to speak of the lesson taught in the next generation regarding the fierce Protestantism which condoned so much evil and disorder, only to be rid of Prelacy.

Nor is it too much to aver that the shadow of this ill-judged act of Charles I. and Laud still hovers over the name of the Stuarts in the land they had then governed since the male line of Robert Bruce became extinct in 1370. The national Covenant abjuring the proposed changes was not only adopted at once by "hundreds and thousands of every age and description" in Scotland, resolved to dedicate life and fortune to the preservation of their faith in its purity; but the violent measures adopted in after years to cope with the smouldering insurrection thus gratuitously created, have been the cause of an abiding prejudice such as nearly obliterated the memory of the previous services of the Stuarts to Scotland. So that, look at the question how one will, Charles's most irretrievable error seems to have been this untoward display of zeal for prelacy.

For the doctrines of Laud and their production at this precise moment in England, it may be urged that, if

Anglicans of the seventeenth century desired to make a historical protest against the idea that the compromise arrived at after the Reformation had obliterated England's ancient Church, they were constrained to lift up their voices before this growing belief, then loudly proclaimed, obtained still wider prevalence.

Just as a similar standard of religious opinion met with high intellectual approval when Newman, Hugh James Rose, and Pusey uplifted it in the nineteenth century, so were men of high-souled piety and deep thought attracted to the patristic lore and religious æstheticism which Charles and Laud sought to popularise, and in default to force on mankind.

It is almost impossible for men living in the nineteenth century to realise what the power of the Established Church was in England when exercised by its ministers 250 years ago in favour of the Crown. It was in truth a mighty engine; Charles himself believed that if the people ceased to obey the dictum of the pulpit, the spirit of the militia —the only military force at his disposal—would soon be antagonistic to the crown, and he exhibited considerable political foresight when uttering this opinion in a letter to the Queen, published late in the last century by Mrs. Catherine Macaulay in her history of this period.*

Not only, then, did Charles I. believe that he was contributing to the conservation of his own authority when supporting Laud in a resuscitation of Church authority and ritual, but there was method in each religious vagary of Cromwell's and Fairfax's soldiery, who from time to time usurped the pulpits of a dispossessed clergy. Had Laud succeeded in his endeavour to raise the Anglican system beyond rivalry, Charles I. might have left to a successor less embarrassed at home, and, we must regretfully add, more vigilant in vital questions of policy abroad, the power to enact a Dictator's part. For enhanced Church authority would have meant increased power to create a military force.

The revival of Anglicanism which Charles I. applauded and succoured, was thrust forward by Laud at a time when multitudes of men were fired with spiritual ideas which took no count of any earthly Church Establishment and revelled in reprobation of prelacy. Moreover, when enjoining

---

* 'History of England from James I. to the Accession of the House of Hanover,' by Catherine Macaulay, vol. iv. p. 420. This work, written by one holding Republican views, contains the results of original research.

uniformity and conformity, Laud withdrew the privilege of meeting for worship, tacitly allowed to certain Protestant communities outside the Establishment, a measure which persuaded many of the more wealthy Independents that the time had arrived to seek a new home beyond the sea. Thus it came to pass that men dreading infringement on the essentials of their faith, were found consorting in the New World across the Atlantic with those who looked askance on government without Parliamentary sanction, such as had been attempted in England after 1629 for several years.

After Marston Moor in 1644, in spite of intervals of hopeful augury, the tide of battle rolled in a direction adverse to the King's party; and, the breach with Scotland being complete, no respite was allowed to the Royalists until the divers interests of Presbyterians, Independents, and the soldiery, as such, clashed after June 1645, when Naseby Field had placed Charles's final triumph outside the range of all things probable. But the desperate condition of the Stuart dynasty had not been brought about without one of the most magnificent efforts for victory the world has ever seen, made on behalf of Charles I. by the Marquess of Montrose, a Covenanter converted by the King's personal influence, in Scotland. To understand the versatility of this great man's genius and realise the audacity of his military plans, one must have trodden the heathery slopes of Aberdeenshire, imbibed the bracing breezes of Badenoch Forest, and above all, threaded the precipitous gorges round Ben Nevis through which the great Royalist commander, in February 1645, swooped down on his arch-enemy, Argyll.*

The crowning victory of Kilsyth, gained on the low country north-east of Glasgow, which for a moment placed all Scotland nominally at Montrose's feet, was won too late —namely, in August 1645—when the Royalist cause had been heavily stricken in England, and when its leaders were unable to stretch out an arm to the mighty Graham's chivalrous advance. Hence at Philiphaugh two months later, where the last battle of Montrose's campaign was fought, this indomitable spirit failed to command success. Far from Highland gorges, and bereft of a large number of those who had fought with him therein, the great captain, surprised by Lesley's superior force and finding no succour from the King, was at last subdued. We have said subdued, because

* See Gardiner's 'Great Civil War,' vol. ii. pp. 79-105, 246-272.

the expedition of 1649, when he was captured and executed, may first and last be described as hopeless, the condition of the Royalist affairs in England making it so.

Notwithstanding the notoriety of the events which brought about this tempestuous result, it is even now difficult to realise how thorough was the civil revolution which, after degrading the Episcopate in 1643, when, being for two years bereft of legislative power, the bishops were dispensed with altogether, finally consummated its policy of violence by bringing about the monarch's destruction. Complicated towards the end of its course by internal dissensions, this revolution resolved itself into a struggle between the Presbyterians, who formed a majority in Parliament, the Independents, and the army, each party desiring an alliance with the Scots, and when neither faction felt certain that by making terms with Charles they could consolidate and sustain power, the men with arms in their hands ended the contest by beheading the King. That Cromwell and his accomplices believed they had Divine sanction for this unscriptural act of regicide, has been adopted as an article of historical faith by most modern writers, who interpret the fantastic, nay apparently *blasphemous* appeals to Providence, which were so common at this period, as a conjunction of piety and patriotism beyond suspicion. It is unnecessary to charge with hypocrisy those whose terrible success had been attained in some degree, and at the earlier stages of the conflict in particular, when defending liberties which Englishmen prize most. But the pretended trial and actual execution of their brave and suffering King must be regarded as an awful crime, a gross infringement of Parliamentary privilege—for had not the Rump usurped the position of a banished majority?—and an egregious blunder. As such it was speedily condemned by the generation which had witnessed that tragic episode.

Vain, indeed, is it to urge as an excuse the harassed monarch's various errors when sold by the Scotch military commissioners, on whose fidelity he relied, to the Parliament; after which, vacillating councils gave some cause to charge him with bad faith. Although the King declined to purchase his liberty from the Scots by signing the Covenant, and never consented, in his *pourparlers* with the Parliament, to do more than tolerate the Presbytery for three years, and leave the future for after consideration, he was yet, in the last instance, prepared to give the Covenanters a free hand,

even in England, in return for Scotch assistance.* But in
the main, despite such wavering, this precious life was lost,
because Charles hesitated to surrender Episcopacy, when an
effective alliance between the Scots and their Presbyterian
sympathisers in England was possible.

Without pressing hard upon one who saw himself entangled
in Cromwell's and Ireton's meshes—for no writer of credit,
after analysing the evidence, has ever pretended that they
were not intriguing to gain that substance of power which
the fallen Sovereign thus erroneously hoped to recover—
it may fairly be said that Charles I. would nevertheless
have placed a better case before the world, either by frank
surrender to Parliament or by flight beyond seas.

The commanding personality of Cromwell, and his great
services in remodelling the Parliamentary forces, together
with his invincibility as general of division, have hindered
Lord Fairfax's military reputation being fairly appraised by
posterity. The campaign of 1646 in the West, for instance,
which led to the annihilation of the Royalists in Cornwall,
enabled this energetic leader to approach Oxford in full confidence of capturing the King's head-quarters, and such
success deserves recognition not only for the professional
skill displayed, but also on account of the great results which
followed.

Firstly, the King resolved to make his escape rather than
be taken captive. Passing by Dorchester in Oxfordshire,
Henley, Maidenhead, Hillingdon, and Brentford, Charles I.,
in company with Hudson, a cleric, and Ashburton, an officer,
reached Harrow-on-the-Hill on April 27, 1646, where tradition says that he paused to survey the distant metropolis.†
This course was adopted at the instance of the French
Minister Montreville, who urged the English monarch to
appeal for support to the Scots, but why—in spite of obvious
objections to a direct journey through the serried ranks of
his foes—Lincolnshire should have been approached viâ
Middlesex in this royal progress, remains to this day an
unsolved problem.

It is believed that the King, while gazing on his distant
capital from the breezy heights which are crowned by St.
Mary's, was mentally revolving the desirability of surrendering rather to the English Presbyterians in London, than
to the Scots in arms at Newark. Possibly, had a bold step

* See Rapin's ' History of England,' edition 1757, vol. x. pp. 432-439.
† Rushworth's ' Historical Collections,' vol. vi. p. 267.

been taken on this occasion, the former countrymen of the hapless British sovereign would have returned to Edinburgh 400,000*l*. poorer than when, in January 1647, they surrendered Charles to the Parliament for that same amount of money taken in repayment of larger monetary claims. But national honour, sacrificed by those Commissioners who acted on the occasion, might have been spared that shock which revolted contemporary public opinion amongst Scots of high and low degree, and is regretted universally in Scotland to this hour. Nor is it just to forget that two years later, viz. in August 1648, the chivalry of Scotland, led by the Marquess of Hamilton, made a despairing attempt to retrieve the unexpiable wrong done to their captive King, pouring over the Border, nearly twenty thousand strong, only to be cut to pieces by Cromwell at Wigan and Warrington.*

As to the projected appearance of Charles I. in London in April 1646, we now are aware that differences existed in that city which might have given him some chance of regaining power. It is very problematical, however, whether the civil dissensions likely to ensue on the King's unexpected arrival might not have led to his close captivity, and possibly have hastened his death.

No study of this epoch is complete without some notice of the vigorous efforts of Queen Henrietta Maria to succour her husband. From the moment when the war began, and she fled across the sea to Holland, and raised money on the royal jewels, to the end of the fatal campaign of 1645,†—when by her husband's command she remained abroad with their children, the same energy, the same devotion, was ever apparent.

But English writers have since taken a somewhat insular view of her conduct when reprobating her conspicuous lack of constitutional sympathy, combined with zeal for the religion in which she was brought up. She is believed to have given the King unwise counsel, more especially in regard to sacrificing Strafford, whom she never liked or trusted, as well as getting one Conn established as unofficial Papal representative in London. This was partly true, inasmuch as the first negotiation with Urban VIII. came through Henrietta Maria's envoy, Sir Robert Douglas; but Charles

---

* Green's 'History of the English People,' edition 1886, p. 552.
† Hume's 'History of England,' edition 1782, vol. vi. p. 414.

and Laud were inexorable in asserting the independence of the English monarchy.* Be that as it may, the would-be friend who seeks to condone Charles's most unpardonable error—viz. the sacrifice of Strafford—by seeking to thrust the responsibility on his wife, places that monarch's conduct before posterity in a worse light than it deserves.

Charles was, moreover, but reaping as he had sown when confronted with Puritan complaints of toleration towards Roman Catholics, because, by a solemn secret treaty made at the time of his marriage, he had not only promised his wife free exercise of her religion, but undertaken to protect those of her communion otherwise subject to pains and penalties.† When the details of this engagement—obscured for a time by shuffle and evasion—became known, the result was to increase Charles's difficulties and enhance the Queen's unpopularity.

Henrietta Maria's sorrows and anxieties had the effect of changing her appearance so completely between youth and a by-no-means prolonged age (for she was but sixty when she died in 1669), that beholders of the two portraits representing her at those several epochs, which appeared at the Stuart Exhibition of 1889, were shocked at the contrast afforded. Owing to the civil wars of the Fronde, Paris was blockaded when Charles I. suffered on the scaffold in 1649, and the Queen underwent a terrible prolongation of an agony of suspense quite beyond realisation. Surely the sympathy granted by Englishmen to Charles and his children, to the high-minded Duke of Gloucester, and the interesting Princess Elizabeth, should not be refused to the trembling fugitive mother, half-forgotten in her native land, where she had taken shelter.

Another phase in the struggle between King and Parliament, concerning which opinion has changed completely, bears reference to Charles's undoubted desire to save his throne by an appeal to the Irish loyalists, irrespective of religion.

To disregard rampant religious prejudices was in the seventeenth century fatal to contemporary success, but at the present day men no more believe that a Roman Catholic should not be called in to defend the Constitution in a period

---

* Lingard's 'History of England,' edition 1838, vol. ix. p. 316.
† Ibid., p. 230. The story of this negotiation, conducted at Buckingham's instance, is very curious.

of rapine and revolution than they credit the fabulous stories which attributed the rebellion of 1641, in Ireland, to royalist machinations. And, indeed, a conviction that the Puritan Parliament of England was inexorable towards their Catholic brethren fanned that revolt into flames.

To this very day, we may add, there is a bitter reparation being demanded as the result of ostracising men in Ireland because of their religion—an evil tradition happily now discarded, but formerly, alas! handed down from age to age.

Searching through the various letters left by King Charles I. in order to conclude this slight sketch of his career with some characteristic penmanship such as might convey a definite idea of the man himself, the writer lit upon a passage from one of the last letters written to the Prince of Wales, afterwards Charles II., during his royal father's sad sojourn in the Isle of Wight in 1648. It will be found in Lord Clarendon's well-abused history.*

This beautiful letter—undoubtedly genuine—presents the most famous Stuart King in all his natural benignity, while at the same time he is seen pointing out to his son the very mistakes and shortcomings which accelerated the political crisis in dealing with which he came into conflict with popular rights, and so helped to create the situation which brought about civil war and his own violent death.

The concluding paragraphs of this remarkable composition are given verbatim. After enjoining mercy towards his enemies should the prince ever be in a position to punish their treason, the King, conscious of nearing the close of his mortal life, says:—

"If you saw how unmanly and unchristian the implacable disposition is in our ill-Willers, you would avoid that spirit. Censure us not for having (in the proposed treaty) parted with so much of our right; the price was great, but the commodity was security to us, peace to our people; and we were confident another parliament would remember how useful a king's power is to a people's liberty; of how much thereof we devested ourself, that we and they might meet once again in a due parliamentary way, to agree the bounds of prince and people. *And in this give belief to our Experience, never to affect more Greatness or Prerogative, than that which is really and intrinsically for the good of subjects, not the satisfac-*

---

* Clarendon's 'History of the Rebellion,' edition 1717, part i. vol. iii. pp. 228-9.

tion of favourites.* If you thus use it, you will never want means to be a father to all, and a bountiful prince to any you would be extraordinary gracious to. You may perceive all men entrust their treasure where it returns them interest; and if princes, like the sea, receive, and repay all the fresh streams the river entrusts with them, they will not grudge, but pride themselves, to make them up an ocean.

" These considerations may make you as great a prince as your father is now a low one; and your state may be so much the more established, as mine hath been shaken. For our subjects have learned (we dare say) that victories over their princes are but triumphs over themselves, and so will be more unwilling to hearken to changes hereafter.

" The English nation are a sober people, however at present infatuated.

" We know not but this may be the last time we may speak to you, or the world, publickly; *we are sensible into whose hands we have fallen;* and yet we bless God, we have those inward refreshments the malice of our enemies cannot perturb.

" We have learned to busy our self by retiring into our self; and therefore can the better digest what befalls us; not doubting but God's providence will restrain our enemies' power and turn their fierceness to his praise.

" To conclude, if God gives you success, use it humbly and far from revenge. If he restore you to your right upon hard conditions, whatever you promise, keep. These men who have forced laws, which they were bound to preserve, will find their triumphs full of troubles. Do not think anything in this world worth the obtaining by foul and unjust means.

" You are the Son of our love, and as we direct you to weigh what we here recommend to you, we do not more affectionately pray for you (to whom we are a natural parent) than we do, that the ancient glory and renown of this nation be not buried in irreligion and phanatick humour; and that all our subjects (to whom we are a politick parent) may have such sober thoughts, as to seek their peace in the orthodox professions of the Christian religion, as was established *since the Reformation* in this kingdom and not in new revelations; and that the ancient laws with the interpretation according to the known practice, may once again be a hedge about

---

* A condemnation of the King's father, James I., in the main lines of a policy taken most unfortunately by Charles I. himself as an example during the earlier years of his reign.

them; that you may in due time govern and they be govern'd, as in the fear of God, which is the prayer of
"Your very loving Father,
"C. R.
"Newport, 25 Nov., 1648."

It is at last safe to declare Charles I. to have written the famous 'Eikon Basilike,' which has been the subject of controversy for so many years. Not only have seven chapters of this work been discovered at Lambeth, which were formerly in Archbishop Tenison's possession, and had been taken by the Parliamentarians after Naseby Field in 1645, two years before the time when Bishop Gauden averred that he began to write the 'Eikon Basilike' himself, but also the second private prayer contained therein has been found in the Record Office, indited in the well-known hand of King Charles I.* We may therefore remember this interesting monarch not only as a good man, and the most unfortunate ruler who ever strove to guide the three kingdoms, but also as a royal author of high ability, whose clear exposition of the reasons which led him to defend what he conceived to be his legal prerogatives, is followed by religious compositions conceived in a spirit of high-souled piety, such as have few superiors in this department of literature, while those are only to be found in that Book of Common Prayer, to spread and preserve which he may be said to have laid down his life. Little wonder, then, if the Church, in whose service he suffered so much, should have once assumed that her dearly-beloved King had gained a martyr's crown.

* See Preface to 1880 reprint of 'Eikon Basilike,' edition 1648, where the editor, Mr. Edward Scott, now keeper of the MSS. in the British Museum, adduces a formidable array of facts bearing on the royal authorship of this book, over and above the two statements mentioned in the text, and which seem so conclusive.

CHAPTER X.

BROKEN PURPOSES.

Charles II., 1649-1685.

THE reign of Charles II. is technically held to have begun on the day when his father suffered death, because the Restoration Parliament in 1660, endeavouring to obliterate the very remembrance of the great Rebellion, had placed the date 1649 on the Statute Book,* though he did not actually reign for twelve years after his father's demise. But for historical purposes, even when the house of Stuart is in question, the weird and eventful period occupied by the Commonwealth and the Protectorate of Oliver Cromwell, cannot be ignored or even lightly regarded if an adequate conception of dynastic events is ever to be entertained.

The wanderings of Charles II. and the Duke of York, (afterwards James II.), for instance, during their exile, have a direct bearing on future history, and form part of the subject in hand ; for who can doubt that alternations of luxury and poverty, such as those experienced by the royal brothers during these adverse times, operated banefully on the characters of men destined hereafter to rule the State?

Of the Revolutionary régime itself, the time has gone by when it is necessary in the interests of truth to stigmatise extravagant excesses which accompanied the successful issue of what, once a popular movement, soon degenerated into government by a fanatical oligarchy, and finally owned a despot's sway. It, so to speak, goes without saying that the tyranny of the Rump proved itself far more detestable to the English mind than the unconstitutional expansion of the royal prerogative which had originally brought the late King into antagonism with Pym, Hampden, and Fairfax, as representatives of public opinion. Moreover, at this distance of time, it is no disloyalty to the Crown which bids one acknowledge freely that the eminence which England gained

* Skottowe's 'Short History of Parliament,' p. 103.

among the States of Europe under Oliver Cromwell's Protectorate unites with the glory gained at sea by the magnificent republican sailor Blake to rescue that administration from the opprobrium provoked by domestic occurrences generally, and especially by the destruction of all constitutional liberty. On the other hand it is but just to the later Stuarts to record how the Protector's leading mistake in foreign policy, when he depressed Spain in the hour of her decline, and allied himself with France, helped to create the situation which, in after years, rendered Louis XIV. a terror of Europe and necessitated the expensive wars of William III. and Queen Anne. He was enticed into this apparently all-conquering, but eventually dangerous course, by the wily political stratagems of Cardinal Mazarin, Minister of France.

Charles II. and James II., confronted with the national dislike to standing armies, found themselves as it were face to face with a gigantic military neighbour, whose ambitions —fatal to a just balance of power—were not to be repressed by any weight Great Britain could bring immediately to bear. It was not, then, altogether the fault of the later Stuarts that the political situation abroad became such that a strong arm alone could cope therewith. Their impotence, for which they were not entirely responsible, tempted them to adopt the subservience to France which became the rule in foreign affairs. The early life spent by the exiled heir of Charles I. had indeed been unsettled. His very birth, on May 29, 1630, was reprobated by the Puritans, who, strange to say, according to the High Church writer Heylin, turned intuitively towards that branch of the Stuart dynasty represented by the Guelphs, and now by Queen Victoria. Heylin relates, how, at a great feast at Friday Street, the expected birth of a child to Henrietta Maria was commented on by a leading Puritan, who said "he could see no cause of joy." "God," he added, "has already provided better for us than we deserve, in giving such a hopeful progeny to the Queen of Bohemia, brought up in the reformed religion; whereas it is uncertain what religion the King's children will follow when brought up under a mother so devoted to the Church of Rome."*

---

* See 'History of England under the Royal House of Stuart' (edition 1730, p. 112), by the author of the 'Critical History of England.' The work in question is full of curious and generally trustworthy details.

There is some doubt, however, as to the actual moment when Charles II. changed his faith, because, although it has been confidently stated by credible authorities that this event occurred in 1654, just before the King left France for Cologne, yet we find the question of religion was made part of the often reprobated secret agreement of 1671 between England and France.*

According to Cunningham's 'History of Great Britain' (vol. i. p. 12), the author being a diplomatist under William III. and Queen Anne, Charles II. was reconciled to the Catholic faith at Fontainebleau just before leaving France in 1654, Sir Henry Bennet (afterwards Lord Arlington) and others following the royal example, while the ceremony was witnessed by the Queen-mother, Henrietta Maria. This account is supported by a deposition of Sir Allen Broderick's, made on his death-bed.

The wretched financial condition into which the royal house of Stuart had fallen after the Cavaliers were defeated, and when Charles I. was near his end, is scarcely to be realised without examining the facts in detail. So bad was the Prince of Wales's credit, that he could not borrow 200*l*. of M. l'Empereur, a banker at the Hague, even when pledging his credit with that of the Duke of York; so that it required the additional bond of a member of the latter prince's suite to persuade another man of business, by name Boyer, to advance the money.†

Lord Crofts and Sir John Denham were also sent as ambassadors to Poland, where the English merchants lent 10,000*l*., while the Czar of Muscovy and the Venetian Senate were solicited in vain in the same high interest. To crown all, we have Cardinal de Retz's assurance that he found the Queen-mother of England living with her daughter the Duchess of Orleans, absolutely without a faggot to light a fire in the apartment of the Louvre which they inhabited.‡ It is also well known that at the request of her father, Charles I., the Princess of Orange lent a sum of money to her royal brother, Charles II., to recover which, William of Orange, her son, paid his first visit to England in the "Merry Monarch's" reign.§

* Dalrymple's 'Memoirs,' edition 1790, vol. i. Appendix, ch. ii. p. 113.
† 'History of England under the Royal House of Stuart,' p. 384.
‡ 'Memoirs of Cardinal de Retz,' p. 142.
§ Cunningham's 'History of Great Britain,' vol. i. p. 15; also 'History of England during the Reigns of the Royal House of Stuart,' edition 1790, p. 549.

Thus alternations of indigence and luxury conspired to ruin entirely a character by no means endowed originally with stability. Of Charles's wit and merry complacency—which, though unmixed with any true nobleness of character, yet rendered him personally popular—there are numerous instances recorded, while the high spirit he preserved during a long train of misfortunes likewise served in his lifetime to condone his lamentable profligacy.* At the close of his first sojourn at the Hague, Charles II. learned how Cromwell's victorious legions had triumphed in Ireland, where the vanquished Catholics were put to the sword ruthlessly during the latter part of the year 1649. Finding that no prospect of immediate reaction seemed about to dawn in England, by the advice of his mother and the Marquess of Hamilton, he accepted an invitation to rule over the Scots. Hesitating slightly, in the vain hope that Montrose might win the northern kingdom back by force of arms, Charles waited until after the final defeat and execution of that hero before he came to terms with the Commissioners, signing the Solemn League and Covenant which bound him to profess and forward the Presbyterian form of worship, and also promising submission to the guidance of the Parliament in Civil matters. By this means relief from immediate impecuniosity was exchanged for a servitude which, to a person of easy-going habits, such as the King, must have seemed simply intolerable. The General Assembly was positively about to make their sovereign do penance for the sins of his family during four hundred years,† when popular attention was called to sterner contests than those of an ecclesiastical type which had led to such an ignominious compact between King and people. Charles came to Scotland in June 1650, and almost immediately tidings reached him at Stirling of Cromwell's advance across the Border by the east coast, under cover of a fleet which followed the English army with provisions. Hence, though it appeared almost certain, after his purposeless sojourn outside Edinburgh, that Cromwell had made a great tactical error, and was in danger of starvation or annihilation during subsequent retreat, owing to uncertain communication with his naval coadjutors, some

* Charles II. declared Isaac Barrow to be the unfairest preacher he ever heard, because he exhausted his subject and left nothing for others to say.
† Arnot's 'History of Edinburgh,' vol. iv. p. 133. Before Charles II. was crowned at Scone, a national humiliation was held for the sins of the Royal Family.

strange fatuity led the Scots to enter into an unnecessary general engagement which resulted, in Lesley allowing Cromwell to "roll up" his line, so that the Scots were utterly defeated at Dunbar, September 3, 1650.

Whether or not Cromwell's great victory was in some degree owing to the ardour of the Presbyterian divines who are said to have forced the battle on,* the result left Charles less trammelled by an irresponsible ecclesiastical tyranny than he was when apparently about to triumph in their name. But this improvement did not take place in his kingly condition until he had endeavoured to escape from the Presbyterian camp, and had taken refuge at Clova in Forfarshire, whence he was persuaded to return and be crowned King o' Scots at Scone on January 1, 1651. His abortive attempt at escape is known in history as "The Start." Upon the occasion of his coronation, Sir Walter Scott, says—"the King, clad in a prince's robe, walked in procession from the hall of the palace to the church, the spurs, sword of state, sceptre and crown, being carried before him by the principal nobility. It was remarkable that upon this occasion, the crown was borne by the unhappy Marquess of Argyll, who was put to death in no very legal manner immediately after the Restoration, using upon the scaffold these remarkable words 'I placed the crown on the King's head, and in reward he brings mine to the block.'" † And indeed it is to Charles's endless discredit that he should have taken the crown from one whose hands were, so to speak, embrued in the scarcely cold blood of Montrose, entering Edinburgh while that noble soldier's head was fixed over the principal gate of the city, and so generally condoning all that Argyll had done to secure that condemnation and execution which in after years the same King avenged without mercy. Nor is it possible to find adequate excuse for the total oblivion of having signed on this occasion the Solemn League and Covenant, affected by the King on his restoration, when he struck ruthlessly at the Presbytery and delivered up the National Church of Scotland to its episcopal assailants;—a notable and glaring case of perfidy in high places.

It is from the gloomy episode of Charles's coronation that

* Sir Walter Scott was clearly of this opinion, and attributed the premature conflict to the interference of the Presbyterian clergy, who insisted on Lesley attacking his opponents upon equal ground.

† 'Regalia of Scotland,' Scott's Miscellaneous Prose Works, 1834, vol. vii. pp. 309-313.

one instinctively turns with relief to the gallant resolve of the King and his able general Lesley to risk all by an irruption into England. This venture, if it led to the overthrow of contemporary Stuart hopes, at Worcester on September 3, 1651, was yet succeeded by an episode creditable to the loyalty of the English people. Doubtless the failure to secure adherents during the southward march of Charles and Lesley, was due to the Royalists being paralysed by dread of Cromwell's military genius, for there is little doubt that a powerful section of Englishmen, comprising all classes, remained at heart loyal.

During Charles's flight through Staffordshire to Whiteladies and Boscobel Oak, on the borders of Shropshire, and thence to the confines of Bristol, and on through Sherborne, Lyme, and Salisbury Plain, to the shores of Sussex and the village Brighthelmstone,* not one needy peasant was found—fifty individuals having been trusted with the secret—base enough to betray his King, notwithstanding that, as Lord Clarendon tells us, 1,000*l*. had been placed on his head. Representative then of the true loyalty of Englishmen will ever remain the names of the Penderell family who secreted the King at Boscobel, and of Colonel and Mrs. Lane, who conducted him safely to Bristol; while the efforts of the Dorsetshire Windhams to secure a vessel for Charles's departure stand equally prominent with that of Captain Tettersell, the Brightonian, under whose care the King embarked.

For the sum of 60*l*. this brave and loyal seaman conducted his sovereign safely from Brighton to Shoreham; whence in Tettersell's little vessel, the *Surprise*, the party escaped to Fécamp, a town on the north coast of France, which lies very nearly due south of Brighton and Shoreham.†

When at last the second Charles did escape beyond sea, we have before us ten years in the life of a neglected adventurer, whom no foreign country cared to protect, although pity and policy conspired to gain him temporary shelter, first in France, and then in Germany, before the Hague became once again the centre of Royalist intrigue on the Continent.

That the Restoration came to pass so soon after Cromwell's death can only be attributed to the natural loyalty of the

---

* The modern Brighton, where the traditions of the Monarch's sojourn in disguise are still vivid.
† Martin's 'History of Brighton,' 1871, p. 35.

English people, the power of which had been discerned by Lord Broghill* (afterwards Lord Orrery), in the spring of 1659, before the certain outcome of a free Parliament revealed itself to Monk's taciturn intelligence. That some doubts as to the permanence of the Cromwellian usurpation occupied Monk's mind so early as August 1655, is made apparent by his conduct after receiving the subjoined letter written by Charles II. soon after his expulsion from France, and headed " Cologne, August 12, 1655."

" One who believes he knows your nature and inclinations very well, assures me, that notwithstanding all ill accidents and misfortunes, you retain still your old affection to me, and resolve to express it upon the seasonable opportunity, which is as much as I look for from you. We must all patiently wait for that opportunity, which may be offered sooner than we expect.

" When it is, let it find you ready; and in the meantime have a care to keep yourself out of their hands, who know the hurt you can do them in a good conjuncture; and can never but suspect your affection to be as I am confident it is, &c. " CHARLES REX."†

Now, the future Duke of Albemarle, although he straightway despatched a copy of this letter to Cromwell, retained the original as an heirloom, which his son Christopher, the second Duke, preserved amongst the choicest treasures he possessed.‡

It did not therefore need much popular persuasion to win over this wily soldier of fortune when the Royalist direction of popular opinion had become evident. Those in authority were aware of this tendency some time before the beginning of the year 1660.

Chief among the reactionists must be named Lord Fairfax, the hero of Naseby Field, and the Parliamentary general who disputed with Cromwell the title of Premier Captain of the forces lately arrayed against Charles I.

Though the names of those who had suffered on the Cavalier side, and received no adequate reward when the King claimed his own again, are legion, one may be pardoned for straying into the byways of history to record the timely

---

* 'History of England under the Royal House of Stuart,' p. 449.

† Guizot's ' Memorials of Monk,' translated and edited by Hon. J. Stuart Wortley, 1838, pp. 83–86.   † Ibid., p. 87.

efforts—unrequited—of two comparatively humble individuals who contributed towards the triumph of the royal cause. One of these seems to have been a nephew of the famous Fairfax, bearing the same surname. Mr. Brian Fairfax, a Cambridge student, chanced to be at Lord Fairfax's house in Yorkshire, Nun Appleton, on December 20, 1659, when his uncle was desirous of communicating with Monk at Coldstream on the Tweed.

Lambert's army being encamped near Newcastle, it was desired to combine, and place his forces between two fires. This Mr. Fairfax effected, after, as he phrased it, "saying his lesson" to the general's chaplain, the Reverend Edward Bowles, of whom hereafter. The messenger passed clean through Lambert's army, and then was assaulted on the highway by Anthony Elliot, a famous moss-trooper, who infested the Border; but Monk's quarters were gained in safety, with the letter which encouraged the general to begin his famous march into England. General Monk promised Brian Fairfax to watch Lambert as a cat watches a mouse.*

Nor is it possible to overlook the remarkable services of the Reverend Edward Bowles, the able coadjutor of Monk and Fairfax in bringing about the Restoration, for there is no doubt that it was greatly on his advice, and after long consideration of the circumstances with him, that the final steps were taken which led Monk to advance on London from York. Mr. Bowles, from long residence in the north, had opportunities of observing the drift of opinion there, and, thoroughly dissatisfied at the turn things had taken under Cromwell, recommended both his master, Lord Fairfax, and the military arbiter of events, to declare for the King before leaving the north.† It is said that Mr. Bowles afterwards regretted that he had been the means of allowing Monk's army to pass through Yorkshire without opposition, and so contributed towards the King's return, for, as a religious nonconformist, he reprobated the flood of impiety and immorality which the careless life and general levity of Charles II. inflicted on the country.‡

* A full account of this mission will be found in the 'Fairfax Correspondence,' edited by Robert Bell, 1849, vol. ii. pp. 146–169.
† 'Fairfax Correspondence,' edited by Robert Bell, 1849, vol. ii. pp. 169–170.
‡ Acknowledgments are due to a descendant, Mr. Sholto Vere Hare, of Bristol, for confirmation of these details. Mr. Hare has certain manuscript letters bearing upon the events in question.

Cromwell dying on Sept. 3, 1658, his son Richard succeeded to the Government apparently as if he had been the representative of an hereditary family; but the calm which prevailed was deceptive, and the very earliest advice the new Protector received partook of a character which undermined his government in a Machiavellian fashion, the very ordinary individual then occupying the seat of supreme power not being acute enough to perceive the craft of his adviser. Monk sent to Richard Cromwell, under the title of "Remembrance of what I desire you to say to his Highness," a minute—by the hands of Clarges, the general's son-in-law—which advised the appointment of certain captains to the ships of war, colonels of regiments, and sheriffs of counties, all men whom the general could trust to follow his commands at a given signal. And so it happened that at Monk's secret desire the call to resign was not made in vain, Cromwell's degenerate son ceasing to be Protector, April 22, 1659.*

How the English people went half mad for joy when their free Parliament recalled Charles II. from the Hague, forms an incident in general history known to all mankind. But there was at that epoch, alas! initiated a régime of degradation and depravity, from which monarchy received a rough shock, while the popular party soiled its escutcheon by trafficking with the French King during the formation of a plot to overthrow Charles II. Even though Algernon Sidney and Lord Russell were most probably ignorant of the design to assassinate the monarch and his brother, the Duke of York, in 1683, when returning from Newmarket; yet when it is known that the first-named statesman received French pay, and that the second patriot was striving to carry out his designs in unison with the Court of Louis XIV., it is difficult not to feel with Sir John Dalrymple, author of the famous 'Memoirs,' who, on seeing the documents in the Paris archives, felt very nearly the same shock as if a son had turned his back in the day of battle.†

For, whatever may be said of the rest of the men involved in that conspiracy, Lord Russell, as well as Algernon Sidney, were, in principle at least, but contending for those limitations of the monarchical system which have rendered the government of England a model for other nations during

---

* MSS. in the possession of Sholto Vere Hare, Esq.
† Dalrymple's 'Memoirs,' edition 1790, Preface, vol. i. p. 24.

the two centuries which followed this strange but instructive epoch.

At first sight it might seem probable that the spark of liberty—preserved to the English almost miraculously during the different phases of revolution which occurred during the civil dissensions culminating in the death of Charles I.—would have perished in this general tumult of loyalty, wherein the populace seemed ready to subordinate every principle to the restored King's prerogative. So long, however, as the faithful Clarendon remained Minister to this sovereign, no serious inroad was made upon the Constitution which had matured under the influence of such arduous experience. On the contrary, securities were obtained which rendered innocuous the designs of the Cabal against the principles of measured liberty; just as subsequent attempts on the Constitution proved to be equally harmless, when Danby corrupted Parliament and the King dispensed with it during the last four years of his reign.

Mingled with the faults of the second Charles's character were to be found elements which rendered him personally popular. Had his training been less irregular and demoralising there is every reason to believe that a different verdict might have been passed upon this reign. In the first place, an ever-ready wit, combined with inexhaustible good nature, conspired to disarm the political opposition which a knowledge of the King's heedless disregard for the Constitution engendered. He would never quarrel with any one, because a time might arrive when the goodwill of the person in question might prove useful.* And although, while bent on following his pleasures, his high sense of the royal prerogative was ruthlessly impressed on those of his subjects with whom he came in contact, yet an exercising of tyranny for tyranny's sake seemed never to accord with the second Charles's taste or disposition. Early in life the King preserved a strong sense of the duty owing to his father's revered memory; and though there appears little doubt that, at the time of his sojourn in Cologne in 1654, the Catholic faith was in reality his own, he strongly deprecated the efforts which were being made in Paris to induce the young Duke of Gloucester to throw off the Anglicanism in which Charles I. had brought him up.

---

* Dalrymple's 'Memoirs,' edition 1790, vol. i. Appendix, pt. i. bk. i. p. 158.

The letter of the then Prince of Wales to the Duke of York, being creditable to the writer, is here given in full:—

"Cologne, Nov. 10th, 1654.

" The news I have received from Paris of the endeavours used to change my brother Harry's religion, troubles me so much, that if I have anything to answer to any of your letters, you must excuse me if I omit it this post. All that I can say, at this time is, that I conjure you, as you love the memory of your father, and if you have any care for yourself, or kindness for me, to hinder, all that lies in your power, all such practices, without any consideration of any person whatever. I have written very home, both to the Queen and my brother, about it; and I expect that you should second it, as I have said to them, with all the arguments you can. For neither you nor I were ever so much concerned, in all respects, as we are in this. I am able to say no more at this time, but that I am yours."

"Cologne, Nov. 10th.

" I have commanded this bearer, my lord of Ormonde, to speak with you at large, concerning my brother Harry. Therefore, I desire you to give him credit, in all that he shall say to you from me, and to do all that he shall desire you. In the meantime, I have nothing more to add to this, but to conjure you to behave yourself as you ought to do, in a thing that concerns both you and me so much. I am yours."*

Never were the counsels of any nation in more terrible confusion than those of Great Britain during the last few years of this reign. The personal influence of the King had been occupied in adjusting the jealousies of his mistresses, while the ministers around him vied with one another in exercising the arts of dissimulation both towards the sovereign himself and the public.

Rein was given to absurd calumnies against the Catholics, whose persons were unsafe in the presence of perjured witnesses such as Oates and Bedloe, while the heir to the throne, the Duke of York, honestly holding these proscribed

---

* Macpherson's 'Original Papers,' vol. ii. Appendix, p. 663.

religious opinions, only escaped the exclusion intended for him by the personal influence of the King, acting on the Upper Chamber of the legislature, where Lord Halifax redeemed the statesmanship of an epoch not famous for the high purpose of its rulers or the wisdom of their measures. Some original letters regarding the Duke of York's sojourn in Scotland, edited by Mr. F. R. Radcliffe, appeared in the 'National Review' of August 1888, and among other matters of historical interest, we find (on page 754) a statement that the Princess of Orange had been expecting an heir to that heritage of land reclaimed from the sea known as the Low Countries. This averment, not to be found elsewhere, expressed hopes of which the realisation might have altered the course of English history considerably. Another interesting notice of the Duke's administration in Scotland would, if it were substantiated, not only convict him of inconsistency, as far as the Test Act of 1681 is concerned,* but also of an unrelenting spirit towards those Covenanters who had been rendered disloyal by the disastrous policy of his brother Charles II. Woodrow, appealing to the Privy Council Records, brings a direct charge of cruelty against James, Duke of York, averring that he attended at the tortures of the unfortunate rebels, who, in accordance with a barbarous law, were questioned thus roughly by the Council of Scotland. Sir John Dalrymple, however, after a full search through those records to which appeal was made, "found no reason for Woodrow's imputation."† Out of this labyrinth of what has been here styled the "Broken Purposes" of those who guided the State during the period succeeding the great Revolution, something has nevertheless survived to make their influence permanently felt.

The traditions of the Commonwealth and Protectorate, if redeemed from obloquy by the genius of Cromwell, and the seamanship of Blake, are not of that constitutional type which England has elected to treasure; while after the Restoration, Clarendon's administration stands prominent, despite venial errors incident to the time, as having been instrumental in regulating the King's prerogative, and creating a Cabinet responsible to Parliament.

Once only in the whole reign of Charles II., after the

---

* 'Stuart Letters,' Appendix I. Paper I.
† Dalrymple's 'Memoirs,' edition 1790, vol. i. pt. i. bk. i. p. 13, note.

Restoration, had the nation's pulse beat high with delight, namely, upon Sir William Temple's success in uniting England with Holland and Sweden in the famous Triple Alliance of January 1668, which for a short time checked the Grand Monarque in his advance on the Low Countries. Towards the end of the King's life there was present around his person the nucleus of that standing army, raised doubtless for his own objects, but which the sovereigns of England have preserved for defence of the realm ever since.* But the presence of nine thousand select troops did not compensate for the waning fidelity of a people once devoted to their King, while alienation from the only one of his natural children whom he loved—the Duke of Monmouth—conspired to darken the close of his pleasure-loving life. Never taking existence seriously, Charles II. had yielded up the reins of government to one Minister after another, only resuming guidance when his purse was light and his pleasures were consequently threatened; while he had incidentally consented not only to a trade war—not on the whole triumphant—with the Dutch, to whom he was indebted for an asylum, but also to a general dependence on France. His death, so inimitably described by Macaulay, came when it was least expected by the revellers who crowded the Court.

The exact facts regarding Huddleston, the priest who had saved the King's person after Worcester fight, being called on by the Duke of York to render that spiritual aid which in the eyes of a good Catholic was necessary at this supreme moment, are told in the second James's own handwriting in the Stuart Papers now at Windsor Castle. James published this narrative in full after he became King, accentuating certain passages which neither give strength to nor take away force from the general meaning. In 'Eikon Basilike Deutera' may be learned this remarkable episode, which on its first perusal astonished many of the homely Country party, who had hitherto attributed any favour to the Catholics not so much to the late King's influence as to that of his Ministers.

Of the various accounts which have appeared detailing the circumstances of the King's death, that given by a sympathetic courtier, Philip, Lord Chesterfield, is the result of personal observation, and is enlivened by some descriptive

* Green's 'History of the English People,' edition 1886, p. 648.

power. The two letters containing this narrative are given at length:—

To the Duke of Ormond.

"Lond., Feb. the 2nd, at 10 at night, 1684.

"My Lord,

"Tho' I know that your grace will receive an express from hence long before this can come to your hands, yet I think myselfe obliged to give your grace this following account of his Majesties dangerous illness. This morning, at eight o'clock, his Majesty had a great trouble and disorder upon him, and often stopped in his discourse as having forgot what he intended to say, which at last he grew sensible of, but immediately after fell down bacwards in his chaire in a sound (swoon), which lasted two howers, wanting seven minutes, with such appopletical simptoms, that all his phisitians despaired of his recovery; but by the force of remedies, it hath pleased God to restore him to his sences, and the doctors doe now think him out of the danger of this fit.

"My Lord, your Grace's, &c.,

"CHESTERFIELD."

To the Earl of Arran.

"London, Feb. the 7th, 1684-5.

"My Lord,

"I writ the last post, at the King's backstairs, a short letter to the Duke of Ormond, when I had so great a trouble upon mee and such a confusion of mind (by reason of my being surprized with His Majesty's desperat condition who wee thought just before out of danger), that I hardly knew then, or doe now remember what I writ; and, seriously I am but little better able to doe it now, tho I have had much more time to recollect myselfe.

"My Lord, I doe not love to be the first declarer of ill newse, and I am confident your Lordship will have heard of the King's death, by an express, long before this paper can come to you; and therefore, I will onely say that, as to the manner of it (of which I was a witness, as having watched two whole nights with him and saw him expire), nothing could be greater; and should I but mention half the remarkable passages that came to my cognisance they would be much more proper to fill a volume with then a letter; and therefore, I will only say, in short, that he died as a good Christian, asking and praying often for Gods and Christs mercy; as a man of great and undaunted courage in never repining at the loss of life, or for that of three kingdoms; as a good-natured man, in a thousand particulars; for when the Queene* sent to aske his pardon for anything that shee had ever done amisse, he answered that shee never had offended him, and therefore needed noe pardon, but, that he had need of hers, and did hope that shee would not refuse it him.

"Hee exprest extraordinary great kindness to the Duke his brother, and asked him often forgiveness for any hardships he had ever put upon him, assuring him of the tenderness of his love, and that he willingly left him all he had; desiring him, for *his* sake to be kind to his poor children, when he was gon.

"Lastly, he asked his subjects pardon for anything that had been neglected, or acted contrary to the best rules of good government, and told those who stood about his bed, how sorry he was for giving them so much trouble by his being so long a dieing; desiring often death to make more haist to free him from his pain, and the byestanders from their attendance. Your Lordship, I am sure, would have thought it very touching to have been a spectator of this dismal scene, and to have seene this brave and worthy prince lye in the horrid agonie of death, with all the paines immaginable upon him, from six a night till twelve the next day, at which time he died. I confess I could not forbeare expressing so effeminat a nature, nor am I able to repeat this now to your Lordship without being very sensible of soe generall a losse; and, therefore, I can say no more but that I am

"My Lord,
"Yours, &c.,
"CHESTERFIELD." †

The sentiments contained in these letters are at least appropriate to the striking scenes recorded of the last hours of Charles II., darkened as they must have been by alienation

---

* Catherine of Braganza.
† Letters of Philip, Lord Chesterfield, edition 1834, pp. 273–279.

from his beloved son Monmouth; while, if other silent doubts oppressed a mind solaced by its obedience to the last dictates of the Catholic Church, there may have arisen the remembrance of having dealt faithlessly with the Presbyterians in Scotland, by suppressing their form of worship, which in the time of need he had sworn to defend.

The success of Lauderdale's arbitrary government does not in the least atone for conduct which has done much to render the Stuarts unpopular in the northern kingdom.

CHAPTER XI.

KING AND EXILE.
James II. of Great Britain and VII. of Scotland, 1685-1701.

THE reign of James II. is approached with mingled feelings by a loyal subject who is also devoted to constitutional freedom and the Protestant religion. Devotion to the throne struggles with national yearning after the preservation of ancestral liberty; while an Englishman's dread of Papal supremacy, as involving a divided allegiance, stifles the respect due to the last Stuart sovereign's undoubted belief in the necessity of defending his ancient faith, which still attracts so many noble spirits throughout Christendom, and in accordance with whose tenets the head of the Church is paramount.

The Test Act of 1673, while its provisions seemed to aim at all religious denominations, was avowedly directed against Roman Catholic subjects. The struggle for a repeal of this measure was therefore nominally conducted in support of that religious toleration now generally accepted amongst ourselves. Therefore, though we know that James II. desired to found an arbitrary rule whereby a hundredth part of the English nation should dominate the whole, we must not be surprised that the King enlisted on his side the sympathies of many, nonconformists included, who desired to see real religious liberty established.

No such considerations can be said to have prevailed in Scotland, where the Covenanters had been dealt with in a summary, if not inhuman fashion; while for every Roman Catholic might be reckoned two hundred opponents of that dispossessed Church, which for ages had found a stronghold amidst the mountains and lakes of Caledonia.

In Ireland, where the vast majority were Roman Catholics, the proceedings of the new king naturally came to be hailed with satisfaction.

So far, then, the element of professed toleration tended to afford excuse for the honest desire of James II. to establish his own faith. There remains an obvious duty, namely, to reprobate most heartily the means by which the attempt to secure this end was pursued. Brought up in the rough school of adversity, the second son of Charles I. had learnt to believe that all the family disasters, including his father's loss of throne and life, were due to a lack of resolution, and that when with Strafford and Laud perished the policy of "thorough," the Stuart dynasty had lost the thread of their influence. This doctrine, fixed in the brain of a brave and obstinate sailor-prince of fair but limited talents, became dangerous when, after his perversion from the Anglican faith, and subsequent elevation to the throne, his theories of government were applied to matters of religion.

Despite the warnings conveyed towards the close of the previous reign, by the debates on the Exclusion Bill, that the people, with all their proved loyalty to the Stuarts, would rather see the line of succession set aside than the reformed faith deposed from its position of pre-eminence, James deliberately prepared to force on these kingdoms the tenets which his conscience assured him were true; and from this course he unfortunately never swerved until the Revolution sent him into exile. How this event was accomplished has become generally familiar to the world through the efforts of Hume, Dalrymple, Lingard, and Macaulay, so it is as superfluous to enlarge thereon as it is to canvass the debated theological questions which agitated England at this period.

Without the magnanimity of Charles I., the new king inherited that lack of breadth which had characterised the vision of his ill-fated father. Never, for instance, was statesmanlike moderation discarded with more palpable recklessness than when a merciless spirit of revenge, indulged without restraint in the hour of triumph, sent an enemy and a nephew to the block, in the person of the vain and ill-advised Monmouth. From that moment, instead of championing a cause broken and discredited, the Prince of Orange became acknowledged leader of a great and increasing Protestant party, many of the members of which were convinced that a struggle impended wherein religion and freedom were at stake. The treason of Monmouth and Argyll was doubtless deep, and in the eyes of a ruler, armed by their very folly with the sword of justice, inexpiable but on the scaffold. It had nevertheless been well for the Stuarts could the remembrance of Sedgmoor, and the Bloody Assize which followed the events of July 1685, have been eliminated from their dynastic history.

Never, from the opening days of the reign, had anticipation pictured a peaceful and prosperous era. At the Coronation, Burnet says—" The crown was not well fitted for the king's head; it came down too far, and covered the upper part of his face; the canopy carried over him did also break."* To these trifling indications, purely fanciful, which men remembered after events had marked their apparent significance, were to be added the far more threatening omens which observers descried among the people of Scotland, owing to the threatened suppression of the religious opinions which Charles II., on his Coronation at Scone in 1650, had sworn to profess and defend. It is hardly credible, but nevertheless true, that administration of the Solemn League and Covenant, or even writing in its defence, was at this time treated as treason, and was therefore punishable with death; while, to use Sir Walter Scott's words, "many other delinquencies were screwed up to the same penalty of death and confiscation."† Well might Holland be crowded with Scotch refugees and malcontents eager to follow any leader hostile to the Home Government, whose title to prominence could stand inspection. But when, with Argyll's capture and death, in June 1685, all hope of immediate deliverance was dissipated the way seemed clear for James's self-imposed task of restoring the Catholic faith in the land of Knox—an undertaking which the Wizard of the North likened to "pushing a stone up-hill."‡

It is noteworthy that the agents employed to carry out this scheme, despite their own fervour for the cause, did not believe in the realisation of their master's hopes. James II. was mistrusted even by the faithful Episcopalians after he had defied the Scottish Parliament, and abolished the Test Oath—which he himself had designed, and forced upon the Presbyterians—by an exercise of kingly prerogative quite remarkable, even in a legislative history not free from memories of royal menace. For, in former reigns, whenever a king had desired to carry matters with a high hand, he was either enabled to persuade the Parliament of Scotland to endorse such proceedings off-hand, or to win over a

---

* 'Hist. Own Times,' vol. iii. p. xx.
† 'Tales of a Grandfather,' edition 1880, p. 241.
‡ Ibid., p. 245.

majority within its walls by gathering around his person leading nobles whose influence effected that which the sovereign had failed to accomplish. The knowledge that he was compelled to ignore the Parliament in Edinburgh should alone have been sufficient to convince James II. of the hopeless nature of the project which he had in hand, when, unlike previous monarchs furnished with executive power, he was unable to persuade his single legislative chamber to endorse the measures he desired to promote. The minister found to be sufficiently bold to recommend this fatal policy, in the teeth of all the warnings which past experience and existing intelligence could afford, was the Earl of Perth, Chancellor of Scotland, and head of the noble family of Drummond, who himself had become a Roman Catholic.

How in the interest of a two-hundredth part of the Scots, an attempt was made to overrule the vast majority by forcibly re-establishing their former faith, is generally known, but few are aware how little the Earl of Perth himself expected his master's policy to triumph. A letter of the Chancellor's own, which appears among the Stuart Papers at Windsor, contains an intimation of his apprehension that the Court had essayed a desperate enterprise. The substance of this interesting document is subjoined. On February 3, 1688, Perth wrote from Edinburgh to the Cardinal of Norfolk at Rome, narrating the difficulties of the Roman Catholic party in the Scotch capital. He had formerly chosen to be silent rather than afflict the Cardinal with the state of affairs, but, owing to the grave crisis existing, had thenceforth determined to write once a month, reporting progress.

The advance had not been rapid hitherto, although the Abbey of Holyrood being restored to the faith enabled them to devote the church to the Order of St. Andrew, while a trustworthy priest was still to be found. The Jesuits hoped soon to get a college established in a house of the Chancellor's which adjoined the Palace ; but jealousies, unfortunately, existed between that Order and the other clergy, although Perth had hitherto kept in good odour with both. Six or seven monks from Germany had arrived, some of them likely to be able missionaries. Conversions however, were rare, here and there "a minister coming in, but very few in towns."

The Edinburgh ministers and the University students the Earl describes as " wild and furious, talking with confidence in a bad cause, so that the people take their assertion for full proof of their veracity." The business of the Duke of Hamilton seemed to be that of "obstructing the Catholic interest." The Earl goes on to say, "others we have here who would fain have us to believe they are our friends, who really are our more dangerous enemies. Especially some in the army, the hundredth man in which is not a Catholic, and we have scarce any officers of that persuasion; not that they are not to be had, but with all the art imaginable the king is diverted from any such design as might bring the army to us." *

Although partial tumults arose immediately these facts were known in the capital,† the ultimate outcome of this conspiracy to change the Presbyterian form of worship into that of Catholicism was not seen until December 10, 1688, when the intensely Protestant populace of Edinburgh arose and destroyed the newly erected images in the house near Holyrood, sacking at the same time that ancient Palace.‡ Thus chasing the Jesuits from their ministrations, they soon rendered all the Earl of Perth's silently formed plans futile, popular fervour of the Knoxian type making accomplishment of the people's will so easy that the work of destruction was performed with just that celerity and completeness with which a modern steam-hammer would crush an egg. And how the Stuarts and their advisers during this last decade of the dynasty could have hoped for any other result, with the history of Scotland before them, is past all understanding.

James's agents north of the Tweed clearly did not act so precipitately and fatally from lack of enlightenment as to the probable consequences of their action; although, with Tyrconnel established in Ireland, and Sunderland Minister for English affairs, the King himself had perhaps some excuse for believing the establishment of his adopted religion to be possible in those countries.

By encouraging James in a fatuous disbelief of the Prince of Orange's projects of invasion, Sunderland did more to defeat his master's aims and bring about his abandonment of the kingdom, than even when during the same administration the Universities and the Established Church were

---

* Stuart Papers, Royal Library, Windsor. (See Appendix I. Paper II.)
† Macaulay's 'History of England,' edition 1849, vol. ii. p. 116.
‡ Ibid., p. 607.

successively attacked—the first by the King forcing a Papist Master upon Magdalen College, and depriving the Fellows; the second by the imprisonment of the seven bishops, because they refused to read the so-called "Declaration dispensing with the Test"—and were thus forced to defend themselves against these inroads upon their independence. On the whole there can be little doubt that it was the prosecution and acquittal of the bishops that brought about the crisis which made so many men of light and leading turn towards the king's nephew, William of Orange, as a national deliverer; but it is extremely doubtful—despite the temporary success of the warming-pan deceit—whether the Revolution of 1688 could have been consummated, but for Lord Sunderland's craft in concealing the Prince of Orange's preparations from James himself.

With full command over the foreign correspondence, he shuffled and misrepresented it at will; and this wily minister added to his own infamy by a pretended conversion to the Roman Catholic faith, thus blinding the falling sovereign's eyes by one of the most notable instances of duplicity in a statesman which modern history records.*

This culmination of ministerial ill-faith occurred, moreover, in an age of deception, and in the course of negotiations not by any means founded on veracity. For indeed, the Protestant champion, William of Orange, sacrificed no advantage which he could hope to attain by an unscrupulous diplomacy, and in the course of his *pourparlers* with foreign courts he deceived the Papal ministers to the extent of inducing them to find him means for what he pretended would be a campaign against France on the Rhine.†

The Emperor of Germany, again, suspicious of designs against a brother sovereign, was pacified by William's promises that he would not accept the British crown. So emphatic and precise was William of Orange upon this point of not becoming King of England, that his words on the subject, contained in a letter to the Emperor Leopold I., are worth preserving.

"I assure your Imperial Majesty by this letter that whatsoever reports may have been spread, and notwithstanding

* See Dalrymple's 'Memoirs,' edition 1790, vol. ii. bk. v. pp. 33-34.
† Ranke's 'History of the Popes of Rome,' edition 1841, vol. iii. p. 181. For full account see Dalrymple's 'Memoirs,' edition 1790, vol. ii. Appendix to bk. v. p. 121.

those which may be spread for the future, I have not the least intention to do any hurt to his Britannic Majesty, or to those who have a right to pretend to the succession of his kingdoms, and still less to make an attempt upon the crown, or to desire to appropriate it to myself." *

Nor had the depth of William of Orange's Machiavellian policy been revealed to the unhappy James himself, whose pleadings for a continuance of war between the Emperor and the Turks † seem strange when addressed to that son-in-law who, in the name of Protestantism, was bent on ostracising Roman Catholic members of the Stuart family, thus inflaming the existing differences which agitated Western Christendom. And indeed these bitter feuds within the Christian Church must have seemed marvellous to the Mohammedans, who profited by them.

What rendered this division of the Christian interest in Great Britain inevitable was the tendency to work, so to speak, underground and away from the light of day, which characterised the Roman Catholic policy. Unfortunately for the Stuarts, James II. relied in the last instance almost solely on the advice of one Father Petre, a fact which, becoming known to the people, rendered that famous Jesuit, so unpopular that his life was in danger when the King deserted the kingdom. Nor is it possible to forget that two British regiments composed of Roman Catholics were in French pay during a considerable portion of this reign, the men having left the Prince of Orange's service at James's instance,‡ their purpose being to defend that monarch against his own Protestant subjects—a condition of things which the generation that expelled the Stuarts never knew.

Reprehensible as were the repeated asseverations of Citto, the Dutch ambassador, that the armament preparing in the ports of Holland was not designed for any attack on England, still more base was the slander disseminated concerning the Prince of Wales's birth at St. James's, which stigmatised

---

* Dalrymple's 'Memoirs,' edition 1790, vol. ii. Appendix to bk. v. p. 132.

† On June 8th, 1688, James II. wrote to the Prince, rejoicing at the hopes of Belgrade being captured; and on May 15 he promised him "to support the peace of Christendom, that the Emperor and the Venetian may prosecute the war against the Turks."—Dalrymple's 'Memoirs,' edition 1790, vol. ii. Appendix to bk. v. p. 160.

‡ Dalrymple's 'Memoirs,' edition 1790, vol. ii. Appendix to bk. v. pp. 134-5. It will be seen that Godolphin was cognisant of this measure.

him as a pretended prince—though his first appearance on the world's stage was attested by many more witnesses than custom enjoined.*

The Lord Chancellor and the Privy Councillors were in the room during the birth of the Chevalier de St. George, whose mother, with natural modesty, desired the King to "hide her face with his head and periwig" in the presence of so many of the opposite sex. Besides the Queen Dowager, Catherine of Braganza, and the Lord Chancellor, there were present on this occasion the Lord President, Lord Privy Seal, the two Chamberlains, Lord Middleton, Lord Huntingdon, Lord Powis, Lord Dover, Lord Peterborough, Lord Melfort, Lord Dartmouth, Sir John Emley, Lord Preston, Sir Nicholas Butler, the Duke of Beaufort, Lord Berkeley, Lord Murray, and Lord Castlemain, together with sundry others not of the Council, who need not be named. Nor should the solemn testimony of the nurse, Mrs. Dawson, as to the birth of Mary of Modena's child at St. James's, be forgotten, when exposing one of the vilest conspiracies which history records.†

And, indeed, whatever the issue of the dissensions which prevailed in the three kingdoms, it was certain that posterity would render justice to the memory alike of the insulted mother and the injured child. No more abominable imposture ever awaited exposure than the warming-pan story, which led weak-minded people to believe the son of James II. to be a suppositious child; and although, owing to his own honesty in cleaving to the religion in which he was brought up, the Chevalier de St. George never received the crown, yet the sympathy of thousands who shared not his religion followed him to the hour of his death. It is impossible to join with thorough heartiness in eulogies of William III., when we know that he rose to his high estate, partly at least, through the temporary success of this infamous device.

In the Stuart Papers, the property of Her Majesty, may be found evidence of the astonishment with which the family of

* Princess Anne's letter to her sister Mary, Princess of Orange, July 24, 1688, quoted in Dalrymple's 'Memoirs,' edition 1790, vol. ii. Appendix to bk. v. p. 179. See also account of Dr. Hugh Chamberlen, who was consulted by James II., 'Hanover Papers,' British Museum, quoted in the author's 'Brunswick Accession,' 2nd edition, p. 52; also 'English Historical Review,' vol. i. p. 768.

† See Appendix IV.

James II. received each successive blow prepared for them by the Prince of Orange's adherents, although neither the desertion of Lord Churchill, nor the acquiescence of the Princess of Denmark in the Revolution, affected Mary of Modena with distress commensurate with the satisfaction inspired by the birth of her son, and his ultimate escape into France after the Revolution. This we learn from a letter to Louis XIV. dated July 10, 1688, where the expression occurs, " Quelque grande ma joye a la naissance de mon fils"; while, after the Revolution had been accomplished, the Prince of Monaco received a communication from her, confessing that the joy of having the King and the young Prince of Wales in safety made her forget everything else. Finally, as regards this dynastic catastrophe, we find Mary of Modena innocently declaring to the Father of the Jesuits how thoroughly religion, and religion alone, had contributed to exile the King and his family. She expressed herself as follows:—" . . . tout le monde d'en juger si la haine de la Religion n'a pas eté la cause de la trahison et de la revolte de nos sujets et si nous n'avons pas perdu nos Royaumes pour y avoir taché d'avancer celui de Jesus Christ." *

The letter-book of this queen, preserved at Windsor, offers ample evidence how much her thoughts ran upon this all-absorbing subject. This state of mind finds expression in sundry letters to the Abbess of Chaillot (a convent which Mary of Modena afterwards chose as her place of retreat), and also to the Abbesses of Dunkirk and Ghent; while in March 1687 her whole energies seem to have been thrown into the candidature of one Father Ferrari of Modena for an inquisitorship in Rome.†

One instrument has escaped the zeal of antiquarian historians who have revelled amongst the papers of Henry, Cardinal of York. It appears that just before the defection of his principal officers, James II. made a will at Whitehall, entrusting the Prince of Wales to his mother's guardianship, and appointing likewise a Council to advise her in the task. The concluding portion of the document relating to those in whom James II. confided, runs as follows:—

" And furthermore for thee especial Trust & Confidence which Wee have in His Royall Highness Prince George of

---

* Stuart Papert, 1688.
† Mary of Modena to the Cardinal of Norfolk, Stuart Papers, March 1687.

Denmark, George Lord Jeffreys, our Chancellor of England, Henry Lord Arundell of Wardour, Lord Privy Seale, Christopher Duke of Albemarle, Henry Duke of Newcastle, Henry Duke of Beaufort, William Duke of Hamilton, William Duke of Queensbury, William Ld Marquess of Powis, Robert Earl of Lindsay, Ld Great Chamberlain of England, John Earl of Mulgrave, Ld Chamberlain of our household, Aubrey Earl of Oxford, Theophilus Earl of Huntingdon, Henry Earl of Peterborow, Philip Earl of Chesterfield, Henry Earl of Clarendon, John Earl of Bath, William Earl of Craven, George Earl of Berkeley, Daniel Earl of Nottingham, Laurence Earl of Rochester, Alexander Earl of Moray, James Earl of Perth, Charles Earl of Middleton, our principal Secretary of State, John Earl of Melfort, Roger Earl of Castlemain, Richard Earl of Tirconnell, Thomas Viscount Fauconborg, Richard Viscount Preston, one of our Principall Secretaries of State, Nathaniel Bishop of Durham, John Lord Bellasys, George Ld Dartmouth, Sidney Lord Godolphin, Henry Ld Dover, Sir John Emle, Knt., Chancellor of our Exchequer, Sir John Trevor, Knt., Master of the Rolls, Sir Edward Herbert, Knt., Ld Chief Justice of our Court of Common Pleas, Sir Thos. Strickland, Knt., Sir Nicholas Butler, Knt., Christopher Vane, Esq., and Silas Titus, Esq.

"Novr 17th 1688 at Whitehall
"James R.

" Witnessed by
Jeffreys. Arundell.
Melfort. Belasys.
Godolphin. Preston.
Wm. Bridgman. Pepys."

This testament was superseded by a later instrument drawn up at St. Germain, but nevertheless remains a curious historical document, showing whom the King really trusted at this critical moment of his reign—a confidence it is well known he at first declined to place either in his trusty friend Lord Balcarres or in the noble Viscount Dundee, who was burning to lead the remaining loyal troops against the Prince of Orange.

James II. was not only allowed by his Minister, Lord Sunderland, to disregard the information of Count d'Avaux, the French ambassador at the Hague, but also to reject an understanding with the Empire which Leopold I. was prepared to enter upon. When at St. Germain, James wrote to the Emperor desiring assistance "for the recovery" of his kingdom, and received in reply a remarkable letter,* in which the following passage occurs:—

"If your Majesty had rather given credit to the friendly remonstrances that were made you by our late envoy, the Count de Kaunitz, in our name, than the deceitful insinuations of the French, whose chief aim was, by fomenting continual divisions between you and your people, to gain thereby an opportunity to insult the more securely over the rest of Christiandom; and if your Majesty had put a stop, by your force and authority, to their many infractions of the peace— of which, by the treaty of Nimegen, you are made the guarantee —and to that end entered into consultations with us, and such others as have the like just sentiments in this matter; we are verily persuaded that by this means you should have, in a great measure, quieted the minds of your people, which were much already exasperated through their aversion to our religion."

The exiled English King must have perused, with horror and disgust, sentences which proved that his isolated position in Europe was owing to the craft of Sunderland, the trusted Minister for Foreign Affairs, who had apparently suppressed the fact that Leopold I., in the interests of his religion, was ready to join hands with James II., provided that French counsels did not remain paramount at St. James's.

But for the mutual hostility of France and Germany, and for the jealousies rampant at Rome, William of Orange could never have organised the expedition which conveyed his army to England. The perils of that undertaking were immense. Bad weather alone might have wrecked his schemes. Once indeed, on October 20th, he was forced by a tempest to put back in a disordered condition to Helvoetsluys; but on the whole, the elements worked in favour of his cause, inasmuch as a change of wind gave him a fresh start and prevented a meeting between the English and Dutch fleets. The former was lying at a rendezvous off Gunfleet Sands, between Harwich and St. Osyth Point, and near the modern Clacton-on-Sea, ready to sail after the heavily laden Dutch transports, while it was expected that William would, according to his original plan, suggested by Lord Danby,† sail north for an attack upon Hull.

---

* 'Harleian Miscellany,' edition 1808, vol. i. p. 23.
† Letter of Lord Danby, in Philip Lord Chesterfield's 'Correspondence;' also Lingard, edition 1839, vol. xiii. p. 174.

It appears from the lately published 'Memoirs of Lord Torrington,' by J. K. Laughton (p. 21), which we owe to the Camden Society, that James II. never approved of this anchorage for his fleet, but feared that in an east wind they might be forced up the Thames by the Dutch, and so be placed on the defensive, while the transports landed their freight elsewhere.

The King preferred, he said, a station between the North Sands Head and the Kentish Knock,* a position which would enable an Admiral to take his fleet with greater facility over into Boulogne roads.

In June 1688 we hear of the King showing great activity, in order to ingratiate himself with the sailors of the fleet, going with Prince George of Denmark—the "Est-il possible?" of Macaulay, even then meditating desertion of his father-in-law—on to most of the ships, "behaving with great affability, and taking notice of every particular officer."†

It was not until the 19th of September that Lord Dartmouth came down and undertook the supreme command, resolving, after a council of war, to reverse the plan of the Vice-Admiral, Sir Roger Strickland, and anchor, despite the King's adverse opinion, near Gunfleet Sands.

The English fleet, as we learn from Mr. Laughton's instructive pages, consisted of 61 vessels, 38 of which were line-of-battle ships. while the Prince of Orange defended his transports, about 323 in number, by 52 ships of the line, and 25 frigates.

When at last, on November 1, 1688, the Dutch fleet weighed anchor for the second time, the same strong east wind which carried the Prince through the Channel prevented the English fleet from coming in pursuit, although six of the invading vessels were seen by the English sailors at Gunfleet. Lord Dartmouth, the British Admiral, although he resolutely refused James's solicitations requiring that the Prince of Wales should be carried out of the country, was yet enthusiastically loyal to the crown, and an engagement appeared imminent had not wind and waves ruled otherwise.‡

* 'Memoirs relating to the Lord Torrington,' edited for the Camden Society, by John Knox Laughton, M.A., R. N., p. 21.
† Ibid., p. 18.
‡ Lord Dartmouth's narrative appears in Dalrymple's 'Memoirs,' edition 1790, vol. ii. Appendix to bk. vi. p. 234.

But the disadvantages which heavily laden transports must
have suffered under, if attacked on their course, were signally
reduced by the presence of Admiral Herbert—deprived of
his English commission for refusing to oppose the Test—in
command of a squadron of Dutch fighting-ships, and by the
prevalence of treason in the English fleet, eight captains
standing prepared to salute their Admiral, Lord Dartmouth,
and join the Dutch.* Torbay was selected as a landing-
place, by advice of the pilots. William owed something to
good fortune, inasmuch as a change of wind carried him into
the desired haven, after his ships had been driven too far
west. But what mattered it where, in the West, William
landed, when, by invitation, he knew that the Comptons and
Cavendishes were with him?†

Further, the shouts of the troops of James II. at Hounslow
after the bishops' acquittal had told of divisions of opinion
in that standing army which the last Stuart King nurtured
so carefully.‡ But the English fleet remaining intact, and
advancing up the Channel under Lord Dartmouth, continued
to give the Protestant leader considerable anxiety; § as, in
the event of any check incurred by the Prince of Orange,
the navy of Louis XIV. would have left its harbours, and,
with the loyal British ships, must have outnumbered the
Dutch. We read, "'Tis thought of no small consequence
to ye suckses of our affaires y^t ye English fleate be forced
in to port least when ye Dutch fleat be returned home
ye K. may call over considerable numbers of ye French
troops." ||

That the Revolution of 1688 was a bloodless one, we owe
to the chance which never allowed the rival fleets to meet in
the Channel, and to the indecision which paralysed James's
vigour of mind as he prepared to cope with his enemies

---

* 'Correspondence of Admiral Herbert during the Revolution,' edited by
E. Maunde Thompson, in ' English Historical Review,' vol. i. p. 527. We learn
in J. K. Laughton's 'Memoirs relating to the Lord Torrington,' p. 26, that
these seceding captains had previously prevented the fleets from meeting off
the coast of Holland.

† Green's 'History of the English People,' edition 1886, p. 604.

‡ Ibid.

§ Russell to Herbert, from Exeter, Nov. 13, 1688. Lord Dartmouth was
in the Downs when he heard that William of Orange had landed in Torbay.
It is to the credit of James II. that he acquitted his faithful servant, Lord
Dartmouth, of any blame, but, with a sailorly insight, attributed this naval
paralysis to the uncontrollable vagaries of winds and waves.

|| Ibid.

ashore, when he saw the reality of the danger. And indeed, each branch of the forces contained desperate loyalists, some of whom, in after years, were ready to imperil all for a cause rendered apparently hopeless when Churchill and the Princess Anne deserted James II.

Lord Macaulay has shown how the jealousies of the rival French diplomatists, Barillon, Sunderland's friend, and Bonrepaux, who acted a hostile part towards that Minister, first led to Lord Rochester's overthrow, and then to the strained situation which preceded the Revolution. In the Appendix to Lingard's 'History' (edition 1839, pp. 236-240) will be found an analysis of the case against Sunderland for betraying James II. to his rival; and without accepting Bonrepaux as an authority, or allowing the lenient judgment of Lingard to be disregarded, it is impossible not to accept what was the latter's tardy conclusion that, to the Prince of Orange, Sunderland did, "occasionally at least," betray "the secrets of his Sovereign," thereby violating alike duty and oath. But for treason in high places, it is probable that the harassed King's later submission to public opinion might have stayed his people's hands. James II. was then, as is well known, ready to yield every point in dispute, "except the Dispencing power which he said he would reserve to a Parliament to judge of."*

How, when the yielding mood proved of no avail to stem these dissensions, the King, after casting the Great Seal into the Thames, escaped down the river to Faversham, where, having been insulted by a mob, and threatened with personal violence by some fishermen, he returned to London and drank in joyfully the pitying salutes of a long-suffering people, is as familiar to Englishmen conversant with national history, as is the sequel which it is necessary to recall.

When the brave old Lord Craven, at the head of the Guards, declined to withdraw his troops from St. James's Park and practically yield up the person of the King, who remained ensconced at Whitehall, the falling sovereign himself sent that order for retreat which sealed the fate of a dynasty and relegated it to a bloodless exile.† For the Queen and Prince of Wales had already fled into France, where James himself,

---

* Burnet to Herbert, Oct. 23, 1688, quoted by E. Maunde Thompson in 'English Historical Review,' vol. i. p. 524.

† Macaulay's 'History of England,' edition 1849, vol. ii. p. 583.

after various delays, soon arrived. But these events, which seem to posterity, to follow naturally upon the choice of high-handed and illegal measures, were by no means consummated without good fortune favouring the Revolution and its instigators. Indeed, it was only after running the gauntlet through many dangers with sundry hairbreadth escapes, that William and Mary, two grandchildren of Charles I., were chosen to rule over the English people in the very banqueting house at Whitehall before which that ill-starred monarch had suffered death.

The popular choice involved a rupture of dynastic continuity which shocked all who held the celebrated doctrine of Divine Right, that is to say, who believed that a king was infallible, and that his subjects had no right to resist him, even if he elected to ignore the law and substitute for it his own will. It is extremely difficult to understand how such a doctrine as this could have been put forward with any assurance by persons who were devoted to the house of Stuart. For the descent from Bruce of itself at once shows, according to our modern notions at least, that their original title was based rather upon national election than divine right. Upon the failure, in 1290, of the direct line of William the Lion, the right of succession reverted to the descendants of William's brother David, Earl of Huntingdon, of whose *second* daughter, Isabella, Robert Bruce was the son, while John Baliol was the grandson of the *eldest* daughter Margaret. Edward I. of England, the arbiter, was clearly right in preferring Baliol's claim, yet the nation ultimately declared in favour of Bruce, and established him and his line upon the throne. The question of degree alone can be urged to vitiate the settlement of 1688, when the eldest daughter of James II. was called to a throne forfeited by her father.

When James II. defied the opinion of the majority of his subjects, and trod the laws under his feet in order to mould religious life and opinion at will, he had furnished abundant grounds for the desire of the English nation that other members of their royal family, possessing the power to check these lawless procedings, should accept the responsibilities and reap the honours of the throne which, it was held, the occupant had forfeited. At the same time, it was not many months before the generous English people, in the absence of those threatened ills against which they had taken such precautions, turned a pitying eye towards the well-meaning but mistaken sovereign who had proved unable to hold his own in Ireland in 1690, at a moment when England's temporary loss of maritime ascendancy in the Channel, after the fight off Beachy Head, was eliciting sympathetic movements in that portion of the realm on behalf of the exiled Stuarts.

The campaign in Ireland which ended at the Boyne forms a subject which it is impossible to deal with satisfactorily in the small space here available; but it is creditable to the ex-King to know that, when the abrogation of Poyning's laws was proposed to him, so that the necessity of initiating laws by the English Council might cease and Ireland become practically independent, he replied:—" I will not hurt my kingdom, although I no longer reign in it."* Moreover, during the siege of Londonderry, when the Irish Parliament, in which there were only six Protestants, resolved to confiscate the lands of certain Protestant proprietors, he aquiesced unwillingly, offering 10,000*l.* out of his private purse to recompense the losers. It is fair to add that this confiscation included also some Roman Catholics."†

It has been frequently averred that James II. before the Revolution desired in a similar way to deal with "The Act of Settlement" of Irish landed property, which had been passed when his brother Charles came to the throne, and which secured fixity of tenure to many Cromwellians whose fathers had been placed on the soil by the Protector. Beyond the *ipse dixit* of Barillon, the French ambassador,‡ who had probably conveyed information received through Sunderland, there is no direct evidence upon this subject.

There can, however, be no doubt that the King of England did, previous to the Revolution, use Tyrconnel as an instrument to advance the Roman Catholic party in Ireland, while troops of that religious persuasion were drafted into English regiments.§ But the policy of eradicating the Saxon possessors of the soil in Ireland, and at the same time conquering England by means of the Celt, was never attempted under James II.

Any permanent result which might have followed the

---

* Dalrymple's 'Memoirs,' edition 1790, vol. ii. pt. ii. bk. ii. p. 70.
† Ibid., p. 68. Dalrymple attributes this to James's consciousness of the injustice done.
‡ Barillon to Louis XIV., Oct. 16, 1687. Dalrymple, vol. ii. Appendix to bk. v. p. 137.
§ Macaulay's 'History of England,' edition 1849, vol. ii. p. 426.

Jacobite endeavours to retain Ireland for the Stuarts, would surely have been prefaced by the success of Viscount Dundee's great campaign in Perthshire, which, however, ended disastrously, though gloriously, at Killiecrankie, on July 27, 1689. It is interesting to know that the brave commander who died there was braced up to his task by a belief that the tide was flowing in favour of his master, James II.; that Londonderry had been captured five weeks before the battle in which he himself actually fell, and also that the French were then masters of the Channel. In each case the wish was father to the thought, and the hopes expressed were never realised.*

Some idea of the estimation in which William III. held Dundee's powers may be learned by the remark he made after Killiecrankie, when the Edinburgh express had been detained a day upon the road by accident. "Then," said King William, "Dundee must be dead, for otherwise he would have been at Edinburgh before the express."†

It is interesting to speculate as to what might have happened in Scotland supposing that the fatal shot at Killiecrankie had missed its aim, and that Claverhouse had immediately swooped down upon the Valley of Forth, and, regardless of Stirling, pushed his way straight to the capital. Regarding the plan to regain Great Britain for the Stuarts as a whole, it is impossible not to see how totally different must have been the position of the English Government with Dundee and his army waiting the turn of events near the Border, the town at least of Edinburgh recovered from the Convention, and the whole neighbouring country owning his sway.

Profiting by Montrose's bitter experience after Kilsyth, Dundee might have adopted defensive tactics, and then William III. would hardly have left for Ireland at all, or even sent troops to oppose James there, in which case the Protestant cause must have become desperate in that country. For although the Irish campaign of 1689-90 is associated in men's minds mainly with the gallant defence of Londonderry and the defeat of James at the Boyne, yet when Claverhouse took up arms in the Highlands of Scotland, the North of Ireland alone seemed likely to resist the tide of Jacobite

---

* Dalrymple's 'Memoirs,' edition 1790, vol. ii. Appendix, pt. ii. bk. ii., p. 96.
† Ibid., p. 89.

reaction in the Emerald Isle, and in default of succour to the sorely-pressed Irish Protestants, there is some reason to think William would have lost Ireland, while his position in England would have been in danger, threatened as he was by the machinations of Louis XIV. and by a powerful minority of the English.

Anyhow, the Great Deliverer could scarcely have continued to disregard the Scots and their interests, but for the inevitable disintegration which ensued after Dundee's death at Killiecrankie. As events turned out, William, trusting to the Earl of Breadalbane to distribute largess amongst the clans within reach of his influence, carelessly issued a commission warranting the massacre of the Macdonalds in Glencoe,* and afterwards silently witnessed the collapse of Paterson's Scotch settlement on the Isthmus of Darien or Panama,† although the Royal assent had been given to the incorporation of the Company: nor did he scruple to subject his foes to that torture which the laws of Scotland still sanctioned.

The sufferings of men such as Nevile Paine, whom no agonies could subdue, and who refused to disclose the secrets of his master, James II., to the hostile legislature in Edinburgh, remain an enduring honour to the victim; as do those of the 150 Lowland officers of the great Dundee—justly rendered famous by Aytoun's Muse—who, preferring principle to advancement, followed James into exile, and cheerfully endured life-long poverty.‡

We read as follows of the torture of Nevile Paine for complicity in Sir J. Montgomery's plot against William's Government:—

"It was surprising to me, and others, that flesh and blood could, without fainting, and in contradiction to the grounds we had insinuat of our knowledge of his accession in matters endure the heavie pennance he was in for two hours. . . . My stomach is truly so far out of tune, by being a witnes to an act so farr cross to my natural temper, that I am fitter for rest than any thing ells; nor could any less then the danger from such conspirators to the person of our incomparable King and the safety of his Government prevailed over me to have in the Councils name been the prompter

---

* Macaulay's 'History of England,' edition 1849, vol. iv. pp. 190, 204
† Ibid., vol. v. p. 219.
‡ Sir Walter Scott's 'Tales of a Grandfather,' edition 1880, p. 269.

of the executioner to encrease the torture to so high a pitch."*

But the time was approaching when the disregarded sympathies of Scotland and the Scots came to be invaluable at Whitehall, amidst the torrent of obloquy which assailed the lately elected King of England—and this within a year of that July 1690, when he won the battle of the Boyne. This reaction was undoubtedly attributable to the detestation with which Englishmen then regarded the Dutch compatriots of the sovereign, seeing that he openly preferred and lavished favours upon them,† and also to the disregard of the popular arts in Government which characterised King William. Absorbed in vast schemes for the safety of Protestant Europe, he seems to have never cultivated the graces which a Court desires to see in its sovereign, while the ordinary civilities of daily life were ignored during the pre-occupation which afflicted him even at the dinner-table.‡ Strong in the power to "grapple to his heart" friends such as Portland, he appeared almost repulsive to other less familiar associates.

The year 1691 had not passed before the discontent in England became very serious, and influential men who had helped to bring about the Revolution were found establishing communications with the ex-King at St. Germain, while in outward appearance they were still supporters of the new Government.

James II. occupied his time in exile at this period by endeavouring to arouse the Roman Catholic world into action on his behalf, and two letters of his at Windsor—written to his friend the Cardinal of Norfolk—describe the situation so clearly, that they are printed here without comment.

"*To the Cardinal of Norfolk.*

"St. Germain, Jan. 15, 1691.

"Some days since I had yours of the 25th November, and do not at all doubt of your continuing of doing your part in advancing my affairs where you are, and if they have not had the success I had reason to expect I am sure it was not for want of your soliciting them, of which Lord Melfort has

---

* Extract from letter of the Earl of Craufurd to the Earl of Melville, Dec. 11, 1690, in 'Leven and Melville Papers,' p. 582.
† Macaulay's 'History of England,' edition 1849, vol. iv. p. 160.
‡ 'Marlborough (i. e. Sarah, Duchess of Marlborough) Letters,' p. 115.

given me an account. The Prince of Orange is making great preparation for the next campaign, and it is sayd by all the last letters from England, intends to head the confederate army in Flanders. He does all he can to advance the Protestant cause everywhere, why should not his Holynesse do the like on his side? The king my brother here does what he can, but he alone cannot do all, having so many enemys to deal with. The Prince of Orange has sent arms into Savoy and Piemont, and money is going now into Switzerland from him, why should not his Holynesse spare me some, to buy arms here, to begin a magazin that for aught I know I may have need of before the summer shall be over, and then I suppose he would be sorry I should want them, which is all I shall say at present.

"JAMES R."

James was exceedingly anxious regarding the probable vacancy in the Papal chair, and makes the remarkable statement to the Cardinal that, anterior to the events of 1688, he had restored the Roman Catholic religion throughout England.

"*To the Cardinal of Norfolk.*

"St. Germain, Feb. 14, 1691.

"The last letter which came from Rome gave so bad an account of his Holinesses indisposition, that it is believed, considering his great age [Alexander VIII. died during this year, 1691, and was succeeded by Innocent XII.], he will hardly recover, which has obliged this king to order all the cardinals in France, except the Cardinal of Furstenburgh, to make what haste they can for Rome. The same reason makes me write so early to you upon that subject. I write also to Lord Melfort, and send him such credentials and instructions as will be necessary for him upon such an occasion. I shall order him to give an account of his instructions, that you may concur with him in doing your endeavour to gett such a choice made as may be for the advantage of holy Church, and the good of all Christendom, which now is in chusing such a one, as may be for the effectual assisting me against the Usurper, and doing his best to draw from him those Catholic Princes who are now in league with him the Usurper, to their owne shame and to the hazard of the Catholic Religion, not only in all my dominions but even in the rest of Europe.

All the world sees the sad effects the Emperors joyning with the P. of Orange has had in Hungary, and had not the King of Spaine and D. of Savoy done the same, in all aperence before this, I had been restored and Catholike Religion established againe as it was in my tyme in all my Dominions. I should think that these considerations should mak all where you are to joyne with you in the choice of such a Pope as would bestir himself for the good of the Church. The most Christian Kings concerns and myne are now so united that all that wish me well must join with his share in the choice which I most earnestly recommend to you to do, and that there may be a good understanding bettwene you and the Car. d'Este for the better coming on of my concerns there, which I am sure you will continue to do, as you always have done, of which I am very sensible.

"JAMES R."

The Stuart Papers at Windsor have provided no data where from we can derive anything new regarding the events of the year 1692, which remains famous for the naval struggle off La Hogue. On this occasion the English Admiral Russell allowed the Court of St. Germain to think him prepared to let the French transport their fleet into an English harbour and land James's French allies in safety, while the English Admiral employed his own fleet in a disembarkation on the coast of France; moreover, he applied in England for leave to make this descent at St. Malo.*

James appears to have kept to himself Russell's entreaty that the two fleets should be prevented from meeting, while acquainting his French allies with the fact that treason existed amongst the British; and it is just to record that Russell gave ample warning of his intention to "fire upon the first French ship" he met, even if he saw the ex-King himself on the deck.† When, therefore, de Tourville, the French Admiral, put to sea triumphantly and appeared off Portland, the situation became such as an English sailor could only escape from at the cannon's mouth. The sea-fight which ensued resulted—after a desperate struggle, conducted with varied success—in the breaking of the French line in several places, the *Royal Sun* (de Tourville's ship) being

---

* Dalrymple's 'Memoirs,' edition 1790, vol. iii. pt. ii. p. 232.
† Ibid.

hauled out of action after a bloody engagement with Russell's flag-ship, while Admiral Carter—another correspondent with James at St. Germain—being mortally wounded, gave orders with his last breath to fight the ship while she could swim.*

A fog brought the battle to a temporary close, and the French ships drifted into shallow water near their own shores, eighteen sail of the line taking refuge under the forts of La Hogue. Five of these escaped, but on the fifth day after the sea-fight, Russell sent Admiral Rooke to carry the remaining thirteen by assault and destroy the vessels, a design fully accomplished, the crews escaping to the mainland.†

The victory of La Hogue, so named from the later operations, was consummated within sight of James himself, who was waiting on high ground near the sea-shore, with the Duke of Berwick and other officers of distinction, amidst the foreign troops designed to invade England.

So complete was the discomfiture inflicted on France, that never again did she appear to be prepared both by land and sea when she was earnestly bent on restoring the elder Stuarts. For when her sympathies for them gained strength, and advanced beyond mere appreciation of the advantage which possession of James's person afforded her, she found herself crippled by the scattered condition of her maritime resources, or by the necessity of facing Germany on the Rhine, and reckoning with an Anglo-Dutch army in the Low Countries.

It is probable that the ex-King of England foresaw this when he crept back to St. Germain, and deserted that ancient palace for the monastery of La Trappe, where the superiority of a future crown eternal over mere temporalities became more than ever impressed on his mind. Thenceforth the exiled king lived in a little world ecclesiastical.

A series of letters from the Abbé de la Trappe, inculcating contentment at a happily changed lot, forms by no means the least valuable of the Stuart collection, the property of the Queen.

That the dissentients in England who reprobated the new Government were more numerous and influential in 1692 than at any epoch during the reign of William and Mary, or in the course of that King's sole occupancy of the throne, is

---

* Dalrymple's 'Memoirs,' edition 1790, vol. iii. pt. ii. p. 241. † Ibid., p. 244.

clear from a study of the Jacobite correspondence in Macpherson and Dalrymple. To the names of Lord Churchill, Admiral Russell, Lord Shrewsbury, Lord Godolphin, and Lord Halifax—powerful men who were prepared to welcome the restoration of James II.—may now be added that of the famous Lady Sarah—the future Duchess of Marlborough—who, Lord Melfort declared, kept him apprised of the changed state of opinion in England.*

But the most important statement which Her Majesty's Stuart Papers of this date contain, is that derived from certain letters written to Rome concerning the establishment of bishops in England, who had been appointed at the instigation of James, when at St. Germain, by the Holy See. At the moment when in matters temporal it was judged advisable both by Louis and his exiled protégé to conciliate the Compounders or moderate party amongst the Jacobites, Lord Melfort, chief of the non-Compounders at St. Germain, writes to Bishop Ellis at Rome, acknowledging that four English Catholic bishops, originally appointed by Innocent XI., were in existence under the ex-King's ægis; and that, although it was intended to renew their faculties, the affair might well be kept secret at such a conjuncture. The letter is of sufficient interest to find a place in this narrative, rather than in the Appendix.

"St. Germain, October 29, 1693.

"My Lord,

"I send you inclosed his Majesty's answer to your Lordship's letter, by which you'l see that his Majesty has conforme to your Desire written to my Ld Cardinall and Mons. Caprara to have the faculties of the four Catholique Bishops of England renued, but as it is of consequence y^t there be no noyse of such matters in this conjuncture, it is necessary y^t ye thing be done as privatly as possible.

"I thank you for y^r Lordship's Corespondence, which I value very much, as I doe your friendship, and do beg the continuation of both, assuring y^r Lordship y^t none is with more gratefull resentment and sincerity, &c.

"MELFORT."

This communication had been prefaced by a letter of recommendation given to Bishop Ellis from Mary of Modena

---

* Lord Melfort to the Cardinal of Norfolk, July 22, 1692, in Stuart Papers, Windsor.

to the Pontiff, as well as by a request from the Bishop to be allowed to continue in charge over the diocese committed to his spiritual care in England. Bishop Ellis seems to have suffered from ill-health, and several notices of his absence from England occur during the ensuing two years, when James himself wrote the remarkable letter which, without regard to chronology, is herewith subjoined. The tone is that of a monarch in the plenitude of power, rather than that of a suppliant to subjects who at the moment were by no means ready to repent of their religious or political actions towards the exiled Stuarts. The letter at Windsor is a holograph.

"My Lord Bishop Ellis,

"The same reasons which at first prevailed with me to desire his Hol^s Pope Innocent XI. that Bishops might be appointed in the severall parts of England for the better service of God and Government of the Church, do now also oblige me to signify to you, that these good intentions of his Holiness and my owne are in great part frustrated by your long absence from that considerable District which was committed to your Charge. That absence at first I know was excusable by reason of a sudden allarme caused by the Revolution, and your want of health since may probably have been a just excuse for your not attending all this while the duty of your charge. You are the proper Judge whither that Impediment does still subsist. What I have to say is, that if your health will now permitt you to execute your office and pastorall function, as it is your duty so to do, it is also mine to require it from you. But if for want of health you still find yourself unable to undergo the fatigue and bear the burden of your charge, it will be necessary that you signify the same to me, that I may accordingly provide and nominate some fitting person for the spirituall government of the District now under your direction. Hereunto requiring your speedy answer,

"I remain,
"Your good friend,
"JAMES R."

According to the account of Bishop Ellis's life in Mr. Leslie Stephen's 'Dictionary of National Biography,' James II. did not wish the prelate to return to the care of his western diocese in England. This is possibly an error, although it is doubtful if he ever performed episcopal duties again in his native land. Philip Ellis had been educated at Westminster School and Douay College, being known both at Protestant college and Roman Catholic seminary as "jolly Phil." His abilities appear to have been considerable.*

Little trace of public events, such as the loss of the Smyrna fleet in the spring of 1693, or the foiled attack on Brest, of which Marlborough, Russell, and Godolphin had apprised James II., and which took place a little more than a year afterwards, are to be found in the Stuart Papers at Windsor, but the letters of Lord Caryll from St. Germain to Bishop Ellis at Rome do certainly describe the situation as it appeared at that time to a Jacobite partisan resident abroad. The tendency was to exercise a credulity regarding James's hopes in England, from which experienced denizens of that country refrained, believing that although men like Marlborough, Russell, Godolphin, and even Halifax, had made themselves safe all round, yet the people generally were adverse to any disturbance of the Protestant Settlement of 1688, and that this feeling had increased since 1692.

An anonymous letter † from a friend, written at Paris after a journey round England, shows why James remained at St. Germain.

It is interesting to contrast with the real situation of affairs in England at this time, which has been briefly indicated, the Jacobite hopes revealed by the Stuart Papers.

Lord Caryll writes to Bishop Ellis on Sept. 6, 1694:—

" All the Royall family are (God be thanked) in perfect health; nor have they at present so much cause to dread a bad peace as formerly; a good one when Right and Religion may take place were indeed at all times to be wished, but to any such I believe our enemys are no ways as yet inclin'd. The blessing which God has bestowed upon France of a very plentifull yeer, has putt his most Ch^n M^{ty} out of ye necessity of seeking a peace, and probably his enemys may be reduced to that sooner than he. In ye meantime ye King our Master, has a great deal of reason to be satisfy'd with ye dayly marks of his most Ch^n brothers kindness to him, who seemes

---
* Dictionary of National Biography,' vol. xvii. pp. 287-288.
† Macpherson's 'Original Papers,' vol. i. p. 450.

to want only an opportunity to complete ye glory of his Reign by restoring him, which would certainly for all ages to come make ye memory of Louis ye Great stand u on an even kiel with that of Charles ye Great.

"This appears ye more likely to come to passe, for that in ye present situation of affairs ther does not seem any other way for France to make a speedy and advantageous end of ye war; so that having those two powerful motives of glory and interest to favour us, we may well hope in some reasonable time to see ye wisht for effect: towards which I doubt not but that we shall have the good wishes, prayers, and benedictions of his Holines, and everything but his mony.

"I am, with due respect,
"CARYLL."

Lord Caryll writes again on October 13th, 1694:—

"I am affrayd we shall find but few just and relligious to that degree, as not to think ye particular concerne of England a lawful sacrifice to ye Peace of Europe, so that we may very well say, 'Nolite confidere in principibus nec in filiis hominum.'

"But since ye discerner of hearts knows his M^{ts} intentions to be as right as his cause is just, we have that Providence to rely upon which still governs ye world under every resort, and in whose hands ye wisest heads and ye strongest arms are no more than ye chisel and ye mallet in ye hands of ye workman. Therefore it is that at this time nobody perhaps acts more for ye interest of our master than ye Prince of Orange, who will come to no peace till France be brought back to ye Pirenean treaty.

"This may in time open ye eyes of our ministeers heer and make them see that they have no way to gett well out of this war but by a vigorous attempt upon England.

"I am, &c.,
"CARYLL."

In a subsequent letter of March 21, 1695, Lord Caryll answers his own arguments and gives good reason why the Pope kept his money in the Imperial Treasury, while continental enemies prevented Louis XIV. from risking his fleets and armies in an attack on Great Britain.

Bishop Ellis is the recipient of another important communication from Lord Caryll, preserved amongst the Stuart Papers at Windsor.

"March 21, 1695.

"I am indeed indebted to ye L S for ye favour of y^{rs} of Feby ye 8th, wherby I perceive ye Austrian spirite and Interest reigns wholy in y^r Court wher you are, and that his Hol^s is so besett with men of that temper and factions, that his owne good intentions towards our King, and even his Conscience are born down by ye violence of ye stream, tho' on the other side his great Age, Naples and Milan at either end of his territory, the Germans at his dore, and Russell at ye mouth of ye Mediterranean, may in some measure excuse his pusillanimity in our behalf.

"All that can be expected of his Holinesse is only to relieve ye extreme necessity of thos Catholic subjects of his Majesty who starve for their Religion and their Loyalty.

"If any impression can be made upon him to open his purse it must be done by my Ld Chancellor of Scotland (Lord Perth) who's quallity, piety and sufferings give him all the credite that any one person can have."

The year 1695 saw Queen Mary, wife of the great statesman and undaunted military leader, William III., laid in the grave at Westminster Abbey. This Princess of the house of Stuart had been for eight years dead to her father in consequence of the events which drove him into a foreign land and left his crown at her husband's mercy. Others, besides partisans, have been found to censure the wife for faithful adherence to her adopted family, and an almost chivalrous championship of the remarkable and illustrious man with whom she had linked her life. And, indeed, without joining in the chorus of Jacobite disparagement which pursued Mary to the end, it is impossible not to feel a doubt whether in her case one Scriptural command —viz. to love, honour, and obey a husband—had not been unduly elevated above the plain duty also sanctioned in Holy Writ, which the Fifth Commandment enjoins on children towards their parents. Charitable feelings towards the departed Queen were not pretended at St. Germain, whence Lord Caryll writes on February 2, 1695, to Bishop Ellis at Rome :—" The Princess of Oranges death begins to produce some good effect in Parliament where Dissolution of Parliament was proposed."

Lord Caryll rejoices in a dispute which occurred in the House of Lords (he had written *Commons* by mistake), while the cup of national indignation seemed to James's adherents almost overflowing in England on account of " the grievance of ye new banke, of sending away ye fleet, and of ye injustice of ye proceedings against ye Lancashire gentlemen."

It must be explained that a new national Land Bank, established on landed security, had been formed, and was exposed to the hostility of the Bank of England.* Again, the Marquess of Caermarthen, stationed with a squadron off the Scilly Isles, mistook certain merchantmen for the French fleet from Brest, and retired precipitately to Milford Haven, in consequence of which the French took British merchantships worth a million sterling.† Prosecutions had been undertaken during 1694, at the instigation of informers, against certain Lancashire gentlemen concerned in James's projected invasion from Normandy.‡

"All this shows" (continues Lord Caryll) "a fermentation which wee hope may augment and produce in time the desired effect." This "effect" so anxiously expected was the invasion of England, for which Louis XIV. again prepared during the year 1696, when 20,000 men were collected at Calais, where James himself waited for a considerable time, until despair of being able to command the Channel with their fleet led the French King's ministers to abandon the project.

The Duke of Berwick had failed to obtain promises of immediate action in England, so that, mindful of the disappointments experienced in 1690 and 1692, when the French navy risked and suffered so much without eliciting the promised Jacobite response, Louis declined to proceed upon so inauspicious an adventure.§

A conspiracy to destroy William III. by assassination tended to weaken the Stuart cause at this moment. Not only did this evil design fail ignominiously, but it has recoiled on the heads of men of honour connected with St. Germain, who wished to draw the sword for the recovery of James's crown, but scorned the idea of any dealings with murderers, such as has been falsely attributed to them.

* Smollett's 'History of England,' vol. i. p. 263.
† Ibid., pp. 245-6.
‡ Ibid., p., 215.
§ Macpherson's 'Original Papers,' vol. i. p. 551.

Public opinion in England could scarcely discriminate at first between the various factions severally engaged in plots against their sovereign's life and throne, so that a Stuart restoration never looked more improbable than just before the mortal blow inflicted on the Jacobite cause by the peace which was concluded at Ryswick in October 1697. With regard to this plot it should be mentioned that the Duke of Berwick had learnt from Sir George Barclay that there was to be an attempt to "seize William the Third's person," and hastily left England lest he should be "confounded with the conspirators." On his way from Calais to Paris he met the exiled King of England, and communicated both the failure of negotiations for a general insurrection, and the private conspiracy against his rival.* Both Bishop Burnet and Lord Macaulay have charged James II. with attempting to profit by a scheme involving murder, which exploded utterly within a few weeks of that discrowned monarch's arrival at Calais. Lord Macaulay suggests that this period of doubt should have been utilised by an attempt to apprise William III. of his danger. Dalrymple is a more charitable historian to James, whose religion and sense of honour are said to have precluded any condonation of murder. Considering that James was not aware of any details, and had heard a mere rumour of conspiracy directed rather against his rival's liberty than his life, the justification seems complete.

The intrigues between the adherents of James at St. Germain and the English Jacobites became necessarily less important after the peace, the resources of France being then no longer pledged to support the Stuart cause. But they also became fewer, and were only initiated in England by people of obscure position after it became known that Sir John Fenwick, sentenced to death for complicity in the latest scheme of proposed invasion from France, had revealed the dealings of Marlborough, Godolphin, Shrewsbury, and Russell with the ex-King.†

It was one thing to be prepared for every eventuality, if the treasonable correspondence involved could only be kept secret; but if these communications involved exposure and probable ruin, then the leading statesmen in England were naturally inclined to let events drift. Towards the close of his life, declining health produced in the exiled King himself

* 'Memoirs of the Duke of Berwick,' vol. i. p. 132.
† Macaulay's 'History of England,' edition 1849, vol. iv. pp. 717-718.

a disposition to adopt a policy of expectant inactivity. He passed his life alternately in the cloister and at that health resort which the waters of Bourbon had created.

William III. astutely availed himself of Fenwick's disclosure by calming the fears of the implicated public servants who were necessary to the carrying on of government, while he let them remain conscious of their detection: and during the last two years of this reign no real danger was apprehended from the Court of St. Germain.

It is true that in the first year of the eighteenth century, when he desired to rekindle war with France, King William, with that adroitness for improving each incident characteristic of him, did simulate dread of an invasion, professing to believe a letter of Lord Melfort's to his brother Lord Perth, in which the danger was intimated.* But Lord Melfort was not amongst the ex-King's counsellors at this period, while the wish seemed to be too clearly father to the thought to count as the expression of any well-considered opinion.

On Good Friday 1701, a fit in his chapel at St. Germain warned mankind that the last English King of the elder Stuart line—a monarch found wanting, maybe, in capacity for government, but who had seen divers battle-fields, frequented many camps, and who was also a brave and able naval commander—was about to close his earthly career. From the field of Edgehill in 1642, where with his hapless father he witnessed the first clash of arms between rival parties in the great Civil War, James Duke of York had passed to the quarter-deck of a flagship during the Restoration, when England was struggling for naval supremacy with the Dutch. He was never timorous, and always ready to tempt fortune in the recovery of his kingdom; nor was it until the last few years of a life which survived sixty-eight summers that his remarkable energy gave place to the repose of conventual retreat at La Trappe.

Judged in either of the several capacities in which he became famous, only in that of an English King is he found wanting in sterling merits; nor have the aspersions cast upon his reputation by partisan historians left thereon any lasting stain.

Pity, and a misplaced magnanimity, led Louis XIV., upon James's death in 1701, to acknowledge James's son, the Chevalier de St. George, as King of Great Britain, thus

* Dalrymple's 'Memoirs,' edition 1790, vol. iii. pt. iii. bk. ix. p. 212.

initiating forty-four years of intrigue dangerous to the Brunswick Dynasty, which only became innocuous after Charles Edward Stuart fled from Culloden in 1745. The immediate result of Louis's bold disregard of the peace of Ryswick was another terrible war, which began at the close of the reign of William III. and was ended by Queen Anne, after the protracted struggle, and in particular the victories of Marlborough at Blenheim, Ramillies, Oudenarde, and Malplaquet, had sorely tried the great resources of France, whilst those of England were also seriously impaired.

Early in March 1702, in the first half-year of this fresh period of Jacobite activity, passed to his grave the greatest sovereign of Stuart descent who had worn a crown since the reign of James I. of Scotland, namely William III. of England, renowned as a resolute warrior and adjudged by posterity to rank high as a statesman. The Revolution of 1688, by which, however brought about, he benefited, is acknowledged as the epoch at which the modern Constitution of England took its birth.

This sketch of the royal Stuarts closes with the death of William III.; as it is unnecessary to repeat here comments on the events of Queen Anne's reign, which have already appeared in print, namely in the present writer's article on the Hanover Papers ('English Historical Review,' vol. i. p. 756), and in his volume on the Brunswick Accession (1887).

The appended collection of Stuart Papers affords very interesting illustrations of the hopes and fears which prevailed at St. Germain during the youth of the Chevalier de St. George.

APPENDIX I.

INTRODUCTORY.

THE correspondence of Henry Stuart, Cardinal of York—now in Her Majesty's possession—contains much that is curious, although its ample bulk comprises a variety of detail possessing little or no meaning at the present time. Unfortunately the series is interrupted by wide chronological gaps. The late Lord Stanhope compiled an interesting appendix to his 'History' mainly from this source, but undoubtedly omitted to print holograph letters of the Chevalier de St. George, the Duke of Berwick, and Lord Bolingbroke, which contain statements and allusions bearing closely on the critical years 1714, 1715, 1716.

A careful study of the Cardinal's correspondence seems likely to clear up more than one debated point which has arisen in connection with the Rebellion of 1715. The period between 1685 and 1688 has been elucidated by several family memoranda belonging to the Stuart sovereigns; while the exile of James II., which never closed before his death in 1701, has been rendered more intelligible by certain letters of that unfortunate monarch to his agents at Rome.

After the death of James II. a paralysis seems to have seized the penmanship of St. Germain, so that during the early stages of Queen Anne's wars nothing is to be learnt from those documents which the exiled court thought worthy of preservation. Not a scrap of information regarding the alleged interference of the Chevalier and his advisers with a view to completing the Scotch Union in 1707,* nor a single detail regarding the attempted invasion of Scotland which occurred the year after, is to be found in this collection; although it should be remembered that the letters of Lord Caryll and Lord Middleton concerning these events—and others which fill up gaps in the Windsor Papers—found their way to the Scotch College in Paris, and were transcribed by Macpherson for his 'Original Papers.'

Hence it is that students in the Royal Library have to content themselves, as regards this particular epoch, with such documents as the Declaration published at St. Germain in 1708, before the Chevalier set out on the errand which, in his sister Queen Anne's court, earned him the name "Pretender." The document in question is more able and liberal in tone than any such production that had previously appeared. But this did not atone for subsequent utter failure, nor relieve the exiles of St. Germain from the poverty in which they were involved when their designs exploded. Their pitiable condition may be inferred from the expression of the rejected heir to England's throne, when from the camp-fire in the Low Countries

* Hamilton's 'Transactions,' p. 41.

he wrote to Mr. Dicconson, the Jacobite Treasurer, on Oct. 11, 1709, thanking him for the " help and care " he tendered to the ex-Queen amidst " all the misery of St. Germains."
That loyal attempts were made by devoted adherents to alleviate this misery is shown by the Stuart Papers. We find that Lady Petre sent Mary of Modena no less than one thousand pounds; and doubtless many smaller offerings represented just as much self-sacrifice on the part of the donors.

It will be seen that the earlier view of the Duke of Berwick, concerning Lord Oxford's Ministry, and their intentions towards the Chevalier, was too sanguine, as he learnt from his experience of their after conduct.

The unpublished letters of this remarkable scion of the Stuarts (the son of James II. and Arabella Churchill, who founded the noble house of Fitz-James in France, and had been by rumour pointed out to usurp, previous to the Chevalier de St. George's birth, the throne on which the nation placed Mary, wife of William of Orange), date from the year 1712, and the salient portions thereof (omitted in the Appendix to Lord Stanhope's 'History') have been collected and printed in this volume with letters, hitherto unpublished, of the Chevalier, Lord Bolingbroke, and others.

At the outset the Duke of Berwick evinces a noteworthy trust in his sister Queen Anne's fidelity to her family, and believed that she wished the Chevalier de St. George to carry on the Stuart Succession, time only being needed to ensure the Restoration; otherwise a letter to the Chevalier, dated Oct. 23, 1712, would not have concluded as follows:—

" Its certain that both your Majesty's affairs and their safety would run great hazard if the Princess of Denmark should unfortunately trip of, before your restauration were secured."

Queen Anne seems to have erred on the side of a family affection, scarcely reciprocated by all the members of the elder branch who needed her aid, and received her private sympathy. In editing these letters the writer has striven to let the various persons concerned unfold the great dynastic drama, without unnecessary comment; but it may be well to mention here the manifest importance which was attached to the hope of securing Marlborough's adherence. That he sent money to St. Germain before the Rebellion of 1715, was known inferentially; but the reader may now learn when that promise was made, together with the fact that the amount was 2000*l*., and how Bolingbroke and Ormond reasonably hoped to meet the restored King with friendly co-operation on the part of England's greatest living captain.

It is also rendered perfectly clear that a Restoration was once more prevented, as it had been in the lifetime of James II., by the refusal of the Stuart exiles to change their religion. The Chevalier and his advisers resolutely avoided the subject in documents meant to become public, while the former privately repudiated what he termed a " dangerous dissimulation " calculated rather to estrange friends than attract foes.

The Marshal, Duke of Berwick, stands out in these pages as a wise and far-seeing counsellor to his unfortunate brother the Chevalier; and one of the direst disabilities under which the Stuart cause laboured after the Grand Monarque paid nature's debt, was the Regent Orleans' disinclination to allow Berwick to conduct the campaign of 1715 in Scotland.

James Francis Edward resented this allegiance to France by his half-brother the Duke of Berwick, and the confusion of counsels which prevailed at St. Germain during the Rebellion of 1715, may in no small degree have been owing to this growing coolness between the brothers. But in justice to the Duke of Berwick it should be remembered that, an outlaw from his native England, he had become a naturalised French subject after James II. died, while he also held high command in the army when Louis XIV. passed away.

The Regent Orleans, when, at Lord Stair's instance, he resolved to preserve at least nominal neutrality between the contending dynasties, deemed it contrary to all the dictates of wisdom and prudence to allow the Duke of Berwick, a French officer, to lead the Chevalier's forces on their desperate errand. Mary of Modena, with her usual fairness and perspicuity, seems to have recognised this, and represented Berwick's case favourably to her chagrined son, the Chevalier.

Of Lord Bolingbroke's enlistment in the Chevalier's cause and his conduct of affairs until he was dismissed in February 1716, a detailed account will be found in these letters; while, in studying the several memoranda and communications of this eloquent statesman, readers will be able to gauge the character of that service which the titular King of England valued so lightly.

Although it is clear from these pages that a jealousy between Bolingbroke and Ormond was rendered dangerous to the cause they served by the vanity and instability of the latter gallant nobleman, yet several other reasons of Jacobite disruption will be discerned by careful students of the subjoined correspondence, which must be left to speak for itself in this particular.

It is remarkable, however, that when the Duke of Berwick was acting as intermediatory at St. Germain between Lord Middleton's mock ministry and the Chevalier, the Duke gave constant advice to his brother on the subject of matrimony, urging an early marriage, and if possible an alliance with a daughter or connection of the Emperor's. The allusions to this possible strengthening of the Stuart influence will be found both curious and novel.

A great danger to the Government of George I. appears to have existed towards the end of July 1715, when, as these letters show, the Chevalier called on Lord Bolingbroke to meet him at Dieppe and embark thence for England. Whether, if the Duke of Ormond, when impeached in Parliament, had acted promptly and joined his associates in the West, the result might have been different it is difficult to decide; although such apparently was the discontent throughout Great Britain that the Chevalier's arrival must have created a feeling of confidence and enthusiasm which did not exist when, after the indecisive battle of Sheriffmuir, he reached Peterhead at the end of the year 1715. The key to this situation is, however, to be found in the fact that George I. commanded a respectably organised military force, even before 6000 Dutch soldiers became available, while his opponents were without any continental allies able to assist them effectively, as, owing to the neutral attitude of France, only a small number of French troops was obtained from that country in 1715.

It is certain, moreover, from these papers that the adherents of the Stuarts in England were consistent in their resolution not to move unless the Chevalier came supported by an armed force.

In fact the Peace of Utrecht, for concluding which the Whig party attainted Bolingbroke and imprisoned Oxford, proved the means of the Brunswick dynasty defending itself with success at a crisis which threatened its very existence.

The Stuart Papers sent to Windsor by the Cardinal of York prove that the attempt of the Chevalier de St. George to regain his ancestral throne in 1715-16 was entered upon without prospect of continental support. There was at the outset of the venture no certain combination between the several portions of Great Britain favourable to a Stuart restoration, and at last, when treachery had completely severed such connection as did exist, Scotland was chosen as the theatre of a conflict depending in a great measure for success on the generalship of the attacking party. Lord Bolingbroke's admirable summary of the situation which is contained in his several letters to the Chevalier, now published, illustrates this most completely.

The Duke of Berwick preferred the title and duties pertaining to a marshal of France, together with the retention of his home at Fitz James, to those shadowy honours which his illegitimate connection with the exiled English dynasty entailed; and although his allegiance to the Government of the Regent Orleans and to the country of his adoption justified his refusal to command the Chevalier's forces in Scotland, yet he thereby renounced the position amongst Jacobite worthies which such cadets of the family as Prince Rupert and George Lord d'Aubigny, the latter of whom fell in 1642 at Edgehill, formerly gained.

Under the circumstances which have been indicated, the prospects of the Chevalier's success were not encouraging, and the personal risk undergone by that unfortunate Prince appears greater than historians have generally allowed. Nor has his dangerous progress from Bar-le-Duc to St. Malo and thence to Dunkirk the same romantic interest in British eyes that the escape of his uncle Charles II. after Worcester field in 1650 presented. Lord Bolingbroke advised his adopted master to follow the precedent furnished by his uncle's interesting adventures, writing these words:—" It is proposed that your Majesty should, in the deepest disguise—such, for example, as saved your uncle King Charles after the battle of Worcester —make the best of your way, with a merchant or some such unsuspected person, whom the Duke of Lorraine would undoubtedly find for you, through Holland, embark on board this vessel, and by the shortest cut pass into Scotland.*

On October 28 the Chevalier left Bar-le-Duc disguised as a servant, and reached the coast near St. Malo. It was a long and dangerous journey this from Lorraine to the sea-coast of Normandy, when the policy of France towards the Jacobites remained unsettled; and the Chevalier did not venture to describe his personal experiences in the almost enigmatical communications to his friends at Paris and Rome, which, written in cypher from St. Malo, contain little bearing on the stirring events pending in Scotland.

But the Stuart Papers show that one unwelcome piece of intelligence greeted the unfortunate grandson of Charles I. when the sea-coast was gained. A certain Colonel Maclean, to whom had been entrusted all details of the Duke of Ormond's conspiracy in Western England, had turned informer, and revealed all he knew to the Government of George I.; so that henceforth the devotion of many ardent sympathisers was neutralised during a struggle which could scarcely issue triumphantly unless the wealth of Bristol, Plymouth, and Exeter was at the service of Jacobite adherents in the surrounding country. In such a case the right arm of

---

* 'Stuart Papers,' September 21, 1715, in Appendix to Lord Stanhope's 'History,' edition 1858, p. 26.

the London Executive would have been paralysed, and so rendered unable to deal effectively with simultaneous outbreaks in Ireland, Lancashire, and Scotland.

As a former invasion in the West had resulted in the flight of the reigning King, and a change of dynasty, the success of the Government in crushing the Duke of Ormond's plot in its inception was of signal importance.

The news of Maclean's treachery, which met the Chevalier at St. Malo, never became known to the Duke of Ormond until, after encountering a storm which caused him to put back towards Normandy, he reached the Devonshire coast. There he was told of the imprisonment of Lord Lansdowne and Sir William Wyndham, which had resulted in the revelations communicated to Lord Townsend's administration.

To land under such conditions, when accompanied by only 150 followers, would—notwithstanding the Duke's great popularity—be equivalent to courting certain imprisonment, and probable destruction; so the only Jacobite who really had the ear of the people was prevented from exercising influence on events.

The Chevalier probably scarcely realised the full weight of disaster which the collapse of Ormond's schemes in the West involved, and he was doubtless cheered by favourable rumours regarding Lord Mar's indecisive battle with the Duke of Argyll's forces at Sheriffmuir on November 13, 1715. Indeed, the engagement in question was spoken of generally in Jacobite circles as a victory, by a pious self-deception which is exposed in the letter of Mr. George Camocke to Lord Mar of January 5, 1716.

After learning the failure of the Duke of Ormond's schemes at Plymouth, Exeter, and Bristol, James Francis Edward was encouraged by his friends to make Dunstafnage, in Argyllshire, the place of disembarkation, to reach which part of Scotland from St. Malo involved a voyage round Ireland.

Again, however, were the Chevalier's dispositions changed by the receipt of intelligence that Argyllshire had remained faithful to the Government of George I., and that an important military disposition of Lord Mar's in that country had been thwarted. Orders were, therefore, secretly given to prepare a vessel for the Chevalier at Dunkirk, in order that he might attempt the shorter voyage from that seaport to the coast of Aberdeenshire at a moment when the British cruisers were for the most part said to be in the Firth of Forth, whence Admiral Byng was endeavouring to prevent communication between Lord Mar's detachments at Burnt Island and Leith with the main body around Perth. The Chevalier's journey from St. Malo to Dunkirk, disguised in sailor's attire, involved considerable hardships; as it was performed on horseback in the midst of a severe winter, while, the main roads being watched, he was forced to travel by the less frequented paths and put up with the poorest accommodation. Reaching Dunkirk in the middle of December he found an English man-of-war outside the harbour, while others were watching the Scotch coast despite the above-named pre-occupation of Admiral Byng in the Firth of Forth.

But to the eyes of uninterested spectators in Europe, ignorant of the defeat of the Lancashire insurgents at Preston on Nov. 13, the same day that Sheriffmuir was fought, the situation did, nevertheless, appear critical for the Brunswick dynasty when at last, about the middle of December 1715, the Chevalier set sail from Dunkirk in company with Lord Tynemouth, the Duke of Berwick's son, together with other followers, and after a week's voyage landed at Peterhead on December 22, 1715.

Although the concert with friends in England was shattered by the above-named surrender at Preston, the suppression of the conspiracy in Western England, and the collapse of Jacobite hopes in Argyllshire and the Isles, yet James Francis Edward's prospects seemed to be by no means desperate as to Scotland; as the Chevalier's letter to the Duke of Gordon, written from Fetteresso on Dec. 28, 1715, will prove.

A very slight success, whereby Inverness and Sutherlandshire could have been relied on as a base of operations, might have secured to James Francis Edward the time to recuperate, and receive help in arms and money from abroad, such breathing space being refused when Argyll pressed forward with his army to Montrose in February 1716 (N.S.). This decisive action on the part of the Government forces was not the least expected by Lord Mar, whose escape into France with the Chevalier is excused in the Stuart Papers. Writing to General Gordon, the unfortunate successor in command of the Jacobite forces, the baffled Mar attempts to justify his conduct in a manner which suggests the French proverb *qui s'excuse s'accuse*. But unfortunately Lord Mar's protestations were not limited to self-justification, and we find him chiming in with the gossip of St. Germain, which attributed the lack of success in Great Britian to Lord Bolingbroke's alleged careless inattention during the Chevalier's absence, when, as the Stuart exiles came to believe, their cause might have triumphed if money, arms, and ammunition within reach of France, had been duly despatched.

Lord Bolingbroke denied these charges in his famous letter to Sir William Wyndham, while the Duke of Berwick declared that the Minister "omitted nothing that it was in his power to do." *

Nor should it go unmentioned that a controversy ensued on the subject between Mr. James Murray, who made the charges of treachery, and Lord Bolingbroke's secretary, Mr. Brinsdon, the final portion of which Lord Mar himself is said to have inspired.† One count in that indictment has alone not been explained away, and the Stuart Papers do lend some colour to the Chevalier's complaint that Lord Bolingbroke never wrote to him during six weeks' absence in Scotland, although allusion to certain missing despatches is made by the accused Minister himself when, on January 31, 1716, he says, "My despatches to the King are so very full."

But in this collection Bolingbroke is silent as regards the Chevalier between his embarkation at Dunkirk and his return to France. On the whole it seems probable that letters of Lord Bolingbroke to his adopted master were either intercepted, or lost, together with a sum of money, on board a small vessel which met with shipwreck off the Scotch Coast. See Paper CIII.

The papers transcribed in this Appendix give a clear idea of the wretched state of the exiles and their adherents in France during March 1716. As all historians have declared that the unfortunate son of James II. landed at Gravelines after the Rebellion of 1715-16 had collapsed, it is surprising to find a letter of the Chevalier's from Boulogne, announcing his intention to proceed to Paris *viâ* Abbeville, and expressing his desire that Lord Bolingbroke should meet him half-way.

The titular King of England seems to have appreciated a good glass of

---

* 'Memoirs of the Duke of Berwick,' translated edition, 1779, vol. ii. p. 256.

† Rapin's 'History of England,' vol. xviii. pp. 516-544.

Burgundy in this depressing condition of his fortunes, while, if Lord Mar's hopes were not buoyed up during his campaign around Perth, it was scarcely for lack of the best Champagne. The letters of General George Hamilton sent to St. Germain to quicken the arrival of arms and ammunition prove this, and are very instructive in other particulars.

So striking, indeed, are the extracts from the later Stuart Papers that they will well repay careful perusal, and it is certain they will afford great assistance to any future elucidator of the events to which they relate.

SELECTION FROM THE STUART PAPERS IN POSSESSION
OF HER MOST GRACIOUS MAJESTY QUEEN VICTORIA,
PRESERVED IN THE LIBRARY OF WINDSOR CASTLE.

PUBLISHED BY HER MAJESTY'S EXPRESS PERMISSION.

PAPER I.

*Act of Council explanatory of the Test in Scotland,
November* 3, 1681.

** His Majesty sent forth this Act with his approbation, but great opposition to the Test continued.

The Earl of Argyll had taken this oath devised by the Duke of York, which bound him to maintain the supremacy of the King in Church matters, and the doctrine of passive obedience, and to devise no alterations in Church and State, but the Whig Earl added an explanation that he mentally reserved the right to promote such changes so far as they were consistent with his religion and loyalty.*

Upon this the following specious analysis of the Test Act appeared, and yet the Earl of Argyll was shortly tried and condemned for the very qualification of his oath which the Council had allowed to pass without observation.† Into such tortuous courses did their ill-advised ecclesiastical policy lead the Stuart Kings in Scotland at that time.

" Forasmuch as some have Entertain'd Jealousies and Prejudices against the oath and Test, appointed to be taken by all Persons in Publick trust, Civil, Ecclesiastick, or Military, in this Kingdom, by the Sixth Act of his Majesty's third Parliament, as if thereby they were to swear to every proposition or Clause in the Confession of Faith therein mentioned, or that Invasion were made thereby upon the Intrinsick Spiritual Power of the Church, or Power of the Keys, or as if the Present Episcopal Government of this National Church, by Law Established, were thereby exposed to the hazard of Alteration, or Subversion; all which are far from the Intention and design of the Parliaments Imposing this oath, and from the genuine sense and meaning thereof.

" Therefore his Royall Highness His Majestie's High Commissioner, and Lords of Privy Council do Allow, Authorise, and Empower, the Archbishops and Bishops to administer

* Dalrymple's 'Memoirs,' edition 1790, vol. i. pt. i. p. 10.   † Ibid.

Appendix I.

this oath and Test, to the Ministers and Clergy in their Respective Dioceses, in this Express Sense: that though the Confession of Faith, Ratifyed in Parliament, 1567, was framed in the Infancy of our Reformation, and deserves its due Praises, yet by the Test we do not Swear to every Proposition or Clause therein contained, but only to the true Protestant Religion, Founded upon the Word of God, contained in that Confession, as it is opposed to Popery and Phanaticisme. Secondly, that by the Test, or any Clause therein contain'd, no Invasion or Incroachment is made or intended upon the *Intrinsick Spiritual Power of the Church, or Power of the Keys, as it was Exerced by the Apostles, and the most pure and Primitive Church in the first three Centuries after Christ, and which is still reserved Intirely to the Church.*

"Thirdly, that the Oath and Test is without any Prejudice to the Episcopal Government of this National Church, which is declared by the first Act of the 2nd Session of his Majesty's 1st Parliament, to be most agreeable to the Word of God, and most suitable to monarchy, and which upon all occasions, His Majesty hath declared he will Inviolably and Unalterably Preserve, and appoints the Arch-Bishops and Bishops to require the Ministers in their Respective Dioceses, with the first Conveniency, to obey the Law, in swearing and subscribing the aforesaid Oath and Test with Certification that the Refusers shall be esteemed Persons disaffected to the Protestant Religion and to His Majesty's Government, and that the Punishment appointed by the foresaid 6th Act of His Majesty's 3rd Parliament shall be Impartially and without delay inflicted upon them.

"Extracted forth of the Records of Privy Council by Will. Paterson, Clerk of the Council."

PAPER II.
*Earl of Perth to the Cardinal of Norfolk.**

** Philip Howard, brother to the Earl of Arundel, known at Rome as Cardinal of Norfolk, was Lord Almoner to Catherine of Braganza, and was the Stuart *confidant* in Rome while James II. and his advisers were attempting to change the faith of Great Britain. The Cardinal was born in 1629 and died in 1694. He was a great favourite of the English Court in the reigns of Charles II. and James II., and also at St. Germain during the earlier years of the latter sovereign's exile in France.

If any students of this epoch accept Dr. Lingard's view of James II.,

* This letter is analysed in the last chapter of this work.

and believe that he only desired toleration for his adopted religion, and not supremacy, they should read this remarkable communication from the Earl of Perth to his friend in the Holy City.

"Edinburgh, Feb. 3, 1688.

" May it please your Eminence,
" For all excuse for my silence these months past, I shall only tell y' Eminence that I had so little good news to offer to y' view that I chused rather to be silent than to afflict you with the progress of affaires here.

" I had long ago Designed my Brother to transmitt such accounts as I gave him of matters relating to this countrie to y' Eminence, and so I cannot but think that you know all I could have said, but if y' Eminence do not considder it as trouble to have things from my hand immediately, I shal not fail for the future to write once a month at least. Since my last letter to y' Eminence, one might have hoped that a considerable progress would have been made in y° advancement of y° Catholick Interest; but I'm very sorry to say that wee have advanced litle or nothing.

. " Wee have indeed got the Abbay of Holyrood house Church (which joyns the pallace here—the nef is only up, for the quire fell under Jo^n Knox' fury) to be the chappell of the order of St. Andrew, and when wee have gott it we cannot find whom to give it to. It cost me A pull to take it from the paroch; but now all is quiet upon the point, and I have made bold to ask as a favor from the Trades of Aberdeen the Church which belonged to y° Trinitarians, and by methods I us'^{d} have gott it with their consent. It is to be putt into the hands of a Clergyman, to be equaly for the use of the Clergy and the Regulars.

" The Jes^{ts} are to sett up their Colledge in a house which formerly lodged the Chancellor (it joyns the pallace too); their schools will be opened next week or y° week after. Some little jealousies have been working betwixt them and ye Clergy, but by some endeavors which I employd, and by the which I lost some Degrees of the favor of both sydes, things keep in a tollerablie peaceable condition. Of late wee have got over 6 or 7 monks from Germany, some of them very good men and like to prove able missioners. They would fain be upon the same foot as y° others, but this y' Eminence knows best how to order, for your Zeal and pious Care of these countries will need no sollicitations for the good of the Church here, and y' prudence needs no insinuation to give you aim;

neither am I so presumptuous as to offer to mention anything of that kind save by way of Information.

"There have been very few conversions of late. Some few Ministers, exemplary men, have come in. Many of the ordinary sort, but few in touns; the Ministers and University men are so wild and furious and talk with that Confidence in a very bad cause that the people take their assertion for full proof of their veracity. Some Debates have been amongst the people who are in ye Gov^t. The Duke of Hamilton (who must stil be complaining) has been exercising that querulous faculty on very frivolous occasions, but the truth is, his business is to obstruct the Catholick interest, which I believe will very fully appeare now very soon. Some others wee have here who would fain have us to believe they are our friends, who really are our more Dangerous enemies. Especially some in ye Army, the hundredth man in the which is not a Catholick, and we have scarce any officers of that persuasion, not that they are not to be had; but with all the art Imaginable the King is diverted from any such design as might bring in the Army to us. This is the true state of our affaires at present. Next week I shal give y^r Eminence A far more particular account which will explain this. In the mean time I must beg that y^r Eminence w^d pardon this Blurrd papers being sent to you by one who has all the Deference and respect thats possible to y^r Eminence, but really I have not time to write it over, and I wil not employ another hand than that of

"May it please y^r Eminence,
"Y^r Eminence'^{s} most obedient,
"Most humble, and most faithful servant,
"PERTH."

PAPER III.

*Chevalier de St. George to Mr. Dicconson.**

"From the Camp of Rui—,†
"Oct. 11, 1709.

"Altho I reckon to be soon with you, yet I cannot differ till then telling you how sensible 1 am of all the pains you take for ye Queen's and my service, and particularly for the help and care you are to her amidst all the misery of St.

* Treasurer at St. Germain.
† The last two or three letters are illegible. The word was probably *Ruille*, for *Rouille*, the name of the person employed by Louis XIV. to negotiate peace just before Malplaquet.

Germain's, which amongst all the obligations I have to you for many years past I shall not look upon as the least. I find you are in no hopes of any mony at all, but our army beginning to be paid more regularly, the rest will I hope come in time.

"If, as I believe, in time, this month I shall not want more than the 4000 livres for October, and upon the whole I think my expence this campagne has not been extravagant, for before I went none of you thought I could make it without retrenching or selling, but thank God wee have rubbed it out without either, by the Queen's help and your care, for which, tho I can now only thank you by words, I hope the time will come in which I may do it by effects.

"JAMES R."

PAPER IV.

Duke of Berwick, regarding Lord Oxford's Ministry.
(Extract.)

⁎⁎ This sentence contains a distinct allusion to Queen Anne's participation in intrigues for her brother's succession, the negotiations breaking off, as history shows, on the question of religion.

"St. Germain, Oct. 23, 1712.

"I do realy believe that they meane well for your interest, and that they intend to act with all speed immaginable, but they are so afraid of its being known before the conclusion of the peace that they are unwilling of trusting anybody with their secret; though at the same time its certain that both your Majesty's affairs and their safety would run great hazard if the Princess of Denmark should unfortunately trip of before your restoration were secured."

PAPER V.

Duke of Berwick to Chevalier de St. George.
(Extract.)

"St. Germain, Oct. 30, 1712.

"I hardly believe Harley will open himself entirely.

"I found the Queen in good health last Thursday, and Madame de Maintenon, who happened to be that same day at Chaillot, gave her the same advice as I did about her coming to St. Germain's, and she seemed to resolve to come back hence after our Lady's feast of November; I believe a word of your Majesty's upon that subject will determine the Queen to make a longer stay in this town, which will certainly be the better for her health than the cold cloysters of Chaillot; besides that, it will be the better for your Majesty's interest and for the comfort of your subjects here.

"The Duchess of Berwick, her brother, and my son are most sensible at the honour your Majesty has been pleased to give them in remembering them in y^r letter to me.

"BERWICK."

PAPER VI.

Duke of Berwick to Chevalier de St. George.

⁂ Several of the following extracts from the Duke of Berwick's letters written in 1714 show how anxiously Marlborough's conduct was watched by the Jacobites before the accession of George I., and also demonstrate the enigmatical character of the great soldier's political procedure.

"St. Germain, Jan. 9, 1714.

. . . "as to M. Malbranche's (Marlborough's) affairs, M. Albert (Queen Anne) consents to his taking a turn to M. Fredeling's house (France), and in that case gives him hopes to leave off all vexations and quarrels, even in time to receive him into favour, but M. Oleron (Lord Oxford) says at the same time he believes M. Malbranche (Marlborough) will not effect what he promised, but I believe he will, for he loves M. Agincourt (the Chevalier)."

PAPER VII.

Duke of Berwick to Chevalier de St. George.

"St. Germain, January 28, 1714.

"I believe your Majesty may have had an account directly from Mr. Foster of his discourse with M. Malbranche (Marlborough), however I shall acquaint you that he finds him not pleased with the answer sent him by M. Talon (de Torcy), and says that his health does not permit him to visit M. Fredeling (France) this winter; to the contrary, he says he must take a turn to his natal aire; this is quite opposite to what he had said before, and I do believe the rumour that lately was passed about M. Prothose (Queen Anne) is the occasion of his having changed his mind. He says he will in a few days give a positive answer, but we can guess by this what it will be."

PAPER VIII.

Duke of Berwick to Chevalier de St. George.
(*Extract.*)

"February 21, 1714.

"In my humble opinion you may answer the A letter without taking the least notice of the article about your relligion. Great assurances of your kindness for your sister, esteem for the first minister, but not mention any other, your love for your country, and countrymen, your resolution to mind entirely their happiness and maintaining them in their liberty, property, and relligion."

PAPER IX.

Duke of Berwick to Chevalier de St. George.
(*Extract.*)

** Marlborough stipulates for pardon in case of a restoration. It will be seen by the preceding correspondence that Marlborough, during his sojourn at Antwerp, went so far as to stipulate for a pardon in case a Jacobite restoration was accomplished, and that in return he received "words," the value of which were duly appraised.

"March 13, 1714.

"I had two letters lately from M. Malbranche's (Marlborough's) friend at M. Forster's (England), which I have sent y^r Majesty; be pleased to let me know what answer I shall make about the pardon. I see no harm in it, and we may give to those sort of people as good as they bring—that is to say, words for words."

PAPER X.

Duke of Berwick to Chevalier de St. George.
(*Extract.*)

"St. Germain, March 28, 1714.

"The Queen told me what the Duke of Lorraine said unto your Majesty at Commercy, and I make no doubt but if you were at home the Emperor would not only consent to give you one of his relations, but would solicit it as a great favour from your Majesty. The chief point would be to try if he would now give you one of his nieces, the youngest has but a portion which w^d not be sufficient to maintain you and children, so that the eldest is the only (*sic*) at this time can be of use to you. She is sole heir to the Austrian family and consequently both your Majesty and your posterity would be sure of a large dominion."

The Duke concludes by suggesting the intervention of the Duke of Lorraine, and points out that despatch is of importance, lest the Prince of Bavaria should offer his son as a husband for the lady in question.

PAPER XI.

Duke of Berwick to Chevalier de St. George.
(*Extract.*)

"January 1, 1715.

"Would it not be proper for M. Rancourt (the Chevalier) to endeavour again by the meanes of M. l'Annarie to begett a more particular friendship with M. Errington (the Emperor), whose alliance is certainly the best; if his sisters be any wayse available, and that he would not give a niece, I should be for taking one of them."

PAPER XII.

Mary of Modena to a Lady.
(*Extract.*)

*** The Chevalier must have seen the lady to whom this letter is addressed, and told his mother that he admired her, the lady also owning tender feelings for the exiled Prince.

"April 5, 1715.

"Tho' I was very well pleased to find by the King's letter that he was charmed with you (it is his own phrase), yett I must own to you I was yett better pleased to find by yours that you were charmed with him and the good quality' God has given him, for I take you to be a good judge and no flatterer."

PAPERS XIII. AND XIV.

Extracts from Letters of Duke of Berwick to Chevalier de St. George.

"M. Malbranche (Marlborough) had writt to his friend that he would be glad to see him next month. I have advised him to make a visit, if it does no good it can do no harm. (April 27, 1714.)

"If M. Oleron (Harley) be a knave, as I much fear he is, he will take that occasion to have at least a vote passed in the two houses against your Majesty.

"I am glad M. Trever is gone to M. Malbranche (Marlborough), for at this conjuncture he may find out what this man thinks. (May 9, 1714.)"

Marlborough's answer was indecisive. (June 22, 1714.)

The Duke of Berwick still harped on the proposed marriage with a daughter of the Emperor.

PAPER XV.

Memorandum of the Duke of Berwick.

"Nov. 28, 1714.

"For the present situation of affairs all that can be said to the King's friends in Scotland is this:—

"That the King is firmly resolved to goe himself in person to them as soon as possibly he can, and to carry me along with him,* that a little time must be allowed for getting together what is necessary, especially for raising of money and for taking measures with friends in England, without which little good is to be expected. The King is now actually about this that for.the better keeping the secret, the King's friends must not insist to know the precise time of disembarking, but that he will give them sufficient warning that they may meet him; in the meane time they must keep up their harts, without giving jealousy to the government, and they must give him regularly an account how matters stand.

"BERWICK."

PAPER XVI.

Duke of Berwick to Chevalier de St/ George.
(Extract.)

"Dec. 7, 1714.

"I do not much reckon upon M. Malbranche (Marlborough), but still we shall soon know his answer to M. Trever."

---

* The Duke of Berwick had leave from Louis XIV. to serve the Chevalier at this time.

Paper XVII.

Duke of Berwick to Chevalier de St. George.
(Extract.)

⁎ The Duke mentions a curious intrigue proposing to gain the fleet, which seems to have come to nought. There is no reply from the Chevalier to this letter to be found among the Stuart Papers.

"St. Germain, Dec. 7, 1714.

"Last night M. Ennis told me of a brother of Arbuthnots starting tomorrow for Port Mahon (Minorca), where he is a captain, and, at the same time, proposed my writing to try if the fleet could be gained. The business is of such consequence that, by the Queen's advice and consent, we determined not to loose this opportunity, and that has made me make use of your Majesty's name, which I trust you will not disown. The Queen had a little scruple in my getting in my letter by your Majesty's order, but I own I think it no lye, for you have often ordered us all to do, on occasions, what was best for your service, and the naming your Majesty in such a material manner was absolutely necessary.

"BERWICK."

Paper XVIII.

Duke of Berwick to Chevalier de St. George.
(Extract.)

⁎ The Duke writes from St. Germain, January 6, 1715, urging the advisability of enlisting Bolingbroke in the Jacobite cause, and pointing out the particular advantages likely to accrue to that Minister thereby. Bolingbroke is to be requested to send his opinion of the situation.

"Jan. 11, 1715.

"Your Majesty desires to know what I think of M. Hatton (Oxford).* I think I have already given you an account of him. Few people know what to make of him. For my part I am persuaded he loves nobody so well as himself, and will never Publickly take any party but that of the Parliament, where he thinks to be always the top man. However, it is good to marry him, and may be he will by degrees be brought further than he is aware. M. Sably (Bolingbroke) is the man I wish would work hartily."

---

* The Duke at this date has doubts as to the amount of support ready in England, but says that Orbec (Ormond) will speak plain and immediately.

PAPER XIX.

Duke of Berwick to Chevalier de St. George.

"St. Germain, January 26, 1715.

"I saw yesterday M. Julie, who told me that in case Sably (Bolingbroke) answered not the first letter, a second ought to be writt; he assures me M. Hatton (Oxford) is still violent for the high church, and is gone to the country about the elections.

"My Lord Stairs came to Paris on Wednesday night. I forgot to give your Majesty an account of my having made the King of France your compliments upon the new yeare; he ordered me to return you his, and with great protestations of kindness.

"BERWICK."

PAPER XX.

Duke of Berwick to Chevalier de St. George.
(*Extract.*)

"January 29, 1715.

"Malbranche (Marlborough) is now omnipotent with Horne (Elector), but I wonder very much that for these three weekes no letter is come from M. Trevers. I fear this latter is fallen sick.

"My Lord Stairs was this day at Versailles, he made me my Lord Churchill's compliments.

"BERWICK."

PAPER XXI.

Duke of Berwick to Chevalier de St. George.
(*Extract.*)

∗∗* This extract contains the first allusion to the money which Marlborough sent to the Jacobites before the rebellion of 1715.

"St. Germain, Feb. 23, 1715.

"Upon the whole, I believe your Majesty will find that nothing is yet in reddiness, nor can be soon; I think no time should be lost in forwarding Hook into Germany, and I wish some one would be found to send into Holland the enclosed M. Dicconson opend, thinking it for himself, but we believe it for your Majesty—it contains very little, only Malbranche's (Marlborough's) small banking suggestions; however, I am glad to find Trevers is not dead.

"BERWICK."

Paper XXII.

Duke of Berwick to Chevalier de St. George.

"St. Germain, March 24, 1714.

"I heare Lord Churchill has refused to receive his pay of Captain-General, so he serves gratis the Elector.

"BERWICK."

Paper XXIII.

Chevalier de St. George to Duke of Berwick.

"March 29, 1715.

"I received yesterday yours of the 13th, and immediately went about the papers you ask for. The power of borrowing mony I have writt over again, and put the signet to it as you desire. As for the Commission, here is as ample a one as Ld Middleton could draw, but as he dos not know the due form those papers should be in, and that in the mean time this is sufficient, why might not you consult Doran about it, or even employ him to draw one, leaving out the name, which I can fill. I know nobody but one Fitzgerald can write the Chancery hand, and am ignorant what coulour of wax should be made use of. In fine, tis impossible with imploying those people to have it done in due form, but if you think that my writing out this in parchment, and fixing the great seal to it, to be sufficient, I can do that out of hand, having here the wax prepar'd for a Declaration or Protestation.

"Ld. Mid. knows nothing of the form of these things, which never pass through the Secretary's Office, and if one is not sure of such a Commission's being done in due form, 'tis needless to go about it, since this I send you is out of form as strong and sufficient as possible.

"I wish Mr. Pemberton may be prevail^d upon to carry over these papers with my letter. My instructions to Cameron will become now useless, besides that some things in them are out of doors. I see 'tis thought he should not go, and indeed Philips is sufficient. I am persuaded he is honest, and he is certainly not disagreeable to Orbec (Ormond), and may be very usefull as he is now necessary.

"I am of your opinion that to avoid tracassaries one should let the different correspondences take their course, but I own to you I am frightend when I see so many people trusted by Orbec (Ormond), who should certainly by prudent means be made more close.

"I give the Queen an account of one I saw from him this morning."

PAPER XXIV.

Duke of Berwick to Chevalier de St. George.
(*Extracts.*)

*** At this time Marlborough sent the promised funds. The important paragraph which mentions his present is distinguished by italics.

"St. Germain, April 14, 1715.

"Your Majesty knows of M. Sably's (Bolingbroke's) arrival. I reckon to see him very soon, he may be very useful to M. Rancourt (the Chevalier).

"I fancy Orbec (Ormond) will soon, whether he will or no, be found to take these measures for his own preservation. I wish he may determine to stand buff at Alencon (England) against Horne (Elector).

"*I have writt to Malbranche (Marlborough) to thank him for his present. Talon (de Torcy) was of opinion that it ought to be received.*

"BERWICK."

PAPER XXV.

Mr. Thomas to Mr. Innes. (*Extract.*)

*** Mr. Thomas, a Jacobite agent, writes from England on April 16th, 1715, regarding the repeal of the Triennial Bill. The Jacobites in England clearly looked hopefully to Marlborough both at home and at St. Germain at this moment.

"As soon as the Bill passes its talkd his Majesty (George I.) designs for Hanover—what sort of Government we shall then have God knows.

"Argile every day gains ground of the Good Duke of Marlborough, nor are there wanting traytors every day to foment mischief."

Paper XXVI.

Chevalier de St. George to Duke of Berwick.
(*Extract.*)

"April 26, 1715.

"I could wish it were in my power to follow Farnham's advice of letting my friends in England prudently know that Orbec (Ormond) is at the head of my affairs, but what considerable friends have I besides himself?"

Paper XXVII.

Chevalier de St. George to Duke of Berwick.

⁎⁎⁎ Bolingbroke comes to France, and is trusted at Ormond's desire.

"April 30, 1715.

"Having writt to the Queen about Cameron, I have nothing to say here but what relates to Bointon alias Sably (Bolingbroke), whom I hope you will have seen long before this comes to you.

"Farnham's letter is, I think, a very reasonble one, and will, I hope determine you. . . .

"I think it is a very good sign that Orbec (Ormond) desires Sably (Bolingbroke) may be trusted, and as the last may be of great use and help, I have at a venture writt the inclosed to him, which, if the Queen and you approve of it, you may deliver or send to him yourself; 'tis certain no time must be lost, and that makes me lose none in writing letters which at worst are but so much pains lost.

"But mony and arms are the point, and in that I can but remember you of them, tho that is, I am sure, very useless when I consider your forwardness and zeal for my service.

"J. R."

Paper XXVIII.

Chevalier de St. George to Lord Bolingbroke.

⁎⁎⁎ This is the first letter from the Chevalier to this remarkable statesman.

"May 1, 1715.

"It hath been a sensible satisfaction to me to hear from good hands of your good inclinations towards me, of which I am the more sensible that I cannot attribute them to the effect of your present circumstances, having solid reasons to believe you have been long since in the same sentiments, and that your zeal for my sister while she liv'd and for the wellfare of our Country join'd with them have rais'd that unjust enemy which obliged you to quit England.

"I do on these accounts share in a particular manner with what hath befaln you, tho I look upon it at the same time as a Providence which by this means affoords me in your person a more prudent adviser and a more powerful sollicitor with the French court than any other whosoever. I hope before this comes to you you will have had some discourse with the D. of Ber., which renders useless my inlarging much on matters here.

"I would very much have wished, as I do yet, to have been able to have seen you myself, but your safety and my service are inseperable, tho if I cannot have that satisfaction I shall be glad at least to hear from you in writing or by a discreet person what your opinion is as to my affaires at present. I shall depend extreamly on your advice, and do not doubt but that you will do your uttmost to serve me in this critical conjuncture; you shall allways find me most sensible of it, and ready when ever in my power to give you the most essentiall proofs of my esteem and kindness.

"JAMES R."

PAPER XXIX.

Duke of Berwick to Chevalier de St. George.
(Extract.)

*** Written after the Duke had seen Bolingbroke. Lord Bolingbroke left England on March 26, and must have been nearly a month in France before he saw the Duke of Berwick, and by committing himself to the Chevalier's cause broke a promise he had given Lord Stair.

On the other hand, the revengeful conduct of the triumphant Whigs in England may be pleaded as having changed the situation even as it existed when Bolingbroke saw Lord Stair immediately after arriving in France.

"May 1, 1715.

. . . " he (Bolingbroke) says Orbec (Ormond) is honest, brave, popular, and willing, but must be guided by some wise people, to which affect he will write to the Bis of Roch (Atterbury), to Lord Lans (presumably Lord Lansdowne), and to Sir Wil Wind (Sir William Windham), of whose honesty by principles he can answerr for.

"Sably (Bolingbroke) said North and Grey was a brave, honest man by principles, but that very few others were so—interest is what has now made them rightly inclined. . . .

"I will send Sably (Bolingbroke) a declaration to examine, he is violent for the prerogative, and never said a word of relligion. He pressed M. Rancourt (the Chevalier) marrying. He said not a word of Montague though I mentioned him on purpose, but said Sir Th. H. (Sir Thomas Hanmer) would be trusted by a great many, even by more than Sir Th. knew of."

PAPER XXX.

Chevalier de St. George to Duke of Berwick.

⁎⁎⁎ The love affair languishes.

"May 3, 1715.

"The account you give me in yours of the 1st of Bellay's (Duke of Berwick's) conversation with Sably (Bolingbroke) is very comfortable, and would well deserve a letter from me had I not sent you one already for him, which being, I think to write a second would be too much, and that the hast I made to write the first ought to be kindly taken by him, so that I think all that is necessary is to Desire you will let him know that after I had writt to him you had given me an account of what passd between you, that I was most sensible of his fresh and reiterated protestations of being ready to serve me, that I hope his solicitations with Mr. Rose (King of France) and his partners would be as effectuall as I was sure they would be pressing on his side, and that tho I should be very loathe to impose any thing on him that he might think dangerous for himself, yet that I could not but desire extremely to have at least one conversation with him. and that I was sure that might be contriv'd with great secrecy. He is soon, I find, about leaving Paris, that nick of time would be the best, and his friend, Long Robin (?) might facilitat his journy, which none here need know but Sir Thomas (Sir Thomas Hanmer) whom he does not seem to be so shy of. Sably (Bolingbroke) seems to have so much trust and confidence in you that I am persuaded you may induce him to what you so much desire, and I may well think myself sure that you will do your part in this after having done it so well already in relation to Sably (Bolingbroke) and all other matters, in which Mr. Rance (Mary of Modena) and Mr. Janson have done you justice, and I am most sensible of it.

"You did very well to oppose his going so far off Paris.

"Since he is so much for Rancourt's (the Chevalier's, i. e. 'my') mariage, why might it not be propos'd to him to go to Blois to stay there, a fine, pleasant country, and where he may have an occasion of seeing pretty Miss and of even negociating that affaire if t'other faills, as I believe it will after what I acquainted the Queen with some days ago.* But this is only a thought of which you will consider with the Queen, and then say as much and as litle to him as you please. The proposing the thing would certainly be agreable to him, because it shows a confidence, tho it should after come to nothing, tho I see no other choice if t'other fails.

"I cannot but approve extreamly all you have agreed on with him, and hope soon a solid plan may be made, in which I think no time should be lost, no more than in Sably's (Bolingbroke's) coming here and soliciting Mr. Rose (France) on the main point, and tying up Hasty's hands when the time comes. I suppose when he desires his correspondence may pass through Tallon's (de Torcy's) hands you are not excluded, so I shall send to you any letters may be proper for me to write to him.

"You have justify'd me so amplley to him Sably (Bolingbroke) that I am (sure) he will no more be shy of me, and if we saw one another I am sure we should part very well satisfyd with one another.

"J. R."

Paper XXXI.

Duke of Berwick to Chevalier de St. George.

_{*} Lord Bolingbroke is very cautious. Marlborough writes to St. Germain.

"St. Germain, May 6, 1715.

"I have received the honour of your Majesty's of the 3rd and 1st instant. I have writt two dayes agoe to Sably (Bolingbroke), and as soon as I have his answer I will not fayle to send him your Majesty's letter for him. He parts the end of this week for Orleans, and M. Talon (de Torcy) is to see him on Thursday next. I will also endeavour to meet with him, though it is difficult, by reason of the great precautions he loves to take. I very much dout that he will venture going to see M. Rancourt (the Chevalier), and realy it would be impossible without being known, for M. Rancourt (the Chevalier) cannot absent himself, nor Sably (Bolingbroke) travel without the knowledge of Lord Stairs. I have just

---

* The "pretty Miss" is probably a daughter of the Duke of Lorraine.

now a letter from Malbranche (Marlborough), which I have not uncyphered. I have sent to Paris to M. Tunstall for the Cypher.

"BERWICK."

PAPER XXXII.

Chevalier de St. George to Duke of Berwick.

"May 9, 1715.

"Booth brought me yesterday yours of the 6th. I did foresee there would be great difficulty in contriving a meeting between Rancourt (the Chevalier) and Sably (Bolingbroke). But if Bellay (the Duke of Berwick) could sometimes discourse with the last, it would supply that, but the journy Sably (Bolingbroke) makes will render that also impossible, and I fear will make the good dispositions. M. Rance (Mary of Modena) says she found M. Rose (King of France) and Talon (de Torcy) in, very much cool, for you know how much importunity may do when from a person esteemed and in vogue as Sably (Bolingbroke) is; but I see no remedy, nor can Sably (Bolingbroke) be hindered from doing what he thinks not only for his own safety, but for my service also.

"I hope you will find some occasion of letting him know that I have deliver'd him from his female teazers,* so that his secret shall be managed as he could wish, and I address to him by no other canals than Talon's (de Torcy) or Bellay's (Duke of Berwick). If others would make use of the same it would be much better for my affairs, and more agreable I am sure to me.

"I think that I have already writt to the Queen that I approv'd Mr. Ines' proposal of making up what Castelblanco (Lord Melfort's son-in-law, and a merchant) proposd to the number of 1000 arms, but the difficulty is to find the mony, and I know of none we have by us but that of M. L'aumarie's, which if Mr. Rance (Mary of Modena) and you agree to it, I consent should be entammé on this occasion, for the time presses, and I am very sure by employing it this way, we shall not act against the intention of the giver.

"I am sorry to hear your health is not quite settled. I hope the country air will not prejudice it, and cannot but take very kindly of you that you intend to take frequent

* First and last, Lord Bolingbroke complained bttierly of the female politicians at St. Germain.

trips to see Talon (de Torcy), for you are my only solicitor, and time presses extremely.

"I hear M. Pemberton is in great streights as to mony, now though I c^d have wished he had not intruded himself so much into business, yet being in it he must be managed and not sleighted. What if 50 pounds were given to young Lesly for him, or had we better stay till we see whether he returns here or not. Pray let me know what you and the Queen think of it.

"J. R."

PAPER XXXIII.

Chevalier de St. George to Duke of Berwick.
(*Extract.*)

*** One Sir John Forester desired to initiate a rising in England.

"June 18, 1715.

"As to Sir John Forester's project of arms, our want of mony dos but too positively decide that question. Besides methinks they are very dear and might be cheaper bought in France, and more easily conveyd from thence, but besides that I cannot pretend to understand these matters, I leave the determination of them entirely to you, when we can get mony for such uses.

"His project for getting officers from Spain and ships to convey them is a very good one if feasible, for since I can have no troops, the more officers I can get the better."

* * * *

"I was overjoyd to hear Mr. Rose's (King of France) indisposition was so well over, for you know how much depends upon his life, what I ow him, and what I expect from him."

PAPER XXXIV.

Chevalier de St. George to Lord Bolingbroke.

"Commercy, July 2, 1715.

"The accounts I have had from the bearer are such that it makes our meeting absolutely necessary, and when you have heard him I beleeve you will have no difficulty in the matter. The bearer will be help to you in conducting you here with all secrecy, and I must conjure you not to lose a moments time in setting out towards me; my impatience to see and discourse with you is equall to the esteem and confidence I have for you, and to the importance of the present conjuncture, in which I should be loath to make some certain steps, or determine any material point without your previous advice. I do not doubt but we shall agree very well when we meet, that we shall find ourselves both of the same mind in most points and equally forward to undertake some thing out of hand. Referring to the bearer, I shall add no more here, but to assure you of the great and sincere friendship and kindness I have for you.

"You know my hand and the bearer knows you, so I beleeve you will like it better that I neither sign nor address this letter."

Paper XXXV.
Chevalier de St. George to Duke of Berwick.

"July 9, 1715.

"I received last night yours of the 4th, and send you here inclosed the letter to the K. of Sweden altered as you desire.* I suppose you have burn'd the credential and letter to Hook. I said so much by Cameron that I can add no more till this new promised messenger comes, after which I hope in God I may soon be able to part myself. I hope means may be found that I may carry some ready mony with me, for what can be done without it or without credit mony, in obtaining which pray lose not a moment.

"I see no reason for thinking affaires seem to lag in England, for I cannot conceive anything wanting but my presence in the Island, therefore neither time nor pains must be spared that I may be once sett a flotte."

Paper XXXVI.
Duke of Berwick to Chevalier de St. George.
(Extract.)

₊ The Duke is speaking of the Chevalier's prospects.

"July 16, 1715.

". . . but be it as it will, he must goe with a little in his pocket rather than not at all, and leave the rest to Providence; his honour is at stake; his friends will give over the game if they think him backward, as no doubt they will, in short, no delay must come on his side."

* At this time the Jacobites were trying to enlist Charles XII. of Sweden in their cause.

PAPER XXXVII.
Chevalier de St. George to Lord Bolingbroke.
"Bar, Friday night, July 18.

"I have ordered Mr. Inese to give you an account of a message I have just receiv'd from our great friend on t'other side (Ormond); you will see the necessity of losing no time, so I shall part the 28th and the 30th at Diepe, where I desire you will be by that time, that we may embark together.

"This messenger knows not of your having been here, so I addressed him to Mr. Inese, to whom I shall refer you, but could not but write, however, these few lines to one who, after having given himself to me in adversity, will, I hope, before it be long, enjoy with me the sweet of better days.
"J. R."

PAPER XXXVIII.
Chevalier de St. George to Duke of Berwick.

⁎⁎* First doubt expressed as to the great French general accompanying his brother in the coming campaign.
"Bar, July ye 23, 1715.

"Father Calahan has decided all things as you will know before this comes to you, so that I have nothing to say in answer to yours of yᵉ 14th, only to explain that I meant yᵉ 10th of August, new stile.

"Nairn has orders also to acquaint you with all particulars, and therefore in yᵉ hurry I am on I shall not repeat them here; I heartily wish your health may be soon established, and that in acting as your heart wishes you will certainly act as I could wish, for, after all, differring your journey eight days after me, is putting yourself in great danger of never getting over at all, and your presence at first in Holland will be, if possible, of yet more consequence than in the suitte; you know what you owe to me, what you owe to your own reputation and honour, what you have promised to the Scotch and to me, of what vast consequence your accompanying of me is, and at the same time no one can know so well as yourself, what Mr. Rose⁸ (King of France) intentions are at bottom, and what he thinks in his conscience and in his heart*; all this being, I cannot but persuade myself you will

---

* Louis XIV. had raised a demur, owing to fear of offending the British Government. See Duke of Berwick to Lord Mar, on Feb. 12, 1716.

take on this occasion the right parte, and it would be doing you wrong to think otherwise, I shall not, therefore, bid you adieu, for I reckon we shall soon meet, and that, after having contributed as much as you may do to my restoration, you may in a particular manner share of ye advantage of it.

"J. R."

PAPER XXXIX.

Chevalier de St. George to Lord Bolingbroke.
(*Extract.*)

*** He creates Lord Bolingbroke an Earl. Although deprecating delay as fatal if prolonged, he does not like to act against the advice of his friends, particularly that of Lord Bolingbroke.

"Bar, July 26, 1715.

"I find too much solid reason and sincere zeal ine y^{rs} of the 23rd,* that I cannot but dayly more and more applaude myself for the choice I have mad of you. I cannot, you know, as yett give you very essential proof of my kindness [but the least I cann do for so faithful a servant, is, in least, in sending you the enclosed warrant, which raises you a degree higher than my sister had done before, and which will fix your mark with me beyond dispute.]† I hope you will take this mark of my favour as kindly as I meane it."

PAPER XL.

Mary of Modena to Mr. Dicconson.
(*Extract.*)

"August 2nd, 1715.

"I know nothing so bad as all these uncertaintys that caus endless Delays, which will at last (and I fear very soon) make the game Desperat; you do very well to writt, tho you have not much to say—pray continue to do it, for I like very well to know the bad, as well as the good of everything, and so dos the King, who would know but litle of anything if William did not writt.

"The relation of St. Germain's misery makes me sad."

She would speak to Madame de Maintenon regarding the comfort of these poor people, and concludes:—

"I pray God give us all more patience, or some suddain relief one way or another.

"M. R."

* Published in Appendix to Lord Stanhope's 'History.'

† The bracketed portion of this letter of the Chevalier was published in a note to Lord Stanhope's 'History,' 5th edition, p. 136.

PAPER XLI.
Lord Bolingbroke to Chevalier de St. George.

⁎ The first letter from Lord Bolingbroke to the Chevalier preserved in the library of Windsor Castle. The pressure put upon Lord Bolingbroke to join the Jacobites by the Chevalier de St. George and his followers had been extremely strong.

"Aug. 3, 1715.

"Sir,

" I did not intend to have writ to y^r Maj^{sty} till this evening, and then to have given you an account of my silence and of ye state of y^r affairs; but the inclos'd letter coming this moment to my hands and there being I hope time to send it by the post, I thought y^t a moment should not be lost in communicating it to you.

" I say nothing of an officer settled att Brussels who is said to correspond with some about y^r Maj^{ty} and to be trusted by people who go backwards and forwards between y^r Court and Mary's (England), because y^r Majesty will have had y^t account already.

" I keep my letter open no longer than to return y^r Ma^{ty} my most humble thanks for ye last instance of y^r goodness, and to assure you that ye uttmost Duty, affection, diligence, and Zeal shall influence me in every step of my conduct for y^r service.

"I am, &c.,
" BOLINGBROKE."

PAPER XLII.
Lord Bolingbroke to Duke of Berwick. (Extract.)
After his first interview with the Chevalier.

⁎ The Duke had written from Fitz James, July 19, counselling delay; as, though Scotland was prepared for the Chevalier's arrival, the arrangements of the Duke of Ormond in England were in a backward state. The Duke of Berwick's health was then indifferent; but he wrote,—" I am doing what I can to be well that I may be in a condition to act as my heart wishes."

" Bar, August 6, 1715.

" I find Rancourt (Chevalier de St. George) very much sett on his journey, and cannot heare with any patience of a long delay. He promised Sably (Bolingbroke) by Cameron that he would have patience for a month counting from thence; but after that, doth he not find things ready on this side; I feare I shall scarce be able to hinder him from passing the sea, as he cann, and as he certainly will, for after all what a conjuncture is this, all this nation (meaning Great Britain) is in a flame, and his person single now will, I am confident, do more good than an army joined to it some months hence."

PAPER XLIII.

Lord Bolingbroke to Chevalier de St. George.
Objects to Ormond seeing the Chevalier.

" Fitz James, Aug. 15, 1715.

" I have nothing more to give your Majesty an account of, only in my last I forgott to speake about M. Rancourt's (the Chevalier's) desire of seeing Orbec (Ormond); this last has also a great mind to it, but Talon (de Torcy), Sably (Bolingbroke), and Bellay (Duke of Berwick) are positively against it, for 'tis impossible Orbec (Ormond) can make that journey without it being known, and it would give a new handle to the Whiggs to make a noise, and even to clapp up many honest men, who by that will become incapable of doing any service.

" BOLINGBROKE."

PAPER XLIV.

Duke of Berwick to Chevalier de St. George.
(Extract.)

"August 20, 1715.

"You will be pleasd to lett me know who shall take of Agincourt (England) in case Malbranche (Marlborough) parts with him. I have writt to-day to Trevers, and I bid insist about Agincourt (England), as also that Malbranche (Marlborough) will repair to Alencon (England) to meet M. Rancourt (the Chevalier) at his arrival there.

" The Duke of Leeds was heare with me some days agoe; he expressed great loyalty, and is full of great projects. I told him he must communicate them to Orbec (Ormond) and Sably (Bolingbroke)."

PAPER XLV.

Lord Bolingbroke to Chevalier de St. George.
(Extract.)

** The Duke of Ormond, when living in great state at Richmond, being impeached in Parliament, neither relied on his great popularity nor

applied the torch to the smouldering insurrectionary movement which threatened to explode iu the West of England, but escaped into France.

" Paris, Monday night,
August 7, 1715.

" S^r,

" Your Maj^{ty} is already informed of ye Duke of Ormond' arrival att this place, and you will hear from ye Bearer ye reasons he has had to alter his first resolution of going direct to attend y^r M^{ty}.

" There will be this advantage through Delay, that he will be able to assist in bringing things to a certainty here, and when he has the honour to see you, to inform you more fully of ye state of y^r affairs."

PAPER XLVI.

Chevalier de St. George to Lord Bolingbroke.

*** The Jacobites had clearly no trust in Marlborough.

" August 23, 1715.

" I write what follows in a sheet apart that you may be able to shew the letter itself to Charles whom I mean by Orbec (Ormond).

" I believe you forgot to send me a letter concerning Marlb., which D. Ber. mentions to me, so I cannot say anything particular as to that more than you know as much as I of that correspondence, and, therefore, I leave it to you and D. B. to send such a message to Marl. as you shall agree on, for 'tis not fitt to let this even for him nice occasion pass without endeavouring to make use of it for the gaining so considerable a man.

" I am glad you give me caution not to name him to Charles (Ormond), though, should Charles know of the Dealings I have with t'other another way, it would be certainly yet more grievous to him.

" Could there be no possibility of uniting these two great men, at least in some measure, for, after all, as to Charles (Ormond), I did not see what jealousy he can have for him, for sure he Charles cannot think that I would ever bring t'other into competition against himself. When I see Charles (Ormond), would it not be proper for me to say something to him as to Marl., which in discourse can be better done than by writing; but 'tis a nice point in which I desire your advice.

" J. R."

Paper XLVII.

Chevalier de St. George to the Duke of Berwick. (Extract.)

₊ The Duke of Shrewsbury, acting with Argyll, had been the means of preventing Lord Bolingbroke from becoming Treasurer after Queen Anne's death, himself accepting the White Staff. His adherence strengthened the cause of George I. at the time of the Brunswick Accession, so that any subsequent change of opinion was specially welcomed by the Jacobites.

"August 23, 1715.

"D. Shrewsbery's being so frankly engaged is a great article, you will do well to forward a kind message to him from me, and such a one as you believe may be most agreable to him; I think that will be sufficient, because of a particular which your mentioning him to me puts me in mind, for 'tis my intention you should be acquainted with all, tho' particular facts do not occur all at once, and so cannot be communicated to you, but present contingencies renew the memory of past transactions.

"As for the pardon mentioned by M. Iberville, there never was such a thing asked for, but some months ago Lady Westmorland writt the good dispositions her nephew was in, and on that I writt a letter to that Lady to be shewd to him, but the whole was only in general terms, and I do not remember I had any return to my letter from D. Shrewsbery, so that your entering into a close correspondence with him will be necessary, for without one enters into details all is time lost.

"This particular of Lady Westm. is only to yourself and Charles (Ormond), because I believe that Lady would be very cautious of the secret of what her nephew may have said to her."

Paper XLVIII.

Chevalier de St. George to Lord Bolingbroke.
(Extract.)

"August 25, 1715.

"The accounts I have of Humphrey's (Louis XIV.'s) state of health are such as threaten a sudden end, and therefore I think nothing ought to be neglected for to court his nephew."

PAPER XLIX.
Lord Bolingbroke to Chevalier de St. George.
(Extract.)

"Vaugirard, near Paris,
"Monday near six in ye evening.
(No date.)

" Sir,
" The Valet de Chambre who brings you this letter is just returned from Versailles, and would no longer defer sending to you, since tho' ye King is not dead, his Death is equally sure. Mons. de Torcy sent me word that ye gangreen is got into his belly, and y^t he must dye in few hours.

" Since this I have seen another who comes with like account from another friend. All centres in Overbury (the Regent Orleans); for God sake let me know whether I should not, or rather Charles (Ormond) ask to see him and speak to him in your name; he is left Regent.

" Tho' I never saw Ld Peterborow, yet his conversation with Iberville seems to answer perfectly the character I have had of him.

" Your intimacy with him makes you the most proper judge of what may most contribute to dipp him."

PAPER L.
Chevalier de St. George to Lord Bolingbroke. The writer is apprehensive of the death of Louis XIV.

" Tuesday, 27th August,
at 8 at night.

" To E. Bol.
" Your Cousin brought me yours of last night an hour ago. I reckon the good King dead before this, and therefore too many advances cannot be made to the Regent. By my last I authorised you to speak to him from me, that is now necessary and more natural for you to do it than another, being in the post I placed you, but that doth not hinder Charles (Ormond) from going also—I even think 'tis proper for you both to do so.

" What is to be said in particular and how far Overbury (the Regent Orleans) should be trusted I leave to friends with you, tho I do not see how trusting him now can be avoided. Talon (de Torcy) can advise you in this, and when the Queen arrives you will concert with her what further is to be done in that respect. Talon (de Torcy) can also advise whether I should write to Overbury (the Regent Orleans), and what is the form with him. When you see the Regent you should mention particularly our pension, which I hope he will continue. Our circumstances are sufficiently known, and for him not to continue it would, methinks, be not a very generous beginning of a Regency. Our pension need be only given to the Queen byr name, by which means hanover can have nothing to say against it. I expect to hear from you by to-morrows post, as you shall from me in that case. At present I have no more to add. The Queens parting from hence was well nick^d. You will, I suppose, discourse with her about the proposal made to you of a mariage, for that would now be of great consequence."

PAPER LI.

Chevalier de St. George to Lord Bolingbroke. (Extract.) The amount of Marlborough's gift to the Jacobite exchequer is mentioned.

"August 28, 1715.

"You did very well to advise Ralph (Duke of Berwick) to make one last effort more with the Lawyer, I mean Samwell (Marlborough), whose two thousand pound I desire may be remitted to Paris and put into Mr. Dicconsons hands, that out of that Andrews landlord mony may be reimbursed.

"Pray let Ralph (Duke of Berwick's) know this, it being all I have to say to him in answer to his of the 25th, being a litle press'd by the posts Departure.

"I wish Ralphs (Berwick's) credit with his new master (the Regent), may be equal to his good will to serve me with him. May I ask you in confidence on what terms they are?

"The Ld Danby has writ me a loyall letter in general terms, which I answer in the same. It seems he has addressd himself to young Lesly; I wonder he did not rather do it to Charles (Ormond) or George (Bolingbroke); however I shall not in my answer name either of them without knowing first their opinion whether they would trust themselves to him.

"I shall follow your advice as to Samwel (Marlborough) when I see Charles (Ormond). The freedom with which you write to me is most wellcom and agreable, your advice necessary, and your great experience of no less advantage to me so new in great affairs. I must confess mine at present seem to press very much, and yet I see no possibility of taking a prudent resolution till I see Charles (Ormond), and know more of Mary's (England's) intentions by him.

"I am very glad Charles (Ormond) secretary and t'other gentleman have made their escape—its to E. Portmore you'l consider what should be said to encourage and manage him. I send to the Queen the English letters you sent me."

PAPER LII.

Lord Bolingbroke to Chevalier de St. George. A letter written piecemeal, and of some importance, being indited when Louis XIV. was dying.

"Sir, "Paris, Aug. 30, 1715.

"I have the honour of your letters, and shall take the best method in my power to execute your orders, and to answer all y^r views. The great danger I was apprehensive of is over; all will certainly submit without ye least struggle to Overbury (Duke of Orleans), and he will by consequence be under no want of assistance from his neighbours, but remain att liberty to pursue the general interest of his own and his neighbours estate.

"George (Bolingbroke) has never had to do either in good or in ill with Overbury (Duke of Orleans), and therefore he imagines yt as there can be no prepossession in his favour, so there can be no prejudice against him in the breast of the latter.

"The trusting Overbury (Duke of Orleans) is of indispensible necessity, if his friendship and concurrence in your cause be so. Besides when Ralph (Duke of Berwick) took occasion two days ago to speak to him concerning your interests, he said that he was appris'd of all that had been done and of ye present state of them.

"There are two or three points in y^r letters which I cannot answer without consulting Talon (de Torcy), and to him I have writ. But I believe the letters to Mr. and Mrs. Stoner were sent, when the last application was made to them by Harry (King of France).

"Bennet arriv'd yesterday. I believe I shall have ye honour of seeing yt person to-night, and shall after that close my letter."

Paper LIII.

Lord Bolingbroke to Chevalier de St. George.
Announcement of the demise of Louis XIV.

"Sep. ye first.

" I had ye honour to wait on Bennet as proposed, but I kept my letter open so long ye next morning in expectation of having somewhat very possitive to write concerning Harry (Louis XIV.) that I lost ye post. Last night Harry (Louis XIV.) continu'd in ye same uncertain languishing way—when I use ye word uncertain, I mean it only wth respect to time —for all recovery is to be despair'd of, but ye progress of ye distemper being sometimes quicker and sometimes slower, ye hour, or perhaps ye day cannot be prefixed.

" It is impossible for George (Bolingbroke) to do anything yet awhile with Overbury (Duke of Orleans) there must be four or five days of convulsion before a settlement.

" As I am writing *precise news* of ye King of France's death and yt my letter may go this night by a Courier, of the Duke of Lorraine, ye former dyed this morning, as ye person tells us, att a quarter after eight.

" I must make haste, but I must tell you that Ralph (Duke of Berwick) has adroitly enough struck into ye interest which joyns to secure Overbury (the Regent Orleans) Power.*

" A certain Battle may perhaps not be forgot, but this is a real service and will cancel former risques. I think in my conscience you have nothing to fear, and a great deal to lose from Overbury (the Regent Orleans).†

" Danby (son of the first Duke of Leeds, and in English parlance second holder of that title) is a madman. I have talked freely with him, because I do not care to have any great reserve, but he can be of no use, except in the moment of Desperate attempt.

" General compliments gain'd him, general compliments will secure him.

---

* The Duke of Berwick's favour at the Regent Orleans's Court led to the permanent naturalisation of Berwick as a Frenchman, and in consequence he refused to accompany his brother the Chevalier to Scotland.

† The Regent trimmed, but threw his influence ultimately on the side of George I., detaining Berwick in France when the presence of that soldier was needed most in Great Britain by the Chevalier de St. George.

"Port— (Lord Portmore) is an officer worth securing. I send compliments from you to him. I am called upon for my letter. I hope it may go by ye Courier, if not it will go by ye post.

"I am, with all duty,
"BOLINGBROKE."

PAPER LIV.

Lord Bolingbroke to Chevalier de St. George.
(Extract.)

"September 3, 1715.

"In ye state of your affairs, your Majesty has little to lose by Treaty; and yet I think it prudent not to admit anything which may hereafter be an incumbrance to you or which might at present, if known, be prejudicial to y^r interest att home.

"The Duke says he will speak to the Regent about my waiting on him, in your Majesty's name as soon as it is proper —in my present hurry it is hardly to be done, att least he will give little attention to Foreign business till his own affairs are entirely settled.

* * * * *

"I think it is plain that no strength can now be found to oppose the Regent. He is absolute master of France. His expressions of friendship to your Majesty, and of good will to your cause, are I am sure very welcome to you; but they seem to me to point to very distant services, and in ye mean while I doubt that things precipitate too fast in England and Scotland to bear much delay."

PAPER LV.

Chevalier de St. George to Lord Bolingbroke.
(Extract.)

"September 3, 1715.

"All seems ripe in that Country, the dangers of delay are great, proposals of foreign help are uncertain and tedious. On t'other side right measures should be taken, some probability of a secure passage and landing, and some sort of concert with friends with Martha (England)."

Paper LVI.

Mr. J. A. Murray to Chevalier de St. George. (Extract). The writer, the second son of Lord Stormont, was then Acting Secretary to Lord Bolingbroke, and afterwards went to Lord Mar in Scotland.

"September 3, 1715.

" Sir,

"Since my Ld Bolingbroke finished his letter to your Majesty he has been taken a little ill and is gone to bed, But commanded me to inform you that Earl Mar was retired privately from London into the Highlands of Scotland and is under great uneasiness, that there is no autherity to act by in that country in case the necessity of affairs should bring things to ane extremity there."

The writer subsequently expresses suspicions regarding Lord Athole's fidelity.

Paper LVII.

Memorandum sent to England by Lord Bolingbroke, September 3, 1715. Reflections on the situation after the death of Louis XIV.

*** Lord Bolingbroke, notwithstanding he was too sanguine regarding the Regent Orleans, had a clear conception of the procedure which he thought should be adopted, and it is worthy of notice that he at this moment expected James Francis Edward to land in Scotland—a view the Minister was subsequently led by the progress of events to discard.

"He (the French King) is dead this morning, Septr 1st, N.S., and the alteration occasiond by his death must be explained.

" Had there been any Dispute in France about the Regency, &c., the Whigs would have had a fair game, there will be none, our Friends may depend upon it, and likewise upon this, that the Duke of Orleans is under no engagements against us, but thinks of English affaires, as his Unkle did.

"It will require some time to settle his Regency and to extricate the Government out of the Difficulty they lye at present under, after which perhaps more is to be hop'd for from France than before. But these views as well as those of money from Spain and Troops from Sweden are distant, and liable to accidents—therefore the King thinks to get ready to come to some parte of the Island as soon as possible, tho he

R

will in all probability come with very few people about him, with little money, and without the additional arms which were hop'd for from France.

"In this case it may be of use that our Friends in Scotland and England lose no time in sending the best advices they can about the place of his Landing (which 'tis thought must be in Scotland), Signals, &c.

"In case they will not have him come yet a while they must determine their intermediate conduct, and regulate his.

"The Duke of Ormonde and Lord Bolingbroke think that it would be for the King's Service for them to be with him, but their Friends are to order them what to do, they are ready to go to him to-morrow or to continue to play less in sight.

"If our Friends resolve to begin immediately they must send notice to all parts to rise at once, and to execute the projects concerted, and they may depend on the King's coming or perishing in the attempt."

PAPER LVIII.

Lord Mar to Gordon of Glenbucket, the Marquess of Huntly's Baily or Factor. (Extract.)

"Sept. 8, 1715.

"You must say nothing of it to anybody except it be L'd Huntly, but I have accounts from Athole that they expect (as they beg) that we may come that way, and much depends on our being soon there, else the Duke may do something to be uneasie to us."

PAPER LIX.

Lord Mar to Gordon of Glenbucket.
(Extract.)

*** This extract from a letter, now at Windsor, will serve to illustrate the Jacobite leader's perplexities. Writing from Invercall (Invercauld), Lord Mar sarcastically laments the moral defection of Farquharson of Invery, the general co-operation of whose followers was necessary to the prosecution of the opposed campaign.

"Invercall, fryday night,
"Sept. 9, 1715.

"That good friend of the King's Invercall has used all the tricks he could to intimidat the people of this country, Bromar (Braemar) and Strathdon, from comeing out, but non of his storys or insinuations have done so much towards it as his makeing them believe that non of our neighbours are to stirr, and particularly my Lord Huntly's men."

Gordon of Glenbucket, as has been said, was Baily to the Marquess of Huntly, and in the absence of the Duke of Gordon, detained by the Government of George I. at Edinburgh, it was of the last importance that the clansmen generally should know of the Gordon fidelity to the Chevalier's cause. Hence the following appeal on Mar's part.

" Let me know as soon as possible what I may expect in this, and for Godsake make Dispatch as to our general meeting, for I have now some of my men here and out of Strathdone together. I'm unwilling to let them seperat again, and it will be hard keeping them if they lay still here long and do not march, and I cannot go into A—le (Athole) w^t these few men of mine alone, or until I know certainly the day you can join me there.

" Thers more depends on our drawing to a head and meeting togither soon than most of our friends seem to be awarr of, wch makes me the more anxious and pressing about it.

" They are so weak at Stirling and so ill-payed that they scarce know what to do, insomuch that their general, Whitham, is gone for London to represent it and is not a thousand pitys that we should loose so luckie an opportunity.

" My most humble service to my Ld Huntly if he be w^t you I know I need not bid you show him this, and if he be not, you'll take care to send him an account of it. I'll be impatient to hear from you and I am

" Your most humble servant,
" MAR."

PAPER LX.

Lord Mar to the Laird of Glengarry.
(Extract.)

"Sept. 11, 1715.

" By all the accounts I have, I hope, in God, our affairs are going well. They write me that the Duke of Orleance (sic) has declaird that he'll assist the King more than ever his Unckle did, and that it is not doubted but he's by this time at sea.

" I have mett w^t aboundance of difficultys and disappointments since you left me, and mostly occasiond by my ungratefull landlord, who beside his own withdrawing, has done all the mischife by his bad example, malicious storys, and otherwise his weak understanding was capable of, tho now, blest be God, I hope the worst of it is over.

"Lord Huntly acts the honourable parte I expected of him, and Glenbucket, his Baily, is very diligent. I have reason to hope that some of the Strathpay people will join him.

"Lord Huntly's men of Badenoch, Strathavine, Glenlivet, Glenrinis, Auchindoun, and Cabrack, as Glenbucket just now writes me, were in armes yesterday, and he writes me too of Clunies diligence, wch w^t you write makes me long to see him and give him thanks in our master's name. The Athole people are reddy against we come near them, and L. Drummond is gone about his men, as I hope, Ld Bredalbain and some others in Perthshire are busie about theirs.

"The low country gentlemen are mostly reddy to join us upon the first advertisement. . . .

"Thers on thing in our scheme of the midle district wch we found necessary to alter since you was here, and that is the makeing our first rendevous in the Highlands and then to march down togither in a body to be joind by the gentlemen in the low country, when we will be able to protect them and ourselves too, wch had we mett in the low country, we would probablie have come in stragling and separat parties, and so been exposed to some danger, and beside, by this way we are now to follow we will take some of our neighbours along w^t us."

PAPER LXI.

Chevalier de St. George to Duke of Ormond, under cover to Duke of Berwick.

"September 15, 1715.

"In answer to yours of the 12 I have nothing to say as to business more than Lord Bolinbroke will acquaint you with, But as to our meeting I am more impatient for it then I can express, and since now there are no more obstacles to it, I shall with impatience expect that satisfaction as soon as you are a little more acertaind of O-brians (the Regent Orleans) dispositions, and that Boll (Bolingbroke) has settled something as to a private business with which none but the Queen and you are to be acquainted, and of that I should be glad to have some account by you, reckoning still that that will not delay your journy many days.

"I hope you will be satisfyd with all that Boll (Bolingbroke) will tell you from me, and convinced that I am far from backward on the present occasion, or in a disposition to give ear to fearfull counsells, had I any, which I thank God I have not. Hoping soon to see you I have no more to add here, but to assure you of my esteem and kindness.

"J. R."

Paper LXII.

Substance of a Memorial sent to England by Lord Bolingbroke. The Regent Orleans veers towards England.

"September 20, 1715.

"That since the last Memorial sent in cypher to Mr. ——— things have been put on a worse aspect in this country.

"That the Duke of Orleans, tho he is possessed of the Regency absolutely, he seems determined to keep the measures with Hanover and the Whigs into which he entered before the death of the late King.*

"That he has ordered the ships at Havre to be unloaded, and has promised not to suffer them to sail.

"That this connivance at the measures which the King shall take is very uncertain, but that his opposition to them, if the secret, or any parte of it, gets the least wind, is very certain. That he has discountenanced some who acted for us here, and expressed disaprobation of the help promised us from other parts.

"That we are at last flatly refused the troops we expected.

"That the money was promised before the King of Frances death, but that since his death the receiving it becomes very dubious, and will prove at best extream dilatory.

"That notwithstanding all these dis-appointments which providence has thrown in his way, the King determines to attempt the getting into Brittain.

"That his friends in Scotland are in the best condition to receive him and in the greatest want of his presence, if the report of the rising of the Highlands be true.

"That wherever he go's the rising must be general in al parts of the Island, so as to distract the forces of the enemy, or he can hope for no tolerable success.*

---

* This paragraph deserves special attention.

"That therefore his friends in England ought to take their resolution once for all, to lose no time in concerting the execution of their designs at home, in concerting measures with his friends in Scotland, and in giving him notice of their proceedings, and of their sence of things, and these points are most earnestly recommended to them."

PAPER LXIII.

Duke of Berwick to Chevalier de St. George.

(*Extract.*)

"September 25, 1715.

"I send your Majesty heare enclosed a letter I received this night from Trevers. It seems to agree with all we have from England, that is (to) say, that the King is expected by everybody. All this concludes for his Majesty's parting as soon as possible. I wish the Duke of Ormonds journey retards not the King's departure."

PAPER LXIV.

Duke of Berwick to Chevalier de St. George.

"St. Germain, Sept. 29, 1715.

"I have not had the honour of writing to y^r Majesty this long while, having been obligd to be running backwards and forwards since the King's death, besides that the Queen has given your Majesty an account of what has passed. We have been doing all we could in the present conjuncture, but all that is to be hoped is that France will not oppose your Majesty in case matters be carry'd on with secrecy; the chief and essential point is your getting through the Kingdom to gain Scotland. Lord Bull (Lord Bolingbroke) has sent Flanningham down to prepare a vessel. As soon as it is ready I do humbly conceive your Majesty ought to loose no time; none can follow you for fear of making a noise that may stopp your journey.

"When Bull (Bolingbroke) leads, Sheldon and Cammock must find ways to meet you on the sea side; and when your Majesty is sail'd, all others must make the best of their way to several ports and get shipps to carry them over to Scotland.

"The Spanish Ambassador will not have an answer this fortnight, but when it comes, if it is to be favourable, money will easily be sent after, and will be alwayse welcome.

Appendix I.

" Belley (Duke of Berwick) would fain part at first, but Fredelings (France) present master seems not willing to allow it; he has desired me to assure your Majesty that if he can possibly find measures to overcome the difficulty he will, with great zeale and hartiness part, but at present he cannot answer positively. Mr. Robinson (the Chevalier) knows that Bellay (Duke of Berwick) proposed to himself about two year and a half agoe. The same reasons of duty and affection subsist, and if he does not goe it will be a most terrible mortification to Bellay (Duke of Berwick).

" I shall write next post to Malbranche (Marlborough) and press him very hard to tell what he will doe if ever M. Rancourt (the Chevalier) visits his friend at Alencon (England) or in the neighbourhood.

" BERWICK."

PAPER LXV.

Chevalier de St. George to Lord Bolingbroke.
(Extract.)

*** The explanation of the Duke of Berwick (see Paper LXIV.) regarding his non-attendance on his brother in the expedition to Britain, was regarded by the Chevalier as vague and unsatisfactory, even allowing for the French citizenship claimed by Berwick, and his high position in the Regent's army.

" Oct. 2.

"It would be doing a great wrong to Bellay (Duke of Berwick) to doubt of his willingness to accompany Robinson (the Chevalier and as Robinson (the Chevalier) knows that nobody can hinder Bellay (Duke of Berwick) if he be resolved to go, so he dos count he will the minut he shows such a desire of it. I have said all that can be on that subject already so I shall add no more of it here."

PAPER LXVI.

Duke of Berwick to Chevalier de St. George, giving reasons for not going to Scotland. (Extract.)

" October 7, 1715.

" The instant it is in my power either to accompany your Majesty, or to follow, I will doe it, but your Majesty knows where the difficulty lyes, and that I am not my own master.

" I find by all the letters that the highlanders are in a good posture, and that Hanover (George I.) is in great concern, not knowing who to trust. If Malbranche (Marlborough) would play him a trick it would make up for the past, though I can hardly hope he will have honesty enough left him for so good and great a deed. We think either Ormond or Bolingbroke should go with the Chevalier."

PAPER LXVII.

Chevalier de St. George to Lord Bolingbroke. (Extract.) Written after receiving the above communication from the Duke of Berwick.
"Oct. 10, 1715.

"Ralph (Duke of Berwick) is incommunicable and incomprehensible, that as the surest way at present is the best, I have directed D. O. (Duke of Ormond) to say nothing to him of the present resolutions. Ralph (Duke of Berwick) is now a Cypher and can do no more harm, and if he withdraw his duty from me, I may well my confidence from him. I must confess I cannot but suspect that he hath been sooner or later the cause of the strange diffidence they have of me at the French court where he never did me good, and where I would never put it in his power to do me harm.

"Duke Ormond will speak to you of him, and of all the rest I have to say. . . ."

PAPER LXVIII.

Mary of Modena to Mr. Dicconson. Written from Chaillot.

⁎⁎* Just at the time of the Chevalier's expected departure from Bar, there was a question as to whether the gold necessary for his journey should be forwarded by post.
"Oct. 16, 1715.

"I did not see Bointon (Bolingbroke) last night, and upon reading again the King's letter, I find he was not to leave Bar till Munday night, so that I cannot hope to see him till tonight, and in this uncertainty I have writt to Mr. Inese to keep the gold in his hands till he hears again from me, but I am convinced it must not be sent by the post, and have writt him word so, which is all I can say till I see Bointon (Bolingbroke).
"M. R."

Appendix I.

Paper LXIX.

Mary of Modena to Mr. Dicconson. Written from Chaillot. (Extract).

"Oct. 21, 1715.

" The Duke of Berwick is writt you from me, I suppose he will tell you the small progress he has made in his affairs, but Ld Bullingbrook has delivered him the King's order and Commission ; he says he must consult mor yet, before he resolves."

Paper LXX.

Duke of Berwick to Lord Bolingbroke. This letter embodies the resolution indicated above.

"October 21, 1715.

"I just now, My Lord, receivd y^r letter with the King's paquet. Nobody can be more sensible of the King's trust and confidence in me, but no-body more mortifyd than I not to be able to obey the King's commands.

" I will try what my conscience and honour will allow me, for my inclination, ambition, and personal glory bids me comply with the King's command and the desire of Scotland."

Paper LXXI.

Lord Bolingbroke[*] to Chevalier de St. George. Written from Paris after an interview with the Chevalier.

" October 18, 1715.

" S^r,

"Mr. Murray attends your Maj^{ty} according to y^r orders with the money and ye Seals, the rest of y^r commands are for ye greatest part already punctually executed as far as relates to me.

" Mr. Campion and Mr. Courtney are actually gone, fully instructed and heartily determin'd to venture everything in y^r service, the first by way of Cherburg into Cornwall, the latter by ye coast of Havre into Devonshire. Att each of these places I have advice that a boat is ready for their

---

[*] Lord Bolingbroke's conduct when directing affairs having been impeached, it is adjudged desirable to place before the public such letters as bear upon the management of the Chevalier's expedition to Britain in 1715-16.

transportation, pursuant to ye directions which I sent Arbuthnot before I waited on y^r Majesty.

"Mr. Kenyon sets out for the North of England, where his acquaintance and interest lyes, tomorrow, and in a few days after Zechy Hamilton shall return to London, the reason of my deferring his journey shall be explained by and by.

"The Duke of Ormonde will be ready to go off from hence on Monday night, and by the care of your faithful servant Arbuthnot, everything will be ready for him as soon as he arrives on ye Coast."

Lord Bolingbroke proceeds to tell how one of the Chevalier's vessels had been denuded of her crew by the threats of the French officials who believed that "ye way to make their Court" was to "appear against" the Chevalier's interest, while the difference between the autocracy exercised in the time of Louis XIV. and government by a Consultative Council or "Board," as prevalent under the Duke of Orleans' régime, is then described.

After stating the desirability of dissipating the hostile atmosphere prevalent in the Regent's Court, by diplomatic measures, and assuring the Chevalier that Lord Ormond's departure should not be delayed by the above-mentioned disappointment at Havre, Lord Bolingbroke sums up the situation in the following masterly sentences. They not only contain the creed of the young-England politicians who flourished in the middle of the nineteenth century, but also embody the views of later democratic Toryism.

["The more I think of it, the more I am convinced that it is absolutely necessary y^t ye Duke of Ormonde should, on his arrival in England, instantly disperse some popular paper among the people, and that declarations and letters should be ready to fly about to all parts in ye very moment of time when y^r Majesty is arrivd, or is upon y^r arrival. This is not my private sence alone, but ye joint opinion of ye Duke and of every man here who knows anything of the present state of that Country. What the methods of carrying business formerly might be I am ignorant, but of late years those have done it best who have by frequent and plausible appeals to ye people gain'd ye nation to their side; since the decay of ye Monarchy and ye great rise of ye popular power without, since the Whig schemes took place, we have been forced to combat them at their own weapon. By these means we brought the bulk of England from a fondness of war to be in love with peace, by ye same means have they been brought from an indolent desponding submission to Hanover to arize and exert themselves in y^r cause. The same methods must be pushed, and ye same topicks must be insisted upon, or the spirit will dye away, and y^r Maj^{ty} will lose that popularity which is, allow me to use the expression, the only expedient that can bring about your restoration.

"I know what may be said, and what perhaps is said, that the Nation is engag'd, and so many considerable men are dipp'd, that popularity is the less to be regarded, that I beseech y^r Maj^{ty} to take ye word of a faithful servant, and to judg of me and others as you find this to be true or false. If the present ferment is not kept up, if ye present hopes and fears are not cultivated by an industrious application of ye same honest art by which they were created, you will find ye general zeal grow cool, and a new set of compounders arise."] *

"The use made of all this is humbly to desire yr Maj^{ty} that you will please to let me have y^r letters to ye Fleet and Army, sign'd by yrself, and ye Declaration too if you shall have approv'd it, and I will undertake in very few days to have them printed off, so as to go with you, or in a day or two after you. I will likewise send you by Cameron letters for ye Universitys and City of London, which you will please to return me, and they shall be ready too.

"Such copy of all these papers as your Maj^{ty} leaves behind you when they are printed, shall be sent several other ways into England, and shall be instantly reprinted att London.

"I keep Zechy Hamilton, whom I shall trust alone in this matter—for ye printer shall not know what he prints—and he shall afterwards proceed to London, and take care of what is to be done there.

"The Duke of Ormonde may go att ye time appointed, but he may likewise be by some accident or other retarded, in all events your Majesty shall have punctual and timely notice. There is a story given out, which I can neither tell how to beleive or disbeleive, of a design to attack ye D. of Ormonde on the road. Mr. Murray will acquaint you with it.

"Certainly Hanover and his faction begin to think their affairs in ill plight; perhaps they may come to imagine that they have nothing else for it but to intercept y^r person.

---

* The bracketed portion has been published by Lord Stanhope in the Appendix to his 'History.'

"I mention this only to repeat ye suggestion I have always dwelt upon, y^t nothing can render y^r cause desperate but an exposal of y^r person in y^r passage.

"I could heartily wish y^t Champion might be come back to ye coast of Britanny, before your Maj^{ty} sail'd, which he will attempt *coute qui'l coute!*

"I shall write more fully to you on this head tomorrow, and shall have some intelligence perhaps to give you.

"I beg y^r Maj^{ty} to take in the best part all I take ye liberty to mention, and ye freedom I use, which proceeds from a heart fully devoted to y^r service. I am, S^r, with respect, y^r Maj$^{ty s}$ most Dutiful subject and faithful Servt,

"BOLINGBROKE."

PAPER LXXII.

Lord Bolingbroke to Chevalier de St. George. (Extract.) This letter, written Oct. 20, two days after the last, instead of one as promised.

** Lord Bolingbroke succeeded in getting the confidence of one M. d'Effiat, and from him elicited the scope of that shifting neutrality, which the great English statesman desired to render both permanent and favourable to the Jacobite interest.

The moment was evidently approaching when events would shape themselves either favourably to the elder branch of the British Royal family, or secure to George I. the throne upon which the mistakes of his English predecessors owning kindred blood had placed him.

Jacobite manifestoes were at this time dispersed over the United Kingdoms of England, Scotland, and Ireland.

"He who I have just nam'd encreases daily in his confidence with me. I met him for ye second time since my arrival here last night—the impossibility of giving that connivance which promis'd unless measures are taken to render ye French passive in ye several ports, and to shew them that it is not the Regent's intention they should in any case, where they have not his positive order, act against your Maj$^{ty s}$ interest, was pres^d upon him.

"He agreed in opinion, assured me that ye D. of Or (the Regent Orleans) was surprisd att what had pass^d at Havre, promisd to renew his instances on this head, and to press ye Marechal d'Huxelles, with whom he does not know y^t I have any concert, to concur with him."

On the whole, Lord Bolingbroke was confident he would retrieve the disaster inflicted on the Jacobite cause by the death of Louis

XIV., while the situation did not seem quite so intolerable as when all the coast was closed.

In a postscript to this letter, indited on October 21, 1715, the Chevalier's distinguished adviser utters these reflections:—

"I broke off my letter yesterday in hopes of news from England, and also because ye Queen thought fit to keep Cameron till to-day, that she might by him give y^r Maj^{ty} an account of ye Duke of Berwick's final resolution to whom y^r paquet has been this morning sent. There are letters of this day seven night from London, which do not answer in all points my expections. Lord Mar encreases in strength, but has not advanc'd so far as we thought.

"Lonsdale, Vivian, and Coulston, and many others are taken up.* The storm grumbles in ye West, but is not yet begun, and Hanover takes what measures he can to prevent it."

Urging that the Duke of Ormond should start for England some time before the Chevalier, Lord Bolingbroke repeats a warning regarding care of his master's person, which appeared in the extracts given from his last letter. He says:—

"Let me most earnestly renew my request that you will leave no possible precaution neglected to disguise y^r person and conceal y^r departure and route.

"I shall be thought timourous by those who take want of foresight for courage, and I confess I am so where ye safety of y^r person is concerned."

Lord Stair is well known to have exercised judicious espionage on behalf of the Government of George I. at this crisis, and we have the fact recorded by Lord Bolingbroke.

"Stair has some jealousy that you or ye D of Ormond and myself, are in motion, or all three. He has people on most of ye roads, and two are this morning gone towards Rouen.

"I believe the posture of affairs in England, as much as any appearances here make him thus alerte. I cannot penetrate yt he has any jealousy of y^r Maj$^{ty's}$ way of going off.

"I will do my uttmost by several little expedients which I have thought of to perplex him and to put him on a wrong scent."

---

* Lord Lonsdale was originally in the interest of George I., but joined the Chevalier's standard.

PAPER LXXIII.

Duke of Ormond to Chevalier de St. George. (Extracts.) Contains an account of the former's interview with the Regent Orleans.

" October 21, 1715.

"I have received the honour of your commandes by my L'd Boll (Bolingbroke), and accordingly design to sett out for Caine (Caen) on Wednesday next in the evening. I am sorry I can't have the honour of waiting on you, but I hope in God that you will have a safe passage and a happy arrival in England, where I shall endeavour to meet you with a good number of your subjects. None will more impatiently wait for your landing than I shall doe. I hope you will take care to be well disguised.

"I must now inform you, S', of what I hope will give you some satisfaction. On Thursday last in the evening I had a private audience of Mr. O'Brien (the Regent Orleans), who made me many excuses for not having allowed me that honour sooner, but gave me the same reasons as most of his countrymen in his business has (*sic*) done, the great measures they were obliged to keep with the people on the other side the water, but att the same time made great professions of his concern and friendship for you, he has agreed to give you a great number of arms and ammunition."

After stating the benevolent neutrality which was to characterise his policy, the Regent agreed that a M. Le Blanc, resident at Dunkirk, should be trusted to work with the Duke of Ormond and arrange the secret aid to the Chevalier's expedition.

The adherents of the elder Stuarts were destined to learn a great deal too much about these "professions" of the new French Ruler.

The Duke of Ormond reserved certain important solicitations for the postscript of this letter.

"I must beg of your Maj'y not to speake of this to any one, Mr. O-Bryen (the Regent Orleans) having made me promise that I should keep the secret, I have only told it to the Queene. L'd Boll (Lord Bolingbroke) knows nothing of this,* it being desir'd by Mr. O-Brien that he should not."

---

* What chance Lord Bolingbroke possessed of performing his duties with success, when promises of "arms and ammunition" were kept secret from that responsible minister, the reader must judge.

Paper LXXIV.

Anonymous. (Extract.)

⁎* It was reported at this time that an Irish Protestant named " Kelli " purposed to assassinate the Chevalier; but beyond the *ipse dixit* of an anonymous French writer, whose written assertion remains to this day amongst the Stuart Papers, the rumour has no foundation. The anxiety of Lord Bolingbroke regarding his master's safety may have proceeded from this mysterious source.

After speaking of the would-be assassin as a Protestant, and describing his appearance, the document runs as follows:—

" Le Kelli, dont le portrait est en dessus, va a Bar pour tuer le Roy d'Angleterre d'un coup de pistolet ou de poignard. Luy mesme s'est offert pour cela determiné a la mort, et content de procurer par là a ses enfants la recompense qu'on luy a promise.

" On pretend qu'il a receu 800 pièces pour les frais de son voyage."

Translation:

" *Kelly, whose description is given above, is going to Bar to kill the King of England with a pistol shot or a dagger. He has offered himself for this, resolved on death, and glad to procure in this way for his children the reward which has been promised him.*

" *It is said that he has received* 800 '*pieces*' *for the expenses of the journey.*

Papers LXXV., LXXVI., LXXVII.

Extracts from three communications of the Chevalier's to Lord Bolingbroke, dated respectively October 21, 23, 25, 1715, the latter having been written three days before he left Commercy for the coast en route to Great Britain. They are contained in one enclosure.

" Commercy, Oct. 21, 1715.

" Mr. Murray gave me last night yours of the 18th, and this goes by a servant of mine who is calld to Paris for his own private business. I am glad you have already dispatchd some of our messengers, and that D. O. (Duke of Ormond) was soon to part, pray God he be not stopp'd at the sea side, for as to what Stairs should have said I think it is not much to be feared, and I own I am not a litle concerned at the ships at Havre being stop'd, as one may well call it, for that shews the generall disposition, and how my own ship can scape that fate I cannot well imagine; however, I trust in Providence it will, and I must certainly take my venture as to that, tho I am clearly of your mind of not setting sail till I hear from England, for all affairs are now in so good a way that we must not spoil all by an ill tim'd impatience."

"October 23, 1715.

"I beleeve you'l wonder to be so long without having an answer from me, but I have been these two days expecting Cameron every moment, and would not send away my express till he came. I begin to hope he may bring me the news of D. O. (Duke of Ormond) being gone with some further assurance from you of an absolute connivance on Overbury's (the Regent Orleans) part. The good news we dayly receive will, I hope, contribute to it, and nothing, I am sure, will be neglected on your side in that respect, and tho the courtship made to Boynton (Bolingbroke) on his return to Paris has more the air of self love than friendship, yet I cannot but draw a good omen from it.

"Ld Mar's behaviour on this present occasion is such that I thought I could not too soon give him marks of my favour, so that I have made a new Draught of the Commission to be drawn in which I give him the title of Duke, and leave out the restricting him to act by the advice of others, for 'tis but reasonable he should have the honour of ending alone what he has so successfully begun."

"October 25, 1715.

"At last Cameron came last night, and I gave him and Murrey their last directions, the last is allready parted, and the first will follow, I hope, before night, tho he be a litle out of order.

"I gave Mur (Murray) the D. B. (Duke of Berwick) letter to you, which I think as positive and as extraord^y a refusall as ever I saw, and I beleeve the Scots when they see it will not regrett that Duke, who I conclude will never go after this so formal a Declar^n, and therefore I bid Murray tell Mar that I did the less regrett D. B. (Duke of Berwick) not going that he has himself managed affaires with so much prudence and success, and that it will be even a satisfaction to me to see him have the honour of ending alone the work he has so prosperously begun.

"So much for Scotland and Ber (Duke of Berwick), whose letter to me I here send you, and shall not make any answer to it, for I think that is the least I can do, and the gentlest return I can make is to name him nor think of him no more, for as to trusting him or employing him, he certainly ought no more to be it, nor will not, I dare say, expect it.

"I am very well pleased with what you write to me in relation to the French Court, where one like you would certainly be very useful in my absence, *tho I still think you would be much more necessary with me*, but as to that, as we agreed in parting, you can best judge where you will be most useful to me, and whether you can meet me on this side of the sea with secresy.

"I approve entirely your destination of the different ships you mention, and which you or somebody els in your absence must see executed, for the article of transporting people after me is of the last consequence. I shall expect with impatience the news of D. O. (Duke of Ormond) parting, which I think presses to a great degree, for tis plain nothing will stirr in Engl^d till his arrival, which alone can put a stop to this fury of imprisoning all our friends, which if it continued would cause inevitable delay at the best.

"I shall give a few days law to D. O. (Duke of Ormond), but as I find by Flanigan that I can ly with great privacy somewhere near the coast on this side I shal still part from hence a day or two after your Couriers arrival, and as I said before wait at that place till I hear from England.

"If that should be at my arrival there, and that I find all is ready to receive me, so much the better. If there should be some delay it would be, I think, of advantage for the security of my passage, for when 'tis once publick that I am no more in this country people will never dream that I am hiding at the sea side, but rather be looking for me in the island or at sea,* and I shall on my side, as you on yours, use all the little *finesses* I can to puzle people as to my true design, and make people beleeve I am gone to Scotland; and on the whole I shall neglect nothing for disguising my person and hiding my march.

"Pray God D. O. (Duke of Ormond) got safe on t'other side, as well as our other friends, and then I shall have very good hopes of our affairs.

"I here return you the Commission to the Lord Grenard altered as you propose, and if they are printed Sir Thomas will send you with this the two letters and the Declaration

---

* This is what actually happened.

printed. If they are not ready my next and last Courier shall bring them to you. Here is a Commission [for] L^d N & G (North & Grey), which tho' it may not be perfectly according to form will I hope be sufficient. I see very few alterations to be made in the new draughts you send me, so I shall get them printed, and sent back to you in a few days.

"As for mony matters I think the more can be carry'd with myself the better, but upon examination I cannot possibly carry the seals along with me, and so I shall be forced to send them back by Booth, and hope you may be able to find a secret way of conveying them to me, if you do not bring them yourself, tho' after all as the secret is the main point, one had better leave them behind than risk tother. This is all I have to say at present.

"JAMES R."

"I cannot get the 3 new letters printed here because of the form of that to the University, so I send you them back with the changes I have made. I will endeavour to make all such papers of a piece, and even in material points, to repeat the same words.*

"If you can you may print them at Paris with all the right forms which we have not, and add yourself the compliment to D. O. (Duke of Ormond). I hope this will find you quite recovered. Pray show the 3 letters I return you to the Queen."

PAPER LXXVIII.

Lord Bolingbroke to Chevalier de St. George. (*Extract.*) †

"October 24, 1715.

"Instead of setting out on notice that ye Duke of Ormonde is gone from Paris I would humbly advise y^r Maj^ty to wait till I send a Courier to inform you y^t he is saild from La Hogue, and to give you such other intelligence as he will send me, in pursuance of what I have concerted with him

---

* These proclamations of considerable length, to the Universities and the Army and Navy, were printed at St. Germain and appear amongst the Stuart Papers. They have, however, far less interest than the various holograph letters of Lord Bolingbroke which adorn these pages.

† Another part of this letter is published by Lord Stanhope in the Appendix to his 'History.'

from ye coast. This I mentioned to ye Queen last night, and she was of opinion y^t ye precaution was absolutely necessary. Thus y^r Maj^{ty} will upon y^r arrival at St. Malo in all probability have some accounts from ye Duke, or from ye two gentlemen first dispatched, to govern y^r self by in ye great attempt you are about to make, otherwise all the measures taken by sending these people before you will be insignificant, you will arrive almost as soon as they, be exposed to ye same uncertainty, and run ye same hazards.

"And this is less to be done now than before, because we have less reason to believe things in ye West disposed for you now, than we had when I attended you last, and receiv'd y^r orders on Hamilton's report.

"Your Maj^{ty} observes that by a parity of reason you must wait as privately as possible when you do arrive at St. Malo, till ye receive ye necessary advices, which one way or other will certainly be sent you.

"I feel myself how disagreeable these uncertainties and these delays must be to y^r Maj^{ty}; but I take true wisdom to consist in bearing cross accidents with temper, and in improving favourable accidents to advantage, and am therefore sure that y^r Maj^{ty} will do both.

"I heartily wish you may have as much occasion to ye latter as you have had to do ye former.

"The Dutch have at last promised Hanover (George I.) the six thousand men which he demands, and thus are foreign forces brought into England against you, tho' none can be promised for you."

Paper LXXIX.

Duke of Berwick to Chevalier de St. George. (*Extract.*)

"November 3, 1715.

"I find the reasons alledged against my leaving France without the Regents leave so strong, that it is with the deepest concern I am forced to ask y^r Majestys pardon for not complying with your commands."

"November 4, 1715.

"I had yesterday a long conversation with the Regent, and afterwards with the Marshal d'Uxelles; they both told me that orders were gone to hinder your Majesty from parting from any port of Normandie or Picardie; the rest was omitted to leave you room to gett away, Ld Bullingbrook (Lord Bolingbroke) will have informed you of the detail. The Marshall d'Uxelles further told me that his opinion was your Majesty cannot part too soon, at least gett on shippboard, for fear Lord Staires should find out where you are, and make his complaint to the Regent, in which case you will be stopped."

PAPER LXXX.

Lord Bolingbroke to Chevalier de St. George. (Extract.)

"Paris, Nov. 8, 1715.

" I am now with the Marx (Marquess) d'Huxelles who sent to speak privately with me since my last dispatch was closed.

" Stair has given a memorial insisting to demand the stopping of y^r Maj^{ty}, who are he says to go either from ye coast of Brittany or Normandy, he has att ye same time taken notice of my being here as contrary to ye Treaty, since I concern myself in ye support of y^r interest.

" The Marx (Marquess) says y^t all y^t can be done shall be done to give y^r Maj^{ty} time, but desires y^t you would lose none.

" I have agreed with him how to banter Stair."

PAPER LXXXI.

Lord Bolingbroke to Chevalier de St. George. (Extract.)

"Paris, Nov. 9, 1715.

" Ye secret of y^r being gone towards ye coast, where you actually are, has so far got wind, that I should have ventur'd to have come to you myself to have assisted in determining this great step and to have received your commands on all ye particulars of Ld Mars letters.

" If y^r Maj^{ty} goes to Scotland, great part of what I should have to do will be needless. If you go to England I shall soon hear from you, and if you should, which God forbid, be stopped, I shall soon see you."

Paper LXXXII.

Chevalier de St. George from St. Malo, most probably to Lord Bolingbroke. (Extracts.) The Duke of Ormond had returned from the British coast, where he received no welcome.

"Nov. 11, 1715.

"On my arrival here on Friday the 8th, it was thought convenient that the Duke of Ormonde and I should waite for fresh accounts from England, and without which it was then thought absolutely impossible for the Duke to return thither after the reception he last met with; but considering the danger of delays, the instances that Staire has made to the Regent, and the little probability we had of having soon accounts from England, the wind being contrary, and the impatience with which the Scots expected me, joynd to the good news of last night received from them, it was resolved that wind and weather serving, I should forthwith embark and set sail and go to the place appointed in the west of Scotland."

* * * * *

"For fear of accidents I send imediately Sir Nicolas Geraldine's son to my Lord Mar to acquaint him that I am set out for Dunstafnage, the place which he appointed me to go to. The Duke of Ormonde will acquaint the Duke of Leeds where he may meet him in England."

Paper LXXXIII.

Lord Bolingbroke to Chevalier de St. George at St. Malo. (Extract.)

"Monday.

"This serves only to convey to you a paper which I cannot imagine how I came to forget to inclose in ye pacquet sent you by Mr. Booth.

"Y^r Maj^{ty} will have heard ye ill news which met ye Duke of Ormond att his arrival on ye coast. Maclean, who has been all along trusted by our friends, and was in ye whole secret of ye rising of ye West, has betrayed them, and by his means ye Government in England has been able to seize of persons and places in such manner and att such time as to defeat all their designs. Notwithstanding this Mr. Savery tells me y^t ye Duke is saild. But y^r Maj^{ty} will have these accounts sooner and better from other hands."

PAPER LXXXIV.

Lord Bolingbroke to Chevalier de St. George at St. Malo.
(Extract.)

"Paris, Nov. 15, 1715.

" I must repeat ye necessity of y^r Maj^{ts} speedy departure. Stair cannot be ignorant of the parts of ye coast from whence you are to proceed, and every moment after he has this knowledge adds to y^r danger."

PAPER LXXXV.

Chevalier de St. George to Lord Bolingbroke. (Extracts.)
From St. Malo.

"Nov. 15, 1715.

" It will be necessary you should go to St. Germaine as soon as you can after you receive this, to concert every thing with the Queen, to whom I wish that all should pass thro' your hands."

After enjoining that the Duke of Berwick, being " useless," should not be trusted, the Chevalier speaks disparagingly as follows of the Duke of Ormond's abilities.

" Our good hearty Duke wants a good head with him. I would have sent Booth with him, but I could not persuade him."

PAPER LXXXVI.

Chevalier de St. George to Lord Bolingbroke. (Extract.)
From St. Malo.

"Nov. 27, 1715.

" D. O. (Duke of Ormond) gott out of the bay last night and sett sail this morning with a fine moderate gale. He will certainly go to Cornwall, which I am sorry for; but after having told him my reasons against it, and inforced yours, I could do no more, for the business is so hazardous that 'tis but just he should himself decide."

Appendix I. 263

PAPER LXXXVII.
Chevalier de St. George to Duke of Gordon. (Copy.)

⁎⁎⁎ Having traversed Normandy, disguised as a sailor, the Chevalier embarked from Dunkirk in the middle of December in a small vessel, once a privateer, in company with Lord Tynemouth, the Duke of Berwick's son, and six others, so that on the 22nd of the month, he wrote to Lord Bolingbroke, from Peterhead, saying, "I am at last, thank God, in my ancient kingdom."

The letter in question being published by Lord Stanhope, we pass on to a scarcely less absorbing communication, which this interesting claimant for a throne indited six days later at Fetteresso.

By this time Lord Mar had fought the indecisive battle of Nov. 13 at Sheriffmuir, which the Jacobites elevated into the dignity of a victory, although their left wing had been driven from the field.

Lord Mar, who is to be commended for the warmth with which, after various alternations of opinion, which gained him the name of "Bobbing John," he embraced and defended the Chevalier's cause, cannot be said to have shown that generalship which the occasion required. Not only was valuable time wasted when 10,000 irregulars enlisted under his banner stood comparatively idle so long before the Royal forces under Argyll, who mustered but 3500; but Lord Mar lost an opportunity of destroying the right wing of the enemy and of capturing the general opposed to him, when, returning from the river Allan after routing Lord Mar's left, weary and tired, Argyll and his soldiers passed by the Highlanders in position on rising ground, and present there in overwhelming numbers.

"Oh, for an hour of Dundee," said Gordon of Glenbucket, the old Killiecrankie warrior; while, "Oh, for a month of the Duke of Berwick," soon came to be a more practical watchword.

"Feteresso, Dec. 28, 1715.

" My safe arrival in this my ancient kingdom will, I believe, be no unwelcome news to you, and tho' I know your own zeal for my service wants no encouragement, yet my presence will inspire, I do not doubt, new life and vigour into the troops you command.

" I shall be very impatient of assuring you by word of mouth of my particular kindness for you, but it is of the last consequence for my service that in conjunction with the Marquiss of Seafort you lose no time in reducing Inverness, which I hope will be no hard task, and that the Earl of Southerland's situation is such that he cannot escape being taken with his troops in a manner at present surrounded by mine. Such a number of prisoners would not only be of consequence for my service, but a great security to our own prisoners in England, for whom I am in great concern.

"Dispatch is requisite on this occasion, and I heartly wish

you the satisfaction of being yourself the first after my arrival that has gained an advantage over the enemy. When that is done you cannot see me too soon at Perth with your following.

"JAMES R."

PAPER LXXXVIII.

Chevalier de St. George to Lord Bolingbroke. (Extract.)

The Chevalier, when in Scotland, changed his mind as to the Duke of Berwick, and from Kinnaird on January 2, 1716, wrote concerning him as follows :—

["His presence here would really work miracles, for they know nothing but good of him; and to please them here I am forced to say he is coming, for the contrary belief would be of the worst consequence."]*

PAPER LXXXIX.

George Camocke to Lord Mar. The writer was a Jacobite agent. He regards the engagement at Sheriffmuir as a glorious victory.

"Morlix, Jan. 5, 1716.

" My Lord,

"Enclosed I send to your Grace, by the comand of the Duke of Ormonde, a copy of my Journal of his Grace'" proceedings between the 31st of October, 1715, and the 6th of December following. The bearer, Cap^{tn} Tho. Sheridan, was on board during the whole voyage. I refer to him to relate to your Grace the maney Fatigues and hazards his Grace of Ormonde hath laboured under for some time past, and could not gain a passage into Cornwall.

" I humbly take leave to congratulate your Grace on your Glorious victory over the Rebels. God give you success in al your undertakings, and grant a favourable occasion to his Grace of Ormonde to put in execution what he hath so long desired and laboured for, is the hearty prayer of him that is, with profound respect,

" My Lord,
" Your Grace' most obedient,
" and devoted humble servant,
" GEORGE CAMOCKE."

---

* Published in Appendix to Lord Stanhope's 'History.'

Paper XC.

Duke of Ormond to Lord Mar.

"France, Jan. 26, 1716.

" My Lord,

" Give me leave to congratulate you on the King's safe landing. I hope it will have the effect that I wish. I am very impatient to doe my part; I am endeavouring it. The King will have acquainted you that I have not been idel, tho I have not had the success that I wish'd for. If our friends will doe their part, I am sure that France will help them with men, ammunition, and armes. I shall soon know their resolutions in answer to what E. Boll (Lord Bolingbroke) and I have sent to them.

" I trembel for poore Ld Lansdowne and for more of our friends.   " With compliments, &c.

" Ormonde."

Paper XCI.

Lord Bolingbroke to Lord Mar. Lord Mar was still believed to be in Scotland.

"St. Germain, Jan. 31, 1716.

" My Lord,

" My dispatches to the King are so very full,* and Mr. Lloyd is so perfectly informed of ye present state of things on this side, that I cannot have much to say to y^r Grace in particular.

" He will communicate a great deal to you, and I beg of you to give him on my account att first all that credit which you will give him on his own when you come to know him. The great point he has to propose requires all possible expedition, and I am apt to think that you will hardly find any person more proper to be sent upon y^r service than Lloyd himself.

" I must entreat y^r Grace to take all possible care that the secret be kept, and on no account whatever, by no accident whatever, that part of it which relates to France get out or rebound back hither.

" Lloyd will explain to you ye meaning of this, ye diffi-

---

* This clause shows that letters were sent which never reached their destination.

cultys I have layn under and am still forcd to struggle thro', how I am every moment exposᵈ to ye necessity of keeping measures equally essential, and at ye same time inconsistent.

"Your Grace can contribute very much to ease me, and I am sure you will, since nothing but ye warmest zeal for our common cause, and ye firmest resolution to live and dye by it, could make me lead ye life which for some months past I have lead, which is at present better, but still bad enough.

"The Duke of Ormond, as well as I, has been without ye least intelligence from our friends in England these maney months. Some letters which I got by ye last posts gave a strange account of ye state of affairs in yt country.

"Every creature who might stand up in ye defence of his country is imprisond, dispersᵈ, or dispirited. Ye people are still ye same, or rather their resentments run higher than ever, but there is not a Duke of Mar amongst ye Nobility or gentry. I shall find a way in very few days of sending to some persons of our acquaintance; it is harder for you to do it, but if you could it would be of singular use.

"I cannot yet be out of pain for Sir John Areskine (Erskine), who ought to have been with you before the King's landing, and who was kept att Calais till twelve days ago. He has two valuable young men and a great sum of gold with him.

"Adieu, my dear Lord; I embrace you with ye warm affection. Depend upon me that nothing which can be done is or shall be neglected.

"I hope—nay, indeed, I am persuaded—yt our Master has an entire confidence in you, for in him, my dear Lord, to what ye present circumstances of his Kingdoms require, you have good sense, good nature, and I trust you will succeed.

"Once more adieu.

"I am till death,
"Yʳ Grace's faithful and obedient servant,
"BOLINGBROKE."

"*P.S.*—I mention to ye King a ship that will soon be dispatch'd with a very large quantity of arms and ammunition, but I forgot to mention that as she will be forc'd to go round Ireland, so unless I hear from yʳ Grace yt there is some particular place on ye North West Coast in ye King's hands, the instructions I shall give the Captains of her will be to sail to ye Lewis, the Isles of Sky, Rum, or Mull, either of which he can first make, and then to follow such orders as he shall receive from ye King, deliver'd by a person who shall come on board and repeat twice 'Bray-Mar.' To put up before he arrives on each topmast head fanes blew and red (streamers blue and red), but to show no flag, and to have only a French flag on board.

"I will give notice by ye first and every opportunity of ye sailing of this ship."

Paper XCII.
Lord Mar to H. S.

⁎ A complete account of Lord Mar's departure from Montrose, sent from the place of landing in France, which is not named. As will be seen in a succeeding letter of the Chevalier, Boulogne was visited, and arrangements made to return to Paris viâ Abbeville, and yet all the historians speak of Gravelines as the spot where the Chevalier disembarked.

"Sir, "February 10, 1716.

"I wrote to you on the 3rd from Montrose, but very quickly after that things took entirely another turn, for then wee thought that wee should have had some breathing time, by the Enemies not marching for some time, but on the contrary, different from the intelligence we had, they marched without stoping at Perth and were within four miles of Montrose and Brichen on Saturday afternoon.

"This sufficiently shewed us that they wer resolvd to follow us on go where wee would. Inverness not being reduced by those it was entrusted to, and by this no time left for us to do it, before the Enemie came up, made the stand wee propos'd to have made there out of view, and should the K (the Chevalier) gone on to that, wee had been in a worse case than at Montrose, without any way for him to gett off, his staying could have been of no use to his friends, but made their condition worse, happen almost what would, so he at last took the resolution of going off that night in a ship that was by accident there which had some time ago come from France.

"He was pleased to order me, Ld Drummond, and Ld Marishall,* positively to go along with him with one or two of his

* James II. in 1458 created Sir William Keith Earl Marischal of Scotland, a hereditary dignity which passed in regular succession to the above-named holder of the title, viz. George, tenth Earl, who joined the Chevalier. The Earl Marischal became a distinguished Prussian diplomatist, and his brother was the famous Marshal Keith, friend of Frederick the Great. The Earl Marischal's account of the flight from Montrose differs from that of lord Mar's (see remarks on Paper CXIII.).

own menial servants, and gave a Commission to Gordon to command in chief with all the Powers necessary, and the armie was orderd to march that minute, being just then assembling. It was more the K. (the Chevalier's) goodness in ordering me along with him, than for any use I am afraid he can find me of here ; but could I have been of any further service either to our friends or the cause there, I am persuaded he would have dispensed with my going along, but my stay would rather have been a loss to them than any service as things stood, which was no small mortification to me, as my going from them also was.

" The K. (the Chevalier) waited on the ships above an hour and an half for Ld Marishall and Clephan ; but by what accident, wee yet know not, they did not come, and there was no waiting longer.

" We had a very good passage, and by great and very remarkable good providence, got safe on this side the water this afternoon.

" I knew you and other friends would be in pain to know what was become us, which made me write this (by order) as soon as wee were got into a house, and I knew no way of sending it, but enclosed to Mr. Morison to forward to you, so I wish it may come safe to your hands.

" You shall hear again, befor long, when I can tell you where wee are, and I will send you an address to write by. The K. (the Chevalier) and wee all are in no small pain to know what has become of our friends wee left behind, and I beg you may send a particular account of it to France, as soon as you can, and from your correspondents there wee shall have it.

" There are two ships ordered, one to Peterhead and another to Frasersburgh, to bring off any of our friends who want such an occasion.

" I hope they will be there soon, and I wish they may be of the use they are designd.

" This is all I can now say, but that I am,
" Yours, &c.,
" MAR."

" I am in great pain about my papers, which are of value. I sent them in two boxes on a horse the day wee came away, but before wee had resolved it, forward (to) Aberdeen by one McNab, of Bræmar, with a letter directed to Pitlodrie younger or his Lady in that town to take care of. I wish heartily they may have come safe to them, tho' I am mightly affraid of some accident happening to them, which would grieve me to the last degree.

"I beg you may inquire about them, and if you can get notice of them, for God's sake let them be taken care of, and kept together without anybody seeing them or medling with them.

"I'l be mighty impatient to know something about them from you.

"The K. (the Chevalier) left a paper with Gordon concerning his going away, of which he has not a copie, therefore I wish you could get it and send it me."

PAPER XCIII.

Duke of Berwick to Lord Mar.

⁎⁎⁎ The reputation of the hero of Almanza was paramount in Scotland, where they clearly mistrusted the generalship of Lord Mar. At the same time, the Duke of Berwick's conduct in not succouring his half-brother in this time of dire need was commented on apparently to the French marshal's disadvantage, leading him to justify himself as follows to Lord Mar. When this letter was written, the Duke of Berwick did not know that the Chevalier's return from Scotland was imminent. The summary of the Duke's case is complete and convincing.

"St. Germain,* Feb. 12, 1716.

"My Lord,

"I find by your grace's letter of the first of January, that the King is in great want of speedy succour from abroad, without which it will be difficult, if not impossible, to maintain the cause. I can assure your grace that whenever it has come in my way, or that I have found an opportunity, I have done my part, and I can also answer for the Earl of Bolingbroke, who, to my certain knowledge, has left no stone unturned, to compass all the King or y' Grace could wish for; if he succeeds not 'tis a misfortune, but none of his fault.

"There was also in your grace's letter another point concerning myself, in which I find you have been misinformed. I know not what those who have been heare backward and forwards may have imagind or sayd; but this I can aver, that I never promis'd to follow the King anywhere, without the proviso of the French Court's giving me leave.

* The Duke of Berwick remained at St. Germain during his brother's sojourn in Scotland.

"The King may very well remember that three yeares agoe, of my own accord, I made him the offer of my services under the above said proviso, his Majesty thought it then so reasonable, that he thanked me for it, and writt to the French Court to obtaine the leave; it was then granted, but after Queen Ann (*sic*) death, the late King of France thought it necessary to avoid any occasion of quarrel with the new government of England, and, therefore, not only recalld his leave, but even forbid me positively from stirring. I did all that lay in my power to obtain the recall of that prohibition, but in vain, as I can prove by an original letter under M. de Torcy' hand, dated of the 19th June last.

"Since the King of France's death, I have usd all my endeavours with the Regent, but to as little purpose.

"This being my present case, all I can say is that I am still ready to part, whenever the Regent will allow me, but 'tis neither consisting with my honour, my duty, my oaths, nor even with the King's interest or reputation, that I should desert like a trooper.

"It was with his Majesty's leave that I became a Frenchman, and I cannot depart from the vast obligations I now have incumbent upon me without breach of public faith and gratitude. Your Grace is too much a man of honour not to approve of this my conduct and resolution. If ever proper occasions offer you shall find me as zealous as any man to render the King service, and of giving your grace real proofs of the great value and esteme I have for your person, being, &c.,

"BERWICK."

PAPER XCIV.

General George Hamilton to Lord Mar. (*Extract.*)
The letter reached Lord Mar at Paris on March 11.

*** General George Hamilton had been sent from Scotland to quicken the efforts of Lord Bolingbroke and his coadjutors at St. Germain in getting arms, ammunition, &c.
The Regent Orleans' Government stood in the way of the latter reaching Scotland in any quantity, but some creature comforts were nevertheless despatched.

"February 13, 1716.

"I have sent your Grace 93 bottells of champagne, which I bought at Montreuil, not finding a drop of good at Calice (Calais).

Appendix I. 271

"Mr. Arbuthnot writs me that he had a ship att Diep (Dieppe) reddy to saile with the first fair wind, and put on board both Burgundie and Champagne, with twentie hogsheads of true Claret, for your Grace, which I hope will come in good season.

"Ther is 6000 weight of powder to be put on board of Capt. Gardiner under the care of Cap^{tn} O Neal, and I have sent him orders to follow his discretions, and Lord John Drummond will follow soon with 8000 armes and 50,000 weight of powder. I wish to God all come saife, then I think you'l be pretty easie for some tym, and I am with all sinceritie and respect, &c.,

"GEORGE HAMILTON."

PAPER XCV.

General George Hamilton to Chevalier de St. George. (Extract.) Memorial detailing the General's experiences when on the mission to France.

⁎⁎⁎ This memorial presents the case of those who believed that due exertions had not been made to supply the Jacobite army. The Regent certainly temporised, but had he desired to see General George Hamilton there could have been no difficulty in so doing. It was probably upon receipt of this memorial that the Chevalier formed the resolution to make a scapegoat of Lord Bolingbroke. The subject of the Duke of Berwick's remaining in France and not joining his brother is discussed, and the familiar explanation given of the Regent's refusal to let him depart.

"When the Duke of Berwick was gone I told my Lord (Bolingbroke) in presence of Lt.-General Dillon, that when I left Perth there was not above 700 weight of powder in the magazine, and asked him whether or not he thought it proper I should wait upon the Regent, and deliver your Majesty's letter according to your intention, otherwise I am sure ther was little or no occasion for me here. I was putt of till next day, and even to this I have not had the honor to see the Regent. Genll. Dillon asked me if he should lay it befor the Regent, to which I reddily agreed, when he was told the state of your magazine he was so much concerned that your Maj^{ties} person and the nation should be exposed to so great danger, that he ordered six thousand weight of powder to be sent immediately, but could not prevaill to get any armes, least the noise, and my Lord Stair, who has spyes everywhere, should have got intelligence of it, then the Regent told him 'comment dit il monsieur d'Hamilton d'estre ice trois jours sans me voir pour quoi me l'avez vous mené vous saviez le chemine,' but as my instructions were to follow the Queen's and my Lord Bolingbroke's orders, I would not doe anything without their permission, and when I waited upon her Maj^{tie} yesterday, she was surprised that my Lord had not procured me access, and the French people of qualitie who know that I have not seen the Regent as yet, and ar not ignorant of his impatience to see me, think that I am not very well used.

"The Comte de Castle Blanco (Lord Melfort's son-in-law), who is entirely devoted to your Maj^{ties} service, complained to me with a great deal of concern, that notwithstanding he had got a warrant from the Regent for the deliverie of the arms and ammunition that were seized at Havre de Grace, upon his giving bale of 2000 crowns not to send those armes either to Scotland or England, yet would have run all hazards and sent them two months agoe if he had not been countermanded."

PAPER XCVI.

Chevalier de St. George to a Mr. Russell.

⁎⁎* The Chevalier, wearied out with hardships suffered on board the small craft in which he sailed from Montrose, at last reached Boulogne in safety.

"Boulogne, 10 at night.
"February 23, 1716.

"I had been in pain for you, had you not let me hear from you; wee have found ourselves very solitary without you, and miss you, but I hope our absence wont be long tho I believe I shall scarce reach St. Germain's before Monday.

"I lye to-morrow at Abbeville, and if you can reach it before nine, I'l stay supper for you; you have all along the road but to ask the road to Paris, and you can't miss your way.

"Roger and I have been drinking your health in Burgundy and the first will acquitt himself of your Commission to your Cousin; I'l provide a lodging for you at St. Germains when I shall await you with impatience. You must write two words to our Swize (porter) at St. Germain's, to lett him know the day you arrive there, that it may be more quiet. *A revoir,* I hope to-morrow night, and so, adieu.

"J. R."

Paper XCVII.

Chevalier de St. George to Lord Mar.

⁎⁎ The titular British King had apparently resolved that Lord Mar should supersede Lord Bolingbroke.

"Paris, March 1, 1716.

"You being to stay here some days after me, I desire all the letters which were directed to me in Holland, and which may be now returned from thence, and any having them are hereby ordered to deliver them to you.

"JAMES R."

"All Pacquets from the Queen you will return to her."

Paper XCVIII.

Lord Bolingbroke to the Chevalier on his arrival in France from Scotland.

"Tuesday, March 3, 2 o'clock.

"S^r,

"Tho I lament extreamly the fatal necessity y^r Majesty was under, yet I most heartily congratulate y^r happy escape and safe arrival. You are well, and ye cause cannot dye, but will in God's good time revive again.

"The Queen writes y^r Maj^{ty} word that she thinks about y^r lying at Malmaison. I defer speaking of y^t, or anything else, till I have ye honour of kissing y^r hand.

"I am ever y^r dutiful and obedient subject and servant,

"BOLINGBROKE."

Paper XCIX.

Lord Bolingbroke to Lord Mar.

⁎⁎ Lord Bolingbroke had evidently heard rumours of the storm destined to break on his head.

The only genius actively engaged in the Chevalier's cause was to be made a scapegoat to satisfy the clamours of the St. Germain *entourage*.

"My Lord, "March 4, 1716.

"According to what was agreed with y^r Grace and ye Duke of Ormonde yesterday, I have writ to ye man we used to employ att Calais, and have sent an officer from his garrison in ye neigbourhood to ye same place, yt he may supervise and quicken ye execution of ye orders.

T

"My letters go to ye Queen open, and if she approves em, will be forwarded with Mr. Dicconson's directions in what manner the merchant shall draw for his reimbursement.

"I see nothing more to be done on my part in this affair which I think so necessary yt I was of opinion all ye ships should not have been stopp'd which were going upon ye King's return.

" It will perhaps, however, be said yt these poor countrymen of ours might have resisted long enough to have made a good capitulation had I taken care to have sent them powder, and if it be, I shall not be much disturbed att ye reflexion. I am enough used to things of this kind to know yt rash censures made without due information last no longer than till ye person concerned shall think proper to give them an answer.

" I mentioned to y^r Grace and to ye Duke of Ormonde some heads of busines which are very capital in my poor opinion, and deserve attention, and some concert. Whenever you have any commands for me, I shall obey them with pleasure, being my Lord, &c., &c.,

" BOLINGBROKE."

PAPER C.

Lord Mar to General Gordon. (Extract.) Written from Paris, March 5, to General Gordon, in command of the Chevalier's army in Scotland.

₊* On March 6, the day after the despatch of this letter, Mary of Modena sent Lord Mar 2,000 livres by Mr. Dicconson, " apprehending that his grace might be in present want of some money." Her liberality towards the exile adherents of her husband and son was from first to last on the amplest scale attainable, and does credit to the reputation of a much wronged woman.

"Since I came to this place I have heard nothing but a general cry against some people for the way we were neglected in nothing being sent us for so long a time, and when ships were sent that no arms nor amunition was sent in them, wch tis plain might have been got.

" Some attribute it to negligence, and others to a much worse reason, which I was unwilling to believe but tis hard to think that negligence alone could have been the only reason, and the King as well as others thinks he has been very ill served."

Paper CI.
Lord Bolingbroke's last letter to Earl of Mar.

⁂ At last James Francis Edward gave way to the clamour at his mock court, and dismissed the man paramount alike in the conduct of affairs and in the graces of a style whereon Chatham moulded himself, and which has influenced all the great political writers and speakers who have since flourished in England.

"My Lord,   "March 27, 1716.

"I have ye honour of y^r Grace's without any date, and I wish you most heartily a good journey. If I had imagined that y^r departure would have been so precipitate, I should have used my best endeavours to have seen and taken leave of you.

"I cannot indeed tell what will be said by friends, for one cannot be at a loss to know what your enemy will say, concerning the residence you are going to; for my own part I shall say and write nothing. I have said little in answer even to all ye vile and groundless calumnys which have been thrown about concerning me.

"I have liv^d long enough and acted well enough in ye world not to pass either for a knave or a driveler, and have therefore as little regarded the calumny as I deserved the treatment which encouraged it.

"Your Grace may be assured that when I receive any answer from Spain—I expect none from any other place—to ye instances made in ye King's name, you shall have an account thereof.

       "I am, my Lord, &c.
             "Bolingbroke."

Paper CII.
Earl of Mar to Lord Kilsyth. (Extract.) Written from Avignon, June 16, 1716, giving an account of Jacobite distresses after the Rebellion.

⁂ The Marquess of Tullibardine mentioned here was one of the first noblemen to proclaim the Chevalier in 1715, afterwards joining in the abortive insurrection of 1719, which came to a close in Glenshiel, while his Jacobite career did not end until after Culloden in 1745. Captured during flight, the Marquess was taken in failing health to the Tower of London, where he died in July 1746. His brother, Lord George Murray, ancestor of the present Duke of Athole, after evincing great military skill as Charles Edward's lieutenant-general, finished life abroad, being one of the Chevalier's favoured adherents. Another brother, Charles, taken prisoner at Preston in 1715, was sentenced to be shot, but received a reprieve.

"I suppose you have waited on the Queen ere now, and received her commands. The King thinks you will be come off before this reach Paris, and you may be sure you are long'd for here, where you may expect all the wellcome a gracious Prince can give you in the unluckie way his starrs have placed him; but I hope better dayes are a comeing both for him and those who now suffer upon the account of his cause and their country.

"I beg you may give my most humble service to the Marquess of Tullibardin, if still with you, who is long'd for here, and others, a Lady who has taken an affection to his name, and was very fond of Ld George upon that account, who she calls Tullibardino. Poor Ld George has not been well almost ever since he came, and has been phisicking, by which he is now better.

"One of the most deplorable things in the King's present situation is that 'tis not his power to give that support to those who have so bravely ventured and lost all for him, that he wyshes he could, but that is his misfortoun, and not his fault."

A bundle of miscellaneous letters dealing with the events of 1716, has been recently investigated at Windsor, from which the following papers have been taken. Their existence was not known to the author in time to place them amongst the preceding papers in chronological order in the first edition of this book, and he has thought it advisable not to disturb the original arrangement.

The letters in question are of considerable historical importance. They deal with Lord Mar's sojourn at Scone and Dundee with the Chevalier, and also expose Simon Lord Lovat's duplicity in intriguing with the Jacobites; while his rewards for outwardly and visibly supporting George I. are likewise announced from Whitehall by no less a personage than General Stanhope.

How these private secrets of Lord Lovat's reached St. Germain must remain a subject of unsatisfied speculation.

The next paper gives evidence that money was lost during this campaign on the coast of Scotland.

PAPER CIII.

Earl of Mar to General Gordon.

"Dundee, Jan. 13, 1716,

"I have just now an express from Jo Erskine, who is at Dundee, and all his crew. The ship was broke to pieces, but the hulk and——(undecipherable), where the gold was, still lies on the sand bank where the ship stranded. They think at the spring tide which is Saturday, Sunday and Monday, it may be dry and so recoverd. Ld. Rothes was advertised of the ships being stranded by the dissaffected thereabouts and Desired to send a party so I'm apt to belive that the party we heard of today at Faukland, have been going there.

"The King thinks it is best for us to appear to give the ship and all that was in her for gone and so to neglect her by recalling the party that was sent to Couper (Cupar) today and letting it be as much known as can be (tho it is not fitt to mention there having been any considerable sum in her in case of that making the enimie look the more narrowly after it)."

PAPER CIV.

Earl of Mar to Marquess of Huntly.

⁎ Lord Mar evinces great anxiety regarding the Chevalier's prospects. It is due to Lord Mar to record that he was adverse to any retrograde movement until such action became absolutely necessary.

"Scone, Jan. 15, 1716.

"By what Lord Seafort is now to do I am persuaded Ldship will find y^r work at Inverness much easier than you expected when you wrote the two last to me and it is of the utmost consequence to the King's service to have it soon over and all joind here with the King, were that once done and before the enimie make any attempt against us I should not be much afraid of them and e'er long by the succours we have good reason to expect from abroad, I believe they will be more affraid of us than we will be of them. The great point is to be able to maintain ourselves as we are til that time, and y^r Lsp finish the affair of the North.

"It was impossible for the King to spare any mon from here, and I hope y^r Lsp will have no occasion for them (*sic*) Lord Seafort being to act his parte. We have much more need of men to join us than to send any away. I wish y^r Ldship could spare y^r horse, there being I presum not much occasion for them of the affair of Inverness."

PAPER CV.
Earl of Mar to General Gordon.

"Scone, Tuesday night, Jan. 17, 1715/16.

"Sir,

"Both the King and I have expected you here all this day and you wou'd be sure to come to-morrow forenoon. Ld. Drummond advises the putting sum mon into the house of Balmanno wch is near the bridge of Earn in case of the enimies takeing possession of it wch I think is right and the more that the enimie have dayly more forces going into Fife —I hear that Cadugan was to go himself to Dumfermling and its very probable he may attempt something tho' he do not march his troops to Perth.

"It is now I think absolutely necessary that more people be quartred at the bridge of Earn and I believe our garison at Faulkland must either be reinforced or withdrawn and I am much against the last.

"I wish you joy of the Desertors that are come to Perth to-day and I wish that of a companys coming may be true.

"I'll say no more till tomorrow but that

"I am y^rs &c.,

"MAR."

PAPER CVI.
Chevalier de St. George to Marquess of Huntly.

"Scoon, Jan. 17, 1716.

"I have just received your packet by Glenbuckett, by whom I shall send you my answer at large. In the meantime as the person that is to carry my last letter to you is not gone, I will not miss this occasion of letting you know how glad I am, that by the 22 your men will al be assembled for I hope then by Ld. Seaforths concurring with you nothing will longer retard your speedy reducing of Inverness which you know is of the last consequence.

"JAMES R."

PAPER CVII.
Earl of Mar to Marquess of Huntly.

"Scone, Jan. 18, 1716.

"I wish heartily that Ld. Reay could be gained to the King's intrest and if anybody can bring that about, it is your Ldship. And Simon (Ld. Lovat) has it now in his power to reconcile himself to the King, wch I am not without hopes he will do and if he did it would make the work easie. I know y^r Ldship will be glad to know that the Regent of France has gone so farr in the Kings Intrest that we have good ground to expect that the first accounts we have of him from France will be his open declairing for him and of troups being sent into England. The two regiments of Dragoons that came to Scotland since our battle and were quartred at Glasgow are marcht back to England by all the accounts we have both from Desertors and otherways and that two other Regiments are gone in place of them from Stirling to Glasgow. The Stocks are falling at London, and Stair has wrote that they may expect an open ruptor with France as soon as they know of the Pretendors being in Scotland, as they call the King, wch I know from a good hand."

Paper CVIII.

Marquess of Huntly to General Gordon.

*** The Marquess of Huntly has been unfairly said to have become a waverer somewhat early in the day, and therefore it seems just to publish this letter. He was still animated with a noble spirit of self-sacrifice, writing as follows even after the Chevalier's army had retreated. The Marquess was at Edinburgh with his father, the Duke of Gordon, on February 8, 1716.

" Kind namesake, " Gordon Castle, Feb. 5, 1716.

" Just now I had y^rs the King's march northwards is very surprising to mee from several hands but one word from the King or Duke of Mar to mee as yet .. its absolutely necessary all my people bee reddy to join the King or not as the King orders and so circumstances happen to bee, but til orders come its not advisable they march not knowing wheare. I hope my friends and myself shall not lessen the reputation wee formarly had of Loyalty and Zeal and Lov for our countary y^r good example cannot but bee of good consequence and I hope that I may yet have oportunitys to show how much Lov and value I have for you and that I am

" Y^r most affec^t friend,
" Huntly."

Paper CIX.

Marquess of Huntly to Lord Lovat.

*** Lord Lovat was certainly playing double, as the Stuart Papers show that even as late as February 8, 1716, he was privy to payment being made to his clansmen by the Chevalier's adherents; still no duplicity on

Lovat's part could save Huntly's home from pillage, and himself from outlawry unless he made terms with Argyll's advancing forces. With Inverness in Government hands, and both the Chevalier and Lord Mar *en route* for France, the situation was hopeless.

"My Lord, "February 14.

" I had the hon^r of y^r Ldship and am sorry I could not thinke myselfe safe from Duke Argels forces upon the assurances made mee since it hindrd me the pleasure of waiting on y^r Lordship and my other friends. I have submitted to the Goverment and my friends but could not in particular to anybody unless D Argil had ordred mee who gav me assurances of life and fortune for myself and friends before I came from Pearth by allowances of the Government. I thank y^r Ldship most kindly and all my friends for their good will towards me and shall bee glad if ever I hav opportunity to return all civilitys done me with gratitued ashur y^r Ldship of my being,

" My Lord,
" HUNTLY."

PAPER CX.

Lord Lovat to General Cadogan. (*Extract.*)

" March 10, 1716.

" The rebellion will not be extinguished in the Highlands, nor the King free from the thoughts of a Rebellion in favour of the Pretender, till the Rebells of those countreys be transplanted or not only their chiefs but likewise the leading men of every clan be made prisoners."

PAPER CXI.

General Stanhope to Lord Lovat.

** General Stanhope announces King George's recognition of Lord Lovat's loyal services; although the Stuart Papers contain no less than eleven vouchers, proving that this treacherous nobleman* was clothing 400 of the Chevalier's soldiers, and doling out money for his cause. A climax of absurdity is reached when a Government agent, one Mr. R. Molesworth, writes from London to Ld. Lovat as follows, on March 23rd, 1716:—

" The King, the Prince and ye D of *Marlborough* (who had sent 2000*l*. to St. Germain) to whom your letters were speedily delivered are fully apprised of your great and Dangerous services."

" My Lord, " Whitehall, March 10, 1716.

" I have the favour of y^r Ldships two lrs of the 10th and 13th which I have laid before the King who as such a sence

* He suffered the penalty of his deep-dyed treachery on Tower Hill after the 1745.

of ye services your Ldship has done him and ye country on this occasion that he has not only signed a warrant for the remission you desired but has also directed me to assure you that you may depend upon such marks of his favour as will be a just encouragement to you to continue Stedfast in y^r Zeale for his maj^{ies} service and make you easie under ye present circumstances, and as I doubt not but all his Majesties servants will heartily concur in promoting your Interest here, none shall be more glad of such an opportunity than myselfe who am

"My Lord, &c.,
"JAMES STANHOPE."

PAPER CXII.

James Welwood (an official in the Metropolis) to Lord Lovat.
(*Extract.*)

"March 17th.

"Now that the rebellion is over . . . I cannot Delay to advyse your Ldship to make what hast you can for this place. Here is the scene now of business, and it may happen in your case as in others out of sight out of mind."

PAPER CXIII.

Lord Southesk* to Earl of Mar at Avignon.
(*Extract.*)

*** The concluding records of the year 1716 which are preserved at Windsor, contain in the first instance an account of the manner in which the Jacobite army fared in Scotland after the Chevalier's departure with Lord Mar, and of its final dispersion at Ruthven Castle in Badenoch close to Kingussie.

There seems to have been much recrimination amongst the lords and gentlemen who led the beaten army, Keith, the Earl Marischal, being specially hard on his fugitive general, Lord Mar, the fact being duly reported at Avignon by a candid friend. Keith had been left on the beach at Montrose by mistake with General Clephane when the Chevalier and Mar left Montrose, and being forced to shift for himself was probably betrayed into using expressions which in more sober moments he would have

---

* James, 5th Lord Southesk, was attainted in 1715, and lost his property in Scotland, although the Government of George I. mercifully provided for his wife out of the estates in 1717. Lord Southesk died in France during the year 1729.

regretted. The author has refrained from reproducing these matters in detail, or repeating the tales of want and woe which reached Mar in his new office of secretary to the Jacobite Chancellerie at Avignon.

There was much devotion evinced to the Chevalier by these distressed people, and an adequate appreciation of their conduct expressed in practical form by the exiled Prince himself, who seems to have freely dispensed money amongst expatriated supporters, although the majority were necessarily in great straits. The full measure of unselfish loyalty seems to be attained in the concluding words of this last document which we print from the Stuart Papers.

"Paris, May 20, 1716.

"My Lord,

"Since I did myselfe the honour to write to your grace by Ld George I have nothing to add to what I then writ only to tell you that I find the same humour still continues among these people. They have been as Col. Hay would inform you to visit E. Bolingbroke and are a taking all the pains they can with the Queen to your graces' prejudice, tho' I'm persuaded to no effect. Our good Duke (Ormond) publickly expresses his dissatisfaction at the change of the Ribbon and way of receiving the saint Andrews and ascribes it all to you. . . . . . .

"It never was out of hopes of reward that I was loyal, for nothing I can lose, nothing I can suffer, nor no slight I can meet with, can ever make me have a repining thought."

APPENDIX II.

The Birth and Childhood of James VI. of Scotland and I. of Great Britain and Ireland.

Although the dignity of history ought not to be allowed to any mere gossiping rumours, it is necessary, when undertaking the task of tracing in outline the career of the Stuart dynasty, to make some comment upon a story current in society, and mentioned more than once in the public press

The remains of a child were said by certain prints, which will henceforth doubtless desire to remain nameless, to have been recently discovered in Edinburgh Castle, under the steps leading to Mary Queen of Scots' room. The first report gave Holyrood instead of the Castle. This story was rendered more sensational by the embellishment that the infant found within was wrapped " in cloth of gold " marked with the letter " J."

Stated by itself, the unearthing of a child's skeleton in any of the Scotch castles, and in Edinburgh particularly—familiar as the old walls must have been with many a tragedy—would not have created any great sensation, but the fact of contiguity to the room where James I. of England and VI. of Scotland was born, started a new theory in some imaginative minds, and it was gravely suggested that an official explanation should be given to satisfy the public that the first sovereign who ruled over the three kingdoms had survived infancy. Now a careful inquiry held on the spot has led to the following information being elicited.

The alleged *recent* discovery was made not lately, but in 1830, and has been known to more than a generation of antiquaries, and to several historians, amongst the latter to the late Dr. Hill Burton, who passed over the event without attributing any importance thereto. He did, however, in his history, note the anxiety with which every act of the young Prince's guardians was regarded, it being known that Bothwell was endeavouring to get the heir to the throne in his possession, while Robertson also records the satisfaction which was felt when the faithful Mar was appointed to the guardianship of this precious child, and removed him to Stirling Castle, of which the said Mar accepted the governorship.

We are now asked to believe on mere conjectural evidence, either that Darnley was wrong when he acknowledged James VI. as his own child, or that the Earl of Mar—famous for personal integrity, whatever his political bias towards the Queen may have been—stood guilty of a State deceit, the discovery of which must have covered his name for ever with disgrace. For a fierce light beat upon the castle at Edinburgh during the period when Scotland's heir remained within its portals. Not only did the city swarm with the secret agents of Queen Elizabeth, while diplomatists in touch with Catherine de Medici and the Guises vied in the collection of information with the emissaries of the Spanish Court; but the various factions interested in anarchy and confusion were likewise fully alive to the leverage which would be won by any seizure, deportation, or despatch of the heir. Indeed, it is not too much to say that had a catastrophe such as the death of James VI. taken place, not only would Mary Stuart and Elizabeth have proclaimed the fact from the housetops during some period of the great drama wherein they were actresses, but Darnley, the Hamiltons (next heirs to the throne), Murray, and Bothwell, would one and all, at different periods, have found it to their interest to place the story on record. Nor is it possible to believe that such an event would have been permanently hidden from the astute Maitland of Lethington, still less from the all-seeing Cecil.

And yet not a whisper of anything at all analogous to the nineteenth century sensational rumour to which we allude has ever before been heard amidst the deluge of Marian writings which fill our historical shelves. And what are the facts whereon this tardily awakened tale of mystery depends?

"Part of the remains of a child and an oak coffin were found on the 11th of August, 1830, in the front wall of the Royal Apartments Square, Edinburgh Castle, nearly in a line with the Crown Room, about five or six feet above the floor.

"A piece of cloth supposed to be woollen, very thick, wove like leather, and another piece of cloth, said to be silk and embroidered with two letters upon it, one of them being according to one account a J, and according to another an I."* If the former, the sepulture probably took place later than the times of Queen Mary, for the letter "J" was seldom used in the sixteenth century—*vide* the "Breeches" Bible, or any printed book extant. If, as Grant, the famous novelist, in his 'Old and New Edinburgh' recounts, the letter was "i," no date being affixed, it is indeed a stretch of imagination to assign its owner the high position in life some would now desire. For it must be remembered that in 1830 the greatest local literary antiquarian whom Scotland ever produced was living, and in the habit of visiting Edinburgh, and yet not a word concerning this matter ever escaped Sir Walter Scott.

Mr. P. H. McKerlie, whose letter we have quoted, says that when a boy "small pieces of the bones and coffin," which were in a state of utter decay, and concerning which so much has been lately said, were given him " to add to a collection of curiosities." He adds that the wood was oak.

One Major-General Thackery of the Engineers, being in command of the Castle in 1830, application was made to Mr. Macdonald, Curator of the Antiquarian Society, and of the Record Department, but no clue to the name of the child entombed in the Castle wall seems to have been elicited. It is certain, however, that any one desirous of putting an infant out of the way, and obliterating all memory of its existence, would never have embroidered initials upon the cloth wherein its body was wrapped.

The Royal Apartments in Edinburgh Castle were erected between 1524 and 1542, in the reign of James V. There is no record who tenanted them during that reign; although the irregular life of the King led to the

---

* Letter of P. H. McKerlie, F.S.A. (Scot.), in the *Scotsman*, Dec. 27, 1888. Mr. McKerlie does not say which came first, the "i" or the erased letter.

birth of numerous illegitimate children all over the country. In 1615 these buildings were repaired, and assumed their present form. The fact that the above-named discovery 'ook place in 1830 is noted in James Grant's 'Memorials of the Castle of Edinburgh,' edition 1850, p. 265, as well as in the work previously mentioned.

There are people in this world who rejoice in mystery of every sort. Some are pleased to believe that Richard II. of England escaped from Pontefract Castle, and was buried years afterwards at Stirling. Others are found to say that Richard III. was not a cruel uncle nor a bad man, and that he did not murder the Princes in the Tower; while, within the memory of most middle-aged men, individuals claiming to represent the main line of the Stuarts have been received as lions in London society. Moreover, how many personators of Louis XVII. of France have turned up in different parts of the world it is difficult to remember. For the first of these historical mysteries there may exist slight grounds for speculative inquiry, while Walpole's researches, conducted for the purpose of white-washing Richard III., are worth reading; but no serious writer will waste his time in attempting to weld them into history, while the other stories to which we have alluded are ridiculous in the eyes of those conversant with the course of events.

The theories recently current regarding James I. of England and VI. of Scotland are as ludicrous as any of the earlier mare's-nests. The controversy upon this subject, which occurred during 1888 in Scotland, is to be found in the *Scotsman* of December 27 and 28 in that year.

Lord Macaulay, it may be remembered, was M.P. for Edinburgh between 1839 and 1847. It is not likely that a historical writer endowed with a capacity for discovering facts regarding the past quite unexampled in his own epoch, and also with an astonishingly retentive memory, would have remained silent upon this subject, had there been a vestige of truth in the theories now put forward. Macaulay veered, it is true, towards the Whigs; but he was not a Court Historian.

APPENDIX III.

THE CASKET LETTERS.

THE casket is said to have contained eight letters and certain French sonnets. The principal evidence against Mary Stuart is, however, contained in the second letter, a communication of great length addressed, as is alleged, to Bothwell at Glasgow. There was originally great difficulty in reconciling the Queen's admittedly short sojourn in that city with the production of such an extended document, and even now the dates render it very questionable whether it could have been indited in the time.

The Privy Seal Register contains two deeds signed by Mary at Edinburgh on the 22nd and 24th of January, while, according to the same Register, the Queen was at Linlithgow on her return from Glasgow.

However, it has been thought possible that Letter II. was written from Glasgow, partly on account of a belief in the old adage, "love will find out the way;" while the diaries of two Edinburgh citizens, one named Birrell, and another, the author of the 'Diurnal of Remarkable Occurrences,' seem to confirm the dates which render the epistolary performance in question possible, giving the 20th as the day Mary Stuart left Edinburgh. But when this Letter II. comes to be critically examined, a very great difficulty assails any believer in the integrity of Murray, Morton, and their coadjutors who vouched for the verity of these writings.

Part of the letter purports to describe to Bothwell a conversation between Mary Stuart (the alleged writer) and Darnley when they met at Glasgow.

The husband is represented as pleading for a re-establishment of his wife's good graces by reason of a resolution to improve his conduct, and claiming an opportunity of amending on account of his youth.

Now it happened that one Crawford, a relation and retainer of the Lennox family, was sent to Glasgow by the Earl to observe details concerning the meeting of Mary and Darnley, and in a deposition made after the murder related what the doomed King had told him of that interview.

The late Dr. Hill Burton, no friend to Mary Stuart's cause, was led to compare this deposition of Crawford's with the above-named passage in Letter II., and wrote concerning them as follows:—" Of the result I can only say that the two agree together with an overwhelming exactness."[*]

Is it not perfectly incredible that Crawford's memory of what Darnley told him about the conversation should tally, almost word for word and sentence for sentence, with the description given by Mary Stuart in a letter to Bothwell?

[*] Burton's 'History of Scotland,' vol. iv. p. 267.

Appendix III.   287

Any lawyer used to deal with evidence would necessarily conclude—as did the late Mr. Hosack—that either Crawford saw this alleged epistle of Mary Stuart's before he made the deposition which included her sentences, or else this portion of the letter was copied from the statement in question.

Our readers must decide for themselves which is most probable, remembering, however, that Crawford had been engaged by Lennox to collect " matter " against Mary when accused of her husband's murder.

Available copies of what are believed to be original French versions of the Casket Letters are these, viz. Nos. III. and V. in the Record Office, and Nos. IV. and VI. at Hatfield.

Number VI. is a compromising document to Mary if it can be proved genuine, because advice is therein given to Bothwell by the writer not to entrust their guilty secret to his "false brother" (in law), viz. Huntly. The same may be said of Letters VII. and VIII., although this nobleman's name is alluded to in regard to less important matters. A great deal has been made of the fact that Huntly never specially denounced the Casket Letters as forgeries when transactions in which he had been mixed up were freely named, but contented himself by averring that Murray and his associates "calumniated the Queen to cloak their own rebellion."*
But is it certain that Huntly and Argyll were allowed to see the documents in question? They were certainly not amongst the chosen few who "sichted" Morton's silver casket, while there is reason to think that Huntly's tongue was tied, inasmuch as it is believed that he was himself privy to the conspiracy to get rid of Darnley, which the Lords initiated at Craigmillar.

It was indeed a touch of genius on the part of any forger who introduced these allusions to Huntly, Bothwell's former friend and brother-in-law, into the text, because he (the concoctor), secure in knowledge of the circumstances, need dread no denial, and yet render his work apparently genuine.

Concerning the alleged "band" for Darnley's murder, Lord Herries † declared that it was found in the silver Casket, an averment by no means disproved because Morton's associates discovered no such paper during the inspection at Edinburgh on June 21, 1567. They probably had but a cursory view of such a mass of manuscript. Nor has anything been elicited to discredit the rumour to which Sir William Drury, the English Governor of Berwick, gave currency, viz. that this compromising document was submitted to the flames towards the close of November 1567.‡

Numbers III., IV., and V. of the Casket Documents are harmless love-letters, and might have appeared in Darnley's cabinet.

But the believers in Hosack's theory have never shown how the Associated Lords got hold of Darnley's private papers, as they must have done to complete the forgeries which Hosack thought he had discovered. Darnley may, it is true, have left some at Holyrood or in Edinburgh Castle, but all that was in the Kirk o' Field probably perished at the explosion.

---

* Proclamation of Huntly and Argyll, Crawford's ' Scotland,' p. 90.

† Hosack's 'Mary Queen of Scots. A Short Statement,' quoting Lord Herries' ' Memoirs,' pp. 99–100.

‡ Sir William Drury to Cecil, November 28, 1567.

There remain the French sonnets for consideration, and of these it is fair to record that Brantôme, the celebrated French chronicler, who was familiar with Mary Stuart's poetical compositions, repudiated the verses contained in the Casket, as incompatible with her style, while Sir David Dalrymple (Lord Hailes, 1726–1792) proved to the satisfaction of Robertson the historian "that they must have been written after the murder of the King, and prior to Mary's marriage with Bothwell."*

In pointing out the difficulties of blindly accepting the Casket Letters as genuine, the writer by no means pretends to speak dogmatically upon a controversy which depends for its outcome on long and arduous analysis of internal evidence—such as that of Malcolm Laing, Goodall, Hosack, Skelton, and Henderson, which has been necessarily avoided here. Whatever might be the opinion arrived at, it could not completely efface the original impression formed by men like Sir Nicholas Bacon and Sir Ralph Sadler, who compared the Casket Letters with Mary Stuart's handwriting before the Westminster Conference, and could see no difference between them.

Although these Elizabethan statesmen and diplomatists were primarily concerned on behalf of their Sovereign's interests, we can have no right to accuse them of deliberate untruthfulness on this occasion.

Mary Stuart's innocence or guilt did not, in Cecil's opinion, altogether depend upon the truth of these writings, although he has erased and altered the several copies at Hatfield (Letters IV. and VI.) until suspicions have been raised in the minds of modern visitors that they beheld the alleged forgeries in process of preparation.

The great Minister, however, based his case mainly on that cursory view of passing events which led the outside world alike to marvel and condemn.

After a brief précis of the points in the Hatfield Casket Letters which Cecil thought might tend to the Scottish Queen's condemnation he makes the following notes on the back of his paper:—

"10 Febru.—Ye K. of Scottes killed.
"5 April.—A contract for mariage signed by ye Q. of Scottes.
"12 April.—Bothwell purged by assise.
"17 April.—Erle Murray cam to Westm.
"19 April.—A band scaled by ye L. of Scotland; a warrant signed ye same day.
          (The Erle of Huntly restored.)
"24 April.—Bothwell toke ye Quene.
"P° Maii.—Devorce began; ended 8 Maii.
"15 Maii.—The Q. marr. to Bothwell.
"15 Junii.—The Q. was taken by her Nobillite."†

Believers in the truth and integrity of the evidence contained in the silver Casket have, however, to explain what became of an alleged warrant from Mary Stuart, requiring the nobles who attended Ainslie's tavern to sign the "band" for her marriage.

This was alleged by the Lords to be in the Casket, and was surreptitiously shown at York, but never has been since heard of.‡

Unless unexpected light should be thrown upon this problem of the

---

* Robertson's 'History of Scotland,' vol. ii. p. 379.
† Hatfield Calendar,' part i. p. 370.
‡ Skelton's 'Maitland of Lethington,' vol. ii. p. 317.

Appendix III. 289

Casket Letters by a subsequent re-arrangement and restoration of the vast mass of manuscript in the Cottonian Library, British Museum, each successive writer on the subject (and they will probably be legion) will stand face to face with an indissoluble mystery; but nevertheless, owing to the late Mr. Hosack, judgment will not go by default against Queen Mary in accordance with the lofty demands of Hume and Froude.

The last tidings of the silver Casket and its contents, after being in keeping of the several Regents Murray, Lennox, Mar, and Morton, comes from the Gowrie family, in whose possession they were before James VI. put the Earl of that name to death in 1584, and seized all his effects.

But whether the Ruthvens or the King destroyed the documents must remain uncertain for all time.

It was not known until late years that any copies existed, either at Hatfield or in the Record Office.

APPENDIX IV.

"I, Margaret Dawson,* tho weake in body, yet of sound mind and memory, for which God be blessed, foreseeing that, by reason of my great age and weaknesse, the time of my dissolution draweth nigh, do here in the presence of God Almighty, before whom I shall shortly appear, make this solemn Declaration that what I have written with my own hand and subscribed to, in a little book concerning the birth of his Royal Highness the Prince of Wales, at which I was present when He was brought into the World by the Queen's Majesty his Mother, is certain and true to my knowledge, and that if God Almighty should vouchsafe to continue me longer in this world, I would most readily and conscientiously attest the same upon oath before any person or persons whatever, whenever I should be called and summoned to give in my Evidence.

"Witnesse this my hand this thirteenth day of February, 1700.
"(Signed) MARGARET DAWSON."

"We whose names are underwritten do testify and declare, y^t Mrs. Margaret Dawson did freely subscribe the declaration above written, after it was twice distinctly read unto her, and after she had declared y^t she distinctly heard the same. We also testify y^t she owned the above said declaration, after she had subscribed the same, to be her act and deed, and likewise that during the severall readings of the said declaration she held the book mentioned in it in her hand.

"Witness our hands, the day, and month, and year above written.
"(Signed) GEORGE HICKES, D.D.
THOMAS SMITH, D.D.
THOMAS BOTELER, A.M.
BRIDGET HARRISON."

Additional MSS., Brit. Museum, No. 33,286.
„   „   „   „   „   26,657.

---

* Margaret Dawson was Bedchamber Woman to Mary of Modena.

INDEX.

ABBEVILLE, 208, 267, 272
Abercorn taken by James II., 44
Aberdeen threatened, 13—gives bond for James I.'s ransom, 29—"Trades" of, 212—mentioned, 268
———, Bishop of, promotes meeting between Livingston and Crichton, 39
Aberdeenshire, 99
Ainslie's Tavern, meeting of Bothwell and adherents at, 109—referred to, 288
Alan, son of Flaald, obtains grant of Oswestry, 1
———, second of the (mythical) Stewards of Scotland, 1
———, second (historical) Steward of Scotland, son of Walter, succeeds his father, 3
Albany, Alexander, Duke of (son of James II.), 46—brother's jealousy, 48—escapes to France and marries, 49—intrigues, *ib.*—design of Edward IV. to make him King, *ib.*—returns to Scotland, 50—driven out, *ib.*—killed, *ib.*—mock siege of Edinburgh, *ib.*—treason, *ib.*
———, Murdoch of, son of the Regent, 21, 23—assumes the Regency, 26—weakness of, *ib.*—arranges ransom of James I., *ib.*, 27—intrigues, 30—retribution, *ib.*—trial, *ib.*—he and sons beheaded, *ib.*
——— of Boulogne, Duke, Regent under James V., position in France, 68—hesitates to accept Regency, 69—makes stipulations, *ib*—represents the French faction, *ib.*—distrusted by Henry VIII., *ib.*—negotiations in France with Francis I., 71—Queen Dowager returns in his absence, *ib.*—invests Hamilton Castle, *ib.*—pardons Earl of Arran, *ib.*—remains in France, *ib.*—returns, 72—hostility of Henry VIII., *ib.*—prepares for campaign, *ib.*—conduct criticised, *ib.*—accepts mediation, *ib.*—goes to France for aid, *ib.*—truce broken by England, *ib.*—obtains French aid, 73—lands and marches to Melrose, *ib.*—advises James V., *ib.*—goes again to France, *ib.*
Albany, Robert, Duke of, and Earl of Fife, son of Robert II., 9—invades England, 14—made governor of the kingdom, *ib.*—governs for Robert III., 15-22—renews league with France, 16—rivalry with Earl of Carrick, 17, 18—receives dukedom, 18—calls a Parliament (1398), *ib.*—charges against, *ib.*—at Calder Moor, 19—charged with nephew's murder, 20—son taken prisoner, 21—becomes Regent, 23—marches to Dingwall, 24—burns a Wycliffite, *ib.*—attacks Roxburgh and Berwick unsuccessfully, *ib.*—estimates of his conduct, *ib.*, 25—dies (1419), 25—his marriages, *ib.*, 26
Albemarle, Duke of. *See* Monk.
Alesta, second wife of Alan, second Steward, daughter of Morgund, 3
Alexander III., Norwegian invasion, 3—death, 4
———, 4th Steward, commands at Largs, 3—marries, 4—buried at Paisley, *ib.*
———, elder son of James I., dies in infancy, 37
———, posthumous son of James IV., 67
——— VIII. dies, 191
Allan (river), 263
Alva, Duke of, 127
American (U. S.) Republic, influence of the religious immigration in moulding its character, 148
Ancrum, skirmish at, 87
Andrew, St., Order of (Knighthood), 282

U 2

Andrew, St., Order of (Monastic), 175, 212
Andrews, 237
Andrews, St., 83, 86—Protestants get possession of castle, 88—destroy monastery, 91
——, ——, Archbishop of, natural son of James IV., killed at Flodden, 65
——, ——, Bishop of. *See* Kennedy or Wardlaw.
——, ——, Cathedral of, marriage of James V. at, 81
——, ——, University founded (1411), 25
Anglicanism, attempted revival of, 147
Angus, Earl of, withdraws from the family (Douglas) camp, 44
——, Archibald Douglas, Earl of, surnamed "Bell the Cat," 50—concludes peace with England, *ib.*—relations with Albany, *ib.*—accusation against the King, 51—taunted at Flodden, 64—dies, 69
——, Earl of (grandson of "Bell the Cat"), marries James IV.'s widow, 68—a competitor for the Regency, *ib.*—sides with the English faction, 69—his wife leaves him, 70—divorce, 71, 74—kills Patrick Hamilton, 71—partisan of England, 72—tool of Henry VIII., 73—with Douglas faction gets possession of James V., 74—besieged in Tantallon, 76—driven to exile, 77—sister burnt, 82
—— shire, 42
Annabella, Countess of Mar, 131
——, Queen of Robert III., anointed, 15—promotes her son's marriage, 18—dies (1401), 19—anecdote of, 22
Anne of Brittany. *See* Brittany.
—— of Denmark, coronation of, 136—favours Ruthvens, 137—James fetches her from Norway, *ib.*—remonstrates at separation from her son Henry, 144
——, Princess, letter to her sister, (n.) 179, 180—acquiesces in the Revolution, 180, 185—Queen, French wars of, 157, 202—fidelity to her family, 204, 214—importance of her life to Jacobite plans, 214—alluded to, 231, 270
Anstruther, town of, 129
Arbuthnot, 219, 250, 271

Archery enjoined, 45
Areskin, Sir John. *See* Erskine.
Argile, 222. *See* Argyll.
Argyll, Countess of, present at Rizio's murder, 101
——, Earl of, killed at Flodden, 65
——, ——, connives at deliverance of James V., 76, 77
——, 5th Earl of, takes part in conference at Craigmillar, 105—supports Bothwell's project for marrying the Queen, 109—with others takes arms against him, 110—an " Associated Lord," 118—betrays his confederates, 119
——, Archibald Campbell, 9th Earl of, tried and condemned under Test Act, 210
——, —— ——, Marquess of, opposed to Montrose, 148—assists at Charles II.'s coronation at Scone, 160—put to death, *ib.*—mentioned, 174
——, John, Duke of, Dutch troops in army of (1715), 93—at Sheriffmuir, 207, 263—advances to Montrose, 208—gains ground of Marlborough, 222—submission of Huntly to, 280
Argyllshire remains faithful to George I., 207
Aristocracy of Scotland, wealth and loyalty, 15th century, 29, 30
Arkinholme (near Langholm, Dumfriesshire), Douglases defeated at, 44
Arlington, Lord, 158
Armada, the, 96, 129, 132
Armstrong and retainers hanged, 77
Army, letters to, from Pretender, 251, 258
——, parliamentary struggle for ascendancy, 149
——, standing, formation of nucleus of, 168—disaffection of, 184
Arnold, Duke of Gueldres and Cleves, 40
Arran, Island of, invaded by Haco, 4
——, Earl of, son of Lord Boyd, 47
——, ——, sent with aid to France, 61, 62—prospects of succession, 69,—pardoned by Albany, 71—escapes at Kelso fight, *ib.*—natural son, treachery of, 74—next in succession, 83—temporises, 86—becomes Regent, 87—signs treaty for Mary's marriage, *ib.*—resigns Regency, and is created

Index. 293

Duke of Chatelherault, 90—follows Knox, 91, 92
Arran, James Stewart, Earl of, favourite of James VI., 131—scheme for a joint government, *ib.*, 132
——, Earl of, letter from Chesterfield, 169
——, Dowager Countess of, daughter of James II., saves Hamilton Castle, 71
Arthur, Prince of Wales, contracted to Catherine of Arragon, 57
——, infant of James IV., dies, 67
——, infant of James V., dies, 83
Articles, Lords of, 30
Artillery, field, first use of, in Scotland, 65
Arundel, Earls of, ancestry of, 2
——, Lord (Henry, Earl of), 120
——, Thomas, Earl of (5th Duke of Norfolk), 211
Ashburton, 150
"Associated Lords," 113, 118, 287
"Athenæum" referred to, (n.) 79, 118
Athole, Walter, Earl of, claimant to throne, 32—put to death, 37
——, Earl of, summoned by James III., 51
——, ——, killed at Flodden, 65
——, ——, entertains James V., 78
——, John, Earl of, visited by Lethington, 104—rises against Bothwell, 110—leads Mary in triumph, 111—present at opening of the Casket, 117—signs warrant for Mary's imprisonment, 118—an "Associated Lord," *ib.*—adheres to Murray, 122
——, Jacobite Duke of, 241
Atterbury, 224
Aubigny. *See* D'Aubigny.
——, Esmé Stuart of. *See* Lennox, Duke of.
Audineham, Arnold, Marshal of France, brings help against Baliol, 7
l'Aumarie, M., 217, 227
d'Avaux, Count, 181
Avignon, 26, 275, 281
Ayala, Pedro de, his personal description of James IV., 57—criticism on 62

Babington's Conspiracy, 128
Bacon, Francis, 142
——, Sir Nicholas, 120, 288
Balfour, Sir James, complicity in Darnley's murder, 117—delivers the Casket to Bothwell's servant, whom he afterwards arrests, *ib.*
Baliol, Edward, overruns the kingdom, 7—quits it, 8
——, John, contests the crown with Bruce, 4, 5—direct descent from William the Lion, 186
Balmauno, house of, garrisoned, 278
Banbury, 143
"Band, the" (a league of Douglases and others), 42—"Band" for murder of Rizio, 101—for marriage of Mary with Bothwell, 192, 288
Bannockburn, battle of, 5, 6, 52
Banquo, traditional Stuart ancestor, 1
Bapst, Edmond, referred to, (n.) 79, 85
Barbour quoted, 5
Barclay, Sir George, 200
Barillon, 185, 187
Bar-le-Duc, 206, 248, 255
Bartholomew, St., massacre of, 127—effect of, 129
Barton, Andrew, helps to create navy, 59—semi-piratical exploits, 61
Basilicon Doron, 139
Bass Rock, Prince James (James I.) at, 21
Bastie, La, murdered, 71
Battles, skirmishes, &c.: Largs (1263), 3, 4—Bannockburn (1314), 5, 6—Halidon Hill (1333), 7—Nevil's Cross (1346), 9—Otterburn, 14—judicial, Clans Kay and Quete (1396), 16—Homildon Hill (1402), 21—Harlaw (1411), 24—Beauge (1421), 26, 28—Verneuil, 26—Western Islanders and Lord Mar (1431), 31—Arkinholme (1455), 44—Sauchieburn (1488), 52—Flodden (1513), 64, 65—artillery at, 64—Kelso (1520), 71—Manuel (1527), 74—Halydon Rigg (1541), 83—Solway Moss (1542), 84—Ancrum (1554), 87—Pinkie (1547), 88—Corrichie, 99—Carberry Hill (1567), 111—Langside, 115—Edgehill (1642), 143—Marston Moor (1644), 146—Naseby (1645), 148—Kilsyth (1645), *ib.*—Philiphaugh (1645), *ib.*—Wigan (1648), 151—Warrington, (1648), *ib.*—Dunbar (1650), 160—Worcester (1651), 161—Sedgmoor (1685), 173—Beachy Head (1690), 187—Boyne (1690), *ib.*

—Killiecrankie (1689), 188 — La Hogue (1692), 192—Culloden (1745), 202, 275—Sheriffmuir (1715), 205, 207—Preston, 207, 275
Bavaria, Prince of, 217
Beachy Head, 187
Beaton (one of "the Queen's Maries"), 90
———, David (afterwards Cardinal), envoy to Francis I., 76, 79, 83—Ministry of, intolerant, 83—concerts hostilities against England, 84—opposes Henry VIII.'s schemes, 85, 87—released and takes refuge at St. Andrews, 86—schemes to become Regent foiled, 87—arrested, *ib.*—thwarts English marriage scheme, *ib.*—burns Wishart, 88—assassinated, *ib.*
———, James, Chancellor of Scotland, 74—consents to deliverance of James V., *ib.*, 76
Beaton's Mill, James III. murdered at, 52
Beatrix, daughter of Gilchrist, 3
Beaufort, Cardinal, 28
———, Jane, 27—married to James I., 28—heroism of, 33—(Queen Dowager) smuggles the King out of Edinburgh, 38
Beauge, battle of, 26, 28
Beauté, Albany's ambassador, 69
Bedford, Duke of, success at Verneuil 26
———, Earl of, 104
Bedloe, the informer, 166
Belgrade, siege of, (n.) 178
Bellenden, John, page of James V., 76
"Bell the Cat." *See* Angus, Archibald, Earl of.
Benedict XIII., 38
Bennet, 238, 239
———, Sir Henry (Lord Arlington), 158
Berwick taken by the Scots (1318), 6—raid on, 24—mentioned, 80, 83, 87
———, Duchess of, 215
———, Duke of, 193—fails in arousing Jacobite action, 200—fears being implicated in conspiracy against William, *ib.*—parentage of, 204—hitherto unpublished letters of, *ib.*—founder of the house of Fitz James, *ib.*—presumptive claim to the throne, *ib.*—letter quoted, *ib.*—his position in 1715, *ib.*, 205—advises the Chevalier to marry, 205—refuses command of 1715 expedition, 206—letter regarding Oxford's ministry, 214—doubts about him, *ib.*—speculations as to Marlborough's course, 215—counsels him to silence as to religion, 216—correspondence with Marlborough about a pardon, *ib.*—urges the Chevalier to influential marriage, 216, 217—fruitless correspondence with Marlborough, 217, 218—anticipation of Oxford's hostility, 218—announces the Chevalier's intention to land in Scotland, *ib.*—attended by himself, *ib.*—doubts about Marlborough, *ib.*—intrigue to gain the fleet, 219—desires to gain over Bolingbroke, *ib.*—opinion of Oxford, 220 — interchanges New Year's compliments between the Chevalier and Louis XIV., *ib.* — Marlborough's influence with the Elector, *ib.*—comments on Bolingbroke's arrival, 222—anticipations as to Ormond's measures, *ib.*—thanks Marlborough for his present, *ib.*—writes the Chevalier account of interview with Bolingbroke, 224—the Chevalier's reply, 225—writes to the Chevalier about Bolingbroke and Marlborough, 226—receives suggestions from the Chevalier to Bolingbroke, and arms and money, 227—Chevalier urges Berwick's preparations for the expedition, 229—Berwick urges action in any case, *ib.*—expostulated with by Chevalier as to difficulty in joining expedition, 230—advises delay, 232—his health, *ib.*—informed by Bolingbroke of the Chevalier's impatience, *ib.*—arrangement for Marlborough to join the Chevalier on his landing, 233—letter from Chevalier respecting Duke of Shrewsbury and Lady Westmoreland, 235—the Chevalier enquires about his footing with the Regent, 237—interview with Duke of Orleans concerning the Chevalier's interests, 238—in favour with the Regent, 239—naturalised in France, (n.) *ib.*—in consequence does not join 1715 expedition, (n.) *ib.*—English expectation of a landing, 246—advises as to preliminary steps, *ib.*, 247—describes

his own wish to share in it, and the obstacles to his doing so, 247—presses Marlborough to declare himself. *ib.* —excuses to the Chevalier, *ib.*, 248— the Chevalier's remarks on the communication, 248—commission and order delivered to him, 249—excuses himself, *ib.*—final resolution, 253— the Chevalier's remarks upon it, 256, 257—apologises for abstention, 259 —informs the Chevalier of measures affecting his embarkation, *ib.*, 260— distrusted by the Chevalier, 262— Chevalier wishes for his help in Scotland, 264—his reputation there, 269 —blamed for not joining the Chevalier, *ib.*—vindicates himself in letter to Mar, *ib.*—subject referred to, 271
Bible printed in Scotland, 130
Birrell, diary of, 286
Bishops, the seven, trial of, 177— reception by the troops of news of acquittal, 184
Black Friars' Monastery, murder of James I. at, 32—destroyed by Knox's followers, 91
Blackness, parley at, 52—Beaton imprisoned in castle, 86, 87
Blair Athole, 78
Blake, Admiral, 157, 167
Blois, 226
"Bloody Assize," the, 173
"Bobbing John," nickname of Lord Mar, 263
Boleyn, Anne, 116
Bolingbroke, Lord, hitherto unpublished letters of, 203, 204—intrigues with Marlborough, 204—his services to the Chevalier, 205—summoned to meet him at Dieppe, *ib.*—attainted, *ib.*—summary of the situation in 1715, 206—exculpates himself from Mar's and Murray's charges, 208— commended by the Duke of Berwick, *ib.*—presumed loss of letters, &c., by shipwreck, *ib.*—desired to meet the Pretender on his way to Paris, *ib.*— overtures to, 219, 220—expected interview with Berwick, 222—letter to Berwick from the Chevalier on the same subject, 223—letter of proposals from the Chevalier, *ib.*— interview with Berwick, 224—breaks promise given to Lord Stair, *ib.*— opinion of Ormond and others, *ib.* —upholds the prerogative; presses the Chevalier to marry, 225—the interview commented on by the Chevalier to Berwick, *ib.*—cautiousness and movements of, 226—difficulty in meeting the Chevalier, 227—complains of female interference, *ib.*—earnest request of the Chevalier for an interview, 228, 229 —requested by the Chevalier to embark with him, 230—created an Earl *in partibus*, 231—letter (the first) to the Chevalier, thanking him and hinting at treachery, 232— informs Berwick of the Chevalier's impatience, *ib.*—statement to the Chevalier of objections to interview with Ormond, 233—Duke of Leeds referred to him, *ib.*—sends messenger to the Chevalier touching Ormond's flight, 234—the Chevalier suggests to him uniting Ormond and Marlborough, *ib.*—letter from the Chevalier anticipating Louis XIV.'s death, and advising courting successor, 235—writes to Chevalier that Louis XIV. is at point of death, 236— asks instruction as to waiting on the Regent, *ib.*—suggests overtures to Lord Peterborough, *ib.*—letter from Chevalier as to making interest with the Regent, particularly as to continuance of pension, *ib.*, 237—to consult with Mary of Modena about marriage proposal for the Chevalier, 237—letter from the Chevalier as to disposal of Marlborough's contribution, enquires as to Berwick's standing with the Regent, and remarks about Ormond, Marlborough, and others, *ib.*—thanked by Chevalier for freedom of advice, *ib.*— letter to the Chevalier respecting Duke of Orleans, &c. (written while Louis XIV. was dying), 238—delay necessary in approaching the Regent, 239—informs the Chevalier of Louis XIV.'s death, *ib.*—of Berwick's relations with Orleans, *ib.*—opinion of Danby and Portmore, *ib.*, 240— letter to Chevalier respecting the Regent and his intentions, 240— letter from the Chevalier, discusses

the landing, *ib.*—being ill, writes through secretary that Mar has retired to the Highlands, 241—reviews situation created by death of Louis XIV., *ib.*—his expectations of the landing of the Chevalier in Scotland, *ib.*, 242—of future help from the Regent, 241—calls upon English adherents to advise as to place of landing, &c., 242—ready to accompany the Chevalier, *ib.*—pledges the Chevalier's coming, *ib.*—summarises the situation under the Regency; failure of assistance from him; urges action in England, 245—makes arrangement for the Chevalier's transit, 246—his going with the Chevalier proposed, 248—alluded to, *ib.*—delivers commission to Berwick, 249—his conduct of affairs, (n.) *ib.*—sends money and the seals to the Chevalier, *ib.*—complains of hostility of French officials, 250—advises as to measures to be taken, *ib.*—asks the Chevalier for letters to fleet, army, universities, and London, and declaration, 251—alludes to designs against the persons of Ormond and the Chevalier, *ib.*—obtains information as to the Regent's intentions, 252—is more hopeful, 253—repeats advice to the Chevalier for care of his safety, *ib.*—endeavours to frustrate Stair's watchfulness, *ib.*—secret aid promised by the Regent kept from his knowledge, 254—grounds for advice to Chevalier to be careful of his safety, 255—communications from the Chevalier, *ib.*—dealings with the Regent, 256—question whether he shall accompany expedition or not, *ib.*—his destination of ships approved, 257—advises waiting for news of Ormond, *ib.*—informs Chevalier of Dutch aid to George I., 259—mentioned, 260—informs Chevalier of Stair's demand to stop him, *ib.*—letter to Chevalier respecting his movements, *ib.*—informs him of Maclean's treachery, 261—urges the Chevalier's departure, 262—letter to Lord Mar on the situation, asking him to receive information from Lloyd, and informing him that a ship will be sent with supplies, 265-267—Hamilton sent to him about supplies, 270—Hamilton's account of interview, 271—probable effect on the Chevalier, *ib.*—to be superseded by Mar, 273—congratulates and condoles with the Chevalier, *ib.*—suspects his coming disfavour, *ib.*—defends himself to Lord Mar, 273, 274—his dismissal, 275—letter to Mar in reference to it, *ib.*—refers to expected answer from Spain, *ib.*—alluded to, 282

Bonkyl, Sir Alexander, 5
Bonrepaux, 185
Booth, 227, 258, 261, 262
Boroughmuir (now Morningside), muster and dispersion of James V.'s army at, 83
Borthwick, commander of artillery at Flodden, 64
—— Castle, 111
Boscobel, Charles II. at, 161
Boteler, Thomas, A.M., 290
Bothwell, Earl of, killed at Flodden, 65
——, James Hepburn, Earl of, 104, 105—his share in Darnley's murder, 106, (n.) *ib.*—created Duke of Orkney, 106—his character, 107—imputed early design (1561) to carry off the Queen, 108—efforts to seize her son, *ib.*—visited by her, *ib.*—accused of Darnley's murder, *ib.*, 109—acquitted, 109—project for marrying the Queen sanctioned by nobles, *ib.*—carries her off, *ib.*—offers single combat, 111—takes flight, *ib.*—doubts as to possibility of divorce from previous marriage, 112—escape connived at, 113—referred to, 114—evidence against in the CasketLetters, 117, 118—Morton's account of Casket, 117—loss of and attempt to recover, *ib.*—alleged design to carry off Prince James, 118, 122—design referred to, in reference to discovery of body in Edinburgh Castle, 283—in connection with the Casket Letters, 286—289

Boulogne, 208, 267, 272
——, Duke Albany of. *See* Albany.
——, Earl of, 49
Bourbon family, attitude towards Scotland, 93

Index. 297

Bowles, the Rev. Edward, an important agent in the Restoration, 163
Boyd ancestry, 2
——, Earl of Arran, 47
——, Sir Alexander, martial instructor to James III., 46—influence over, *ib.*—treasonably carries him off, 47—arrogates power, *ib.*—beheaded, *ib.*
——, Lord, of Kilmarnock, influence over James III., 46—hints of his treason, 47—escapes to England and dies, *ib.*
——, ——, supports Bothwell's project for marrying the Queen, 109—an "Associated Lord," 118—betrays his associates, 119—Mary's Commissioner, 120
Boyne, battle of the, 187
Branksome Moor (Flodden), 68
Brantôme declares sonnets in Casket not Mary's, 288
Breadalbane, Earl of, 189
"Breeches Bible" in reference to use of letter J., 284
Brentford, 143
Brest, 73, 89—attack on, 196, 199
Brichen, 267
Brighthelmstone, 161
Brinsdon, Bolingbroke's secretary, 208
Bristol, 86, 161, 206, 207
Brittany, Anne of, anecdote of, 35—fatal influence over James IV., 58, 61
Broderick, Sir Allen, 158
Broghill, Lord. *See* Orrery.
Bruce, Marjory. *See* Marjory.
——, Robert, contests crown, 4, 5—Elizabeth, wife of, 5—Marjory, daughter of, *ib.*, 6—her death, 6—regulates succession, *ib.*—fidelity to, shown by general acceptance of Stuart dynasty, 11—tactics of, 66, 72—succession of, indirect, 186
"Brunswick Accession," (n.) 179, 202
Buccleuch family concerned in rescue of James V., 74
Buchan, Earl of, half-brother of Robert III., 15—set over Highlands with his son, *ib.*—savage conduct of, 16
——, John Stuart, Earl of (son of Regent Albany), acquires Earldom of Ross, 24—conquers at Beauge (1421), 26, 28—killed at Verneuil, 26
Buchanan, George, quoted or referred to, (n.) 43, 51, 63, 70, 73, 77, 79, 97, 100, 107, preceptor to James VI., 131

Buckingham, George Villiers, Duke of, James VI. and Charles I. under influence of, 141—journey to Spain with Charles, *ib.*—murder of, 142
Burgundy, Dukes of, 40
Burnet, Bishop, omens at coronation of James II., 174—charge against James II., 200
Burnt Island, 207
Burton's History of Scotland quoted or referred to: in reference to Regency of Walter Stuart, 7—to candidature of Douglas, 11—character of Robert II., 15—Rothesay's murder, 18—position of the Regent Albany, 24—estimate of his conduct, 25—doubts as to Richard II., *ib.*—murder of James I., 33—Douglas alliances, 40—murder, (n.) 43—James III. and his favourites, 50—strength of army, 62—field of Flodden, 64—on alliance against France, (n.) 72—authorships ascribed to James V., 77—Chastelard, 97—Dundrennan Abbey, (n.) 116—Casket Letters, 119—remains of child, Edinburgh Castle, 283—remarks on No. 2 Casket Letter, 286
Bute, Island of, 4, 7
Byng, Admiral, 207

CADUGAN (Cadogan), 278, 280
Caen, 254
Caerlaverock Castle, James V., at, 84
Caermarthen, Peregrine, Marquess of, naval mistake of, 199
Caernarvon, Exchequer at, 2
Caithness, Earl of, summoned by James III., 51
——, ——, killed at Flodden, 65
—— supports Bothwell's project for marrying the Queen, 109
Calahan, Father, 230
Calais, 199, 266, 270, 273
Calder Moor, 19
Calvinists, outrages by, 91
Cambuskenneth Abbey, James III. and Margaret buried there, 54
Camden's History referred to, 97
Cameron, 221, 223, 229, 232, 253, 256
Camocke, Mr. George, 207 (Cammock), 246, 264
Campbell, Colin, of Lochow, takes Dunoon, 7
Campion, Mr., 249, 252

Canongate, death of Mar at, 49
Caprara, Monsieur, 194
Carberry Hill, battle of, 111
Carlisle besieged, 13—mentioned, 72,84
Carlyle supports Bothwell's project for marrying the Queen, 109
Carrick, Earl of. *See* Rothesay.
Carter, Admiral, killed, 193
Carthusian Monastery at Perth burnt, 91
Caryll, Lord, correspondence with Bishop Ellis, 196-199
"Casket, the," story of, 117, 118—
—successive custodians of it, 289
"Casket Letters," handed to Murray by Morton, 116 — examined by Morton and others, 117, 118—genuineness vouched for, 118—examination of controversy respecting, 119, 120—possible tampering with, 120—discussion of in Appendix iii., 286-289
Cassilis, Earl of, killed at Flodden, 65
——, ——, supports Bothwell's project for marrying the Queen, 109
Castelblanco, Comte de, 227, 272
Castle-Stewart, ancestry of Earls of, 26
Catesby, 139, 140
Catherine, Queen of France (1420), 28
—— of Arragon, contracted to Arthur, Prince of Wales, 57
—— of Braganza, 170, 179, 211
—— de Medici, Regent of France, 94
—unfriendly to Queen Mary (Stuart), 102
Catholic League of 1565, 96—of 1577, 128
Catholics (Roman) and Protestants, iniquities of, 129
Caxton, 67
Cecil, Robert, Earl of Salisbury, 142
——, William Lord Burleigh, his statements touching treaty with Mary and Francis II., 93, 94—letter from Randolph, 95, 96—letter from N. White, 98—from Throckmorton, 100—pacific influence, 115—hostility towards Mary, 116— has Morton's deposition, 117 — Commissioner in matter of Mary Stuart, 120, 121, 128, 133—his opinion on the Casket Letters, and annotations on them, 288
Cecilia, daughter of James II., 46
——, daughter of Patrick, Earl of Dunbar and March, 5

Chaillot, 214, 215
——, abbess of, 180
Chalmers referred to: sale of title of Steward, 2—Bothwell and the Queen, 108
Chalons, Margaret, daughter of James I., dies at, 35
Chamberlen, Dr. Hugh, (n.) 179
Charles I. prejudiced by his father against the Presbyterians, 136—birth of, 137, 138—intended murder of, 139—journey to Spain, 141—marriage, *ib.*—failure of his policy, 142—attempted arrest of the five members, *ib.*—imminence of war, *ib.* —character and measures, 145—at advantage with the enemy, 146—defeated at Marston Moor by Scotch help, *ib.*—zeal for prelacy his irretrievable error, *ib.*—opinion of political influence of the Church, 147—reverses, 148— putting him to death an infringement of parliamentary privilege, 149—sold by the Scotch, *ib.*—escapes from Oxford, 150—hesitates whether to surrender to the Scotch, *ib.*—doubtful chances in London, 151—his wife's efforts, *ib.*—secret compact for protection of Roman Catholics, 152—beheaded, *ib.*—projected appeal to Irish loyalists, *ib.* —letter to his son Charles, 153
—— II. goes with his father to York, 142—technically king on his father's death, 156—evil influence of the circumstances of his exile, *ib.*—subservience to France partly forced by circumstances, 157—Puritan dissatisfaction with his birth, *ib.*—uncertainty of when he became a Roman Catholic, 158—poverty, *ib.*—raises money from English merchants in Poland, *ib.*—his character, 159—invited to Scotland, *ib.*—signs the covenant, *ib.*—intention of his doing penance, *ib.* —" the Stuart," attempt to escape known as, 160—crowned King of Scots at Scone, *ib.*—perfidy towards National Church of Scotland, *ib.*—enters England and is defeated at Worcester, 161—concealed at Boscobel, *ib.*—escapes to Fécamp, *ib.* —overtures to Monk, *ib.*—the Restoration, 164—plot to assassinate, *ib.*

—dispenses with Parliament, 165— personally popular, his faults notwithstanding, *ib.*—to prevent conversion of Duke of Gloucester, *ib.*— nucleus of standing army, 168— leaves government in hands of his ministers, *ib.*—war with the Dutch,*ib.* —subservience to France, *ib.*—death, 168-171—referred to, 206
Charles V. of France, 12
—— (Emperor), offers matrimonial alliances to James V., 79
—— VI., Emperor of Germany, projected matrimonial alliance of the Pretender with, 205, 216
—— IX., minority of, 94—requested to be sponsor for child of Queen Mary and Darnley, 103
—— XII. of Sweden, Jacobite hopes from, 229
—— Edward (the Young Pretender), 93, 275
Charlotte, daughter of Francis I., (n.) 79
Chartier, Alain, 35
Chastelard put to death, 100
Chatelherault, Dukedom of, 90—Duke 91, 129
Chattan (or Quete) Clan, 16, 17
Chaucer, 34
Chepman, Walter, introduces printing into Scotland, 67, 129
Cherbourg, 249
Chesterfield, Philip, Lord, letters describing death of Charles II., 169-171
Chevalier de St. George, James Francis Edward, birth of, and witnesses thereto, 178-180—acknowledged by Louis XIV., 201—declaration of, 1708, 203—distresses of, *ib.*—refuses to change his religion, 204, 214—dissatisfaction with Duke of Berwick, 204,205—attitude of Jacobites in England in 1715, 205—personal danger in journey to Dunkirk, 206, 207—sails from Dunkirk, 207—lands at Peterhead, *ib.*—fallacious hopes in Scotland, 208—escapes to France, *ib.*—complaints against Bolingbroke, *ib.*— landing at Gravelines, *ib.*—curious discrepancy, *ib.*—desires Bolingbroke to meet him on the way to Paris, *ib.* —letter of thanks to Dicconson, 213, 214—counselled by Berwick to silence as to religion, 216—urged by Berwick to form influential marriage, 216, 217—receives contribution from Marlborough, 220, 221—letter to Berwick about written power to borrow money and written commission, 221, 222—alarmed at Ormond's want of secrecy, 222—communication by Berwick as to Ormond, Bolingbroke, and Marlborough, *ib.*—regrets inability to communicate with English adherents, 223—writes (first letter) proposals to Bolingbroke, *ib.* —comments to Berwick on interview with Bolingbroke, 225—discusses marriage, *ib.*, 226 — difficulty in meeting Bolingbroke, 227—delivers Bolingbroke from "female teazers" at St. Germain, *ib.*—comments on Forester's project of insurrection and Louis XIV.'s illness, 228 — urges Bolingbroke to an interview, *ib.*, 229 —immediate expectation of setting out for England, 229—invites Bolingbroke to embark, 230—expostulation with Berwick concerning difficulty in joining in expedition, *ib.*—flattering letter and earldom to Bolingbroke, 231—impatience at delay, 232—Berwick arranges for Marlborough to join the Chevalier on his landing, 233—writes to Bolingbroke suggesting the uniting of Ormond with Marlborough, 234—letter to Berwick respecting Duke of Shrewsbury and Lady Westmoreland, 235—letter to Bolingbroke touching expected death of Louis XIV., *ib.*—from Bolingbroke suggesting paying court to the Regent, 236—from the Chevalier directing him and Ormond to do so, and suggesting his own writing to him; anxious about continuance of pension, 236, 237—allusion to a marriage proposal, 237—directs Bolingbroke that Marlborough's remittance should be sent to Dicconson, *ib.*— inquires of him the footing of Berwick with the Regent, *ib.*—remarks as to Ormond and others, *ib.*, 238— thanks Bolingbroke for freely advising, 237—informed by Bolingbroke of Louis's death, 239—of Berwick's favour with the Regent, *ib.*—and as

to Danby and Portmore, *ib.*—information from Bolingbroke about the Regent and his intentions, 240—writes to Bolingbroke as to chances of success, *ib.*—receives information of Mar's retirement, 241—and of doubts of Athole's fidelity, *ib.*—his personal coming pledged by Bolingbroke, 242—desires interview with Ormond, 244 — alludes to some private arrangement, *ib.*—intelligence from Berwick, 246—advised as to means of getting away from France for the purpose of the expedition, *ib.*—remarks on Berwick's hesitation, 247—receives explanation, *ib.*, 248—is dissatisfied with it, 248—advised by Bolingbroke to take care of his person, 252, 253—movements watched by Lord Stair, 253—reported scheme for assassination of, 255—fears of French interference with expedition, *ib.*, 256—hopes for connivance, 256—approval of Mar's behaviour, *ib.*—makes him a duke, *ib.*—comments on Berwick's refusal, *ib.*—approves of Bolingbroke's arrangements, 257—his plans for getting across, *ib.*—the enemy on a false scent, (n.) *ib.*—returns to Bolingbroke commissions to Lords Grenard and North and Grey, and printed declaration, 257, 258—proposes to return seals, 258—Lord Stair insists on stoppage of his embarkation, 260—discouraged at Ormond's ill-success, 261—resolves to sail for Scotland, *ib.*—sends intelligence to Lord Mar and Duke of Leeds, 261 — departure urged by Bolingbroke, 262—desires Bolingbroke to concert with Mary of Modena, *ib.*—distrust of Berwick, *ib.*—disparages Ormond, *ib.*—sails from Dunkirk, lands at Peterhead, 263—congratulates himself, *ib.*—calls upon the Duke of Gordon to join with Marquess of Seaforth to reduce Inverness, *ib.* — wishes for Berwick's presence in Scotland, 264—place of disembarkation in France, 267—circumstances of re-embarkation described by Mar, *ib.*—reaches Boulogne and proceeds to St. Germain, 272—intentions towards Mar and Bolingbroke, 273—directs Mar to return packets to Mary of Modena, *ib.*—proposed lying at Malmaison, *ib.*—letter to Marquess of Huntly respecting attempt on Inverness, 278—in flight, 280—flight alluded to, 281—declaration of Margaret Dawson touching his birth (Warming-pan story), 290

Chevalier, the Young, Charles Edward, 202, 275

Chieftains, subjugation of, by James I., 30, 31

Christian I., 47, 48

"Christ's Kirk on the Green," 77, (n.) 78

Church, English, power of in 17th century, 147

Churchill, Arabella, 204

—— (Sarah), lady in correspondence with Lord Melfort, 194

——, Lord, deserts James II., 180, 185—intrigues for his restoration, 194. *See* Marlborough.

Citta, Dutch ambassador, duplicity of, 178

Clarence, Duke of, design of David II. to put him in succession, 10

——, ——, defeated at Beauge, 26

Clarendon's History of the Rebellion, 153, 161

Clarendon Lord, upright statesmanship of, 165—develops constitutional government, 167

Clarges, Monk's son-in-law, 164

Claverhouse. *See* Dundee.

Clement VI. gives dispensation for marriage of Robert Stuart (Robert II.), 9

—— VIII., 38

Clephane, General, 268, 281

Clergy of Scotland, lax morals of, 38, 138

Clinton and Saye, Lord, 120

Clova, 160

Clyde, the, 3, 73, 80

Cochran, favourite of James III., 48—traduces Mar, *ib.*—hanged with others, 50

Cockburn, Sir James, of Skirling, 120

Coinage regulated temp. James I., 34

Coldingham Priory, revenues confiscated, 51—destroyed by the English, 88

Coldstream, 73, 163

Index. 301

Colville, Lord, retainers massacred by William Douglas, 41
Commercy, 216, 255
Commissioners of Inquiry into charges against Mary Stuart, 120, 125
Commonwealth, the, 156 — estimate of, ib.—traditions unconstitutional, 167
"Compounders," moderate Jacobites so called, 194
Confederated Lords march to attack Bothwell, 111—send the Queen to Holyrood, 112—accuse her of adhering to Bothwell, ib.
Conference of Lords with Queen at Craigmillar Castle, 105, 106, 113, 114, 124, 125
——, for inquiring into Mary Queen of Scots' conduct. See York and Westminster.
Congregation, Lords of, accept James Stuart, 90—destroy ecclesiastical buildings, 91—obtain Elizabeth's interference, 92—attitude of England towards, 115
Conn, papal representative, at Henrietta Maria's instance, 151
Constance, Council of, 38
Constitution in peril under Charles II., 165
Corriche. See Battles.
Corstorphine, 74
Coulston arrested, 253
Council directed by Albany not to make peace with England, 73—advice of, to James V., 79—action of, 83
——, the, consents to residence of the young Queen in France, 90
—— of Government chosen, 93
Courcelles, de, French ambassador, referred to, 133
Courtney, Mr., 249
Covenanters, persecution of, 167, 172, 174
Craigmillar Castle, confinement of Mar at, 49—conference at, 104–108, 113, 114, 124, 125
Craufurd, Earl of, description of tortures of James II.'s adherents, 189, 190
Craven, Earl of, refuses to withdraw his troops, 185
Crawford, spy of Lennox's, deposes to account given him by Darnley, 286

—suspicious identity of this statement with letter in Casket, ib.
Crawford, Earl of (the Tiger Earl), confederacy with, sought by William Douglas, 42, 43—submits himself, 44
——, ——, summoned by James III., 51
——, ——, killed at Flodden, 65
Crichton, Sir William, James II. smuggled from his custody, 38—kidnaps him, 39—meeting and compact with Livingston, ib.
Cromwell, Oliver, religious vagaries of his soldiery, 147—modern writers' judgment of, 149—intrigues for power, 150—defeats Hamilton, 151—protectorate of, 156—England's eminence in Europe under his rule, ib.—ill consequences of alliance with France, 157—cruelty in Ireland, 159—advances into Scotland, ib.—conquers at Dunbar, 160—dread of, paralyses Royalist action, 161—receives from Monk copy of letter from Charles II., 162—dies, 164
——, Richard, 164
Culloden, battle of, 202—mentioned, 275
Cumberland, raids into, 13
Cumyns, the, resign their claim, 4
Cunningham's History of Great Britain, 158
Cupar, 277

DACRE, LEONARD, rebellion of, 126
——, Lord, Warden of the Marches, diplomacy of, 72—breaks truce, ib.—at Solway Moss, 84
Dalgleish, George, sent by Bothwell for the Casket, 117—arrested and tortured, ib.—execution, 123
Dalkeith, 58, 87
Dalrymple, Sir David (Lord Hailes), referred to, 1—statement respecting sonnets in Casket, 288
Dalrymple's, Sir John, "Memoirs," 164, 200
Danby, Lord (Earl of). See Leeds, Duke of.
Darien, Paterson's settlement at, 189
Darnley family, 5
——, Henry, Lord, 69, 86—Mary resolves to marry him, 100—schemes

as to succession, 101—conspires for Rizio's murder, *ib.*—escapes with Mary, 102—insolence, *ib.*—complicity in murder becomes known, *ib.* —letter to Cardinal de Guise, announcing birth of son, 103—demands Lethington's dismissal,104—estrangement of the Queen, *ib.*—opposed to Morton's return, *ib.*—plans for his removal, 105 —murdered, *ib.*, 106 —attitude towards Roman Catholic faction, 107—retreat to France meditated, *ib.*—ill-feeling between him and Mary, 108—mentioned, 114, 116, 118, 120, 121, 122—his knowledge of French and Latin, 124—his private papers, 287
Dartmouth, Lord, takes command of fleet, 183—eluded by the Dutch fleet, *ib.*, 184—refuses James's wish for the Prince of Wales to be carried abroad, 183—some of his captains prepare to desert him, 184
D'Aubigny, John, Lord, 86
——, George, Lord, 206
Dauphin, the (afterwards Louis XI.), 35
——, ——, son of Francis I., 80
——, ——, son of Henry II. *See* Francis II.
David I., reign of, 1—makes grant to Walter, first Steward, 3
—— II., twice married, 6—dies childless, *ib.*—an exile in France, 7—returns, 9—defeated and taken prisoner at Nevil's Cross, *ib.*—wishes to put Duke of Clarence in succession, 10—returns from captivity, *ib.*—distrusts Robert Stuart, and wishes to alter the succession, *ib.*—divorced, *ib.*—dies, *ib.*
——, Earl of Huntingdon, 186
Dawson, Margaret (bedchamber woman to Mary of Modena), at birth of heir, 179—dying deposition of, 290
Denmark, 47, 79
——, Anne of. *See* Anne of Denmark.
——, Prince George of, 183
——, Princess of, wife of Prince George. *See* Anne, Princess.
Derby, Charles Edward at, 93
Dicconson, Jacobite treasurer, letters from the Chevalier to, 204, 213—opens by mistake letter from Marlborough, 220—Mary of Modena thanks him for intelligence, 231—the Chevalier directs Marlborough's gift to be handed to him, 237—instructions for transmission of gold, 248—informed of Berwick's hesitation, 249—money arrangements, 274 —transmits money from Mary of Modena to Mar, *ib.*
Dieppe, 80, 205, 230, 271
Digby, Sir Everard, 140
Dillon, Lieut.-General, 271
Dingwall, 24
"Diurnal of Remarkable Occurrences," 286
Divine Right, doctrine of, 186
"Doctrine of a Christian Man, the," 79
Donald of the Isles defeated, 24—retires, *ib.*—claims to Earldom of Ross, *ib.*—ally of England, 25
Doran, 121
Douay College, 196
Douglas, Andrew, present at opening of the Casket, 117
——, Archibald, killed (1455), 44
——, ——, Earl of, daughter marries Duke of Rothesay, 18—enmity towards Rothesay, 19—charged with his murder, 20—taken prisoner, *ib.*
——, ——, ——, governor of the kingdom, dies, 39
——, Catherine, heroism of, 33
——, George, threats to James V., 74
——, ——, aids Mary's escape, 115
——, James, son of James the Fat, connects himself with the Yorkist party, 44—defeated at Arkinholme, *ib.*—and brothers killed, *ib.*
——, —— Earl of, dispute with John de Vienne, 12—dies victorious at Otterburn, 14
——, ——, ——, assistance of, asked by James III., 53
——, ——, the Fat, Earl of, dies, 40
——, Margaret, Countess of Lennox, daughter of James IV.'s widow by second marriage, mother of Darnley, 69—her birth, 70—marriage to Lennox, 86
——, Sir Archibald, embassy under, to Paris, 12
——, Sir Robert, envoy of Henrietta Maria, 151
——, William, Earl of, pretensions to the succession, 11

Douglas, William, Earl of, and David entrapped and murdered, 39, 40
——, ——, ——, son of James the Fat, succeeds him, 40—his haughty character, ib.—Lieutenant-Governor of Scotland, ib.—marries Fair Maid of Galloway, ib.—lawlessly storms Lord Colville's castle, 41—and family popular, ib.—present at tournament, ib.—pilgrimage to Rome, ib.—combination against him, ib.—returns and makes submission, ib.—proposes alliance with Crawford and Ross, 42—goes under safe-conduct to Stirling, ib.—murdered, 43—presumed skeleton, (n.) ib.—adherents burn Stirling, ib.—widow married by brother, 44
——, ——, conducts Mary's escape, 115
——, House of, 3—rivalry with that of Stuart, 40—designs baffled, 75—anger of James against, 76, (n.) 79—partisans of the English, 86, 87
—— and Angus faction, 74
Douglases, feud of, with Hamiltons, 71—battle with, ib.—English partisans, 72
—— and Stuarts, comparative influence of, 3, 42—Stuarts' supremacy established, 44
Dover Castle, hostages for James I. confined in, 29
Drummond. See Hawthornden.
——, Lord, 244, 267, 278
——, —— John, 271
——, Margaret, Euphemia, and Sybilla, death of, 56
—— family, 56, 175
Drury, Sir William, his statement that the "boud" for Darnley's murder was burnt, 287
Dryburgh Abbey ruined by the English, 88
Dugdale's Baronage referred to, 2
Duke, title of, imported, 18
Dumbarton Castle, 7, 69, 86, 108, 115
Dunbar, 69, 102, 110, 111
——, battle of, 160
—— (poet), 58
——, Gawyn, tutor of James V., 76
Dunblane, Bishop of, agent of the league sent to Queen Mary, 96
Dundee, gives bond for James I.'s ransom, 29—the Chevalier at, 276—wreck at, ib.
Dundee, Viscount, 181—killed, 188—William III.'s opinion of, ib.—speculations on what might have happened had he not been killed, ib.—150 officers follow James into exile, 189—alluded to, 263
Dundonald Castle, 9
Dundrennan Abbey, 116, (n.) ib.
Dunfermline, 13, 278
Dunkirk, 206, 207, 254, 263
——, abbess of, 180
Dunoon Castle taken, 7
Dunstaffnage, 207, 261
Dutch troops in Argyll's army (1715), 93, 205

EARN, bridge of, 278
Edgehill, See Battles. Alluded to, 146, 201, 206
Edinburgh recovered from Baliol, 8—burnt (1385), 13—threatened, 19, 74—mentioned, 39, 47, 51, 56, 58, 84, 87, 91, 93, 99, 102, 109, 122, 132, 159, 175, 279, 286—fortified, 67—treaty of (1560), 95
—— Castle, 38, 39, 49, 50, 55, 74, 92, 103, 117, 118, 129, 287—alleged recent discovery of remains of child at, under steps leading to Mary Queen of Scots' room, 283-285
—— Ministers furious with James II.'s measures, 175, 213
Edmond, Father, 96
Edward the Confessor, 1
—— I., designs upon Scotland, 4, 5—rightly prefers Baliol's claim, 186
—— III. buys title of Steward of Scotland, 2—overruns Scotland, 7—invades France, 8—truce with Scotland (1381-4), 12
—— IV., 45, 46, 49
—— VI., 66, 82
d'Effiat, M., 252
Eglington, in connection with Bothwell's project for marrying the Queen, 109
Eikon Basilike, authorship of, 155
—— —— Deutera, 168
Elder, the Rev. John, 124
Elector of Hanover. See Hanover Elector of.
—— Palatine, 79 (n.) ib.

304 Index.

Elizabeth, Queen, 91—sends an expedition against Leith, 92—attempts abrogation of Mary's succession, 93—protests against the Darnley marriage, 100—interferes concerning Mary's treatment by confederates, 112, 115—probable sincerity, 116—disputed legitimacy, *ib.*—situation, 119—names commissioners to investigate touching Mary Stuart, 120 — negotiates for surrender of Mary, 122, 127—displeasure at Mary's projected marriage, 127—internal conspiracies, 128—detention of Mary unjustifiable, *ib.*—sends Killigrew to the north, 129—strife with Mary at its crisis, 133—foreign policy, 141
Elizabeth, daughter of Charles I., 152
———, Queen of Bohemia, 137—conspiracy to proclaim her Queen of United Kingdom, 139, 140—James VI. hesitates to give assistance to, 141—Puritan hopes of her children's succession, 157
Elliot, Anthony, a moss-trooper, 163
Ellis, Bishop, correspondence of Lord Melfort and James II. with, 194, 195—some particulars of his career, 196—letters from Lord Caryll to, 196—198
Elphinstone, Sir Alexander, 66
England, state of war with, 11—alienation from Rome, 78—passage through refused to James V., 81—war with Scotland foreshadowed, *ib.*—likelihood of James V. succeeding to throne of, 82—alluded to under pseudonyms, 222, 232, 233, 238, 240, 247
English fleet ravages coast of Forth, 87
"English Historical Review," 179
Ennis, Mr. *See* Innes.
Episcopacy abolished in Scotland, 93—Scotch hatred of, 146—efforts of Charles I. and Laud for, 145-148
Erasmus, 65
"Erection of the King" (1524), (n.) 74
Erroll, Earls of, 2
———, Earl of, summoned by James III., 51
———, ———, killed at Flodden, 65
Erskine, Lord, 89
———, David and Adam, 131

Erskine, Jo., captain of wrecked treasure ship, 276
——— (Areskine), Sir John, 266
———, Margaret, wife of Douglas of Lochleven, 85—her son (afterwards the Regent Murray) by James V., 89—her custody of Queen Mary at Lochleven, 113
——— family, education of Prince Henry by, 144
Eschina de Loudiniis, 2
Esk, the, 44, 72, 84
Essex, Earl of, interrupts the King's march on London, 143
Euphemia, Countess of Ross, 24
——— Ross, 12
European war imminent, 72
Eva, first wife of Alan, second Steward, 3
Exclusion Bill, debates on, 173
Exeter, 206, 207

FAIRFAX, religious vagaries of his soldiery, 147—threatens Oxford, 150—favours restoration, 162
———, Brian, medium of communication with Monk, 163
Fala Muir, 83
Falconberg, Neville, Lord, 45
Falkland, 75—palace, 85
——— Castle, Rothesay imprisoned in, 19
———, Viscount, 143
Farnham, 223
Farquharson of Inverey, 242
Faukland (Faulkland), 277, 278
Fayette, Count de, 70
Fécamp, 161
Felton, Buckingham's murderer, 142
Fenwick, Sir John, reveals trafficking with James II., 200
Ferdinand and Isabella, schemes of, 57
Fetteresso, 208, 263
"Field of the Cloth of Gold," 71
Fife, Earl of. *See* Albany.
Fitzalan, Walter, first historical Steward, 1-3
———, Richard, makes over title of Steward to Edward III. (1335), 2
Fitzgerald, 221
Fitz James family, 204
Fitzwilliam, Sir William, Admiral of English fleet, 73
Flaald, or Flathald, 1

Index. 305

Flamborough Head, 21
Flanigan, 257
Flanniugham, 246
Fleance, traditional Stuart ancestor, 1, 2
Fleet, the, letters to, from Pretender, 251, 258
Fleming (one of "the Queen's Maries)," 90
———, Sir David, murdered, 21
Flodden, battle of, 64, 65—calamitous effects of, 67—mentioned, 68, 84, 129
Fontainebleau, 158
Forbes, Lord, 51, 56
———, son of Lord, put to death, 82
Ford (encampment near), 63
Fordun quoted or referred to, 8, 25—remarks on, (n.) 34
Forester, Sir John, proposes insurrection, 228
Forman, Andrew, 61
Forth, Firth of, 7, 12, 54, 87, 207
Fotheringay, 128, 133
Fountainbridge, 109
France, office of Seneschal in, 2—traditional connection with Scotland confirmed, 12—sends aid, 7, 12—league with, maintained by Robert of Albany, 25—by James IV., 60, 61—threatened rupture with England, 72—mentioned, 73—ancient league with Scotland weakened, 92, 93—James VI. solicits aid, 132—negotiations of James VI. for offensive alliance, *ib.*—effects of battle of La Hogue upon, 193—alluded to under pseudonyms, 215, 247
———, Queen Dowager of, 70
Francis I., overtures of, for renewed league, 71—amity with England, *ib.*—makes peace with, 72—alluded to, (n.) 79, 80, 81
——— II. marries (when Dauphin) Mary Stuart, 90—measures in relation to Regency and to England, 93—death of, 94, 95—his rights in Scotch succession, 101—referred to, 117
Fraser, Lord, 51
Fraserburgh, 268
Frederic II. of Denmark, 137
Frederick the Great, (n.) 267
French assistance, dissatisfaction with, 13, 14

French fleet brings money to Dumbarton to arrest Catholic cause, 86
——— troops raised by Albany, 73—repulsed at Werk, *ib.*
——— Paris, Bothwell's page, tortured and hanged, 123
Froissart quoted, 12, 13, 14, 40—referred to, 40
Froude quoted or referred to, 83, 84, 119, 124, 126, 289
Furstenburgh, Cardinal, 191

"GABERLUNZIE MAN, THE," 78, (n.) *ib.*
Galloway, ancestry of Earls of, 5
Gardiner, Capt., 271
———, Professor Rawson, quoted, 143, 145
Gauden, Bishop, 155
Gaunt, John of, 12
George I., his military expedition in 1715, 205—alluded to, 220, 221, 222—expected to leave for Hanover, 222—his situation described by Berwick, 248—by Bolingbroke, 251—his measures, 253—Dutch troops promised, 259—rewards to Lord Lovat, 276, 280—forbearance towards Lord Southesk's wife, (n.) 281
———, Prince (George II.), joins in thanks to Lovat, 280
Geraldine, Sir Nicolas, his son, 261
Germain, St., refugees at, 190, 192-194, 196, 199-204, 208, 209, 211, 214, 219—misery of, 204, 213, 214, 231—female politicians at, 227—mentioned, (n.) 258, 262, (n.) 269, 270, 272, 273, 276
Germany, monks imported from, to Aberdeen, 212
Gesualdo, Carlo, Prince of Venosa, 34
Ghent, abbess of, 180
Giles, St., church of, Edinburgh, (n.) 20, 39
Glamys, Lady, burnt, 82
Glasgow, Archbishop of. *See* Dunbar, Gawyn.
———, Mary Queen of Scots and Bothwell at, 286
Glencairn, Earl of, killed at Flodden, 65
———, ———, attempts rescue of James V., 74
———, ———, supports Bothwell's project for marrying the Queen, 109—

X

present at the opening of the Casket, 117—warrant for Mary's imprisonment signed by, 118—an "Associated Lord," *ib.*
Glencoe, massacre of, 189
Glenshiel, 93, 275
Gloucester, Henry, Duke of, 152— attempted conversion of, 165
Godfrey de Bouillon, 1
Godolphin, Lord, British troops in French pay, 178, (n.) *ib.*—intrigues for restoration of James II., 194, 196, 200
Golf and football discouraged, 45
Goodall, 120, 288
"Goodman of Ballengiech," 77
Gordon, Catherine, married to Perkin Warbeck, 57
——, Duke of, the Chevalier's letters to, 208, 263—importance of his attitude to Jacobites, 243—mentioned, 279
——, General, Jacobite commander, 208—left in command of the Chevalier's flight, 268, 269, 274— informed of loss of treasure ship, 276 —military directions from Mar, 278 —receives promise of support from Marquess of Huntly, 279
—— of Glenbucket, letters of Mar to, 242, 263—mentioned, 244, 278
—— of Lochinvar, 120
——, Lord, 56
Gowrie, Earl of, holds the young King in restraint, 136—mentioned, 139
—— Plot, the, 136—Gowrie and Ruthven killed, *ib.*, 137—the Casket in their possession, 289
Graham, Malise. *See* Menteith, Earldom of.
——, Sir Robert, plots against James I., 32, 33—execrated, 33—tortured and put to death, 37
——, the Master of, present at opening of the Casket, 117—warrant for Mary's imprisonment signed by, 118
Grange. *See* Kirkaldy of.
Grant's "Old and New Edinburgh," 284—"Memorials of the Castle of Edinburgh," 285
Gravelines, 208, 267
Gray, Lord, 49, 50
——, the Master of. *See* Keith, Sir William.

Green, Professor, quoted, 143
Gregory XII., 38
Grenard, Lord, 257
Gueldres. *See* Mary of.
Guelphs, English, Elizabeth of Bohemia progenitrix of, 138, 140, 157
Guise, Cardinal de (Lorraine), 90, 94— Darnley's letter to, 103—mentioned, 128
——, Duke of, 81, 90, 94, 128
——, Mary of. *See* Mary of Lorraine.
Guises, the, 76, 90—urge the Queen Regent to persecution, 92—mentioned, 127
Guizot's Memorials of Monk, 162
Gunfleet Sands, 182, 183
Gunpowder Plot, 139, 140—imputed to the Roman Catholics, 140
Guy Fawkes, 139, 140

HACO, King of Norway, 4
Hague, the, centre of Royalist intrigue, 161
Hailes, Lord. *See* Dalrymple, Sir David.
——, ——, Governor of Edinburgh Castle (1488), 55
Halidon Hill, battle of, 7
Halifax, Lord, statesmanship of, 167— intrigues for restoration of James II., 194, 196
Halydon Rigg, 83
Hamilton of Bothwellhaugh, 126
—— Castle, 71, 115
——, Duke of, obstructs the Catholic interest, 176, 213
——, Gavin, 120
——, General George, letters of, 209— informs Mar of despatch of wines and powder, 270 — informs the Chevalier of difficulty in getting audience of the Regent as to arms, &c., 271
——, Marquess of, defeated, 151 — advises Charles II. to accept offer of the Scotch crown, 159
——, Sir Patrick, slain, 71
——, Zechy, 250, 251
Hamiltons desert the Douglases, 44— feud with, 71—fight with, at Kelso, *ib.*—Manuel, 74—place in succession, 83, 101—march to rescue the Queen, 111—assist in her escape, 115
Hampden, John, 143, 156

Hanmer, Sir Thomas, 225
Hanover, George I. expected to visit, 222
——, Elector of. *See* George I.
"Hanover Papers," 202
Harbotle Castle, 70
Hare, Mr. Sholto Vere (descendant of the Rev. Edward Bowles), MS. letters in his possession, (n.) 164
Harlaw, battle of, 24
Harley. *See* Oxford, Earl of.
Harrison, Bridget, 290
Harrow-on-the-Hill, Charles I. at, 150
Hasty, 226
"Hatfield Calendar" quoted or referred to, (n.) 92, 93, 288, 289
Havre, 249—the Chevalier's ships interfered with at, 252, 255, 272
Hawthornden, Drummond of (History of Scotland), referred to, 26—remarks of, on influence of James I.'s tastes, 34—on James I.'s personal appearance, 36—and influence, *ib.*—on the Douglas murder, (n.) 43—on death of Mar, 49—on authorship by James V., 78
Hay, Colonel, 282
Helvoetsluys, 182
Henderson, Mr., 118, 122, 288
Henrietta Maria, 141, 147—escapes to Holland, and makes efforts for Charles, 151—mischievous influence, *ib.*, 152—promised free exercise of her religion, 152—sufferings and death, *ib.*—present at reception of Charles II. into the Romish Church, 158—poverty, *ib.*—advises Charles II. to accept Scotch Crown, 159—written to about conversion of Duke of Gloucester, 166
Henry I. (of England), 1
—— II. (of France), killed, 90—fascinated by Mary Stuart, 98
—— III. (England), 4
—— —— (France), 128, 132
—— IV. (England), invades Scotland, 18, 19—mentioned, 23
—— —— (France), 141
—— V. (England), negotiation with, 23—takes James I. to France, 28—intrigues with Albany, 30
—— VI. takes hostages for James I.'s ransom, 29—exile in Scotland, 46

Henry VII., daughter married to James IV., 56—peaceful designs of, *ib.*—attitude towards France, 61
—— VIII., grievances of James IV., 61—hostility to Regent Albany, 69, 72—project of marrying Princess Mary to James V., 70—meeting with Francis I., 71—intrigues in Scotland, 73—strained relations with James V., 78—leans towards Reformation, 81—meeting with James proposed, 82—demands, 83—meeting frustrated, *ib.*—prepares for war, *ib.*—desires custody of Mary Stuart, 85—tampers with Scotch prisoners, 86—arranges for marriage of his son to Mary Stuart, 87—thwarted by Beaton, *ib.*—revenges himself on Scotland, *ib.*—dies, 88—his will, Scotch succession passed over in, 90—validity of marriage with Anne Boleyn, 116
——, Prince of Wales, 137—promising character and education of, 144, 145—intention of reconciling Puritans to the Church, 144—peril of his seizure by a faction, *ib.*
Hepburn family, 51, 53, 55
——. *See* Bothwell.
Herbert, Admiral, being deprived of his commission, serves Prince of Orange, 184
Hermitage Castle, 108
Heron, Sir William, wife of, 63
Herries supports Bothwell's project for marrying the Queen, 109—escorts her after Langside, 116—Mary's commissioner, 120—statement that the "bond" for Darnley's murder was in the Casket, 287
Hertford, Lord, ravages at and near Edinburgh and the Tweed, 87, 89
Heylin, Peter, 157
Hickes, George, D. D., 290
Hogue, La, battle of, 192—mentioned, 258
Holland, alliance with, 168—refugees in, 174—letters for the Chevalier in, 273
Holyrood, 20, 37, 40, 46, 74, 85, 87, 99, 101, 102, 103, 112—sacked, 176, —remains of child said to be discovered there (really Edinburgh Castle), 283—Darnley's papers, 287

x 2

Holyrood, Abbey of, restored to the Roman Catholics, 175, 212
Home (author of "Douglas") quoted, 41
——, Lord. *See* Hume.
Homildon Hill, battle of, 21
Hook, 220, 229
Hosack, Mr., 119, 120, 124, 126, 287, 288, 289
Hostages for James I., 29
Hotspur, 23
Howard, Philip. *See* Norfolk, Cardinal of.
Huddleston, Father, gives the viaticum to Charles II., 168
Hudson, 150
Hugh, Earl of Ormond, killed, 44
Huguenot massacres, 96, 127
Hull, 182
Hume, Lord, supports Bothwell's project for marrying the Queen, 109—present at opening of Casket, 117—an " Associated Lord," 118
——, ——, Warden of the Marches, beheaded, 70
——, David, alluded to, 289
—— family, 51, 53, 55, 70
Hungary, Queen Dowager of, 79
Huntingdon, Earl of. *See* David.
Huntlaw, 2
Huntly, 3rd Earl of, summoned to join James III., 51
——, 4th Earl, killed at Flodden, 65—attitude towards Reformation, 94—becomes insurgent; accidentally killed, 99
——, George, 5th Earl, takes part in conference at Craigmillar, 105—supports Bothwell's scheme for marrying the Queen, 109—carried to Dunbar, 110—defection of, 129—alluded to in Casket Letters, 287—his behaviour in reference to them examined, *ib.*—doubtful whether he actually saw them, *ib.*—complicity in Craigmillar conference may have silenced him, *ib.*
——, Alexander, Marquess of, 242, 243, 244—attempt on Inverness, 277, 278—unfairly said to be a waverer, 279—letter to General Gordon, promising to move if required, *ib.*—letter to Lord Lovat, informing him of his submission, *ib.*
d'Huxelles, Marechal, 252, 259, 260

IBERVILLE, M., 235, 236
Inchcolm, Abbot of, 34
Inchmahome, Island of, 89
Independents contemplate settling in America, 148—struggle for ascendancy, 149
Innes, Mr. (Ennis), 219, 222—proposal as to money and arms, 227—ordered to communicate with Bolingbroke, 230—instructions to, about gold, 248
Innocent VI., 26
—— XI., 194, 195
—— XII. succeeds, 191—appoints English Bishops, 194—Jacobite hopes from, 197
Invermeith supports Bothwell's project for marrying the Queen, 109
Inverness, 99, 263, 267, 277, 278, 280
Ireland, rebellion of 1641, 153—designs regarding—187, 188—satisfaction of, with James II.'s measures, 172
Ireton, intrigues of, 150
Isabella of Denmark, 79
——, second daughter of David, Earl of Huntingdon, 186
Isles, Lord of the, 31

JACOBITES, French attitude towards, 93—wretched state of, in France, 208—expectations from Marlborough in 1715, 222—their mistrust of him, 234—distresses following 1715, 275, 276—fate of army after the Chevalier's flight, 281
James I. of Scotland, captive in England, 21—succeeds, 23—negotiations for release, *ib.*—possible influence of rumour as to Richard II., 25—maintains correspondence with leading subjects, 26—particulars of captivity, 27, 28—enamoured of Jane Beaufort, *ib.*—marries her, 28—carried into France, *ib.*—ransom settled, *ib.*, 29—hostages given, 29—resolves on subjugation of predatory chiefs, 30—domestic policy, 31, 32—combinations against, *ib.*—effects reform, 32—taxes impair his popularity, *ib.*—plot against, by heirs of Robert II., *ib.*—assassinated, 33—character and accomplishments, 34—wise measures, *ib.*—gives his daughter Margaret in marriage

to the Dauphin, 35—develops Parliaments, *ib.*—Drummond's description and remarks on, 36—age, *ib.*—attributed authorship, (n.) 78—referred to, 114—Jane, widow of, 122

James II. succeeds when seven years old, 37—his father's murderers punished, *ib.*—crowned, *ib.*—detained in Edinburgh Castle, 38—smuggled to Stirling, *ib.*—kidnapped by Crichton, 39—compromise between Crichton and Livingston as to his custody, *ib.*—Douglases enticed to meet the King and murdered, *ib.*—the King innocent, 40—rivalry of the Douglas faction, *ib.*—marries Mary of Gueldres, *ib.*—insolence of William Douglas, 41—presides at tournament at Stirling, *ib.*—gives free conduct to Douglas and retinue, 42—stabs him, 43—meditates flight, *ib.*—advised by Bishop Kennedy, 44—takes Abercorn, *ib.*—victorious at Arkinholme, *ib.*—legislation, 45—injudicious policy with England, *ib.*—breaks truce, *ib.*—killed, *ib.*, character, *ib.*—attitude towards Papacy, 46—personality, *ib.*—burial-place, *ib.*—offspring, *ib.*—referred to, 77, 114, 202, (n.) 267

—— III. succeeds, 46—carried off by the Boyds, *ib.*, 47—approves it, 47—strives to free himself, *ib.*—marries Margaret of Denmark, *ib.*, 48—instability or duplicity, *ib.*—favourites, 48—alienated from his brothers, *ib.*—by Cochran's influence, *ib.*—parsimony; imputed timidity, *ib.*—dissensions, *ib.*—listens to Cochran, *ib.*—death of Mar, *ib.*—flight of Albany, 49—measures against threatened invasion, *ib.*—favourites hanged, 50—attitude towards Albany, *ib.*—effects of his tastes, *ib.*, 51—confiscates revenues of Coldingham, 51—confederacy against, *ib.*—alleged design to destroy the nobility, *ib.*—summons his supporters, *ib.*—confederates get possession of the Prince, 52—encounter with the rebels, *ib.*—death, *ib.*—character, &c., of, *ib.*, 53—asks help of James of Douglas, 53—rumour of his survival, *ib.*—buried at Cambuskenneth, 54—complicity of his son with rebellion, 55—mentioned, 77, 114

James IV. succeeds, 55—his remorse, *ib.* — the revolts against him, 56—bad influences upon, *ib.*—attachment to Margaret Drummond, *ib.*—marries daughter of Henry VII., *ib.*, 58—plot to betray him, *ib.*—personality and acquirements, 57—exaggerated chivalry of, 58—marriage festivities, *ib.*, 59—pacification of Highlands, 59—remarkable ride, *ib.*—improves navy, *ib.*, 60—vigilance, 60—adheres to French alliance, *ib.*, 61—sends aid to France, 61—incompetence in generalship, 62—prepares to invade England, *ib.*—pretended apparition, 63—haughty reply to Surrey, *ib.*—unjust one to Angus, 64—death at Flodden, 65—defects of character, *ib.*, 66—circumstances of interment, 66—doubts of his death, *ib.*—children, 67—widow married to Angus, 68—referred to, 69, 71, 108, 114, 138, 144

—— V., long minority, 67—evil effects of, 68—competition for Regency under, *ib.*—Albany of Boulogne appointed, 69—proposed English marriage, 70—remains at Stirling, *ib.*—carried to Holyrood; "Erection of the King," 74—debasing influence employed on, *ib.*—rescue attempted, *ib.*—violence threatened near Manuel, *ib.*—resentment of, *ib.*—escapes from Falkland, 75—summons his supporters, *ib.*—education of, 76—asserts himself, *ib.* — revenge upon Angus, *ib* — arrests recusants, 77—hangs Armstrong, *ib.*—divided effect of severity, *ib.*—popularity, *ib.*—adventurous character, *ib.*—popular and assumed names of, *ib.*—opposed to the nobles, *ib.*—avarice unfairly imputed, *ib.*—low state of national resources, *ib.*—entertained by Athole, 78—strained relations with Henry VIII., *ib.*—abortive scheme for conference between, 79—alliance matrimonial, offered by Charles V., *ib.*—evades offer, *ib.*—prefers French alliance, *ib.*—hesitates about the Reformation, but adheres to Rome, *ib.*—

Mary of Bourbon proposed as wife, *ib.*—matrimonial intrigues during captivity, (n.) *ib.*—voyages to France, 80—prefers Madeleine, *ib.*—courtship and marriage in Paris, *ib.*, 81—returns with his wife, 81—passage through England refused, *ib.*—wife dies, *ib.*—marries Mary of Lorraine, *ib.*—this alliance hostile to England, *ib.*—"Knight of Snowdoun," *ib.*—unmerciful, 82—prospects of succeeding to English throne, *ib.*—religious intolerance, *ib.*—refuses Henry VIII.'s demands, *ib.*—rigorous administration, 83—desires to introduce French centralisation, *ib.*—loses his sons, *ib.*—meeting with Henry VIII. frustrated, *ib.*—prepares for war, *ib.*—disaffection, and causes of it, of army, 84—retires, but concerts fresh enterprise, *ib.*—gathers army, *ib.*—Sinclair, incompetent leadership of, *ib.*—defeated at Solway Moss, *ib.*—supposed cause of absence from the field, *ib.*—constitutional bravery of, 85—illness; birth of daughter (afterwards Mary Queen of Scots); dying words and death, *ib.*—encouragement of science and art, *ib.*—lax morality of, *ib.*—dispensation for marriage with Margaret Erskine asked for, *ib.*—buried at Holyrood, *ib.*—referred to, 89, 107, 108, 113, 114, 138, 144

James I. of England (and VI. of Scotland), dictates to Camden, 97—education of, 131—unsettled opinions and policy, *ib.*—scheme for a joint government, *ib.*—solicits French aid, 132—danger of Spanish alliance, *ib.*—intercedes with Elizabeth, *ib.*—enforces prayer for his mother, 133—personal characteristics of, 135—insincerity of religious utterances, 136—dislike to Presbyterianism justified, *ib.*—under restraint by Gowrie, *ib.*—list of children, 137—real name Charles James, 138—abilities and opinions, 139—his welcome to England, *ib.*—Arabella Stuart, *ib.*—breach of faith towards Roman Catholics, 141—influenced by favourites, *ib.*—hesitation in succouring his daughter, *ib.*—quarrel with Spain, *ib.*—illness and death, *ib.*—deserves praise for education of his son Henry, 144—his later measures hasten civil war, 145—unreasonable suspicion, founded on discovery of remains in Edinburgh Castle, that he died in infancy, 283-285—alluded to in connection with the Casket, 289

James II. of England (and VII. of Scotland), Duke of York, 142—evil influences of circumstances in his exile, 156—subservience to France greatly forced by circumstances, 157—plot to assassinate, 164—appealed to by Charles II. respecting conversion of Duke of Gloucester, 166—unpopularity of, 167—charges of inconsistency and cruelty, *ib.*—position and measures examined, 172—impolitic vindictiveness, 173—circumstances at coronation, 174—mistrusted by the Episcopalians, *ib.*—ignores Scotch Parliament, 175—deceived by his ministers, 177, 181—Magdalen College and the seven bishops, 177—regiments in French pay, 178—birth of son (the Pretender), *ib.*, 179—will of, providing for son's guardianship, 180, 181—correspondence with Leopold I., 181, 182,—visits his fleet, 183—number of fleet, *ib.*—wishes the Prince of Wales to be carried out of the country, *ib.*—exonerates his admiral, (n.) 184—indecision, 185—offers concessions, *ib.*—throws Great Seal into the river, and escapes to Faversham, *ib.*—insulted, and returns to London, *ib.*—orders withdrawal of his guards, *ib.*—retires to France, *ib.*, 186—reaction of public opinion in favour of, 186, 187—patriotic speech of, 187—offers compensation to the Irish Protestants, *ib.*—imputed wish to tamper with "the Act of Settlement" (Irish), *ib.*—action to advance Roman Catholic party in Ireland, *ib.*—appeals to the Roman Catholic world, 190—letters to the Cardinal of Norfolk, 190-192—claims to have restored Roman Catholicism, 192—at La Hogue, 193—retires to La Trappe, *ib.*—concerned in appointment of English bishops by Rome, 194—letter to Bishop Ellis, *ib.*—

Index. 311

remarkable letter to Bishop Ellis, 195
—meets the Duke of Berwick, 200—
charges of complicity in conspiracy
to murder William III., *ib.*—probable
groundlessness of charge, *ib.*—
closing years of, inactive, 201—has
a fit, *ib.*—career and character, *ib.*—
death, *ib.*—alluded to, 203, 204—
deviser of Test Act, 210
James, infant son of James IV., dies, 67
———, infant son of James V., dies, 83
——— Francis Edward Stuart, the Old
Pretender. *See* Chevalier de St.
George.
———, 5th Steward (1283-1309), 4, 5
—Regent, 4—surety for Robert
Bruce, 5—associated with Wallace,
ib.
———, the (ship), 62
Jane, widow of James I., 122
Janson, Mr., 225
Jean, heiress of James, son of a Lord
of Bute, 4
Jedburgh harried, 72—Mary at, 108
Jerusalem, 67
Jesuits in Edinburgh, 175, 176
Joanna, Queen of David II., 6, 9
John (Robert III.). *See* Robert III.
——— (brother of 5th Steward), pro-
genitor of the Darnleys, Earls of
Lennox, and of the Earls of Gallo-
way, 5
——— XXIII., 38
Johnson, Dr., opinion as to Casket
Letters, 124
Johnston, Saint, old name of Perth, 32
Julius II., 60

KAUNITZ, Count de, 182
Kay Clan, 16, 17
Keith, George, 10th Earl Marischal,
left at Montrose, 267, 268—his
indignation at the same, 281
———, Marshal, 267
———, Sir William, sent to intercede
with Elizabeth, 132
———, William, 1st Earl Marischal, his
career, 267
———, de, Sir William, daughter of, 26
Kelli (Kelly), alleged intended assassin
of the Pretender, 255
Kelso, 46, 66, 71, (Abbey) 88
Kennedy, Bishop, counsels James II. of
Scotland, 44—intrigues of, *ib.*—as

minister, 45—wise ministry in
minority of James III., 46—secures
truce, *ib.*—appoints instructor to the
young King, *ib.*—dies, *ib.*
Kennedy, Gilbert, tutor of James III., 47
Kentish Knock, 183
Kenyon, Mr., 250
Ker of Faudonside assists in Rizio's
murder, 102
Killiecrankie, battle of 188
Killigrew, H., secret instructions to,
(n.) 127—mission, 129
Kilmarnock, Earls of, 2
Kilross, murderers of Abbot of, pun-
ished, 77
Kilsyth, battle of, 148
———, Lord, 275
Kilwinning, Commendator of, 120
Kincardineshire, 42
"King of the Commons" (James V.),
77, 82
——— ——— ——— (Pym so called), 143
"King's Men," 131
"King's Quhair, the," quoted, 28
Kinnaird, 264
Kirkaldy, 80
——— of Grange and others combine to
rescue the Queen, 110—offers combat
with Bothwell, 111—receives surrender of the Queen, *ib.*—scruples
silenced, 112—pursues Bothwell,
113—military talent, 115—an
"Associated Lord," 118—death of,
129
Kirk o' Field, 105, 113, 287
Knox, John, taken prisoner and put to
the galleys, 88—his agency in the
Reformation, *ib.*—inflames the populace, 91—supported by the nobility,
ib., 92—gains support by hopes of
plundering the Church, 94, 96, 97—
malevolence towards Queen Mary,
98, 99—insults her, 99—accusations
against her, 100, 107—alluded to,
131, 132, 212

LADIES' HILL, Stirling, tournament at,
41
Laing, Malcolm, 119, 288
Lambert, General, encamped at New-
castle, 163
Lammermuir Hills, 83
Lancashire Jacobites prosecuted, 199
Lancastrian Party, 44, 45, 57

Land Bank, establishment of, 199
Lane, Col. and Mrs., 161
Langside, battle of, 115
Lansdowne, Lord, imprisoned, 207—Bolingbroke vouches for, 224—his danger, 265
Largs, battle of, 3
Laud, Archbishop, imprisonment and death, 142—his resolve to restore Episcopacy in Scotland, 146—motives, *ib.*—withdraws from outside sects, privilege of meeting, 148
Lauder, conclave in church of, 49—bridge of, 50, 51
Lauderdale, 171
Laughton, J. K., Memoirs of Lord Torrington, 183
League, Catholic. *See* Catholic.
Learning, revival of, in Scotland, 67
Le Blanc, 254
Le Croc, French ambassador, 104—account of Queen Mary's wedding-day, 110
Leeds, Thomas Osborne, 1st Duke of, corrupts Parliament, 165—suggests attack on Hull, 182
——, 2nd Duke of, 233—letter to the Chevalier, 237—Bolingbroke's account of, 239, 261
Lees, J. Cameron, "Albany's Aisle," (n.) 20
Leicester, Lord, 120
Leith, 80, 81, 87—stout defence of, 92, (n.) 96, 207
Lennox, Earls of, ancestry of, 5
——, Esmé Stuart, Duke of, favourite of James VI., 131, 132
——, Lord, revolt of, 56
——, Earl of, killed at Floddon, 65
——, ——, stabbed, 74
——, —— (Matthew), treachery of, 86—father of Darnley, *ib.*, 109—accuses Bothwell, *ib.*—regency of, 127, 130—the Casket in possession of, 289
——, Lady (Darnley's mother), 100, 128
Leopold I., Emperor of Germany, letter of William of Orange to, 177 —correspondence with James II., 181, 182
Lesley defeats Montrose, 148—beaten at Dunbar, 160—invades England, 161—defeated at Worcester, *ib.*

Leslie, Bishop of Ross, 104, 120—unguarded statement of, 125
——, Norman, kills Cardinal Beaton, 88
Lesly (young), 228, 237
Lethington. *See* Maitland of.
Letters and Papers in Appendix No. 1 (Nos. i to cxiii. pages 210 to 282)
Anonymous, lxxiv
Berwick, the Duke of, to Lord Bolingbroke, lxx
——, ——, on Lord Oxford's ministry, iv
——, ——, to Chevalier de St. George, v, vi, vii, viii, ix, x, xi, xiii, xiv, xvi, xvii, xviii, xix, xx, xxi, xxii, xxiv, xxix, xxxi, xxxvi, xliv, lxiii, lxiv, lxvi, lxxix
——, ——, to Lord Mar, xciii
——, ——, Memorandum of, xv
Bolingbroke, Lord, to the Duke of Berwick, xlii
——, ——, to the Chevalier de St. George, xli, xliii, xlv, xlix, lii, liii, liv, lxxi, lxxii, lxxviii, lxxx, lxxxi, lxxxiii, lxxxiv, xcviii
——, ——, to Lord Mar, xci, xcix, ci
——, ——, Memorandum of (after death of Louis XIV.), lvii
——, ——, Memorial respecting the Regent, lxii
Camocke, George, to Lord Mar, lxxxix
Chevalier de St. George to the Duke of Berwick, xxiii, xxvi, xxvii, xxx, xxxii, xxxiii, xxxv, xxxviii, xlvii
—— —— —— to Lord Bolingbroke xxviii, xxxiv, xxxvii, xxxix, xlvi, xlviii, l, li, lv, lxv, lxvii, lxxv, lxxvi, lxxvii, lxxxii, lxxxv, lxxxvi, lxxxviii
—— —— —— to Mr. Dicconson, iii
—— —— —— to the Duke of Gordon, lxxxvii
—— —— —— to the Marquess of Huntly, cvi
—— —— —— to Lord Mar, xcvii
—— —— —— to the Duke of Ormond, lxi
—— —— —— to Mr. Russell, xcvi
Hamilton, General George, to Chevalier de St. George, xcv
——, ——, to Lord Mar, xciv

Index. 313

Letters and Papers—*continued*.
 Huntly, the Marquess of, to General Gordon, cviii
 ——, —— to Lord Lovat, cix
 Lovat, Lord, to General Cadogan, cx
 Mar, Lord, to General Gordon, c, ciii, cv
 ——, ——, to Gordon of Glenbucket, lviii, lix
 ——, ——, to H. S., xcii
 ——, ——, to the Laird of Glengarry, lx
 ——, ——, to the Marquess of Huntly, civ, cvii
 ——, ——, to Lord Kilsyth, cii
 Mary of Modena to a lady, xii
 —— —— to Mr. Dicconson, xl, lxviii, lxix
 Murray, Mr. J. A., to Chevalier de St. George, lvi
 Ormond, Duke of, to Chevalier de St. George, lxxiii
 ——, ——, to Lord Mar, xc
 Perth, Earl of, to the Cardinal of Norfolk, ii
 Southesk, Lord, to Earl of Mar, cxiii
 Stanhope, General, to Lord Lovat, cxi
 Test Act, Act of Council explanatory of, i
 Thomas, Mr., to Mr. Innes, xxv,
 Welwood, James, to Lord Lovat, cxii
Leven, Scotch commander at Marston Moor, 146
Leven and Melville Papers, 190
Lindores, Monastery of, 53
Lindsay, Lord, banished; hatred to Darnley, 102—offers combat with Bothwell, 111—an "Associated Lord," 118
Lingard's History of England referred to, 185, 211
Linlithgow, 47, 48, 52, 63, 89, 126, 286
"Lion, the" (cannon), 45
Livingston (one of "the Queen's Maries"), 90
——, Sir Alexander, 38—meeting and compact with Crichton, 39
——, Lord, in charge of Mary Stuart, 89—mentioned, 120
Lloyd, Mr., 265
Lochleven, 113, 116, 122

Lochleven, Douglas of, 85
——, Prior of. *See* Wynton.
Lochmaben, 84
Logie, Margaret, wife of David II., 6, 10—divorced, 10
London, letters to, from Pretender, 251
——, Tower of, records in, 2—James I. confined in, 27—James I.'s hostages confined in, 29
Londonderry, siege of, 187—reported capture of, 188
Longueville, Duchess of. *See* Mary of Lorraine.
Lonsdale, Lord, arrested, 253
Lorraine, Cardinal de. *See* Guise.
——, Duke of, 206, 216, 217—hint of project of marriage of the Chevalier with a daughter of, (n.) 226
Louis XII., enemies of, 60—asks aid from James IV. against England, 61—allied with, 64
—— XIV. a terror to Europe, 157—intrigues with Sidney and Russell, 164—Triple Alliance against, 168—fleet prepared to act against William of Orange, 184—Jacobite hopes of assistance from, 196, 197—intended invasion of England frustrated, 199—acknowledges the Chevalier, 201—gives permission to Berwick to serve the Chevalier, (n.) 218—civilities with the Chevalier, 220—favourably disposed to him, 227—illness, 228—demurs to Berwick commanding expedition of 1715, 230—expected death, 235, 236—death, 239—effect of death estimated, 241, 252, 253—promises made in his lifetime, fulfilment of doubtful, 245—alluded to under pseudonyms, 215, 247—his commands to Berwick, 270
Louise, daughter of Francis I., (n.) 79
Lovat, Simon Fraser, Lord, duplicity of, 276, 279—rewarded by George I., *ib.*—Mar hopes for his adherence, 278, 279—letter to Cadogan advising severe measures, 280—thanked for his supposed loyal services, *ib.*—advised to repair to London to press for reward, 281
Luther, 79
Lyndsay, Sir David, Lion King at Arms, 76

MACADAM, Roger, 8
Macaulay: description of death of Charles II., 168—charge against James II., 200—silence of, as to story of James I.'s death in infancy, 285
———, Catherine (historian), referred to, 147
Macbeth (1043), 1
Macdonald, Alexander, Lord of the Isles, 31
———. *See* Glencoe.
———, Mr., Curator of the Antiquarian Society, 284
McCrie. *See* Melville, Andrew.
McKerlie, P. H. (F.S.A.), some particulars as to remains discovered in Edinburgh Castle, 284
Maclean, Colonel, turns informer, 206, 207—consequences, 261
Maclellan, a Stuart adherent, put to death by William Douglas, 41
McNab (of Braemar), 268
Madeleine (or Magdalen) of Bourbon, (n.) 79, 80—marriage with James V., 81—lands in Scotland, *ib.*—dies, *ib.*—mentioned, *ib.*, 85
Magdalen College, Fellows of, deprived, 177
Maintenon, Madame de, 214, 231
Maitland of Lethington, 90, 91, 92, 95, 98—dismissal demanded by Darnley, 104—retires to Perthshire, *ib.*—takes part in conference at Craigmillar, 105—carried off by Bothwell, 110—violence of Bothwell towards, *ib.*—with others takes arms against him, *ib.*—present at opening of the Casket, 117—warrant for Mary's imprisonment signed by, 118—an "Associated Lord," *ib.*—death of, 129
———, John, minister of James VI., 137
Malcolm confirms grants to Walter, first Steward, 3
Malmaison, 273
Malo, St., 192, 206, 207, 259, 261, 262
Malplaquet, (n.) 213
Manuel. *See* Battles.
Mar. *See* Murray.
———, Earl of. *See* Morgand.
———, ———, at Harlaw (1411), 24—defeated (1431), 31
———, John, Earl of, guards Queen during confinement, 103—present at opening of the Casket, 117—warrant for Mary's imprisonment signed by, 118—an "Associated Lord," *ib.*—dealings with Elizabeth, 122, 127—Regent, death of, 127—regency, 130—alluded to in connection with discoveries in Edinburgh Castle, 283—custody of Casket, 289
Mar, Earl of, at Sheriffmuir, 207—failure in Argyllshire, *ib.*—at Perth, *ib.*, 209—escapes to France, 208—blames Bolingbroke, *ib.*—retires to the Highlands, 241—dukedom conferred by the Chevalier, 256—praises of, *ib.*—letters, 260—informed of sailing of the Chevalier, 261—bad generalship at Sheriffmuir, 263—nicknamed "Bobbing John," *ib.*—letter from Bolingbroke, 265—account of flight of the Chevalier and himself from Montrose to France, 267—anxiety about missing papers, 268—generalship mistrusted, 269—wines and gunpowder, 270, 271—to supersede Bolingbroke, 273—to return packets to Mary of Modena, *ib.*—letter of defence from Bolingbroke, *ib.*, 274—money sent to him by Mary of Modena, 274—complains of negligence or treachery in supply of arms, *ib.*—last letter from Bolingbroke, 275—at Scone and Dundee with the Chevalier, 276—sends Gordon news of loss of treasure ship, *ib.*, 277—letters to Huntly on the situation, 277, 278—military directions to Gordon, 278—in flight, 280—indignation of Keith, Earl Marischal, 281
———, Annabella, Countess of, preceptress of James VI., 131
———, Lady, preceptress of Prince Henry, 144
March, Earl of, his daughter's marriage broken off, 18—demands redress, *ib.*—revolts to the English, *ib.*
Margaret Bonkyl, 5
———, daughter of Christian I., 47, 48—buried, 54
———, eldest daugter of David, Earl of Huntingdon, 186
———, daughter of James I., married to the Dauphin (afterwards Louis XI.), and dies, 35—kisses Alain Chartier, *ib.*

Margaret, daughter of Henry VII., married to James IV., 56, 58—festivities, 59—marries Angus, 69—English party, *ib.*—influences Henry VIII., 70—quarrels with and quits Angus, 71—mediation of, 72—interference of, 74—divorce; marriage with Henry Stewart, *ib.*—in the Highlands, 78—proposes conference, 79

" Margaret " (ship), 62

Marian persecution, 91

" Maries, the Queen's," 90

Marischal, Earl, of Scotland. *See* Keith, George; Keith, William.

Marjory Bruce, 5—marriage with, brings the Stuarts into succession, 6—James V.'s dying allusion to, 85, 138

Marlborough, Duke of (*See also* Churchill), 196—implicated in Fenwick's plot, 200—victories of, 202—sends money or promises of, to St. Germain, 204, 220, 222—Jacobite anxiety as to his course, 215—ambiguous attitude of, *ib.*—stipulates with Berwick for pardon, 216—alluded to, 217, 218—omnipotent with the Elector, 220—civilities to Duke of Berwick, *ib.*—refuses pay as Captain-General, 221—loses ground, 222—letter in cypher, 227—expected to join the Chevalier on his landing, 233—Chevalier wishes to unite him and Ormond, 234—remittance of 2000*l.* to the Chevalier, 237—pressed by Berwick as to his intentions, 247—Berwick's doubts of him, 248—joins in thanks to Lord Lovat, 280

———, Duchess of. *See* Churchill, Lady.

Marston Moor, battle of, 146

Mary of Bourbon, 79, 80

——— (afterwards Queen) of England, 79—dies, 91

——— of Gueldres, married to James II., 40—buried, 46—resolute conduct at Roxburgh as Queen Dowager, *ib.*

——— of Lorraine (or Guise) married to James V., 81—gives birth to daughter (afterwards Mary Queen of Scots), 85—opposes Henry VIII.'s schemes, *ib.*—Beaton, her minister, 87—becomes Regent, 90—set at defiance by Knox, 91—fortifies Leith, *ib.*—dies, 92—mild character of, *ib.*—mentioned, 98, 107, 146

Mary (daughter of James II.), 46, 71

——— of Modena, gives birth to heir, 179—letters of, 180—retires to convent of Chaillot, *ib.*—appointed guardian to her son, *ib.*—recommends Bishop Ellis to the Pope, 194—receives help from Lady Petre, 204—mediation of, between the Chevalier and Duke of Berwick, 205—Berwick's advice for her health, 215—writes to a lady concerning the Chevalier's marriage, 217—shares in intrigue to gain the fleet, 219—receives from the Chevalier intelligence from Ormond, 222—the Chevalier submits to her approval his letter to Bolingbroke, 223—participates in the negotiations with Bolingbroke, 225—and marriage projects, 226—account of Louis XIV.'s goodwill, 227—consulted as to raising money, &c., *ib.*, 228—thanks Dicconson for news as to events, and as to distress at St. Germain, 231—the Chevalier's suggestion as to pension, 237—Bolingbroke to consult with her about proposal for the Chevalier's marriage, *ib.*—English letters submitted to, 238—cognisant of some private matter, 244—alluded to, 246—directions to Dicconson as to transmission of gold, 248—account of Berwick's hesitation, 249—the Chevalier's proclamation submitted to her, 258—Bolingbroke to concert with her, 262—receives Hamilton's report of difficulty in seeing the Regent, 272—packets from, to be returned to her, 273—Malmaison, *ib.*—letters from Bolingbroke for approval, 274—sends money to Mar, *ib.*—general liberality, *ib.*—alluded to, 282

——— of Portugal, 79

——— Queen of Scots, minority alluded to, 76—birth of, 85—desire of Henry VIII. to gain custody of, in minority, *ib.*—his designs foiled, 86—treaty for marriage with Prince Edward signed, but not ratified, 87—In Stirling Castle, 89—taken to France, *ib.*—reared with her half-brother (afterwards Regent), *ib.*—"the Queen's Maries," 90—is placed for education in a convent, *ib.*—becomes Queen of France, *ib.*—prompted by the Guises, quarters the English arms, *ib.*—she and her husband not to use arms of England, 93—they acknowledge Elizabeth as Queen of England, *ib.*,—presumptive succession to England, attempt by Elizabeth to abrogate it, *ib.*—her husband dies, 94, 95—begins actual reign in Scotland against advice, 95—her attitude towards the Church and the Reformation, 96—desire for toleration, *ib.*, 97—her character, opinions of, 97—her personal fascination, *ib.*,—acquirements, 28—suppresses Huntly's rising, 99—insulted by Knox, *ib.*—Chastelard, 100—Rizio, *ib.*—resolves to marry Darnley, *ib.*—Murray revolts, *ib.*—and is defeated, 101—Darnley's character and schemes, *ib.*—Rizio's murder, *ib.*—escapes to Dunbar with Darnley, 102—plan to force her abdication or her apostacy, *ib.*—discovers Darnley's complicity in Rizio's murder, *ib.*—wishes vainly to retire to France, *ib.*—son born in Edinburgh Castle, *ib.*, 103—estrangement from Darnley, 104—consents to Morton's return, 105—the Craigmillar Conference, *ib.*—proposal at it for removal of Darnley, *ib.*—compromised fatally, 105, 106—proofs of complicity in Darnley's murder, 106—imputed affection for Bothwell, 107, 108—visits him, 108—attacked by fever, *ib.*—carried off by Bothwell, 109—measures for her rescue, 110—her wedding-day, *ib.*,—contemplates suicide, *ib.*—she and Bothwell driven to Dunbar, 111—takes disguise as a page, *ib.*—surrenders to Kirkaldy at Carberry Hill, *ib.*—carried through Edinburgh, *ib.*—popular sympathy, 112—probability of issue by Bothwell, *ib.*—question of legality, *ib.*—alleged communications with Bothwell, *ib.*—imprisoned at Lochleven, 113—abdication, *ib.*—visited by Murray, *ib.*—Elizabeth's intervention in her favour, 115—schemes for escape, and escape, *ib.*—confederacy in her favour, *ib.*—battle of Langside, *ib.*—escapes into England, 116—accusations against, *ib.*—Casket Letters, *ib.*—at Melrose, 118—alleged consent to Bothwell's abducting of her son, *ib.*—attitude of Roman Catholic powers, 119—Commission of Inquiry, 120, 121—acquittal by, 121—alleged statements of Bothwell's page, 123—position after acquittal by Commissioners at Westminster, 125—grants pension to Murray's murderer, 126—negotiation by Murray, and afterwards by Morton, for her surrender by Elizabeth, 127—Elizabeth's displeasure at projected marriage with Norfolk, *ib.*—supposed to be a party to the "League," 128—detention in England unjustifiable, *ib.*—her mother-in-law exonerates her, *ib.*—her son's attitude towards Spain, *ib.*—defection of Huntly and the Hamiltons, 129—joint government proposed, 131—her death, 134—attempt to connect her with remains in Edinburgh Castle in 1830, 283—evidence of the Casket Letters examined, 286-288

Mary (William and Mary), expectation of an heir, 167—called to throne, 186

Matheson, Sir Alexander, 59

Maxwell, Warden of the Marches, 84

Mazarin, Cardinal, 157

"Medici, Archives de," quoted, 96

Melfort, Lord, 190, 191—correspondence with Sarah Churchill, 194—letter to Bishop Ellis, *ib.*—to Lord Perth, 201—his son-in-law, Castelblanco, 227

Melrose burnt by Richard II., 13—mentioned, 73, 118—ruined by Lord Hertford, 88

Melville, Andrew, McCrie's Life of, quoted, 128

——, Sir Andrew, Master of Queen Mary's Household, last farewell of the Queen to, 134

——, Sir James, carried off by Bothwell, 110—disbelieves accusations against Mary, 123

——, ——, Memoirs of, quoted or referred to, 104, 110, 112, (n.) 113, 120, 123, 125, 126, 130

Index. 317

Ménage quoted, 35
Menteith family, ancestry of, 4
——, Isabella, Countess of, 26
——, Earldom of, to Malise Graham, 32
Meriadet, a Flemish knight, prevails at a tournament, 41
Merrimonth, William, "King of the Sea," 59
"Michael, the" (great ship), 60—sold to the French, 62
——, St., church of, London, 66
Middleton, Lord, 205, 221
Milford Haven, 199
Mill, Walter, burnt, 91
Molesworth, Mr. R., 280
Molla, 2
Monaco, Prince of, 180
Mondovi, Bishop of, 96
Monk, General George (Duke of Albemarle), early expectation of a Restoration, 162—double-dealing, *ib.*—receives Royalist communications and marches into England, 163—treacherous advice to Richard Cromwell, 164
Monmouth, Duke of, 168, 171, 173
Mons Meg, 45
Montague, 225
Monteith, Lake, 89
Montgomery, Count de, causes death of Henry II., 90
——, Sir J., plot against William III., 189
Montreville, French Minister, advises Charles to surrender to the Scotch, 150
Montrose, 208, 267
——, Earl of, killed at Flodden, 65
——, Marquess of, wins battle of Kilsyth, 148—beaten at Philiphaugh, *ib.*—captured and hanged, 149, 159
Moray, Sir Andrew, joint Regent, 7—dies (1338), *ib.*
——, Archdeacon of. *See* Bellenden.
——, Bishop of, promotes meeting between Livingston and Crichton, 39
Morgand, Earl of Mar, 3
Morison, Mr., 268
Morningside, James IV. at, 61—failure of James V. at, 83
Morton, Earl of, killed at Flodden, 65
——, ——, 95—banished; hatred to Darnley, 102—recalled from exile, 104, 105—privity to Darnley's murder, 106—supports Bothwell's project for marrying the Queen, 109—with others rises against Bothwell, 110, 111—offers combat with Bothwell, 111—commits the Queen to the custody of Murray's mother, 113—reason for conniving at Bothwell's escape, *ib.*—military talent, 115—gives the Casket to Murray, 116—deposition, 117—examination of Casket, *ib.*, 118—warrant for Mary's imprisonment signed by, 118—an "Associated Lord," *ib.*—assertion respecting Casket, 119—possible tampering with, 120—Regent, 127—becomes predominant, 129—pacific policy, *ib.*—anomalies in his life, 130—encourages printing, *ib.*—estimate of his character, *ib.*—beheaded, *ib.*, 132—the Casket in custody of, 289
Murdoch, son of the Regent Albany. *See* Albany, Murdoch of.
Mure, Elizabeth, 8—probable date of marriage, 9—issue, 11, 12
Muriella de Keith, 26
Murray, James Stuart (afterwards Earl of Mar and Murray, and Regent), his character and conduct, 89—accompanies his sister to France; returns, and is chosen a Lord of Congregation, *ib.*, 90—mentioned, 92, 95, 96—Earl of Mar, 98—made Earl of Murray, 99—threatens rebellion because of the Darnley marriage, 100—defeated and driven into England, 101—takes part in conference at Craigmillar, 104, 105, 108—supports Bothwell's project to marry the Queen, 109—his party take arms against Bothwell, 110—reasons for conniving at Bothwell's escape, 113—cruel behaviour to the Queen at Lochleven, *ib.*—styled the "Good," *ib.*—made Regent, 115—intervention of Queen Elizabeth, *ib.*—military talents of, *ib.*—receives Casket from Morton, 116—he and adherents charged with Darnley's murder, 121—produces letters, &c., *ib.*—receives douceur, *ib.*—intrigues with Norfolk for marriage with Mary, *ib.*—suspicions of complicity in

318   Index.

Darnley's murder, 125—assassination of, 126—estimate of his character, ib.—negotiations for surrender of Mary by Elizabeth, 127— anomalies in his career, 130— question of his integrity in the matter of the Casket, 286—his custody of the Casket, 289
Murray, Lord George (ancestor of present Duke of Athole), career of, 275—illness of, 276
——, —— Charles (brother of above), career of, 275
——, J. A., Bolingbroke's secretary, 241, 249, 251, 255, 256
——, James, his charges against Bolingbroke, 208
—— of Tullibardine, 111—present at opening of the Casket, 117—an "Associated Lord," 118
——, Captain William, 137
Muscovy, Czar of, 158
Musgrave, 84
Musselburgh, 89, 111

NAIRN, Mr., 230
Naseby, battle of, 148
"National Review," 167
Neville, Lord Falconberg, 45
Nevilles and Percys, quarrel between, 14
Nevil's Cross, battle of, 9
Newark, 150
Newbattle, 58
Newcastle, 83, 163
Newman, Cardinal, 147
Niddry, 115
Nimeguen, treaty of, 182
"Non-compounders," extreme Jacobites so called, 194
Nonconformists, partial sympathy of, with James II., 172
Norfolk, Cardinal of, 175—letters from James II. to, 190-192—in correspondence with Bishop Ellis, 194—particulars respecting, 211
——, Duke of, 83, 120 — projected marriage with Mary Stuart, 121, 127 —intrigue with Spain, ib.
——, Dukes of, 2
Norham Castle, 63
North and Grey, Lord, 224 258
North Inch, 16
North Sands Head, 183

Northumberland invaded (1388), 14
——, Earl of, rising of, 126
Norway, 47
——, Maid of, 4—death of, ib.
Notre Dame (Paris), 81
Nottingham, James I., confined at, 27

OATES, TITUS, 166
Ochiltree. See Arran, James Stewart, Earl of.
Ogilvy, Lord, 51
—— supports Bothwell's project for marrying the Queen, 109
Oliphant supports Bothwell's project for marrying the Queen, 109
O'Neal, Captain, 271
Orange, Mary, Princess of, lends money to Charles II., 158
——, ——, ——. See Mary (William and Mary).
——, William, Prince of, visits England, 158—becomes head of a great and growing Protestant party, 173— projects of invasion, 176—unscrupulous policy, 177, 178—disclaims designs upon English Crown, 178—Warming pan plot, 179—profits by foreign political situation, 182—perils of the expedition, ib.—number of fleet, 183. See William and Mary and William III.
Organs used in Scotland, temp. James I., 34
Orkney Isles, 47
——, Duke of. See Bothwell.
Orleans, 226
——, Duchess of, 158
——, the Regent Duke of, his attitude towards Jacobite cause in 1715, 204, 205—Bolingbroke suggests paying court to him, 236—also the Chevalier, particularly in the matter of the pension, ib., 237—his situation, 238, 239 —hesitates, but sides with George I., and prevents Berwick from leading 1715 invasion, (n.) 239—situation and intentions as estimated by Bolingbroke, 240—his dispositions to be sounded, 244—sides with George I.; refuses troops, and delays the money promised before death of Louis, 245 —disapproves of certain interferences of officials, 252—promises secret aid, 254—measures in relation to the

Chevalier's embarkation, 260—his prohibition of Berwick from joining the Chevalier's invasion, 270—interference with warlike stores for Scotland, *ib.*—Hamilton's difficulty in getting audience, 272—orders powder but no arms, 271—Mar expects open assistance from, 279

Ormond, Earl of, killed, 44

———, 1st Duke of, bears Charles II.'s letter to Duke of York, 166—letter to, 169

———, 2nd Duke of, intrigues, 204—jealousy towards Bolingbroke, 205—impeached, *ib.*—conspiracy revealed, 206—his landing frustrated, 207—the Chevalier alarmed at his want of secrecy, 222—Berwick's expectation of measures to be taken, *ib.*—the Chevalier regrets want of means to inform adherents that Ormond is at head of his affairs, 223—recommends the Chevalier to trust to Bolingbroke, *ib.*—Bolingbroke's account of, 224—summons the Chevalier, 230—his arrangements backward, 232—his wish for interview with the Chevalier objected to, 233—Duke of Leeds referred to him, *ib.*—escapes to France, 234—letter from the Chevalier to Bolingbroke respecting uniting him and Marlborough, *ib.*—suggestion for his seeing Duke of Orleans, 236—his doing so directed by the Chevalier, *ib.*—escape of his secretary, 238—willing to accompany the Chevalier, 242—the Chevalier desires meeting with, 244—alluded to, 248—his starting arranged, 250—rumoured design of intercepting him, 251—to start before the Chevalier, 253—movements watched by Lord Stair, *ib.*—informs the Chevalier of his immediate departure, 254—gives account of audience of the Regent, who promises secret aid which Bolingbroke is not to know of, *ib.*—danger of his being stopped at the seaside, 255—his going, 256—anxiety of the Chevalier for news of his success, 257—compliment to, 258—ill received in England, 261—to inform Duke of Leeds where to meet the Chevalier, *ib.*—sailing of, *ib.*—disparaged by the Chevalier, 262—sails, intending to make for Cornwall, *ib.*—sends Mar account of proceedings, 264—letter to Lord Mar on the Chevalier's landing and prospects, 265—without news from England, 266—mentioned, 273, 274—dissatisfaction of, 282

Ormonde, Lord (Earl). *See* Ormond, 1st Duke of.

Orrery, Earl of, 162

Oswestry, Castle of, 1—Lords of, 2

Otterburn, battle of, 14

Overy, St. Mary, 28

Oxford, 150

———, Harley, Earl of, imprisoned, 205—his ministry, intentions of, 204, 214—Berwick's mistrust of, 218—opinion of him, 219—violent for High Church, 220

PAINE, Nevile, torturing of, for conspiracy, 189

Paisley Abbey (founded 1164), 3, 4—Alexander, 4th Steward, buried at, 4—Paisley mentioned, 6—Robert III. buried at, 21

Palatine, Princess. *See* Elizabeth of Bohemia.

Papal dispensations, 9, 85, 112

Paris, 80, 81, 208, 220, 258, 267

Parliament, English, dispensed with by Charles II., 165

——— at Perth, 18—at Holyrood (1402), 20—remarks, general, concerning, *ib.*—power to James I., 30—action of, developed by James I., 34, 35—at Edinburgh (1440), 39—declaration of James III. to, 47—summoned at Edinburgh (1469), *ib.*—Edinburgh (1488), 51—" the Healing," 56—altered nature of, 68—being appealed to, trusts Albany, 70—co-operation with James V., 77—appoints Council, 93—attitude towards James II., 175

———, Irish, confiscates lands of Protestants, 187

Paterson. *See* Darien.

———, Will., 211

Paul IV., 126

Pemberton, Mr., 221, 228

Penderell family, 161

Percys and Nevilles, quarrel between, 14

Perth taken by Robert Stuart, 7—burnt by Richard II., 13—gives bond for James I.'s ransom, 29—assassination of James I. at, 32—Knox at, 91—mentioned, 267—lack of powder at, 271—deserters at, 278—mentioned, 280
——, Earl of, Chancellor of Scotland, despairs of James II.'s policy, 175, 176—influence with the Pope, 198—letter from Lord Melfort, 201—letter to Cardinal of Norfolk detailing Roman Catholic encroachments, 211
Perthshire, 42
Peterborough, Lord, 236
Peterhead, 205, 207, 268
Petre, Father, unpopularity of, 178
——, Lady, sends money to Mary of Modena, 204
Philip of France, 7—assists the Scotch, ib.
—— II., 96, 132
Philiphaugh, battle of, 148
Pinkie, battle of, 88
Pitlodrie, 268
Pitscottie quoted or referred to, 53, 60
Pius II. (Piccolomini Æneas Silvius), 46
—— V., Bull against Elizabeth, 126
Plymouth, 206, 207
Poland, 158
Pontefract Castle, 25, 285
Port Mahon, 219
Portmore, Lord, 238, 240
Potter Row, Edinburgh, 117, 118
Poyning's Laws, proposed abrogation of, 187
Presbyterians struggle for ascendancy, 149
Presbyterianism established in Scotland, 93, 94
Preston, Lancashire insurgents defeated at, 207
Printing, introduction of, 60—into Scotland (1509), 67
Privy Council safeguards Queen Mary in view of birth of an heir, 103—proclamation for her rescue from Bothwell, 110
Protestant party and Protestantism, 87, 89—gloomy prospects of, 90—Marian persecutions in England, 91—supporters among the nobles, 94

—who were swayed by hope of plunder, ib.—iniquities of members of, 129—rising of, in Edinburgh, 176
Pusey, Dr., 147
Puttenham (Eng. Poes.) referred to, 35
Pym, John, 143, 156

QUEEN DOWAGER. See Beaufort, Jane; Margaret, daughter of Henry VII.; Mary of Gueldres.
"Queen's Maries, the," 90.
"Queen's Men," 131
Queen Mother. See Mary of Lorraine.
Quete (or Chattan) Clan, 16, 17

RADCLIFFE, Mr. F. R., "Stuart Letters," 167
Raleigh, Sir Walter, implicated in the Arabella Stuart plot, 140
Ramorny, Sir John, 19
Ramsay, John, of Balmain, 50—insolence of, 51—treachery, 56
Randolph, letter to Cecil, 95—assertion of, 96—suspects Elizabeth's acquiescence in the Darnley marriage, 100
Ransom of James I., 29
Reay, Lord, 278
Rebellions: against James I., 32—James II., 44—James III., 51—partial, against James IV., 56—under Queen Mary, 99, 101—in Ireland (1641), 153—of 1715, Jacobite, 204—entered upon without continental or other adequate support, 235—alluded to, 275—of 1719, ib.
Reformation, the, approach of, 57, 68, 79—in Scotland, ib.—Henry VIII. and, 81—Knox, mainspring of, in Scotland, 88—gains ground, 91—divisions, 135
Regents. See Stuart, Robert, and Moray, Sir Andrew (joint Regents); Stuart, Robert (sole Regent); Albany, Robert, Duke of; Albany, Murdoch, Duke of; Albany of Boulogne, Duke; Arran, Earl of; Mary of Guise, Queen Mother—Regency declared in abeyance, 93—Murray, Earl of; Mar, Earl of; Morton Earl of; Lennox, Earl of.
Renfrewshire, ancient patrimony of the Stuarts, 3—confiscated, 7
Resby, John, burnt, 24

Restoration, the, anticipations of, 162—immorality following, 163—popular joy at, 164—plot to overthrow, *ib.*
Retz, Cardinal de, 158
Revolution of 1688, 173, 184—birth of English constitution, 202
Richard II. marches to the Border, 12—burns Melrose, Edinburgh, and Perth, 13—besieges Stirling unsuccessfully, *ib.*—threatens Aberdeen, *ib.*—deposed and imprisoned, 18
—— II. (of England ; a pretended), 25—burial at Stirling, *ib.*—story alluded to, 285
—— III., and Walpole's version of his character alluded to, 285
Richelieu, 142
Rizio, David, 100—opposes Darnley's schemes, and is murdered, 101
Robert (7th Steward : afterwards King Robert II.), born under Cæsarean operation, 6—prospects of succession, 6, 7—at Halidon Hill, 7—acts against Baliol, *ib.*—successes of, *ib.*—joint Regent, *ib.*—defeat of, *ib.*—sole Regent, *ib.*—applies to Philip of France, *ib.*—occupies Perth, *ib.*—besieges Stirling, 8—Fordun's description of him, *ib.*—marries Elizabeth Mure, kinswoman within prohibited affinity, *ib.*—dispensation from Clement VI., 9—son John (Robert III.) born, *ib.*—second son (Duke of Albany) born (1339), *ib.*—accused, *ib.*—honourably acquits himself during captivity of David II., 10—succession jeopardised, *ib.*—becomes King, 11. *See* Robert II.
Robert II. (*See also* Robert, 7th Steward) : succeeds, 11—pretensions of William, Earl of Douglas, *ib.*—issue by first wife, 11, 12—by second wife (Euphemia Ross), 12—succession imperilled, *ib.*—obscurity as to dispensation, *ib.*—dispensation first mentioned (in literature) by A. Stuart, *ib.*—embassy to Charles V., *ib.*—unable to take the field, *ib.*, 13—character, 15—buried at Scone, *ib.*—second family of, pretend to Crown, 32—alluded to, 114
—— III., birth of, 9—created Earl of Carrick, 10—crowned, 15—and his Queen, *ib.*—real name John, *ib.*—a cripple, *ib.*—presides at judicial fight, 16—homage claimed by Henry IV., 18—wife dies, 19—son murdered, *ib.*—surviving son (James I.) taken prisoner, 21—dies, *ib.*—character and anecdote of, 22—mentioned, 114
Robertson of Struan beheaded, 70
Robertson's History of Scotland referred to, (n.) 107, 119, 283
Rochester, Lawrence Hyde, Earl of, 185
Roman Catholic party in France, 81—Perth's account of proceedings in Scotland, 175, 176, 211-213
Roman Catholics in peril from Oates's and Bedloe's accusations, 166
Rome, alienation of England from, 78
Ronsard, 98
Rooke, Admiral, destroys French vessels, 193
Rose, Hugh James, 147
Ross, Bishop of. *See* Leslie.
——, Countess of, 18
——, Earldom of, contention as to, 24
——, Earl of, confederacy with, sought by William Douglas, 42, 43
——, Euphemia, 12
Rosse Hecat supports Bothwell's project for marrying the Queen, 109
Rothes, Earl of, summoned by James III., 51
——, ——, killed at Flodden, 65
——, ——, son of, stabs Beaton, 88
——, ——, supports Bothwell's project for marrying the Queen, 109
——, Lord, in service of Pretender, 277
Rothesay, Duke of, and Earl of Carrick, son of Robert III., Steward of Scotland, 17—rivalry with Earl of Fife, *ib.*—character, *ib.*—profligacy, 18—receives dukedom, *ib.*—made the King's lieutenant, *ib.*—marries Elizabeth, *ib.*—in command, Edinburgh, 19—gives offence to Douglas, *ib.*—imprisoned, *ib.*—starved to death, *ib.*
Rouille (or Ruille), 213
Roxburgh, 8, 31, 32, 45, 46, (Abbey) 88
Rudolphi, 127
Rump Parliament, 149—tyranny of, worse than the King's, 156
"Runabout Raid, the," 101
Rupert, Prince, 143—at Marston Moor, 146—alluded to, 206

Y

Russell, Admiral, double-dealing of, 192 —obliged to fight the battle of La Hogue, 192—intrigues for James's restoration, 194—temporising conduct of, 196—implicated in Fenwick's plot, 200
———, Lord, intrigues with the French Court, 164—scope of his designs, *ib.*
———, Mr., 272
Ruthven, Alexander, 137—mentioned, 139
———, Beatrice, 137
——— Castle, 281
——— family, Calvinistic, 136—their cause championed by Anne of Denmark, 137
———, Lord, assists at Rizio's murder, 102—banished, *ib.*—hatred to Darnley, *ib.*—an "Associated Lord," 118
Ruthvens, ancestry of, 3. *See also* Gowrie.
Rymer (chronicler) referred to, 28
——— (compiler of Fœdera) referred to, 30, 56
Ryswick, peace of, 200—broken, 202

SADLER, Sir Ralph, Henry VIII.'s ambassador, 82—foiled, 86—obtains treaty for Mary Stuart's marriage, 87—enquiry respecting Mary Queen of Scots, 120, 288
Salisbury, Earl of. *See* Cecil, Robert.
Sanquhar, 116
———, Lord, present at opening of the Casket, 117—warrant for Mary's imprisonment signed by, 118—an "Associated Lord," *ib.*
Sauchieburn, 52
Savery, Mr., 262
Schism in the Western Church (1378), 38, 57
Scilly Isles, 199
Scone, 37—Abbey and Palace of, destroyed, 91—Charles II. crowned at, 160—the Chevalier at, 276
Scotland, Norwegian invasion, 4— miserable condition of (1341), 9; (1385) 14; (1396) 17—invasion by Richard II., 13—tournaments, 17 —invasion of, by Henry IV., 18, 19— lawless state of, at return of James I., 30—weakness of consecutive, 38— suffering from lawlessness of the Douglases, 41—yet favourable to them, *ib.*—north of, hostile to Crown, 43—influence of James III. on, 50, 51—war with England imminent, 61—effect of Flodden on, 67, 68— printing introduced (1509), 67— anarchy, 70—not included in peace between England and France, 72— intrigues in, 73—nominally peaceable (1535), 78—Lutheran controversy, 79—hostile to Protestant cause, 82, 85—Beaton arbiter of Catholic policy, 87—ancient league with France weakened, 92, 93—religious war is averted by death of Francis II., 94—opinion hostile to French or Spanish alliance, 132—reduced population, 138—hostile to James II.'s measures, 174—readiness for rising of 1715, 232, 240—the Chevalier's arrangements for landing, 246
"Scotsman," 285
Scott, Mr. Edward, preface to the reprint of Eikon Basilike, 155
———, Sir Walter, quoted or referred to, 6, (n.) 17, 26, 44, (n.) 50, 64, 82, 85, 135, 160, 174—silence respecting discovery of remains, Edinburgh Castle, 284
Seafort, Marquess of, 263, 277; (Seaforth) 278
Sedgmoor, battle of, 173
Semple, Lord, supports Bothwell's project for marrying the Queen, 109 —present at opening of Casket, 117— warrant for the Queen's confinement signed by, 118—an "Associated Lord," *ib.*—author of partisan ballads, 122
Seniscalcus (Steward), derivation of, 2—powers of, *ib.*—in France, *ib.*
Seton supports Bothwell's project for marrying the Queen, 109—assists in her escape, 115
——— (one of " the Queen's Maries "), 90
Seymour, William, 140
Shaw, Governor of Stirling, 51—gives up Prince James, 52
Sheen, in Surrey, 66
Sheldon, 246
Sheridan, Captain Thomas, 264
Sheriffmuir, 205, 207, 263, 264
Shetland Isles, 47
Shoreham, 161

Shrewsbury, Douglas taken prisoner at 20
——, Duke of, foils Bolingbroke, 235 —message to, from the Chevalier, *ib.*
——, Lord, intrigues for restoration of James II., 194, 200.
"Sichted," meaning of, 118
Sidney, Algernon, receives French pay, 164—scope of his designs, *ib.*
Sieges and Occupations mentioned: Berwick (1318), 6—Dunoon, 7— Perth, *ib.*—Stirling (1339), *ib.*— Edinburgh (1341), *ib.*—Roxburgh (1342), *ib.*—Edinburgh,13—Stirling, *ib.* — Carlisle, *ib.* — Edinburgh (threatened), 19—Roxburgh, 31— (1460), 45, 46—Edinburgh (1481), 50 —Norham and Werk Castles (1513), 63—Hamilton Castle (1517), 71— Werk Castle (1524), 73—Tantallon Castle (1528), 76—Edinburgh (1554), 87—St. Andrews (1547), 88 —Leith (1560), 92—Banbury (1642), 143—Belgrade (1688), (n.) 178—Londonderry (1689), 187
Simon, ancestor of Boyd family, 2
Sinclair supports Bothwell's project for marrying the Queen, 109
——, Oliver, 84
Skelton's "Maitland of Lethington" quoted or referred to, 91, (n.) 92, (n.) 94, 100, 120, 126, 288
Smith, Thomas, D.D., 290
Smyrna fleet, loss of, 196
"Snowdoun, Knight of" (James V.), 81
Solway Moss, battle of, 84—subsequent career of prisoners taken at, 86
Somerset, Earl of, 27
——, Duke of, Protector, defeats the Scotch at Pinkie, 88
Southesk, Lord, letter to Mar informing him of petty intrigues, &c., and professing his own disinterested loyalty, 281, 282—his estates confiscated, but provision allowed to his wife, (n.) 281—his death, *ib.*
Spain, Scotch friendliness towards, 128, 129—Cromwell's policy towards, 157—proposal to ship officers, for Pretender's service, 228—Jacobite hopes from, 241—expected answer from, 275

Spanish prisoners taken at Glenshiel, 93
"Spectator" referred to, 85
Stair, Lord, 205, 220, 224—watchfulness, 226, 253, 255, 260, 271— insists upon the Chevalier being stopped, 260—knowledge of the Chevalier's movements, 262—expects rupture with France, 279
Stanhope, General, conveys the King's thanks to Lord Lovat, 276, 280
——, Lord. *See* Stuart Papers.
Stanley, Sir Edward, 65
"Start, the," 160
Stephen, Leslie, "National Dictionary of Biography," 145, 195
Stewards of Scotland (mythical, 1124 —1370). *See* Walter, son of Fleance, and Alan, son of Walter; Walter (first historical), son of Alan; Fitzalan, Richard; Alan (second), son of Walter; Walter (third), son of Alan; Alexander (fourth); James (fifth, 1283-1309); Walter (sixth); Robert (seventh, afterwards King Robert II.); Carrick, Earl of, and Rothesay, Duke of, son of Robert III.
Stewart, Alexander, James VI. threatens to hang, 133
——, Henry, married to Queen Dowager, 74—surrenders Edinburgh Castle, *ib.*
Stirling, 8, 13, 25, 30, 37, 38, 39, 40– 43, 51, 52, 73, 74, 77, 83, 91, 104, 109, 118, 144, 285—Court of, 81
—— Castle, 51, 55, 70, 75, 88, 89, 283
Stoner, Mr. and Mrs., 238
Stowe quoted or referred to, 57, 66, 67
Strafford, Wentworth, Earl of, career and fall, 142—imputed enmity of the Queen, 151
Strathearn, Earldom of, grievances as to, 32
Strickland, Miss, describes marriage of James VI. and Anne, (n.) 137
——, Sir Roger, Vice-Admiral, his advice over-ruled, 183
Strozzi, Leo, takes St. Andrews Castle, 88
Struan, Robertson of, 70
Stuarts, traditional ancestry of, 1— descent from Alan the Norman, *ib.*, 2 —Bute, island of, their property, 2— and Douglases, comparative influence

of, 3—Renfrewshire their patrimony, *ib.*—confiscated, 7—supremacy established, 44—foreign policy, keystone of, 60—their attempts to regain English throne, 93—remarks concerning, 138, 139—succession of, indirect, 186—recent claimants of descent from main line, 285

Stuart, A., "Genealogical History of the Stewarts" referred to, 12

——, Arabella, scheme for her succession, 139—treatment of, and death, 140

——, Charles Edward. *See* Chevalier, the Young.

——, James. *See* Murray, James Stuart.

——, ——, the Black Knight of Lorn, 122

——, —— Francis Edward. *See* Chevalier de St. George.

——, John. *See* Buchan, Earl of.

——, Sir John, ancestor of families of Darnley and Earls of Galloway, 5

——, Margaret, daughter of James II., 69

——, Murdoch. *See* Albany, Murdoch of.

——, Robert, joint Regent, 7—sole Regent, *ib*. *See* Robert II.

——, Lord Robert, Bishop of Caithness, 124

——, Walter, 26—beheaded, 30

—— Exhibition, the (1888-9), 53, 135, 152

—— Papers at Windsor referred to, 168, 175, 192, 193, 194, 196, 203, 208—Stanhope, Lord, his limited use of, 203, 204—clear up some debated points, 203—silent on many important points, *ib.*—some in the Scotch College at Paris, transcribed in Macpherson's "Original Papers," *ib.*—references to, 206—value of the extracts from, 209

Succession, dispute concerning, averted, 4—regulated by Robert Bruce, 6—controversy respecting, 10—conspired against, 32—Henry VIII.'s will passing over Scotch line in succession to England, 90—presumptive, of Mary Stuart, 93—place of the Hamilton's in, 83, 101—Darnley desires to supplant them by obtaining

the "Crown Matrimonial," 101—indirect, of the Stuarts, 186

Sully, description of James VI., 135

Sunderland, Robert Spencer, Earl of, misleads James II., 176, 177, 181, 182, 185—pretends conversion, 177—probable information to Barillon, 187

Surrey, Lord, at Flodden, 63-65—evacuates Scotland, 68

Sussex, Lord, 120

Sutherland, Earl of, summoned by James III., 51

——, ——, his troops threatened by the Pretender's, 263

——, ——, supports Bothwell's project for marrying the Queen, 109

Swan, progenitor of the Ruthvens, 3

Sweden, 47—alliance with, 168—Jacobite hopes from, 241

TANTALLON CASTLE, 76

Temple Newcome, Yorkshire, 124

——, Sir William, 168

Tenison, Archbishop, 155

Terregles, 116

Test Act (1673), scope of, 172—abolition of, 174—declaration dispensing with, refused by the seven bishops, 177

—— —— (1681, Scotland), 167, 210

Tettersell, Captain, 161

Thackery, Major General, 284

Thomas, Mr. (Jacobite agent), writes to Mr. Innes touching Triennial Bill, &c., 222

Thor, 3

Throckmorton, Sir Nicholas, sent by Elizabeth to protest against the Darnley marriage, 100—letter from, *ib.*—mission to Lochleven, 115

Till, the, 64

Todd, Sir Thomas, 56

Torbay, landing of William III. at, 184

Torcy, de, 215, 222, 226, 227, 228, 233, 236, 237, 238, 270

Torrington, Lord, Memoirs of, referred to, 183

Tournaments, many in Scotland, 17—notable, at Stirling, 41—Duke of Albany killed at one, 50

Tourville, de, French Admiral defeated at La Hogue, 192

Townsend, Lord, administration of, 207

Index. 325

Trappe, Monastery de la, 193, 201
——, Abbé de la, 193
Trever, M., 218, 220, 221, 233, 246
Triennial Bill, Repeal of, 222
Trinitarians, Church of, at Aberdeen, 212
Triple Alliance, the, 168
Tullibardine, Laird of. *See* Murray of.
——, Marquess of, career and death in the Tower, 275
Tunstall, 227
Turks, war with, 178
Turnham Green, 143
Tutbury, 98
Tweed, the, 73, 84, 88
Twisell Bridge, 64
Tynemouth, Lord, 207
Tyrconnel, 176, 187
Tytler quoted: sons of Robert II., number of, 12—character, &c., Robert III., 15, 22—doubts as to pretended Richard II., 25
—— (the Elder), Casket Letters, 120 124

UNIVERSITIES, letters to, from Pretender, 251, 258
University students furious at James II.'s measures, 175, 213
Upslo, 137
Urban VIII., 151
Utrecht, Peace of, 205
d'Uxelles. *See* d'Huxelles.

VALLEY, the, at Stirling, tournament in, 41
Valois, House of, 7, 93, 95
Vendôme, Duc de, 80
Venetian Senate, 158
Venice at war with Turks, 178
Verneuil, battle of, 26
Versailles, 220
Victoria, Queen, erects monument to James III. and wife, 54—descent from Elizabeth of Bohemia, 157
Vienne, John de, with a French force in the Firth of Forth, 12—dispute with Douglas, *ib.*—with the Scotch advances south, and retreats, 13— detained with others in requital for damage, 13, 14, 69
Villiers, George. *See* Buckingham, Duke of.
Vivian arrested, 253

WADE, Sir William, 140
Wallace, Sir William, 5
Walpole, Horace, alluded to, 285
Walter (mythical), Steward, son of Fleance, 1, 2
—— (historical) Fitzalan, first High Steward, son of Alan the Norman, 1, 2—grants to, 3—founds Paisley Abbey, *ib.*
—— (son of Alan), third Steward, 3
—— (son of James), sixth Steward, father of Robert II., 6—commands at Bannockburn, 5—marries Marjory Bruce, 6—dies, *ib.*—saves Berwick, *ib.*
Warbeck, Perkin, protected by James IV., 57
Wardlaw, Bishop of St. Andrews, tutor of James I., 21
Warine, 1
Warming-pan story, 179—dying declaration of Margaret Dawson, 290
Warrington, battle of, 151
Welwood, James, 281
Wemyss Castle, 100
Wentworth, Sir Thomas. *See* Strafford.
Werk Castle, 63, 73
Western Islanders, 31, 77
Westminster Abbey, 198
Westminster Conference, inquiry concerning Mary Queen of Scots, 117, 121, 125, 288
Westminster School, 196
Westmoreland, raids into, 13
——, Earl of, rising of, 126
——, Lady, and nephew, 235
Whitehall, 186, 276
Whiteladies, 161
"White Rose." *See* Gordon, Catherine.
Whitham, General, 243
Whithorn, Prior of. *See* Dunbar, Gawyn.
Wiesener, Professor, referred to, 96
Wigan, battle of, 151
William the Conqueror, 1
——, progenitor of the Fitzalans of Arundel, 1, 2
—— the Lion, 5—failure of direct line of, 186
—— III. (*See also* Orange, Prince of) and Mary II.: William's (and Anne's) wars, 157—succeed James II., 186—attitude of William towards Scotch, 189, 190—massacre of Glencoe, 189—cruelties to James's

adherents, *ib.*—reaction against, 190—Mary dies, 198—political effect of her death, *ib.*—alluded to, 204
William III. (*See also* Orange, Prince of), conspiracy to assassinate, 199, 200—behaviour towards persons implicated, 201—professes fear of invasion, *ib.*—war with France, 202—death, *ib.*
Windhams of Dorsetshire, 161
Windsor, 26, 27
Wishart, George, burnt, 88
Wolsey, Cardinal, 69, 70, 73
Wood, Sir Andrew, 54—bold conduct of, 59—assists in improving navy, 59, 60
Woodrow, charges against Duke of York, 167
Worcester, battle of, 161—alluded to, 206
Wycliffite martyrdom, 24

Wycliffites not tolerated by James I., 34, 38
Wynd, Henry of the, 16
Wyndham, Sir W., imprisoned, 207—Bolingbroke's letter to, 208—Bolingbroke vouches for, 224
Wynton, Prior of Lochleven, 18, 21, 24, 25

YORK, 83, 84, 142
———, inquiry at, concerning Mary Queen of Scots, 121, 123
———, Duke of (Prince Charles). *See* Charles I.
———, James, Duke of. *See* James II.
———, Henry, Cardinal of, Papers of. *See* Stuart Papers, alluded to, 206
Yorkists, 44, 45, 57
Young, a glazier, carries off James IV.'s head, 66
———, Peter, 131

WORKS BY THE SAME AUTHOR.

1.

THE BRUNSWICK ACCESSION.

SECOND EDITION.

One Volume, 8vo, Cloth. Price Six Shillings.

2.

FOREIGN SECRETARIES OF THE NINETEENTH CENTURY.

SECOND EDITION.

Three Volumes, 8vo, Cloth. Vols. I. and II., 32s. 6d.; Vol. III., 18s.

www.ingramcontent.com/pod-product-compliance
Lightning Source LLC
Chambersburg PA
CBHW030004240426
43672CB00007B/815